THE SEARCH FOR A
SOCIALIST EL DORADO

THE SEARCH FOR A SOCIALIST EL DORADO

Finnish Immigration to Soviet Karelia from the United States and Canada in the 1930s

Alexey Golubev and Irina Takala

Michigan State University Press

East Lansing

♾ The paper used in this publication meets the minimum requirements of ANSI/NISO Z39.48-1992 (R 1997) (Permanence of Paper).

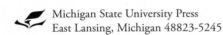 Michigan State University Press
East Lansing, Michigan 48823-5245

Printed and bound in the United States of America.

20 19 18 17 16 15 14   1 2 3 4 5 6 7 8 9 10

LIBRARY OF CONGRESS CATALOGING-IN-PUBLICATION DATA

Golubev, Alexey.
    The search for a socialist El Dorado : Finnish immigration to Soviet Karelia from the United States and Canada in the 1930s / Alexey Golubev and Irina Takala.
        pages cm
    Includes bibliographical references and index.
    ISBN 978-1-61186-115-0 (print : alk. paper)—ISBN 978-1-60917-405-7 (ebook) 1. Finnish Americans—Russia (Federation)—Karelia—History—20th century. 2. Finns—Russia (Federation)—Karelia—History—20th century. 3. Karelia (Russia)—Emigration and immigration—History—20th century. 4. United States—Emigration and immigration—History—20th century. 5. Canada—Emigration and immigration—History—20th century. 6. Soviet Union—History—1925–1953. I. Takala, Irina. II. Title.

DK511.K18G65 2013
305.894'54104715—dc23   2013023031

Book design by Scribe, Inc.
Cover design by Erin Kirk New
Cover art is "A Ski Workshop" by Heinrich Vogeler circa 1933 and is used courtesy of the National Museum of the Republic of Karelia (http://kgkm.karelia.ru/).

ɡ green Michigan State University Press is a member of the Green Press Initiative and is committed to developing
  press and encouraging ecologically responsible publishing practices. For more information about the Green
  INITIATIVE Press Initiative and the use of recycled paper in book publishing, please visit www.greenpressinitiative.org.

Visit Michigan State University Press at www.msupress.org

Contents

Preface

THIS BOOK AROSE FROM OUR PARTICIPATION IN TWO RESEARCH PROJECTS THAT STUDIED emigration from Finnish communities in the United States and Canada to the USSR during the early 1930s. Life trajectories of these Finnish American and Canadian emigrants are a fascinating case that gives multiple novel perspectives on the turbulent history of the first half of the twentieth century. They crossed the Atlantic twice, first emigrating from their native Finland in search of a better life in the New World and from there moving back to Europe, to the Soviet Union, which, it seemed to them, promised a just social order and better opportunities to work, to raise children, and to preserve their language, culture, and identities. To their new socialist home, Soviet Karelia, they took critically needed skills, tools, machines, and money—much was put to use and transformed certain sectors of the Soviet Karelian economy, but much was lost through inefficient Soviet bureaucratic management. Educated and skilled, American and Canadian Finns were regarded by Soviet authorities as agents of revolutionary transformation who would not only modernize the economy of Soviet Karelia but also enlighten its society. North American immigrants, indeed, became active participants of the socialist colonization of what Bolshevik leaders perceived as a dark, uneducated, and backward Soviet ethnic periphery. In Soviet Karelia, they created a unique culture based on the Finnish language and revolutionary aspirations of their generation; however, just as it became an important factor in the cultural transformation of Soviet Karelian society, immigrant communities were severely affected by witch-hunting campaigns of the late 1930s, targeted and victimized by the same regime that had recruited them for socialist building, and then finally destroyed in the course of the Second World War. With their lives, North American immigrants to Soviet Karelia stitched into one whole three different worlds—Finland, an Old World nation-state; the United States and Canada, two countries of seemingly endless opportunities for European immigrants that, after the Great Depression, turned unfriendly and even hostile to many of them; and what they thought was the first workers' state, the Soviet Union. The history of these Finnish immigrants is, in a way, a history of the world—of its Atlantic part at least—in upheavals and tragedies of the twentieth century.

It is hardly surprising that the history of Finnish emigration from North America to Soviet Russia appeared recently in research in the four countries affected by it: the United States, Canada, Finland, and Russia. In 2006, the Canadian-Finnish-Russian project Missing in Karelia: Canadian Victims of Stalin's Purges was launched, headed by Varpu Lindström from York University in Toronto and supported by the Social Sciences and Humanities Research Council of Canada. It aimed to collect biographical data on Canadian and American Finns who had emigrated to Soviet Karelia in the early 1930s. The project team developed the website Missing in Karelia, which presents the gathered information. It coincided with the research project North American Finns in Soviet Karelia from the 1920s to the 1950s, headed by Irina Takala from Petrozavodsk State University, one of the co-authors of this book, and supported by the Russian Foundation for Humanities and the Government of the Republic of Karelia. Its participants looked at the history of the North American immigrant community in Karelia to better understand Soviet regional history and focused on the impacts of American and Canadian immigrants on the cultural, economic, and social development of Soviet Karelia during the turmoil of the 1930s and 1940s in the Soviet Union. These research problems have not yet been properly addressed in contemporary scholarship, and the fates of hundreds of immigrants, many of whom became victims of political repression and ethnic cleansing in the late 1930s in the USSR, still remain unknown. Even in Karelia, where these events occurred, few knew about the people who were agents of prominent political, economic, and cultural change in this Soviet republic and who, in the early twentieth century, twice changed their homeland in search of their El Dorado.

This book would never have been written without the help of many people. We are particularly indebted to Varpu Lindström at York University in Toronto whose commitment to creating an international research network on the history of Finnish emigration from North America to the USSR was instrumental in pushing us to write this book. We are very sad that it is too late to express our deep gratitude to her in person. Thanks to the network that she created, we were able to present and discuss different parts of our research at conferences and meetings in Canada, Finland, Sweden, and Russia. At these meetings, our other Canadian colleagues, Börje Vähämäki (University of Toronto) and Evgeny Efremkin and Samira Saramo (both at York University), were a very receptive audience for our ideas.

In Finland, Markku Kangaspuro, the director of research at the Aleksanteri Institute of the University of Helsinki, arranged a series of opportunities for us to present and discuss our arguments, and our debates with him have greatly enriched our work. Timo Vihavainen (University of Helsinki) and Auvo Kostiainen (University of Turku) also gave us stimulating responses and ideas during the process of writing. Our correspondence and personal meetings with Alexis Pogorelskin (University of Minnesota Duluth) and Stella Sevander (Umeå University) allowed us to sharpen our arguments and broaden our evidence, while Geneva Wiskemann at the Michigan Oral History Association inspired us, back in 2007, to embark on a six-year-long venture of writing in English about the emigration of American and Canadian Finns to the Soviet Union. Financial support from Gerda Henkel Stiftung (Project AZ 03/SR/10) allowed Alexey Golubev to undertake two research trips to the University of Freiburg in 2011 and 2012, where the hospitality of Dietmar Neutatz and Julia Obertreis and the riches of the university library were priceless for the completion of this book. Golubev's participation in the Open Society Institute-funded project The Soviet in Everyday Life made our analysis of primary sources more nuanced, and Nick Baron's (University of Nottingham) cutting-edge research on Soviet spatial politics in Soviet Karelia gave us new theoretical perspectives on our material. Help from Tadeo Lima (University of British Columbia) came at the last and most exhausting stage of our writing and was thus especially valuable.

In 2002, the North Karelian Regional Film Association (Finland) launched the film project American Finns in Soviet Karelia headed by Pekka Silvennoinen. During 2002 and 2003, students from Joensuu and Petrozavodsk under the supervision of Jouko Aaltonen, a producer with the Finnish film production company Illume Oy, recorded a number of interviews with American and Canadian Finnish immigrants as part of this project, and we are deeply grateful to the project organizers for their permission to use these materials in our research. Archival work was a key part of our research, and in the National Archive of the Republic of Karelia Elena Usacheva and Liudmila Makarevich gave us valuable advice and aid in our search for documentary evidence. The director of the archive, Olga Zharinova, was very helpful when we asked to use its extremely rich collection of photographs to illustrate our book. We are also grateful to the family of Lekanders for kindly permitting us to reproduce photos from their family album. The National Museum of the Republic of Karelia kindly supplied us with the images used for the book cover. We also received financial support from the Program of Strategic Development of Petrozavodsk State University. Finally, we would like to thank our colleagues, the faculty and staff of the Department of History of Northern Europe at Petrozavodsk State University, including Leo Suni, Ilya Solomeshch, Aleksander Tolstikov, Aleskander Osipov, Irina Nesterova, and Nina Saburova, whose collegial support created a very friendly environment for us to research and write this book.

To our deep regret, it is too late to express personally our indebtedness to Mayme Sevander and Eila Lahti-Argutina, pioneers in this field of study of Finnish emigration from North America to Soviet Karelia.

Portions of Chapter 4 were previously published in Alexey Golubev and Irina Takala, "The Harsh Reality of Fine Words: The Daily Implementation of Immigration Policies in Soviet Karelia," *Journal of Finnish Studies: A Special Double Issue* (*Victims and Survivors of Karelia*) 15, 1–2 (2011): 125–43. Parts of Chapter 8 were published in Irina Takala, "The Great Purge," *Journal of Finnish Studies: A Special Double Issue* (*Victims and Survivors of Karelia*) 15, 1–2 (2011): 144–57. We gratefully acknowledge the permission of the *Journal of Finnish Studies* to reproduce certain parts of these articles in this book.

We used the Library of Congress Russian-language transliteration system for Russian names and original spellings (with diacritics) for Finnish and Swedish names. References to Russian archival sources are given in accordance with Russian standards: name of the archive, a collection to which the document belongs (indicated as f. from Russian *fund* or "collection"), inventory number of the box with files (indicated as op. from Russian *opis* or "inventory"), number of the file itself (indicated as d. from Russian *delo* or "file"), and the page within the file containing the actual document (indicated as l. from Russian *list* or "sheet"). References to Finnish archival sources are provided in accordance with Finnish archival nomenclature. The National Archive of the Republic of Karelia is abbreviated in footnotes as NARK, the Archive of the Office of the Federal Security Service (former KGB) in the Republic of Karelia as Archive of the UFSB RK (based on its Russian abbreviation АРХИВ УФСБ ПО РК), and the Russian State Archive of Socio-Political History as RGASPI (based on its Russian abbreviation РГАСПИ). We retained the Soviet nomenclature of terms related to the Soviet Communist Party: RKP(b) (1918–25), VKP(b) (1925–52), and KPSS (after 1952) refer to the party itself, while *obkom* refers to a regional party committee that supervised a large territorial unit, such as a republic (Karelian *obkom*), and controlled policies and activities of its regional authorities. For ease of reading, we have translated most terms denoting Russian and Soviet territorial divisions into equivalent English notions; where clarity is required, we have mentioned original terms in brackets in transliteration.

This book is our expression of respect to those Finnish American and Canadian immigrants who helped to build Soviet Karelia and our dedication to all innocent people who perished there in the ordeals of the Great Terror and the Second World War.

Introduction

HISTORICALLY, THE NEW WORLD WAS THE DESTINATION FOR NUMEROUS WAVES OF emigrants. Seemingly endless opportunities made the United States and Canada incredibly attractive to people seeking to emigrate from their home countries. In the nineteenth century and during the first two decades of the twentieth century, emigration from Europe to North America surpassed in volume all other population movements in the world; most emigrants landed in the United States, but Canada also received its share of new citizens. Between 1815 and 1930, at least 54 million Europeans left the Old World. Of them, 37 million eventually settled in the United States, 5 million in Canada, and the rest in South America and Australia.[1]

Nordic Europe was an integral part of this migration: at the turn of the twentieth century, Norway and Sweden were near the top of the list of European nations by the ratio of emigrants to their populations, a ratio that was larger only in Ireland. The number of Swedes who emigrated between 1851 and 1930 reached an astonishing 1.2 million, the overwhelming majority of them landing in the United States, where roughly every fifth Swede lived by the early 1900s.[2] Approximately half a million people left Norway for the United States between the 1880s and the outbreak of the First World War.[3] Numerous Finnish communities emerged in North America at the same time. From the late 1860s to 1914, over 300,000 Finns, or 10 percent of the total population of the Grand Duchy of Finland, then part of the Russian Empire, emigrated to North America.[4]

Wars and revolutions in the early twentieth century shook Europe, destroying the Russian Empire in the process and greatly accelerating migration. A new revolutionary force, Soviet Russia, emerged on the political map of the world in 1917, proclaiming itself as the first state of workers and peasants. For the first time in history, a large wave of emigrants crossed the Atlantic from west to east, when tens of thousands of people driven by different motivations set sail from North America for a new proletarian state.

Despite the rhetoric of emancipation, immigration to the Soviet Union was based on a hidden hierarchy. The top-ranked group were political immigrants, among whom there were famous intellectuals and activists of the Communist movement such as Georg Lukács, a renowned Marxist philosopher; Georgi Dimitrov, future general secretary of the Comintern and first Communist leader of Bulgaria; Ho Chi Minh, a Vietnamese revolutionary leader; and many others. In Soviet Russia, political immigrants enjoyed certain social benefits provided by the Soviet government, for they were regarded as powerful disseminators of Communist ideas in their own countries and across the world. They were nevertheless a minority in the flow of immigration to Russia. The largest group of immigrants consisted of foreign workers and technical specialists who came to Soviet Russia and later the USSR to help the Soviet people build a shining Communist future. Most of them were sincere in their beliefs and motivations. Faith in socialist ideals was strong among many workers in the world, and the Great Depression that swept through Europe and North America in the 1930s only reinforced it.

Their hopes were never fulfilled. Their shattered illusions and their disappointment in the "free society of emancipated labor" came quickly. Many re-emigrated, and in the second half of the 1930s many immigrant workers and specialists became victims of political repression, which grew uncontrolled in the Soviet state.[5]

Finns comprised one of the largest immigrant groups in the first two decades of Soviet history. They settled mainly in Soviet Karelia, an autonomous republic in northwestern Russia bordering Finland itself. During the period 1920–35, it was headed by Finnish political immigrants, or so-called Red Finns, who developed and carried out an immigration policy aimed at bringing large numbers of left-leaning Finns to Soviet Karelia. Before the turn of the 1930s, most immigrants to Soviet Karelia came directly from Finland. In the early 1930s, however, several thousand Canadian and American Finns arrived and immediately found themselves in the midst of drastic social and economic transformations.

As a consequence, the history of North American immigration to the Soviet Union reflected most of the characteristic features of development of pre-Second World War Soviet society: social, economic, and national policies of the central and regional authorities that drastically changed both society and state, reactions of the population to these revolutionary transformations, as well as peculiarities of regional development and interethnic relations in Soviet Karelia. To translate this into contemporary academic discourse, power and culture, center and periphery, ethnicity and nation, migration and diaspora, labor and class—all these and many other categories can effectively be explored by addressing the case of American and Canadian Finnish emigration to Soviet Karelia. Its close study offers novel perspectives on issues of interwar Soviet history such as competition among regional economies and their slow and by no means complete integration into the centralized economic system built in the 1930s; competition among different visions of how to transform Soviet ethnic peripheries; and Soviet appeal to Western visions of modernity embodied in the skills, culture, and very bodies of immigrants in efforts to realize the socialist project. The background and course of their immigration; their roles in economic, national, and cultural changes in a Soviet ethnic periphery; and their fates in Soviet Russia are the research questions that this book aims to examine.

One particular region of the Soviet Union, the Karelian Autonomous Soviet Socialist Republic (KASSR), or Soviet Karelia, is the focus of this book. Soviet Karelia was that socialist El Dorado to which thousands of Finnish Americans and Canadians set sail in the early 1930s. Located in the northwest of Russia and occupying the lengthiest part of the Soviet-Finnish border, Soviet Karelia had a long history of cross-border contacts and conflicts, first as part of the Russo-Swedish medieval and early modern struggle for hegemony in the Baltic Sea area, then, after the last Russo-Swedish War of 1808–9, when Sweden ceded its Finnish counties to Russia, as part of the Russian-Finnish dialogue and struggle over the status and place of Finland in Russian imperial politics. After 1917, when Finland became independent, this struggle moved once again into the sphere of international relations, addressed in detail in the third section of the first chapter.

Because of its position as a border territory with a large share of non-Russian population and contested by a foreign power, Soviet Karelia occupied a specific place in Soviet regional politics. In many ways, it was not a typical Soviet region—but the Soviet Union had hardly any "typical" regions. Neither was it a sociocultural space unified and solidified by a common Communist ideology. Although that ideology was a powerful force, to its demise the Soviet Union existed as a patchwork of local ethnicities, cultures, bureaucracies, and practices.

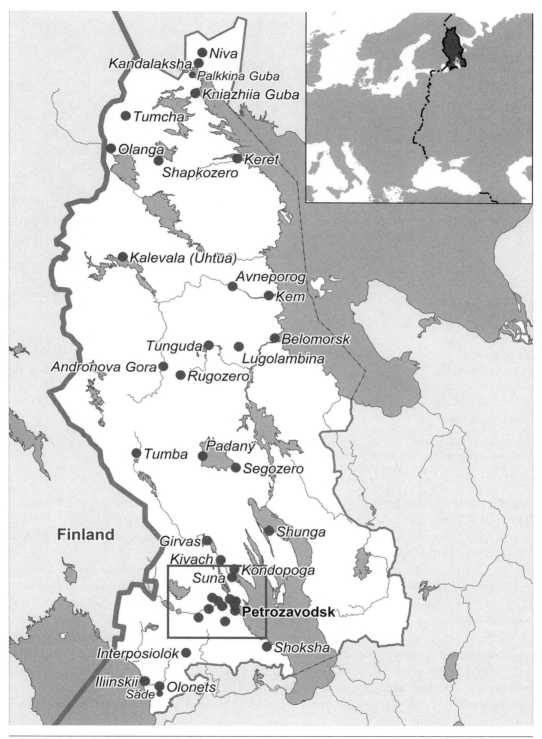

MAP 1. SCHEMATIC REPRESENTATION OF SETTLEMENTS WITH SIGNIFICANT NORTH AMERICAN FINNISH COMMUNITIES IN SOVIET KARELIA DURING THE 1930S. CREATED BY IRINA TAKALA AND ELENA LYALLYA. (COURTESY OF THE GEOGRAPHIC INFORMATION SYSTEMS DEPARTMENT AT PETROZAVODSK STATE UNIVERSITY.)

MAP 2. SCHEMATIC REPRESENTATION OF SETTLEMENTS WITH SIGNIFICANT NORTH AMERICAN FINNISH COMMUNITIES IN THE SURROUNDINGS OF PETROZAVODSK. CREATED BY IRINA TAKALA AND ELENA LYALLYA. (COURTESY OF THE GEOGRAPHIC INFORMATION SYSTEMS DEPARTMENT AT PETROZAVODSK STATE UNIVERSITY.)

Equally, Soviet politics never took shape as a projection of the omnipotent will of Moscow on the regions; instead, the politics were formed through never-ending negotiations between center and periphery, and, no matter how passive and receptive the latter seemed on a superficial level, such negotiation deeply influenced political, economic, social, and cultural practice in the USSR. The case of Karelia in Soviet foreign and domestic policies of the 1920s and 1930s, and the story of North American emigration to this region, are, in this way, typical for Soviet history in their atypicality, and hopefully their examination will yield new insights into the turbulent periods of the Soviet 1920s and particularly 1930s.

Until recently, Finnish emigration from North America to Soviet Karelia has been surprisingly neglected in scholarly research. The only monograph that addressed this phenomenon was written by Finnish scholar Reino Kero and published in 1983 in the Finnish language.[6] While providing an excellent analysis of the background and course of the immigration, Kero, who had no access to Soviet archives, was inevitably less specific on the lives of immigrants in Soviet Karelia. Before this volume and other works published by Kero in the 1970s, the Karelian fever (what emigration to Soviet Karelia was called in Finnish communities in North America during the early 1930s) had been nearly completely forgotten. In one of his early works, Kero attributed this situation to a number of complicated problems that hampered a careful study of the Karelian fever. Restricted access to Soviet materials was one problem, but a much more significant one was reluctance among American and Finnish researchers to address the social dimension of this historical phenomenon. Finnish emigration from the New World was a clear indication of a deep social conflict between Finnish immigrants, on the one hand, and American and Canadian societies, on the other, and according to Kero it was difficult for scholars from Finland and the United States or Canada to approach this issue from academic perspectives.[7] This gap in historical writing was partly bridged by memoirs, but they were also scarce.[8]

The collapse of the Soviet regime gave both Russian and Western researchers access to formerly restricted archival collections. This access initiated a new wave of studies on the emigration of American and Canadian Finns to Soviet Karelia[9] and encouraged a radical re-examination of the early history of Soviet Karelia, particularly in Finland.[10] This interest among Finnish historians resulted from the fact that, between 1920 and 1935, the development of Soviet Karelia followed, to a considerable degree, strategies shaped by Finnish émigré politicians, and references to Soviet Karelia of this period as an "alternative Finland" became common in historical research.

In the Soviet Union, the first publications about North American Finnish immigrants appeared during the relative and brief liberalization of historical writing in the early 1960s.[11] Written in the Soviet historical paradigm, they explained the phenomenon of Finnish immigration to Soviet Karelia in terms of world proletarian solidarity with the USSR, failing to mention equally (if not more) important reasons for the immigration, to say nothing of the fates of immigrants during the Great Terror. Only after perestroika did it become possible to carry out more careful and insightful research on this issue.[12] New journalistic books based on memoirs and interviews of North American Finns,[13] as well as a comprehensive register of Finnish victims of the Great Terror, including North American immigrants,[14] were also published during this period.

In the 2000s, Russian and Western researchers of Finnish American and Canadian immigration to the Soviet Union finally established contact with each other. At conferences in 2004 in Thunder Bay (Canada), in 2006 in Eskilstuna (Sweden), and in 2008 in Petrozavodsk (Russia), scholars from Canada, the United States, Finland, Sweden, and Russia discussed the Karelian fever as an international phenomenon that stretched over the Atlantic and connected, in a number of surprising ways, global, national, regional, and personal histories in both the Old World and the New World. This research cooperation opened the way for new publications, which became important contributions to this field.[15]

This book is the result of our participation in two international research projects mentioned in the Preface. While working on these projects, we were able to become acquainted with research perspectives on this subject originating in North American academia and to identify and examine earlier unknown sources stored in the National Archive of the Republic of Karelia, to analyze the regional Karelian press of the 1930s, and to collect oral history interviews from American and Canadian immigrants and their children.[16] Sources stored in the National Archive were particularly useful for our research. Throughout the history of this immigration, it absorbed documents of Finnish American and Canadian labor and socialist organizations between 1908 and 1930, documents of Soviet party and government bodies responsible for immigration, materials related to official inspections of immigrants' living and working conditions, and personal files of immigrants. Our experience of other research perspectives and our discovery of new sources allowed for a new, more coherent, and complete narrative of the history of immigration of American and Canadian Finns to Soviet Karelia.

Our research agenda involved returning agency to political and social groups other than the central Soviet leadership. Although appeals to overcome the totalitarian model formulated after the Second World War by Karl Popper and Hannah Arendt have sounded loudly in the field of Soviet history for several decades,[17] the explanatory framework that renders all agency behind Soviet historical phenomena during the 1930s to the early 1950s to Communist leadership in general, and to Stalin in particular, remains influential in academic writing and, even when challenged rhetorically, reveals itself through unconscious choices of concepts, rhetorical strategies, and models of argumentation. Our opinion is that, though this model was heuristic in the 1940s and since then has helped to produce important knowledge about Soviet history, by now it can only reiterate rather well-known truisms. New knowledge in the field of Soviet history, including the Stalinist period, is now created by research projects that examine it as a complex web of central and regional agents and as a never-ending process of negotiation among them. It is also created by attempts to historicize emotions, rational ideas, life strategies, and symbolic spaces of Soviet people—something that we attempted to do in this research, taking North American immigrants as a case and placing it into a wider political, economic, and social context of Soviet history of the 1920s and 1930s.

Since we attempted to write a comprehensive history of the immigration of North American Finns to Soviet Karelia, we had a hard time finding a middle ground between building a narrative that would cover different themes related to this immigration and our desire to problematize the material that we had extracted from a mass of primary and secondary sources. The price of this compromise was that in some cases we had to sacrifice detailed analysis to keep our narrative pace smooth and avoid an overemphasis on certain problems at the expense of others. Yet the discipline of history is genealogically rooted in storytelling, and we had what seemed to us an interesting story to tell, so we are ready to accept the disadvantages of this compromise to reap the fruits of its advantages.

The book consists of nine chapters and is structured along both chronological and problem-oriented lines. The first chapter presents the general historical background of the Karelian fever: the emergence of the Finnish diaspora as a result of emigration from Finland to the United States, Canada, and Russia (Sweden is omitted because it is not relevant to our research agenda). Its third section focuses on the role of Finnish Communist émigrés in early Soviet regional and ethnic politics that resulted in the establishment in 1920 of a new autonomous ethnic region, Soviet Karelia, where Finnish Communists became the political elite. The second chapter examines, in three narrowing circles, early Soviet immigration policy. It starts with the general Soviet context, then looks at the role of immigration policy in economic and cultural visions of the Finnish leadership of Soviet Karelia, and finally investigates how these visions, combined with economic and political factors, sparked the Karelian fever in North American Finnish communities. In the third chapter, we analyze the heyday of Finnish emigration from the United States and Canada to Soviet Karelia, including operations of the Karelian Technical Aid Committee, an organization established to assist the immigration process, disputes among different forces in the Soviet bureaucracy over this immigration flow, and the motivations of Finns that urged them to emigrate from their American or Canadian communities to unknown, but picturesquely imagined, Soviet reality.

Chapter 4 discusses causes of the failure of immigration policy of Soviet Karelian authorities, focusing, in particular, on their inability to defend their vision of ethnic, cultural, economic, and political development of Soviet Karelia against competing visions of other bodies of Soviet bureaucracy. Its third section also addresses the disappointment of immigrants themselves on confronting a reality that had little to do with the imagined Soviet Karelia. Chapter 5 details the contributions of Finnish immigrants to the Soviet Karelian economy and, through it, to the transfer of knowledge and technology from the West to the USSR. Chapter 6 provides a similar analysis, focusing on how a new Soviet Karelian culture interwove Finnish nationalist, Marxist internationalist, and North American cultural influences brought by the immigrants. In Chapter 7, we address the issues of cross-cultural communication between Finnish immigrants and the local Soviet population, a situation that served as a litmus test highlighting stereotypes and prejudices—but also goodwill and cooperation—of both groups.

The last two chapters discuss the most traumatic and disturbing episodes in the history of North American Finnish immigration to the USSR: the Great Terror and the Second World War. Chapter 8 examines the background of the "Finnish operation" of the NKVD during the Great Terror, the course and consequences of the operation itself, and, in the final section, the attempt to disguise the repression of American and Canadian Finnish immigrants from the international labor movement, particularly in Canada. Chapter 9 explores the fates of North American Finns in the turmoil of the Second World War, which for them was split into the Soviet-Finnish (or Winter) War of 1939–40 and the war against Nazi Germany and its allies, of which Finland was de facto, if not entirely de jure, one. Its last section addresses in passing the postwar history of North American Finnish communities in Soviet Karelia.

Finnish emigration from the United States and Canada to Soviet Karelia was a phenomenon that spanned national, regional, and personal levels of Soviet interwar history. In many ways, North American Finnish immigrant communities in the USSR turned out to be a middle ground between East and West, Moscow and Soviet periphery, and indigenous and immigrant groups in Soviet society, while Soviet Karelia became in this process a contact zone between capitalist and socialist worlds in their 1930s versions. This book explores this middle ground and contact zone to better understand the grand scale of processes in the 1930s on both sides of the Atlantic and the ways in which people made sense of them to build their lives.

CHAPTER 1

Finnish Immigrants in North America and Russia

AMERICAN FEVER

THE FIRST FINNISH SETTLERS ARRIVED IN NORTH AMERICA AS EARLY AS THE SEVENTEENTH century,[1] but in general large-scale emigration from Northern Europe to the New World did not occur until the nineteenth century. "American fever" broke out in Norway in the 1820s, struck Sweden in the 1840s, and appeared in the mid-1860s in the Grand Duchy of Finland, then a part of the Russian Empire. Economic problems in Finland at that time were the key to a sharp rise in the number of Finnish emigrants sailing across the Atlantic in the mid-nineteenth century.

In the second half of the nineteenth century and into the early twentieth century, Finnish economic development was plagued by contradictions between its traditional agricultural economy and fundamental demographic changes. In the early twentieth century, approximately 70 percent of the Finnish population still earned their living through agriculture, while only 10 percent worked in industries and crafts.[2] The stability of this mostly rural society was undermined by rapid growth of its population starting early in the nineteenth century. By 1870, the population of the Grand Duchy had more than doubled compared with that of the beginning of the century: from 863,000 people in 1810 to 1,770,000 in 1870. Between 1870 and 1910, the population of Finland was increasing rapidly, by approximately 300,000 people every decade, and by the outbreak of the First World War it exceeded 3 million people.[3] The resulting overpopulation had a dramatic impact on the quality of life, primarily in rural areas that could no longer support an increasing number of tenants because of existing legislation. According to the law, land could not be divided among heirs: even in large families, only one of the children could inherit it, while the rest had to earn a living by other means. Industry and small Finnish towns were unable to provide enough work, and emigration became inevitable for many of of the landless population.

By the late 1880s, American fever spread through all of the western provinces of Finland, most notably affecting Pohjanmaa, territories northeast of the Gulf of Bothnia, since they had no large industrial centers to attract those of the redundant rural population. Traditional economic activities of Finns living in the provinces of Uleåborg and Vaza[4]—production of tar and pitch, shipbuilding, timber processing—declined throughout the nineteenth century: along the Bothnic coast, most forests had been cut down, while wooden sailing ships were gradually replaced with metal steamships. As a result, out of 302,800 emigrants who left Finland between 1870 and 1914, 206,000 (68 percent) were former residents of these two western provinces.[5] Emigration was also inspired by stories of Finnish sailors who, upon return from their voyages, praised the conditions of life and work in the United States as well as by letters from relatives and friends who had already emigrated there.[6]

The United States indeed seemed an extremely attractive destination for European immigrants. Distribution of unoccupied lands outside the original thirteen colonies under the Homestead Act of 1862 seemed like a fairy tale for hungry peasants of the Old World. Gold rushes in California and Alaska ignited hopes of becoming rich quickly and easily. Freedom of enterprise as well as plentiful work in the mines of Michigan and Minnesota, in the ports of the Great Lakes, in railroad building, and in the timber industry—for many Finns, these opportunities became the driving force behind the decision to emigrate.

In the 1880s, approximately 25,000 people moved from Finland to the United States for permanent residence there.[7] Gradually, Finns from the central and eastern parts of Finland joined the flow of emigration from its western provinces. The Finnish Lutheran Church as well as the imperial administration and Finnish authorities condemned emigration and made numerous efforts to prevent the outflow of population from the Grand Duchy, but these efforts proved futile.[8] Emigration peaked in 1902 when crops failed and Russian imperial authorities intended to introduce conscription into the Russian army for young Finnish men.[9] During that year, 23,000 people permanently left Finland. In total, between 1880 and 1910, approximately 280,000 people emigrated from Finland to the United States, and by the First World War the total number of emigrants had risen to 302,000.[10]

During the Great War, the scale of emigration from Finland was very small, and in the early 1920s the immigration policy of the United States changed significantly. In 1921, Congress passed the Emergency Quota Act, which limited the annual number of immigrants from European countries to slightly over 350,000. Separate quotas were also set for every country. They were calculated on the basis of the 1910 United States Census: the number allowed entry from any country was restricted to 3 percent of the total number of people of that nationality living in the United States in 1910. Three years later annual immigration quotas for European countries were reduced again, to 164,000 people. The Immigration Act of 1924 limited the number of immigrants from any country to 2 percent of the number of people of that nationality living in the United States in 1890, according to the census of that year. The annual quota for Finnish immigrants was set as low as 471 (according to the 1921 Emergency Quota Act, it was 3,921).[11]

After the passing of these laws in the United States, the main flow of Finnish immigration turned to Canada. From 1901 to 1920, Canada welcomed slightly more than 20,000 Finns, and from 1921 to 1930 that number increased to 36,000 Finns. Half of them arrived in Canada just before the Great Depression (18,448 people from 1926 to 1929). Since they did not have enough time for proper adaptation, they became the most vulnerable group during the upcoming economic crisis.[12]

A general overview of Finnish immigration to the United States between 1870 and 1930 shows that men constituted 63 percent of the flow, that approximately 70 percent of immigrants were aged between fifteen and thirty-four, and that almost all of them (over 90 percent) were former rural dwellers.[13] About a third of Finnish immigrants returned to Finland.

FIGURE 1. ONE-YEAR-OLD AARE LEKANDER, THE FIRST CHILD IN THE FINNISH CANADIAN FAMILY OF VALTER AND AUNE LEKANDERS, RESIDENTS OF SASKATCHEWAN, CANADA, SEVERAL MONTHS PRIOR TO THEIR EMIGRATION TO SOVIET KARELIA (GOLUBEV AND TAKALA, *USTNAIA ISTORIIA*, 119).

According to census data, the number of Finnish-born immigrants with their children was 320,500 in the United States in 1930 and 43,600 in Canada in 1931.[14]

Finnish immigrants tended to settle in the areas where climate and landscape resembled their native land. In the United States, the largest Finnish communities formed in Michigan and Minnesota (41.2 percent of the overall Finnish population, according to the census of 1930), while in Canada Finns settled mostly in Ontario (62.3 percent of all Finnish Canadians in 1931).[15] Men worked in mines, in lumber camps, and on railroad construction; many were employed in large factories or established their own farms.

Integration into a new society proved difficult for many Finnish immigrants. They were slow to adapt to new realities, the primary reason being the difficulty of the English language for them: unlike most other European languages, including English, which are part of the Indo-European language family, Finnish belongs to the Uralic languages. This had a considerable impact on the Finnish diaspora—Finns tended to stick to their communities, settling compactly and establishing numerous religious and social ethnic organizations, societies, clubs, and communes in which they could speak their native language. Many immigrants who arrived in North America at the turn of the twentieth century never learned to speak English since they spent their lives in entirely Finnish-speaking communities. Linguistic contact between Finnish immigrants and the surrounding English-language environment resulted in a new pidgin, so-called Finglish, spoken rather widely during the 1920s and 1930s. Described in simplified terms, Finglish was a mixture of Finnish syntax and morphology with English vocabulary, which meant that English words were used with Finnish verbal or case endings, resulting in phrases such as *karalla raidemme dauntaunille* ("we are going to downtown by car") that much amused native English speakers.[16] The local population considered

FIGURE 2. A FINNISH AMATEUR THEATER TROUPE, SASKATCHEWAN, CANADA, LATE 1920S OR EARLY 1930S (GOLUBEV AND TAKALA, *USTNAIA ISTORIIA*, 119).

the Finns a rather strange people who were hard to understand and did not like to go outside their close communities.[17]

Yet in their communities Finnish immigrants organized an active social, political, and cultural life. The first influential social organizations of American Finns were temperance societies under the auspices of the Finnish Lutheran Church. Later, by the turn of the twentieth century, the entire Finnish diaspora became split on the basis of religious and political views. On the one side were Finns who adhered to religion and a conservative political position and criticized socialism not only because of its economic foundations but also because of its hostility toward religion. As a rule, they tried to preserve their Finnish Lutheran identities and wanted to become an organic part of American society. On the other side were Finns attracted to political and religious radicalism because of their failed dreams and their disappointment in the "country of rhinoceroses," a sarcastic nickname for the United States used by many of them.[18] The growing popularity of radical views (according to various sources, they were shared by up to 25 percent of Finnish immigrants[19]) was boosted by numerous Finnish political, social, and cooperative organizations as well as by workers' Finnish-language press.[20] The activities of the radicals provoked anti-Finnish sentiment in American society and caused growing suspicion among American and Canadian authorities. This worsened living and working conditions of Finnish immigrants and caused further growth of radicalism among them.[21]

The Russian Revolution of 1917 and the Finnish Civil War of 1918 intensified the hostility between these two groups of North American Finns. During the 1920s, the period preceding large-scale Finnish emigration to Soviet Karelia, the Finnish diaspora in North America split into two social worlds that would not overlap each other for decades to come.

FIGURE 3. A BUILDING HOSTING A FINNISH WORKERS' CLUB, SASKATCHEWAN, CANADA, LATE 1920S OR EARLY 1930S (GOLUBEV AND TAKALA, *USTNAIA ISTORIIA*, 119).

EMIGRATION TO THE EAST

Large-scale Finnish emigration to Russia started in the first half of the nineteenth century, almost immediately after Finland became part of the Russian Empire. Like the later emigration to North America, its main cause was rural overpopulation. Huge numbers of poor people were unable to find permanent jobs and were often tried under rather harsh laws for vagrancy. The Russian labor market provided good opportunities for many of these people. Finns were also in a more favorable position compared with Russian peasants, at least before the emancipation of serfs in 1861, since all inhabitants of Finland were personally free, unlike a large part of the Russian rural population. Finally, emigration was also stimulated by frequent crop failures that led to famine and financial ruin for many Finns.

In the late 1880s, the flow of Finnish emigrants to Russia dropped considerably, and minor increases were observed only under favorable economic conditions in the late 1890s and during the First World War with construction of the St. Petersburg-Murmansk railroad. The decrease in emigration was caused by changes in the economies of both Finland and Russia, by growth of the Russian industrial proletariat, and by a more complicated political situation caused by tsarist assaults on Finnish autonomy. At the turn of the twentieth century, emigration from the Grand Duchy changed its main direction toward North America.

Emigration to Russia during the nineteenth century can be characterized as a boundary migration, for the majority of Finnish emigrants, mainly inhabitants of eastern Finland, settled in the Russian northwestern provinces, namely St. Petersburg, Olonets, and Arkhangelsk.

According to the 1897 Russian census, about 36,000 Finns resided in the Russian provinces of the empire, with 98 percent (ca. 35,000) living in the European part of Russia.[22]

The most important regions of immigration were St. Petersburg city and St. Petersburg province,[23] which hosted over 80 percent of all Finns living in the Russian Empire. St. Petersburg, the capital of the empire, was a huge metropolis located only thirty-two kilometers from the Russian-Finnish border as established in 1812. Consequently, it had a major influence on the population on the Finnish side of the border, providing a huge market for land and sea trade, transportation, and crafts. In the mid-nineteenth century, over 10,000 business trips between Finland and St. Petersburg were registered annually. Because of these tight contacts, Finns interested in emigration to the imperial capital had no difficulty learning about living and working conditions that they would encounter there. The favorable economic and labor situation there further stimulated Finnish emigration.[24]

It is hard to determine the exact number of Finns in St. Petersburg at any given time because the migration flow was always active both ways. The Finnish immigrant community in St. Petersburg was heterogeneous. One part of it was permanently on the move between their work in St. Petersburg and home in Finland. Others stayed to work in Russia for extended periods of time, but eventually moved back to Finland. Yet others planned to settle down in St. Petersburg city or province permanently. The Finnish population of the Russian capital seemed to reach its peak by the early 1880s, with about 22,000 Finns registered in 1881. Then it began to decrease, and by 1910 the number of people of Finnish origin (with their children) in St. Petersburg was about 15,000.[25]

Over 80 percent of all Finns in St. Petersburg were employed in industry and crafts. Their most common occupations were weavers, spinners, shoemakers, tailors, and carpenters. Many Finns worked in metallurgy, and over half of all chimney-sweeps in the capital were Finns. St. Petersburg was also important as a place where Finns could master new crafts less developed at that time in Finland, such as watchmaking and gold working.[26] In the area around St. Petersburg, Finns were occupied in transportation, crafts, and trade.

Social conditions and short distances encouraged Finnish women to emigrate, and their share of the emigration flow to St. Petersburg varied between 50 percent and 60 percent in the second half of the nineteenth century. Finnish women worked mostly as housemaids (over 60 percent of all Finnish immigrant women) as well as in industry (primarily textiles) and various crafts.[27]

Most Finnish immigrants stayed in St. Petersburg city or province only temporarily. Having earned enough money or learned some professional skills, they moved back to Finland. Finns almost never mixed with the multi-ethnic community of St. Petersburg. One reason was language, for most immigrants did not bother to perfect their Russian; a second reason was religion, for the Finnish community was consolidated around the Lutheran Church. For Finns, parishes served as centers of national culture, as places where they felt unity with their homeland. Immigrants had their ethnic associations, which maintained tight contacts with Finland, and their newspapers, which were printed in Finnish.[28] Finally, ethnic unity was also preserved because of the normal demographic structure of the Finnish community, which promoted inside marriages and prevented interethnic ones. During the revolutions of 1917 and the ensuing civil war of 1918, a majority of these immigrants moved back to Finland.

Emigration of Finns to other regions of European Russia—Olonets and Arkhangelsk provinces[29]—was caused by different factors, as reflected in the social structure of this emigration flow. The primary motivation for Finns who moved to these northern regions of the

Russian Empire was frequent crop failure. This was evidenced, first, by the coincidence of high emigration with hungry years in the Grand Duchy and, second, by the mostly peasant origins of emigrants to Arkhangelsk and Olonets, who came mostly from Finnish rural areas, a noticeable contrast to Finnish emigrants to St. Petersburg, who came mostly from Finnish urban centers.

Finnish settlers first arrived in Olonets province in the 1830s, and in the second half of the century their number increased significantly. By the turn of the twentieth century, the Finnish population of Olonets province reached 3,000 people and remained at that level in 1917 (1 percent of the total population of the province). There was parity between male and female Finns in this area; children and youth below twenty constituted a high share at over 40 percent.[30] Men were employed in industry, crafts, construction, timber cutting and rafting, farm work, and river transportation (including barges). Women worked in rich households. Most Finns in Olonets province regarded immigration as a temporary stage in their lives, as did those in St. Petersburg province. At the end of the nineteenth century, first-generation immigrants in the Finnish community in Olonets province still comprised 90 percent. In 1917 and 1918, approximately 70 percent of Finns returned to their homeland.[31]

The largest concentration of Finnish settlers in Arkhangelsk province was in the Kola Peninsula on the arctic coast. Their first settlements emerged there in the 1860s, which were hungry years in Finland. Emigration was also stimulated by decrees of the Russian government issued in 1868, 1876, and 1890 that offered privileges to colonists of the Kola Peninsula—both to Russian nationals and to foreigners, to the latter on the condition that they become Russian citizens. Because of the special status of the Grand Duchy of Finland, Finns belonged to this second group. Unlike Finns in St. Petersburg and Olonets provinces, Finns who emigrated to the Kola Peninsula intended to take permanent root there. Most colonists settled along the coast of the Barents Sea (the Kola Bay) and along the Tuloma River.[32] By the end of the nineteenth century, there were a number of Finnish rural settlements that maintained a traditional lifestyle.

In 1897, the number of Finns in the Kola Peninsula was 1,276 (645 men and 631 women). Only half of them (650 people) were first-generation immigrants (83 percent originated from Uleåborg province). The share of those who kept Finnish citizenship was even lower, 428 people, or 33 percent. The Finnish community in the Kola Peninsula had a normal demographic structure with a favorable outlook for further growth, for children and youth below twenty comprised 50 percent of the community.[33] Kola Finns were mostly engaged in fishing and hunting (55 percent of the gainfully employed). They also worked in farming, various crafts (woodworking, food processing, cloth making), and construction. Unlike Finns in St. Petersburg city, those in the Kola Peninsula maintained traditional gender roles: 80 percent of women over twenty depended financially on their husbands and were responsible only for the household and children.[34] During the First World War, the Finnish population in the Kola Peninsula increased considerably because of construction of a railroad between St. Petersburg and the arctic seaport of Murmansk, and in 1915 it reached 2,793 people, who constituted 19 percent of the total population in the region.[35] Unlike in other Russian provinces, revolutions in 1917 did not cause a mass exodus of immigrants back to Finland; most of them stayed in the Kola Peninsula.

The Russian Revolution and the ensuing Finnish Civil War led to drastic changes in the Finnish population of Russia. Many Finns returned to their homeland, and during the Soviet time the eastern Finnish diaspora actually formed anew. The period 1918–35 saw three large waves of emigration for a number of political and economic reasons following the Russian Revolution and the declaration of Finnish independence. The causes of emigration, the temporal frameworks, and the places of exodus for Finns to Soviet Russia allow us to divide them into three main groups: namely, political immigrants (Red Finns), illegal immigrants or border hoppers (*loikkarit* in Finnish), and North American immigrants.

The first large wave of emigration from Finland occurred at the end of and immediately after the Finnish Civil War of 1918, in which Social Democrats and their allies, or "Reds," confronted nationalist forces, or "Whites." The war was relatively short, lasting less than four months, but caused numerous casualties and had a deep negative impact on Finnish society, a trauma that lasted for decades. The policy of terror implemented by both sides, as well as postwar persecutions of former Red guards by their victorious White enemies resulted in about 30,000 victims (about 25,000 belonging to the Red camp). After the victory of the Whites, over 60,000 people were sentenced to various terms of imprisonment; although by the end of 1918 most of them were free under conditional releases, political repression still loomed over former Red combatants of the Civil War.[36] As a result, thousands of participants in these events and members of their families fled Finland. A certain number of emigrants moved to Sweden or other Western states, but the majority preferred to seek protection in Soviet Russia. During April and May 1918, 6,000 refugees arrived in Petrograd.[37] Initially, they were accommodated there and the town of Buy (БУЙ), where a special point of evacuation was established. From there, Finns were sent all over Russia to Vologda, Kostroma, Murom, Moscow, Nizhny Novgorod, Murmansk, Petrozavodsk, the Urals, and Siberia. By the end of the summer, most immigrants had found employment, while almost all men fit for military service formed voluntary ethnic Finnish detachments of the Red Army. After the Russian Civil War, the majority of political immigrants concentrated in the northwestern part of European Russia.

Political immigrants and their families kept on emigrating from Finland to Russia until the beginning of the 1930s. The precise number is difficult to determine since Red Finns were the most politically active part of the Finnish diaspora: the majority of them were members of the VKP(b) and employed in the Soviet bureaucratic apparatus. Consequently, they often changed their places of work and residences following orders from party authorities. Overall, various estimates suggest, the number of Finnish political immigrants in Soviet Russia was between 10,000 and 13,000.[38]

Two other large waves of Finnish emigration took place in the first half of the 1930s. One resulted primarily from the economic and political crisis in Finland. For several years starting in 1930, large groups of Finns chose to escape hunger and unemployment in their homeland by illegally crossing the border between Finland and the USSR. A propaganda campaign launched by Soviet Karelian authorities and Finnish Communists to increase the labor force for Soviet Karelian industry convinced many Finnish workers that fleeing across the border was the best possible alternative to unemployment or low-paid work in Finland. Between 1930 and 1934, between 12,000 and 15,000 Finns, according to different sources, hopped across the border into the USSR.[39] They were immediately placed in quarantine camps of the OGPU[40] (Soviet political police). After inspection, they were sent to work in various regions of the USSR or to the gulag system of camps: at that time, punishment for illegally crossing the border could be as high as three years of forced labor in camps. After 1932, the majority of illegal immigrants were allowed to work in those parts of Soviet Karelia or the Leningrad region that were not adjacent to the Finnish border. Unlike other Finnish immigrants, illegal immigrants found themselves in unfavorable conditions that were slightly better than those in the gulag camps. They lived in special settlements, were under constant supervision of the OGPU, were not issued passports or any other documents, and were unable to leave their workplaces on their own wishes. Almost all of them were used in hard jobs such as construction, timber cutting, or mining, disregarding their professional skills.[41]

The last but not least wave of Finnish emigration to the USSR came from the United States and Canada. Although the first groups of North American Finns started to arrive in Soviet Russia in the early 1920s, this did not become a large-scale phenomenon until a decade later. Their destination, as it was for the majority of Finnish political and illegal immigrants, was Soviet Karelia—an autonomous republic in the Russian northwest.

RED FINNS AND THE MAKING OF REVOLUTIONARY KARELIA

Karelia, a historical region divided by the border between Russia and Finland, belongs to that common type of European border region, such as Alsace, Schleswig, or Galicia (Halychyna), that often became a bone of contention between neighboring states and changed national affiliation several times during its history. Permanent settlements first emerged in Karelia in the early ninth century. By that time, Karelians had become a distinguished ethnic group who separated from the larger group of Finnic peoples. Their ethnic territories comprised the Karelian Isthmus and area to the west and north of Lake Ladoga. The period of early united Karelia lasted until the early fourteenth century, though already since the early twelfth century Karelian lands had become a battlefield between Sweden and the Russian republic of Great Novgorod. The western part of the Karelian Isthmus came under the influence of Sweden, which enforced Catholicism among western Karelians, while eastern Karelians found themselves a part of Novgorod's sphere of interests and, consequently, Russian Orthodox. Officially, they became the subjects of two different states for the first time in 1323, when Sweden and Novgorod divided Karelia according to the Treaty of Nöteborg.[42] Since then, the state border for many centuries divided western and eastern Karelians, with the borderline changing multiple times in the aftermath of Russo-Swedish and later Soviet-Finnish conflicts.

Between the fifteenth and seventeenth centuries, Karelians, many of whom were eager to escape from dangerous border territories, began to resettle northeast of the Karelian Isthmus, colonizing together with Novgorod Russians vast territories between Lakes Ladoga and Onega and the White Sea. By the early nineteenth century, when, during the last Russo-Swedish war of 1808–9, the Russian Empire conquered Finland from Sweden, eastern Karelians inhabited the territories of two Russian regions—Olonets and Arkhangelsk provinces (lands populated by Karelians in these provinces were known as Olonets Karelia and White Sea Karelia respectively). White Sea Karelia played a significant role in the history of Finnish culture, for it was there that during the 1820s to 1840s Elias Lönnrot discovered and transcribed most of the folklore material that he later used to create the Finnish national epic poem "Kalevala."[43] Since the northern Karelian dialect was particularly close to the nascent Finnish literary language, in the mid-nineteenth century Karelia became a source of inspiration for Finnish writers, poets, artists, and composers (a cultural phenomenon called Karelianism).[44] Thus, during the nineteenth century, Karelia turned into an imagined world of Finnish nationalism, and its cultural images contributed to the making of Finnish national identity.

Interest in Russian Karelia also gradually penetrated the political agenda of Finland: in the second half of the nineteenth century, Karelianism transformed from a national cultural trend into irredentist political aspirations encapsulated in the concept of a Greater Finland (or its variation natural Finland), which referred to a unified territorial entity comprising Finland, eastern Karelia, and the Kola Peninsula.[45] In this way, the irredentist agenda of Finnish nationalists was part of similar nationalist irredentist aspirations that followed the rise of nation-states in nineteenth-century Europe and helped to mobilize nationalist audiences and construct "imagined communities." In the early twentieth century, the doctrine of a Greater Finland appeared in the international arena in the form of the eastern Karelian question, an active propaganda campaign by Finnish volunteers among eastern Karelians, which from the beginning combined enlightening ideals with pro-Finnish ideological pragmatism.[46]

Between 1918 and 1922, Finnish nationalists made several attempts to incorporate parts of the territories inhabited by eastern Karelians by military and diplomatic means.[47] One of the arguments used by Finnish nationalists to justify their attempts to annex territories of "kindred" Karelian people was the lack of autonomy and self-determination for eastern Karelians in Soviet Russia. This became one of the reasons that led the Soviet leadership to declare the establishment of Soviet Karelia as an autonomous federal territory of Russia in 1920.[48] Initially, its official name was Karelian Workers' Commune and since 1923 Karelian Autonomous Soviet Socialist Republic (KASSR). By early 1922, when Finland disputed the international status of Soviet Karelia in the League of Nations, arguing that the right of self-determination for the Karelian people had been violated by the Soviet government, the latter had a weighty counterargument to repel Finnish claims: Karelian ethnic autonomy as a voluntarily chosen form of national self-determination for Russian Karelians.[49]

Diplomatic considerations, however, were only part of the story. By 1920, the Russian Civil War was drawing to its end, and victorious Bolsheviks faced a whole set of new problems related to peace-time administration of vast territories that they had inherited from the Russian Empire. Military subordination by the Red Army, such as in northern and some western parts of Soviet Karelia, was obviously not enough, taking into account the limited economic and human resources that the Soviet government possessed; more importantly, Bolshevik leaders did not want to rely on military power as a basis for territorial administration. Instead, they implemented complex measures that combined compulsion with persuasion and appointed trusted Communists to key positions in administration, economy, culture, and education that allowed for overall control of national life in a country where the majority of citizens remained skeptical of, if not hostile to, the new power. In many respects, Bolshevik tactics after 1920 resembled methods of colonial administration, with the main difference that functions of colonial officials were performed by the Communist bureaucracy, and these colonialist practices were directed at Russia's own population in a kind of internal colonization.

Introduced among scholars of Russian history by Aleksandr Etkind, the concept of internal colonization was initially meant to facilitate a reinterpretation of Russian imperial spatial politics[50] and was later applied to studies of Soviet history,[51] implying a specific relationship between the Russian/Soviet state and its subjects, wherein the former regards its own territory as a colony, rather than as a metropolis, and its population as people requiring proper civilization and acculturation. Dark, illiterate, petty bourgeois, and sometimes openly counterrevolutionary post-Civil War Russia had to be colonized by new Soviet ideas, a new Soviet way of life, and new Soviet people who could be forged from "old" people but also come from elsewhere. In Soviet Karelia, these new people were Finnish Communist émigrés. To get the idea of an autonomous Karelia off the ground, the Soviet government appointed Red Finns, who had actively been advocating the idea of Karelian autonomy, to govern the newly created region. The policy of this new Red Finnish leadership of Soviet Karelia, which shaped its further development for over a decade, was determined by Edvard Gylling, a former member of the Finnish Parliament, a prominent member of the Finnish Social Democratic Party, and a doctor of philosophy.

Gylling was born in 1881 in Ikaalinen into a well-to-do Swedish Finnish family and was bilingual from his early childhood. In 1903, after three years at the University of Helsinki, he defended his master's thesis on the economic situation of agricultural workers in Ikaalinen parish. His doctoral thesis addressed an issue of major importance to Finland in the early twentieth century, the so-called *torppari question* (a *torppari* was a tenant of a small land plot in Finland similar to a crofter in England).[52] Apart from statistics and economy, during his university studies, Gylling became interested in Social Democratic ideas widespread among students at that time. In 1905, he became a member of the Finnish Social Democratic Party, and because of his expertise on the peasant question he was soon a leading expert of his party in agrarian policy. In the 1908 parliamentary election, he won his first seat in the Finnish Diet for the Social Democrats, and he was re-elected twice, in 1911 and 1917.[53] He also had a successful academic career, holding since 1910 the position of associate professor in statistics at the University of Helsinki.

As a member of the Finnish Social Democratic Party, Gylling persistently advocated the idea of a coalition with the Agrarian League to implement social reforms. He was one of the few Finnish politicians who, after the proclamation of Finnish independence in December 1917, did their best to prevent a towering confrontation between socialists and nationalists in order to avoid a civil war. Gylling, in particular, was one of only two Social Democratic leaders to vote against the takeover of power inspired by the radical wing of the party at the end of January 1918. After the Finnish Civil War broke out, Gylling expressed his protest initially by not taking any appointment in the revolutionary government. Only after he became convinced that most rank-and-file Social Democrats did not support his isolationism did he accept the post of minister of finance in the Red Finnish government. His hopes for compromise with the Whites and national peace were finally destroyed when the White government appealed for help to the German Empire to ensure a decisive defeat of the Reds. After the landing of the German expeditionary force in Finland on 3 April 1918 and subsequent defeats of the Finnish Red Guard by the combined White Finnish and German forces, the Soviet government recommended that Red Finns give up their resistance and emigrate to Russia. This time, however, Gylling stubbornly supported continuation of the struggle.[54] He was the only leader of the Reds who refused to flee to Russia, instead going first underground and then, when he no longer had any hope in the success of the Red cause, moving to Sweden.

In Sweden, Gylling became interested in the future of Russian Karelia, a question that he had already dealt with in negotiations with the government of Soviet Russia in early 1918, during the time of a short-lived revolutionary government of Finland. At first, he was skeptical about a Bolshevik victory in the Russian Civil War and projected a unification of Scandinavia into a federation, in which Russian Karelia would become an autonomous entity.[55] After Gylling was finally convinced that the Bolsheviks were triumphant because of what he believed was wide popular support, he planned a new project in which autonomous

Russian Karelia was supposed to remain a part of Soviet Russia and become a kind of bridgehead for expansion of the socialist revolution into Northern Europe. According to Gylling, by establishing a "separate Karelian commune with the borders in the White Sea, Lake Onega, Finnish border and . . . Arctic Ocean," the Soviet government would be able to solve two troublesome issues: first, satisfying the nationalist aspirations of the Karelian population; second, eliminating the basis of Finland's claims regarding eastern Karelia.[56] He also believed that these ideas had to be implemented by those with expert knowledge of the Karelian question, namely Red Finns.[57]

These plans and Gylling's negotiations with Soviet People's Commissar of Foreign Affairs Georgy Chicherin, and later with Lenin and Stalin, all this with Finnish territorial claims in the background, resulted in the Soviet government's decree of 1920, which merged territories of Olonets and Arkhangelsk provinces populated by Karelians into a new autonomous region initially called the Karelian Workers' Commune. Edvard Gylling became the first head of the autonomous Karelian republic, a post that he held for fifteen years, until 1935.

Thus, Soviet Karelia resulted from a curious tangle of ideas that came from nationalist rhetoric, diplomatic negotiations, colonialist practices, and revolutionary aspirations. Nineteenth-century Finnish nationalists started to think of Russian Karelia as a territory that deserved self-determination; their twentieth-century counterparts used the collapse of

FIGURE 4. TWO PROMINENT RED FINNISH LEADERS OF SOVIET KARELIA: EDVARD GYLLING (FOURTH FROM THE RIGHT, WITH A CANE), THE CHAIRPERSON OF THE COUNCIL OF PEOPLE'S COMMISSARS (EQUIVALENT TO HEAD OF THE GOVERNMENT), AND KUSTAA ROVIO (THIRD FROM THE RIGHT, IN A BLACK COAT), THE FIRST SECRETARY OF THE KARELIAN REGIONAL COMMITTEE (*OBKOM*) OF THE VKP(B), AT THE MAY 1ST PARADE IN PETROZAVODSK (1930) (PHOTO BY G. A. ANKUDINOV; COURTESY OF THE NATIONAL ARCHIVE OF THE REPUBLIC OF KARELIA).

the Russian Empire for military incursions into and diplomatic claims for Karelian territories, which forced the Soviet government to come up with a response framed in terms of ethnic autonomy for Karelians. It is a speculative question whether an autonomous Karelia would have appeared on the Soviet political map in 1920 without this Finnish factor, but concepts and categories (and even the actual borders) were partly borrowed from Finnish nationalist rhetoric, with Red Finns acting as translators of Finnish nationalist ideas into Communist rhetoric and practice.[58] The need to control the Karelian population and "reforge" it into proper Soviet subjects led the Soviet government to appoint Finnish Communist émigrés as a sort of colonial administration of Soviet Karelia, and for them this was only natural since their intellectual background in nineteenth-century Karelianism also made them think of Soviet Karelia in terms of a dark territory that had to be raised to the level of the civilized West, only that the West was now framed in socialist terms. Finally, in the long run, both Moscow and Red Finns planned that northern Russia would become a bridgehead for a future world revolution, with Soviet Karelia destined to turn into a "model socialist republic, which will contribute to revolutionize neighboring Finland and Scandinavian countries."[59]

Although the first Finnish political immigrants came to Karelia as early as 1918, initially the number of Red Finns in Soviet Karelia was relatively small. By 1920, no more than 500 political immigrants resided there, most of them members of the Finnish Social Democratic Party and of the Finnish Communist Party founded in 1918 in Moscow. They were supposed to assist in the establishment of the Karelian Workers' Commune and to secure Bolshevik power among the Karelian population. In the early 1920s, the inflow of Red Finns to Soviet Karelia intensified, with an average of 100 to 120 people arriving annually.[60] By 1926, the number of Finns in Soviet Karelia reached about 2,500 (0.9 percent of the total population). The political immigrants tended to settle in Petrozavodsk, the capital, and around it (the region comprised 49 percent of the Finnish population of Soviet Karelia, with half of this number living in Petrozavodsk), as well as in areas with a dominant Karelian population—the regions of Ukhta in the north (20.4 percent of their total number in Karelia) and of Olonets in the south (13.2 percent).[61]

In the early 1930s, the Finnish population of Soviet Karelia experienced a significant increase from new waves of immigration—illegal immigration from Finland and labor recruitment from North America. By 1935, about 15,000 Finns lived in the republic (half of the overall Finnish diaspora of the USSR). Finns who came from the United States and Canada made up a third of this amount.[62]

Although in the early 1920s Finns composed less than 1 percent, and in 1933 only 3.2 percent, of the total population of Soviet Karelia, they took prominent positions in the Soviet and Communist bureaucracy; ran large factories, state institutions, and branch offices of paramilitary organizations such as the Assistance to Defense and Aviation Construction of the USSR (OSOAVIAKHIM); and worked in cultural, academic, and educational spheres. Many of them were professional soldiers with experience in the Finnish and Russian Civil Wars, so they constituted a significant part of the rank and file and almost the entire officer cadre of the Karelian Jäger Brigade, a national detachment of the republic. This made the ethnic and political situation in Soviet Karelia in the 1920s to early 1930s unique, for the region predominantly populated by Russians and Karelians (the latter, though the republic was named after them, since the administrative reform of 1922, were no longer a majority in it) was headed by a small group of Finnish political immigrants, put in charge of the development of autonomous Karelia. This situation was only possible as long as the Soviet leaders openly and enthusiastically supported Red Finns in their activities at the head of Soviet Karelia. When in the mid-1930s the attitude of Moscow toward the border republic and the policies of Gylling's government changed, it heralded the end of the Finnish period in the history of Soviet Karelia.

Two Perspectives on Soviet Immigration Policy
Moscow and Petrozavodsk

IMMIGRATION POLICY OF THE SOVIET GOVERNMENT

SINCE THE EARLY MODERN PERIOD, RUSSIAN RULERS WHO ASPIRED TO MODERNIZE their state were always confronted with the challenge of an insufficient labor force in terms of qualification, distribution, and even number: there was always a shortage of qualified technical specialists, but even farmers and unqualified workers were in high demand in the spacious territories. Recruitment of foreign nationals was one response to this challenge that Russian authorities had regularly tried since the time of Ivan the Terrible (1533–84), when new foreign quarters emerged in a number of Russian cities. During the reign of Peter the Great (1682–1725), the inflow of foreign specialists to Russia significantly increased; in the time of Catherine the Great (1762–96), German farmers were invited to colonize vast and sparsely inhabited lands along the Volga River and the Black Sea coast.[1] The economic migration of Koreans, Chinese, Norwegians, Finns,[2] and representatives of other ethnic groups to border regions of the Russian Empire in the late nineteenth century was another notable phenomenon. The government granted significant privileges to colonists and immigrants who settled in virgin lands: in particular, they were exempt from compulsory military service and taxation.

The Bolshevik leadership was confronted with the need to develop its own immigration policy since the early days of the revolution. During the Russian Civil War, popular movements grew in many Western countries in support of the "republic of workers and peasants." At meetings organized in its support, workers often declared their willingness to emigrate to Soviet Russia to help build a new society. Perhaps many of these resolutions were made purely for rhetorical purposes during strikes to scare employers or governments with radicalism, but at least some of them were sincere. Among those who actually wanted to leave for Soviet Russia were thousands of Germans, whose country was struck by a severe post-First World War economic crisis. Many of them ended up emigrating to Soviet Russia without any permission from either the German or the Soviet side.[3]

In 1919, the Soviet leadership started discussing possible recruitment of labor from Western Europe for employment in Russian industry and agriculture. During the spring of 1920, the Soviet government passed a number of laws that set conditions of immigration for farmers and workers from Western Europe.[4] Initially, they targeted immigrants from Germany but later became the basis for drafting agreements with other groups of immigrants. The main idea of all documents related to the immigration of qualified German workers was that immigrants had to be organized into groups to work in factories and communal farms in order to increase industrial and agricultural production. Immigrants were granted a number of privileges compared with other Soviet citizens, including exemption from national and regional taxes for five years and exemption from military service on the condition that they obey laws and meet standards of production. Higher wages and additional food supplies were also provided given that they were directly linked to increases in labor productivity. Preference was given to unmarried workers and those with small families.[5]

The desire of the Soviet government to recruit labor immigrants, who would be equipped with tools in short supply in Russia and have critically needed job skills, was hindered from the beginning by its own bureaucratic system as different Soviet organizations tried to avoid paying benefits to foreigners.[6] This reluctance among Soviet organizations to accept immigrant workers, as well as the overall economic collapse of Soviet Russia during the Civil War, led early researchers of Western emigration to the USSR to conclude that it was driven entirely by ideological motivation and had no economic basis.[7] However, Bolshevik leaders themselves emphasized the economic aspect of labor immigration to Soviet Russia. Lenin, in particular, publicly argued that "a dozen, a hundred of high-qualified foreign workers could teach a hundred or a thousand of Russian workers by working with them," and advocates of labor immigration reiterated that the recruitment of immigrant workers was both desirable and necessary in economic terms.[8] Of course, ideological implications were still omnipresent: Lenin, for example, feared that immigrants, if unprepared for the harsh economic conditions of Soviet Russia, would re-emigrate in large numbers, thus damaging the Soviet image abroad. He therefore insisted on obtaining written acknowledgments from German delegates who visited Russia for negotiations on immigration; they had to confirm that they were familiar with all the difficulties of workers' lives in Russia.[9]

Apart from Germany, another source of mass emigration to the Soviet Union was from the United States and, though to a lesser extent, Canada. Here desire and intention to move to Soviet Russia were more widespread among recent immigrants, including those of Russian origins, who had not adapted well to life in North America. Re-emigration sentiment spread under the slogan of help for restoration of the Soviet economy and because of practical desires to escape unemployment. During several months in late 1920 and early 1921 alone, about 16,000 American emigrants moved to the Soviet Union, often without proper permissions. American and Canadian emigrants took with them technical equipment and enough supplies for two years, both on their own initiative and as a condition of entry into the USSR.[10]

The demand for qualified workers in Soviet industry was indeed great because, from 1917 to 1920, the number of workers in Russia declined from 2.6 to 1.2 million. Many people left towns and moved to the countryside because of the lack of food.[11] In the meantime, Soviet agriculture remained very outdated: as late as 1928, 5.5 million peasant farms used plows, and half of the crop was harvested with reaping hooks and scythes.[12] In this sense, the immigration of farmers from Europe and North America who used modern agricultural technologies seemed very opportune for the Soviet government. In general, labor immigration was encouraged for both ideological and economic reasons until late 1921.

At the same time, the course and experience of early immigration to the USSR demonstrated that Soviet plans to organize large-scale immigration were initially unrealistic since the country was not prepared to accept a large number of immigrants. Practical implementation of the immigration project ran into serious difficulties, such as famines and housing shortages, and a drastic decrease in industrial production because of the Civil War and international isolation could not accommodate an extra labor force in the form of immigrant workers and brought about conflict, rather than solidarity, with the Soviet proletariat.[13] As a result, in 1921 the first restrictions on labor immigration were imposed in Soviet Russia.[14] In May 1922, the Council of Labor and Defense (the supreme body for economic management) passed a resolution that aimed to "reduce immigration to a minimum and give entry permits only to those groups of workers who can surely find appropriate work in the [Soviet] republic."[15] In practice, this law effectively stopped all immigration, except from America, since the relatively large scale of immigration from there was economically profitable for the Soviet government. In the first part of the 1920s, American miners became prominent in Kuzbass, a center of Soviet coal production in Siberia,[16] and American agricultural communes sprang up in different parts of the USSR.[17] According to two Soviet authors, about 20,000 American and Canadian immigrants entered Soviet Russia from 1920 to 1925, of whom about 10,000 Americans arrived in a short period between September 1921 and September 1922.[18] The first American Finnish immigrants to Soviet Russia were part of this large flow. In 1922, a large group of American immigrants, dominated by Finns, established the commune Seiatel, also known by its Finnish name Kylväjä (Sower) in the region of Rostov,[19] and later founded the communes Säde (Sun Ray) in southern Karelia in 1925 and Työ (Labor) near Leningrad in 1927.

The immigration regulations that the Soviet government started to introduce in 1921 were aimed at keeping away poor immigrants who would be unable to sustain themselves for a certain period of time. Since 1923, potential immigrants were required to import enough capital for the establishment and initial operations of their communes. The amount and form of capital were to be determined by individual contracts between immigrant farmers and Soviet authorities. The Soviet government, particularly interested in the cultivation of virgin lands, granted those farmers who agreed to settle on them a number of privileges. Agricultural innovations could also reduce high rental rates.[20]

During 1923–24, what started as a powerful flow of industrial immigration to the Soviet Union was reduced to a miserable trickle. Many factories were closed because of a general industrial crisis, followed by unemployment, and Soviet governments ceased to provide subsidies for travel expenses of immigrants and transportation of their equipment. Immigrants could still buy tickets at reduced rates and import their equipment free of customs duties, but the only direct privileges that they retained were exemption of certain taxes and military service. In 1925, in addition to existing restrictions, a new condition of entry permission was introduced for labor immigrants: only members of agricultural communes, workmen's associations, and cooperatives could now apply for immigration permits.[21] Immigration to the Soviet Union stopped completely in 1927 when Soviet authorities, perhaps in the context of debates over agricultural policy among the party elite, introduced a ban on agricultural immigration.[22]

A new turn in immigration policy was caused by the accelerated campaign of industrialization launched by Soviet authorities in 1929, which drastically increased the demand for industrial workers and, in particular, qualified technical specialists. Although the restrictive immigration legislation of the previous period remained in force, the Sixteenth Congress of the VKP(b) (26 June–13 July 1930) set an official course for "extension of the practice of sending workers and specialists abroad and inviting foreign engineers, foremen, and qualified workers to the USSR"[23] and initiated a new wave of immigration to the Soviet Union.[24] At the congress, the

Communist leadership set a goal of recruiting 40,000 foreign workers and specialists. Such party resolutions had the force of law in a single-party state.

However, a single, centralized system for the recruitment of immigrant workers was never established, and Soviet organizations, ministries, and provincial governments were responsible for finding and using their own channels to recruit specialists. The scale of their recruitment efforts can be illustrated by the Soviet embassy in Germany where, in the early 1930s, seventy people were employed to manage the recruitment of immigrant workers and specialists.[25] By the end of the First Five-Year Plan in 1932, there were at least 20,000 highly qualified immigrant workers and specialists in the USSR.[26] A significant number of them were Finnish North Americans who had responded to a recruitment call from their compatriots standing at the helm of Soviet Karelia.

ECONOMIC PLANS AND THE IMMIGRATION PROGRAM OF RED FINNS

The first plans to recruit Finnish Americans for the Soviet economy were formulated soon after the Bolshevik Revolution when, as early as May 1918, two Finnish Communist émigrés, Eino Rahja and Edvard Vasten, discussed the idea with Lenin.[27] Edvard Gylling, another Finnish Communist, who became the leader of the Karelian Workers' Commune in 1920, saw the recruitment of Finnish immigrants abroad as a solution to two problems: the shortage of labor and a decreasing share of Finno-Ugric people in the population of Soviet Karelia, which endangered the very idea of building ethnic autonomy. During 1921 and 1922, the government of Soviet Karelia established contacts with the Finnish trade union movement, which assisted in the employment of qualified Finnish workers in the forest industry of Soviet Karelia, primarily in timber harvesting and transportation.[28] At the same time, the first American Finns arrived in Soviet Karelia when in 1922 a fishing commune from the United States settled in its northern part (Kniazhia Guba, near Kandalaksha), and three years later a group of Canadian workers and farmers founded the agricultural commune Säde near Olonets in southern Soviet Karelia.

The shortage of qualified labor was indeed one of the biggest challenges for the modernization plans of the Red Finnish government of Soviet Karelia. After the Civil War, which ravaged much of its territory from 1918 to 1920 and returned, in the form of a peasant uprising, to northern parts of Soviet Karelia in the winter of 1921–22,[29] its economy lay in ruins. The population decrease was also significant, especially in northern Soviet Karelia, where after a failed peasant uprising in the winter of 1921–22 more than a third of its population fled to Finland from the Red Army. Those who stayed behind had no horses to cultivate land, and famine soon followed.[30]

The newly appointed Red Finnish government of Soviet Karelia was able to convince central Soviet authorities that a faster and more effective revival of the collapsed economy required economic autonomy. Political experience and personal connections among the Bolshevik leadership helped Gylling to secure for Soviet Karelia a privileged position within the economy of Soviet Russia and later the USSR, a feat of diplomacy much facilitated by the border location of Soviet Karelia.[31] In 1921 and 1922, upon requests from Gylling, the government of Soviet Russia passed decrees that introduced urgent measures for the reconstruction and revitalization of the Karelian economy. These decrees granted an autonomous budget to Soviet Karelia, a privilege that no other ethnic autonomy of Soviet Russia could boast. Soviet Karelia was granted the right to set its own budget independently of the state budget of Soviet Russia and later the Soviet Union, was exempt from national taxes until 1924, and received large long-term loans to finance construction of a pulp and paper plant and a power plant in Kondopoga, to stimulate development of the mining industry, and to purchase food for the regions most affected by hunger. Besides, the authorities of Soviet Karelia were granted the right to use 25 percent of revenues from the export of timber for the import of commodities and equipment that could not be purchased on the domestic market.[32]

These measures proved effective, and from 1922 the economy of Soviet Karelia underwent fast growth based on the forest industry, which, by the end of the 1920s, had increased its production nearly fourfold compared with that of 1914.[33] In the autumn of 1922, a state trust aimed to monopolize the timber industry and named Karelles, or "Karelian Timber," was established under the direct control of the government of Soviet Karelia to run forest harvesting and timber processing.[34] Apart from earning money for the Karelian budget, Karelles provided an additional source of income for local peasants unable to earn a living only by farming.

In 1929, the Kondopoga pulp and paper plant was finally launched after six years of construction. It was powered by the Kondopoga hydroelectric power plant, also launched in 1929, which accelerated the electrification of Soviet Karelia. As a result of the fast development of the timber industry and the introduction of new industries, industrial production in the GDP of Soviet Karelia grew from 7 percent in 1923 to 62 percent in 1929. In contrast, agricultural production, also severely affected by the Civil War, reached the level of production of 1913, the last prewar year, only by the end of the 1920s. In general, because of large investments in industry, the annual economic growth in Soviet Karelia during the 1920s reached a remarkable 10 percent,[35] while the per capita income grew from thirty-four rubles in the 1924–25 budget year to 136 rubles in 1930.[36]

A special program aimed at accelerating the development of Karelian border regions played a particularly important role in the economic growth and sociopolitical stabilization in Soviet Karelia during the 1920s. Gylling, its main advocate, believed that ethnicity would determine a special place for Soviet Karelia in Soviet and international politics and was much worried by an imbalance between what he regarded as a backward ethnic Karelian periphery and economically and culturally developed ethnic Russian regions of Soviet Karelia. A product of nineteenth-century rationalism, Gylling believed that this imbalance could be eliminated if Karelian peasants would "upgrade their primitive households to more rational forms of agricultural production."[37] His government granted numerous privileges to border regions populated by ethnic Karelians and developed plans for their industrialization, including a major increase in forest harvesting, the building of new timber-processing facilities, organization of geological exploration, development of the mining industry, electrification of agriculture, and state support of crafts.[38] By the turn of the 1930s, this "border policy" was extended to all ethnic Karelian regions with a total population of approximately 100,000 people.[39]

To sum up, the Red Finnish government of Soviet Karelia believed that, through careful planning and the rational use of natural resources, especially forests, it could achieve accelerated and proportional development of all branches of the economy. Gylling, in particular, advocated the decentralization of management, demanding that all economic plans be "discussed in detail with local level authorities."[40] At the initial stage, funding for the implementation of these plans was expected from the Soviet state budget as loans, and later the Karelian economy was supposed to become self-supporting because of its large export potential. This model of the development of Soviet Karelia was inspired by neighboring Finland, which had demonstrated fast economic growth based on skillful management of its forest resources.[41] The borrowing of Finnish experience was revealed by many measures implemented by the government of Soviet Karelia, especially plans for railroad building in border areas,[42] though the source of these inspirations was never discussed publicly.[43]

Only a few plans developed by the Red Finnish government of Soviet Karelia reached the stage of implementation. Budget privileges granted to Soviet Karelia were designed from the beginning as temporary measures, initially due to expire as early as 1924. In the second half of the 1920s, they were prolonged annually upon requests from Karelian authorities, but their spheres of application were gradually narrowed until they became empty formalities by 1928. Soviet Karelia was consequently unable to finance its economic development through its own resources and regularly had to appeal for economic support from the Soviet state budget. Soviet people's commissariats (or ministries) also retained control over the activities of those industries of Soviet Karelia that belonged to their particular branches of the economy.[44] Central economic authorities also kept control over the railroad between Petrograd (Leningrad since 1924) and Murmansk, the most important traffic artery in Soviet Karelia. Moreover, administration of the railroad received a large part of Karelian territory for its economic needs in the form of the so-called Murmansk industrial and colonization complex (*transportno-promyshlennyi i kolonizatsionnyi kombinat*), when 3.3 million hectares, or 22.5 percent of the territory of Soviet Karelia (146.3 square kilometers), were removed from the economic jurisdiction of its government.[45]

Despite these restrictions, in June 1927 the Soviet leadership officially appraised the economic development of Soviet Karelia, which had "met all expectations and achieved outstanding results," for it had demonstrated the best economic growth rates among all autonomous regions of the USSR.[46] Gylling argued that the main factor in this success was economic autonomy granted by Moscow. He also emphasized that the economic system of Soviet Karelia, based upon privileges in the form of an autonomous budget, would demonstrate even greater advantages in the next five years. At that time, his arguments convinced the Soviet leadership to extend economic autonomy to Soviet Karelia for another year.[47]

After 1928, conceptions of how proper economic relations between the Soviet center and periphery should look underwent a drastic transformation, reflecting a power struggle between supporters of Stalin and those of Bukharin in the Bolshevik leadership. Although Bukharin argued in favor of retaining limited market mechanisms and some economic autonomy of Soviet regions, the majority of rank-and-file party members supported Stalin, who advocated elimination of the market and centralization of economic and regional management.[48] The introduction of five-year planning in 1928, aimed at accelerated industrialization with an emphasis on heavy industry, heralded a greatly increased role of the state in economic processes at all levels. Political centralization followed. This was a serious threat to national development of Soviet ethnic republics and autonomies since it undermined the already established economic order in them. For Soviet Karelia, an autonomous budget meant that during the 1920s its leaders could stimulate economic development in the territories with the predominantly ethnic Karelian population in order to reinforce the socioeconomic basis of the nascent socialist Karelian-Finnish ethnicity that they aspired to build. Now, with the introduction of the First Five-Year Plan (1928–32) and the subordination of the Karelian *obkom* of the VKP(b) to the Leningrad *obkom* in 1928, all attempts at building an economy that would spur national development of Karelian regions gradually vanished.[49] Although formally Soviet Karelia retained its special budget rights until the late 1930s, they became de facto defunct when it was included in the First Five-Year Plan, for its economy now had to pursue goals set by Moscow rather than Petrozavodsk. The economic authority of Gylling's government gradually shrank to control over implementation of orders given by central economic authorities.

In the grand scheme of accelerated economic modernization of the Soviet Union envisioned in the First Five-Year Plan, Soviet Karelia was given the role of an exporter of raw materials, both for sale on international markets and as work material for industries located in more developed Soviet regions.[50] During the winter of 1929–30, timber harvesting was greatly increased, but to sell the timber for hard currency on shrinking markets in the early Great Depression the timber industry trust of Soviet Karelia, Karelles, had upon orders from Moscow to sell timber abroad at prices that did not cover expenses, thus operating at a loss.[51] It was part of a wider export strategy of the Bolshevik leadership, since it used all possible resources, including agricultural produce, to earn foreign currency necessary to purchase equipment for the accelerated development of the USSR, a policy that would soon lead to the terrible famine of the early 1930s. In September 1930, Karelles, the largest source of revenue of the Karelian economy, was resubordinated to the all-union timber industry association Soiuzlesprom run by the Supreme Council of the National Economy.[52] The loss of timber export revenues meant the ultimate loss of economic autonomy for Soviet Karelia.

Henceforth, the only remaining justification for the existence of Soviet Karelia as an autonomous region was its ethnic and cultural peculiarities. However, they were also under threat, since increased timber harvesting demanded by the First Five-Year Plan led to large-scale migration to Soviet Karelia from other regions of the USSR. The Red Finnish government of Soviet Karelia was much worried about this tendency, since increased centralization in Moscow of all spheres of life could endanger the project of national and cultural development of Soviet Karelia.

In 1920, when the Karelian Workers' Commune was founded, Karelians constituted an ethnic majority (60 percent).[53] Between 1922 and 1924, however, the territory of Soviet Karelia grew significantly larger by incorporating several neighboring regions with ethnic Russian populations, which changed the ethnic makeup of Soviet Karelia. According to the 1926 census, the total population of Soviet Karelia was 269,700 people, including 154,000 Russians (57.2 percent), 100,800 Karelians (37.4 percent), 8,500 Vepsians[54] (3.2 percent), 2,500 Finns (0.9 percent), and 3,500 people who claimed another ethnicity (1.3 percent).[55]

To make things worse, at least from the perspective of Red Finns, most new migrants of the 1920s were Russians, which further eroded the ethnic foundation of Karelian autonomy.[56] Migration was a necessary evil since the sparse population of Soviet Karelia was unable to provide a sufficient labor force to carry out its economic modernization. Throughout the 1920s, the authorities and industries of Soviet Karelia launched annual recruitment campaigns in neighboring regions of Soviet Russia: the seasonal nature of timber harvesting created a huge demand in labor only during winter and early spring months that could be satisfied by peasants from surrounding regions. However, as production plans for the Karelian timber industry gradually increased on orders from Moscow, the annual recruitment of tens of thousands of seasonal workers became more expensive and less effective.[57] Karelian authorities repeatedly addressed the Soviet leadership with requests for a drastically different recruitment policy, one that would create a permanent cadre of professional forest workers. In one of their requests, they argued that

> a fast rate of socialist building and economic reconstruction of Karelia and its transformation into an industrial center demand the quantity of labor force that is impossible to satisfy with our current population. The situation is aggravated by the extreme deficiency of qualified workers. Moreover, Karelia lacks not only its own ethnic proletariat—it does not even have a nucleus that could be used as the basis to forge this proletariat.[58]

In order to prevent further "de-ethnicization" of Soviet Karelia through labor immigration, the Red Finnish government suggested that a new migration policy be implemented to target Finnic peoples of Russia (Karelians from the Tver region, Vepsians and Ingrian Finns from the Leningrad region) as well as Finns abroad. In particular, a recruitment campaign among Finns in North America was perceived as a measure that would help to solve both problems of an insufficient labor force and a gradually decreasing share of Finno-Ugric people in the ethnic composition of Soviet Karelia. Karelian authorities expected that the Finnish diaspora of 300,000 in the United States and Canada would provide a large number of highly qualified specialists to constitute the nucleus of an "ethnic proletariat" in Soviet Karelia.[59]

Initially, proposals of the Karelian leadership to organize a recruitment campaign among Finns abroad were rejected by the Soviet authorities, including the OGPU of the USSR, People's Commissariat of Foreign Affairs, and Council of People's Commissars of the RSFSR. Other than security considerations, they were most likely worried that failures similar to those of early Soviet labor immigration could happen again and explicitly referred to the previous experience by saying that "using foreign workers in the Soviet conditions proved ineffective."[60] But already several months later resolutions of the Sixteenth Congress of the VKP(b) concerning employment of foreign labor in the Soviet economy radically changed the situation and prepared a legal basis for a large-scale recruiting campaign that drove thousands of American and Canadian Finns to Soviet Karelia.

PRELUDE TO KARELIAN FEVER

Initially, the Red Finnish government of Soviet Karelia relied on Finland as the main source of labor immigration. In December 1929, it sent an official inquiry to the Soviet leadership describing its proposal. In this inquiry, Karelian authorities described the hard situation in the timber industry caused by an insufficient labor force and suggested that, "in order to accelerate formation of the workforce and to create shock groups of labor [*udarnyie gruppy*], we currently plan to recruit a certain number of qualified lumberjacks from northern and central Finland, where a numerous proletarian class of lumberjack already exists. They are known for high qualification and work efficiency and are, besides, accustomed to the climate and conditions of northern Karelia."[61] This was a preamble to a request for immigration permits for 300 Finnish lumberjacks and their families who were supposed to settle in northern Soviet Karelia (Ukhta and Kestenga).

This proposal immediately faced robust opposition from central Soviet bodies. The strongest objection was expressed by the People's Commissariat of Foreign Affairs and OGPU. The former commented that resettlement of Finnish lumberjacks to Soviet Karelia would, first, weaken the Finnish working class and, second, lead to an outflow of Soviet currency from the USSR, since Finnish workers would support their relatives remaining in Finland. Besides, officials were concerned with inadequate living conditions in places where immigrants were supposed to work, stressing that they could "give reverse results, as [settlers], due to difficulties in a new place, will become much less disposed to the Soviet order." Then re-emigration would certainly follow and impair the image of the USSR among the Finnish proletariat.[62]

At the same time, the leadership of Soviet Karelia carefully probed the question of possible recruitment of Canadian workers—an issue that also caused objections among Soviet security organs, though in this case the factor of border proximity could be disregarded.[63] As Karelian authorities tried to defend their initiative, they explained that a proposal had been sent to them by a group of Canadian lumberjacks who wanted to come to Soviet Karelia as labor immigrants, and they would bring "their work equipment" and "rapidly introduce American[64] working methods in forest harvesting."[65]

These initial failures to secure Moscow's support for their immigration policy did not discourage Karelian authorities. In March 1930, they sent another official request to the Soviet government in which they even more strongly insisted on the need to radically reorganize the Karelian timber industry and to form a permanent cadre of industrial workers, ideally of Finnish ethnicity. They argued that Finnish lumberjacks from Canada, because of their experience in the Canadian timber industry, were known for "the highest labor productivity in the world" and would bring cutting-edge technologies in the industry. Also, if permitted to settle in Soviet Karelia, they could help local workers "rapidly learn foreign methods of forest harvesting."[66]

In the same letter, Karelian authorities outlined a draft agreement with Canadian lumberjacks, including their working and living conditions. The group comprised fifty people, all of whom had been participants in the Finnish Civil War on the Red side and were now members of either radical workers' organizations or the Communist Party of Canada. Each lumberjack would provide $300 for transportation, work clothes, and tools. At the same time, the directorate of their employment organization, Karelles, took into account that most immigrant workers were currently jobless because of the Great Depression and would provide 10,000 rubles to cover their travel costs and $5,000 to purchase equipment for the Karelian timber industry. Finnish Canadian immigrants were to reside in a specially built settlement located close to one of the best collective farms in Soviet Karelia that would provide the Canadian workers with food. The quantity of production would be set annually in a special agreement. Karelles planned that the Canadian lumberjacks would work in their own teams, not be split up in groups with local workers. To monitor the quality and quantity of their work, Karelles intended to appoint a representative who, however, "would not have a right to interfere in their work process or in the organization of work."[67] This would avoid the negative experiences of earlier Soviet recruitment campaigns, in which foreign workers, dissatisfied with the poor management of local authorities and language problems, re-emigrated from the USSR.

After several months of negotiations, permission for the entry of this group was granted, and on 25 September 1930 the first small group of Finnish lumberjacks from Canada arrived in Soviet Karelia. Numerous newspaper articles and even several books were written about this group,[68] and they were often mentioned in official documents,[69] but the irony of the situation was that different sources indicated different numbers of its members, varying from sixteen to fifty people, and almost none of them mentioned the names of these first immigrants.

Using archival materials, we were able to identify the names of twenty-one people in the first group. Nearly all were relatively young. The oldest, Albin Kukko, was forty-eight at the time of arrival, while the youngest man in the group was his nineteen-year-old son Akseli.[70]

The Canadian logging crew was assigned to a harvesting camp near a settlement called Matrosy (Matroosa in Finnish), recently established thirty-five kilometers from Petrozavodsk. Before the arrival of the Canadian lumberjacks, the workforce there was mostly peasants recruited in central Russia who had no previous experience in the timber industry and who consequently demonstrated low productivity. New tools for and techniques of logging brought by the immigrants, as well as the introduction of ice roads for the transportation of timber, led to a sharp increase in production. The crew used bow and crosscut saws of a new design for felling trees, sledges and skidders for pulling cut trees out of a forest, and horse- and tractor-driven derricks for loading, unloading, and piling of logs. Already in January 1931, Väino Järvi, one of the crew members, wrote to the newspaper *Punainen Karjala* (Red Karelia) that the experience and skills of the Canadian lumberjacks had to be disseminated among all Karelian forest workers to increase work efficiency.[71] Soon Matrosy, as well as some other timber industry settlements where North American lumberjacks were employed (Vilga, Interposiolok, and the logging camp Lososinskii), became centers of the transfer of modern technologies of logging and timber transportation to Soviet workers.

This first group of Canadian lumberjacks paved the way for the mass immigration of American and Canadian Finns to Soviet Karelia. Industries and organizations in Soviet Karelia started to send numerous applications to the Karelian government indicating their needs for qualified immigrant labor. On the other side of the Atlantic, many Finns were eager to move to Soviet Karelia. By August 1930, before the news of recruitment in Soviet Karelia actually spread around Finnish communities there, 176 applications had been received in Soviet Karelia from Finnish workers in the United States and Canada. Applicants were lumberjacks,

Figure 5. One of the first groups of North American Finns on their way to Soviet Karelia, 1931 (photographer unknown; courtesy of the National Archive of the Republic of Karelia).

builders, mechanics, electricians, smiths, and so on. Of them, 140 people had already formed organized groups under the leadership of members of the American and Canadian Communist Parties.[72] Upon learning about this enthusiasm in North American Finnish communities, Karelian authorities prepared plans for the immigration of 1,000 Finns based on current recruitment demands of Karelian industries. At the end of September 1930, these plans were discussed and approved in Moscow by the Council of People's Commissars (SNK[73]) of the RSFSR, which granted to Soviet Karelia permission to recruit 885 workers from the United States, Canada, and Sweden (1,485 with family members) before 1 October 1931.[74]

Although this was an important breakthrough, the immigration policy of Karelian authorities in the face of continuing opposition from Soviet security organs could become a reality only if supported by the supreme party leadership. Gylling was able to secure this support. In the margins of his letter to the Politburo of the Central Committee of the VKP(b) on the issue of immigration to Soviet Karelia was his handwritten note: "According to the information directly from Kirov,[75] the approval is given. I have received preliminary support in this question from Stalin and Molotov."[76] The final decision was made on 5 March 1931. Resolution No. 35, passed by the SNK of the USSR, stated that "the government of Soviet Karelia is permitted to recruit up to 2,000 qualified workers from Canada for forest harvesting operations in Karelia."[77] In September 1931, Soviet authorities agreed that an additional 785 workers could come to Soviet Karelia as labor immigrants.[78] These permissions granted by the top Soviet authorities were later used by Gylling's government to repel attempts by various state bodies (OGPU, People's Commissariat of Foreign Affairs, Supreme Customs Administration, etc.) to reduce or stop the immigration to Soviet Karelia.

The practical course of immigration soon brought significant changes in the immigration policy of Karelian authorities. More Finns would arrive in Soviet Karelia from the United States than Canada, and, most importantly, the government of Gylling, because of a changed conjuncture of Soviet domestic and foreign politics, would be unable to achieve the desired rate of immigration and the original objectives of its immigration policy.

CHAPTER 3

To Karelia!

THE KARELIAN TECHNICAL AID COMMITTEE

THE IMMIGRATION POLICY OF KARELIAN AUTHORITIES BECAME POSSIBLE ONLY BECAUSE there was an enthusiastic response in Finnish communities in Canada and the United States. The ground for the Karelian fever had actually been prepared long before 1930 by propaganda originating on both sides of the Atlantic. Ethnic radicalism was perhaps the most important factor of all. American and Canadian leftist press and organizations were immensely popular and influential among Finnish communities, and Finns were often mentioned as the most radical ethnic group in North America, constituting, for example, 44.7 percent (6,803 members) of the Workers Party of America, a legal party of American Communists from 1921 to 1929.[1] Many North American Finns consequently supported or at least sympathized with socialist and communist ideas. After the Karelian Workers' Commune was established in 1920, the Finnish immigrant press, particularly the newspapers *Työmies* (United States) and *Vapaus* (Canada), published numerous materials advertising the achievements of Soviet Karelia and coordinated early fundraising activities in support of the newly established republic.[2]

In 1921, the Soviet Karelia Relief Committee was established in New York City. It was headed by Yrjö (George) Halonen, a member of the Communist Party USA (CPUSA). The committee issued and distributed bonds for a total of $20,000 US. The money raised through the sale of bonds was used in financial operations, including on the real estate market, supposedly to increase the capital stock. Revenues were then partly transferred to Soviet Karelia and partly used to purchase necessary equipment and supplies. These financial activities of the committee were supervised by Matti Tenhunen, a major figure of the Karelian fever, who at that time was even nicknamed "needle-monger" for his commercial initiatives.[3]

Tenhunen left Finland for the United States in 1905 at the age of eighteen. For many years, he worked at the Työmies Society, which was responsible for the publication of Finnish-language Communist materials, including the daily newspaper *Työmies,* and as a member of the CPUSA he supervised party activities in Superior, Wisconsin.[4] He visited the Soviet Union several times in the late 1920s at the behest of the Comintern, and it was probably then that he established contacts with the Red Finnish government of Edvard Gylling, which would make him one of the main propagandists of emigration to Soviet Karelia from the United States in the early 1930s.

The Central Committee of the CPUSA was suspicious of the Soviet Karelia-related activities of Halonen and Tenhunen, generally because of a strained relationship between the American Communist leadership and Finnish Communists, who stuck to their language-based organizations and resisted attempts at centralization and bolshevization.[5] Likely because of this tension and at the insistence of the Central Committee of the CPUSA, the Comintern summoned Halonen to Moscow in 1922 and demanded that he dissolve the Soviet Karelia Relief Committee.[6] In 1930, Halonen was expelled from the Communist Party after he opposed his party bosses in their attempts to use funds of the Finnish cooperative movement in the western Great Lakes region to finance party activities. Tenhunen, who supported him in this conflict, was summoned to Moscow for questioning.[7]

His visit, however, proved to be much more substantial than just giving explanations of a conflict in the American labor movement. In the summer of 1930, the Sixteenth Congress of the VKP(b) called for the organization of labor immigration to the Soviet Union, and the Comintern obviously decided to use this new agenda to strengthen the Finnish Communist Party, based in the Soviet Union, with Finnish American and Finnish Canadian Communists. Tenhunen, turning all of a sudden from prey to predator, was assigned a special role in the organization of the emigration of Finns from the United States to Soviet Karelia. The Central Committee of the CPUSA could do nothing but accept this decision. Tenhunen returned to New York, where for several months he supervised the publishing activities of the Central Committee of the CPUSA. After Soviet authorities granted formal permission for immigration to Soviet Karelia, Tenhunen started working as a representative of the People's Commissariat of Labor of Soviet Karelia at the Soviet consulate in New York. In February 1931, he moved to Petrozavodsk, but two months later he returned to New York on a special assignment from the government of Soviet Karelia—to create a formal organization that would coordinate recruitment efforts in the United States and Canada.[8]

On 1 May 1931, the Karelian Technical Aid Committee (KTAC) was founded in New York for the recruitment and emigration of Finns to Soviet Karelia. From late 1931 to 1932, the

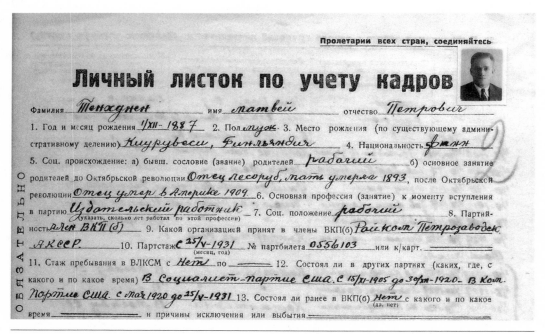

FIGURE 6. THE FIRST PAGE OF MATTI TENHUNEN'S PERSONAL VKP(B) FILE (NARK, F. P-3, OP. 6, D. 10792,1. 2) (COURTESY OF THE NATIONAL ARCHIVE OF THE REPUBLIC OF KARELIA).

committee was headed by Kalle Aronen and between 1932 and 1934 by Oscar Corgan. KTAC had a second office in Toronto and was represented in several US states with large Finnish populations.[9] The Toronto office was continuously headed by John (Jussi) Latva.

Aronen, Corgan, and Latva were members of Finnish sections of their respective Communist Parties, but they reported all issues related to the organization of emigration to the Soviet Union directly to the government of Soviet Karelia, since they were official employees of the Resettlement Administration established in Petrozavodsk in the autumn of 1931. Tenhunen was appointed head of the Foreign Department of the Resettlement Administration and coordinated all activities of KTAC. This situation greatly irritated the Central Committee of the CPUSA and caused its negative attitude toward the immigration policy of Karelian authorities. The situation in Canada was different since its Communist Party and the Finnish Organization of Canada actively cooperated with Tenhunen and Latva. Still, they were also worried about the prospects of mass emigration of Finnish Communists and activists to Soviet Karelia.[10] The leadership of the CPUSA and CPC feared that a large-scale exodus of Finns, who played prominent roles in both parties, would damage the Communist movement in North America. Yet for the time being they were unable to stop the recruitment policies of Karelian authorities, and the efforts of a few activists of KTAC ignited a burst of socialist enthusiasm in North American Finnish communities that became known as the Karelian fever (*karjalan kuume*).

In October 1931, the Resettlement Administration of the Council of People's Commissars of Soviet Karelia was established in Petrozavodsk to manage the immigration flow to Soviet Karelia. It was responsible for coordination of recruitment and reception of immigrant labor, control over conditions in which immigrants were to work and live, and registration of all foreigners arriving in Soviet Karelia.[11] The heads of KTAC in the United States and Canada—Kalle Aronen, Oscar Corgan, and John Latva—were officially employed in the Resettlement Administration, though their salaries were actually paid from commission fees charged by shipping companies for the passengers provided by KTAC.[12]

Apart from recruiting, the Karelian Technical Aid Committee was responsible for the purchase of equipment and supplies for industries in Soviet Karelia. The committee was funded by several sources. First, there were voluntary contributions and donations from American and Canadian citizens. Second, it reached an agreement with the Swedish American Line, a steamship company that carried immigrants across the Atlantic to the USSR. According to this agreement, the Swedish American Line paid commissions to KTAC amounting to $11.50 US for every adult and $5.75 US for every child. And third, contributions from immigrants themselves comprised the main source of the committee's income. They deposited money in dollars in the so-called Equipment Fund, intended for the purchase of machines and equipment for Soviet Karelia, and in return they received receipts signed by the head of KTAC guaranteeing that the deposited sum would be reimbursed in the USSR in rubles at the official rate of two rubles for one dollar. Archival evidence shows that the total sum of money deposited in the Equipment Fund from 1931 to 1934, the period of most active emigration to Soviet Karelia, amounted to $162,146 US. According to a later estimate, a male emigrant typically contributed between $100 and $300 US, and sometimes significantly more, in the Equipment Fund.[13] In return, the Resettlement Administration in Petrozavodsk paid 304,629 rubles to immigrants upon presentation of the receipts signed by Aronen and Corgan.[14] For unclear reasons, approximately $20,000 remained uncompensated.

Equipment was purchased by the committee both through Amtorg, the Soviet trading representative in the United States, and independently. Since initially the import of equipment with American and Canadian immigrants was spontaneous and infringed on the monopoly of Soviet foreign trade, the government of Soviet Karelia formed the so-called Foreign Currency Committee, which began to coordinate the purchase of equipment by assembling orders from Karelian economic organizations.[15] It legalized, from the perspective of Soviet laws, the commercial activities of KTAC and allowed for a more orderly organization of imports.

Purchased equipment was delivered to Soviet Karelia with immigrant groups, which reduced transportation expenses and, more importantly, customs fees. This was made possible by a resolution of the Soviet government that allowed immigrants to import free of duties not only personal belongings but also a certain category of machinery and tools, as approved by the People's Commissariat of Foreign Trade. Once delivered to Petrozavodsk, the equipment was initially transferred to the Karelian government, which compensated its purchase by immigrants in rubles. The government then resold the equipment through the Resettlement Administration to those industries that had ordered it with a 50 percent premium added to the original price. This surplus was intended to be used to improve the living conditions of foreign workers.[16] In 1934, when the flow of immigrants was drying up and contributions to the Equipment Fund almost completely ceased, the Karelian authorities tried to stimulate both: workers who agreed to deposit their money in the Equipment Fund were guaranteed by the Karelian government that it would reimburse their travel expenses from the United States or Canada to the USSR and, after the expiration of their labor contracts, back.[17]

Apart from equipment purchased by the Karelian Technical Aid Committee, Finnish immigrants themselves also imported equipment and tools on their own. After their arrival in Soviet Karelia, the Resettlement Administration compensated their costs at the same official rate of two rubles for one dollar spent. By the autumn of 1935, American and Canadian Finns had brought in equipment and tools worth about $50,000 US since compensations amounted to 100,000 rubles.[18] However, as in the case of money deposited in the Equipment Fund, some immigrants never received reimbursements for imported equipment.[19]

To understand the scale of the financial contribution made by North American immigrants to the Karelian economy, it is necessary to consider the purchasing power parity between the American dollar and the Soviet ruble, rather than their official exchange rate, at which the Karelian government reimbursed immigrants' investments. The latter, as set in the USSR in the early 1930s, was 1.95 rubles to one dollar. The real purchasing power of the US dollar, however, was much higher: a state-run company, Torgsin, which operated a network of stores from 1931 to 1936 that sold goods in short supply in the USSR for hard currency, gold, or jewels, set its internal rate at 5.75 rubles to one dollar. American economists estimated the ruble to be even lower, arguing that its purchasing power was equivalent to four to ten cents in the early 1930s. In this ratio, one US dollar was worth ten to twenty-five rubles.[20] At the Torgsin rate, based on a comparison of purchasing power for consumer goods, contributions made by North American Finns to the Karelian economy amounted to about 1,200,000 rubles. However, immigrants invested mostly in hardware, for which the purchasing power of the dollar in the United States, where the equipment was bought, was much larger compared with that of the ruble, so our estimates of their contributions can be doubled or even tripled. For all this, immigrants were reimbursed only a fraction of the value of their investments. For comparison, the 1931 budget of Soviet Karelia set capital investments in industry at 5,687,000 rubles and in the economy overall at 18,417,000 rubles.[21]

The selection of applicants, at least during the first two years of emigration, was divided into several stages. Those who wanted to move to the Soviet Union had to submit an application to one of the local Finnish workers' organizations, which served as regional representations of the Karelian Technical Aid Committee, and receive a letter of recommendation from it. Information about resettlement opportunities in Soviet Karelia was disseminated through the Finnish-language socialist newspaper *Työmies,* by recruiters working on behalf of KTAC, or via rumors circulating in Finnish communities. This effectively limited the Karelian fever to Finnish communities in North America, though the campaign also caught the eye of a small number of Swedish immigrants who then applied for immigration to Soviet Karelia.[22] Documents were examined in the central KTAC offices in New York and Toronto by a committee that included the head of the particular office, a representative of the respective Communist Party, and a representative of one of the Finnish democratic or trade union organizations. These committees compiled lists of the people whom they recommended for emigration to Soviet Karelia and sent these lists to Petrozavodsk. The Karelian government and *obkom* of the VKP(b) examined them and, after formal approval, sent them to Moscow, where entry visas were issued.[23] During all these stages, major criteria for the selection of candidates were their professional training or experience and political views. However, committees in New York and Toronto sometimes took other considerations into account when recommending certain people for emigration. In certain cases, there was a corporate approach: that is, preference was given to a relative or friend of someone who had already been included on the emigration lists; in other cases, which were more common, KTAC approved candidates who could contribute large sums of money to the Equipment Fund. In this respect, it was characteristic for application forms to start with a question regarding the amount of a possible cash contribution.[24]

Emigrants were supposed to pay travel expenses to Petrozavodsk themselves, though several hundred people, mainly lumberjacks from Canada who did not have enough money to pay their travel costs, went to Soviet Karelia at the expense of the Karelian Technical Aid Committee or were funded by their friends. Emigrants signed labor agreements for the period of two years.[25] Most of them, however, planned to leave North America forever: they sold their properties and closed their bank accounts, which made return all the more problematic. Even those who knew for certain that living and working conditions in the USSR would be much worse than those in North America emigrated to Soviet Karelia. In the summer of 1932, Aronen, head of the New York office of KTAC, arrived in Soviet Karelia. Two years later, when the recruitment campaign almost stopped and those Finnish North Americans who had returned from the Soviet Union spread terrible stories in Finnish communities, Corgan, his successor, went to Petrozavodsk. Perhaps his decision was the last argument that KTAC could offer in support of emigration policy, which was on the verge of failure. Matti Tenhunen, Kalle Aronen, and Oscar Corgan were later executed during the Great Terror. Among the leaders of the Karelian Technical Aid Committee, only Jussi Latva, who stayed in Canada, survived.

WHAT CAUSED THE KARELIAN FEVER?

The question of what caused a relatively large-scale emigration from North American Finnish communities to Soviet Karelia was often asked during the emigration itself, and the more that it claimed attention among researchers the more explanations were offered to interpret the

A. K. C. C. P.
HAPKOMTPYDA
Työasiain Kansankomisariaatti,
Petroskoi, U. S. S. R.

K. A. S. N. T:n tulevien henkilötiedot

a) Tulijalta vaaditaan todistus joltakin vasemmist. työväenjärjestöltä.

Todistukset miltä järjestöltä .... Canadan S Järjestöltä

b) Tulijalta vaaditaan lääkärin todistus, että on työkykyinen ja vapaa tarttuvista taudeista.

Todistus ....

c) Onko perhettä? Kuinka monta jäsentä? Perhe saa tulla, mutta tulija maksaa itsensä ja perheensä kyydit.

Vastaus .... vaimo ja kaksi lasta

d) Jos voi, niin minkä verran voi antaa rahaa: a) Yleiseen konerahastoon: $.......... b) Mistä arvosta työkaluja $.......... 50.00

Jokaisen perheen jäsenen, 16 vuotta vanha tai yli, on itsensä persoonakohtaisesti täytettävä tämä kaavake ja vastattava seuraavat kysymykset:

1) Tulijan täydellinen nimi .... Julius August Seppälä

Isän nimi .... Akseli Seppälä

2) Syntymäpaikka .... Seinäjoki .... Aika 19.... p. 9 .... kuuta, vuonna 1894

3) Perhesuhteet. Selostus .... Vaimo ja kaksi lasta

4) Tulijan kansallisuus .... Suomen

5) Mitä kouluja käynyt ja päättänyt .... Kansakoulun

6) Ammatti. Kuinka laaja kokemus milläkin ammattialalla? .... Metalli ja puutyömies

7) Minkä maan passilla matkustatte? .... Suomen

8) Milloin voisi tulla? .... Kutsun saatua

9) Mihin työhön haluaa tulla? .... Metalli tai puutöihin, eli missä tarvitaan

10) Onko ennen ollut U. S. S. R:ssä taikka vanhalla Venäjällä .... ei. Jos, niin missä paikassa ja millä asialla

11) 16 vuotta nuorempien lasten nimet ja iät. (Sitä vanhemmat perheen jäsenet panevat itse hakemuksen) ....

12) Mihin puolueeseen kuuluu? .... Mistä asti? .... Mihin muihin järjestöihin? .... Canadan S Järjestöön .... Mihin on ennen kuulunut? Amattiliitton Suomessa

13) Milloin on matkustanut Amerikaan? .... 1921 .... Mistä? .... Suomesta .... Minkä sataman kautta? .... Halifaxin

14) Onko palvellut sotaväessä? .... ei. Jos on, niin minkä maan sotaväessä ja millä rintamalla? ....

.... Missä saanut sotilasopetuksen? .... ei

15) Onko ollut oikeudessa syytettynä? .... ei .... Jos, niin mistä asiasta? ....

16) Omistaako S. N. T. Liitossa omaisuutta? .... ei .... Jos, niin missä ja kuinka paljon? ....

17) Onko sukulaisia S. N. T. Liitossa? Nimet ja osoitteet .... ei

18) Mikä järjestö suosittaa tulemaan Neuvostoliittoon? .... Canadan S Järjestö

19) Kuka yksilö suosittaa? Nimi ja osote .... John Stahlberg Box 69 Sudbury Ont.

20) Mukaan liitettävä kolme passikuvaa.

JA Seppälä

(Hakijan allekirjoitus.)

Box 153. Copper Cliff

(Täydellinen osote.)

Архив
Национальный

FIGURE 7. AN EXAMPLE OF A FORM THAT AMERICAN AND CANADIAN FINNS SUBMITTED TO APPLY FOR IMMIGRATION TO SOVIET KARELIA (NARK, F. R-685, OP. 2, D. 205,1. 21) (COURTESY OF THE NATIONAL ARCHIVE OF THE REPUBLIC OF KARELIA).

phenomenon of the Karelian fever. This situation in the scholarship seems to reflect the true complexity of the migration process.

Although all researchers admit that multiple motives stood behind the Karelian fever, they generally do not coincide in their emphases. Some scholars stress the importance of economic motivations and argue that the main factor in making the decision to move to the USSR was the Great Depression that struck America and Canada in 1929.[26] Others consider that the major factor in this decision was a propaganda campaign launched in the Finnish-language leftist press and by Karelian recruiters[27] as well as genuine socialist enthusiasm among North American Finns for the ideals of Communism.[28] Yet others dispute these arguments and claim that national and ethnopsychological factors were more important.[29] They argue that North American Finns were eager to respond to the Karelian recruitment campaign because of their general isolation and alienation in the New World. Among the factors that contributed significantly to the Karelian fever, the split in Finnish communities over religious and political issues is also mentioned.[30] A number of works advocate the idea that Finnish immigrants were treated unfairly in the United States and Canada.[31] They argue that American society was unable to appreciate the contributions of Finnish immigrants to its economic and social order. Finns felt discriminated against compared with immigrants from other countries, such as Swedes, Germans, and Danes, to say nothing of Anglo-Saxons. Their great disappointment resulted in emigration back to Finland or in searches for a better life in the Soviet Union.

Interpretations of the immigration policy of the Karelian government are similarly various. For some, Edvard Gylling and those Finnish Communists who were responsible for the organization of emigration on the American and Canadian side were genuine Marxists, deeply devoted to socialism.[32] They really wanted to build a country of "equality and brotherhood for all," and they were not to be blamed that these attempts ended in the Great Terror. Others argue that the immigration policy of the Red Finnish authorities of Soviet Karelia was driven by nationalist, rather than Communist, ideas since they tried to make Soviet Karelia an ethnically homogeneous Finnish-populated region and dreamed of a "Greater Red Finland."[33] For yet others, the initiative of recruiting Finns in North America belonged entirely to the Comintern, which hoped to push forward the idea of worldwide revolution,[34] while a fourth group of researchers stresses purely economic factors—primarily the interest of the Karelian government in securing a qualified foreign labor force along with new technologies and tools.[35]

The scholarly debate over the Karelian fever has been hampered by the narrow empirical basis of this topic. For a long time, documents stored in Russian archives were unavailable to researchers: the Soviet government claimed all materials related to immigration to the Soviet Union as classified already in the spring of 1932.[36] After the Great Terror, which had a severe impact on Soviet Finnish communities, these materials became nearly inaccessible. The sources remaining open to access, such as newspaper articles or memoir accounts, were conspicuously biased. Materials of the Soviet and American or Canadian press of the 1930s did not even try to provide a somewhat balanced picture of the immigration/emigration, each pursuing its own political and ideological agenda of defending or attacking the Communist cause. Soviet newspapers, for example, in response to the American and British boycott of Soviet timber exports,[37] published speeches by Finnish immigrants from the United States and Canada in which they praised socialist ways of life and labor and attacked Western newspapers and politicians for their "slander."[38] The Finnish-language press in North America also published numerous witness reports about life in Soviet Karelia, but these reports were from immigrants who were so disappointed with their Karelian adventures that they returned home, embittered and disillusioned, after several months or years of life there. There was also at least one book-length personal account of immigration published in the immediate aftermath of the Karelian fever,[39] but it remained unnoticed until recently.[40]

Another important source on the life of the American-Canadian colony in Soviet Karelia were immigrant letters, which represented a diverse picture of immigrants' lives and avoided black-and-white judgments and stereotypes typical of the press. One can find in them a spectrum of emotions, from naive dreams and spirited enthusiasm to disarray, confusion, and finally disappointment. Many immigrants were afraid to speak openly of hardships in Soviet Karelia, so they wrote to friends and relatives in a rather Aesopian language that the latter "should wait a little with their journey to Karelia." However, even the harsh reality of Soviet Karelia could not disillusion all immigrants. Many of those who mentioned hardships in their letters still believed that all problems were temporary and would soon be resolved. They were satisfied with their jobs and the attitudes of local people toward them, and they invited their friends to visit Soviet Karelia. These letters informed Finnish communities in North America about the lives of friends and relatives in Soviet Karelia during the 1930s, and were the only source of news after the Second World War, but only recently has this important group of sources been engaged by researchers.[41]

Those immigrants who stayed in Karelia and survived the Great Terror and the Second World War were devoid, for a long time, of any opportunity to speak publicly about their lives, to say nothing of writing their memoirs. The first memoirs that discreetly mentioned the contributions of North American Finns to the development of the Karelian economy during the 1920s and 1930s were published in Petrozavodsk in 1976, forty years after the events described.[42] It was only in 1989, in the heyday of perestroika, that Mayme Sevander, a daughter of Oscar Corgan, one of the primary organizers of the emigration from North America, published a letter titled "American Finns, Answer!" in the two central Karelian newspapers. The response was an avalanche of letters from immigrants and their children, and in the wake of this response Sevander published several long articles on Finnish American immigration to Soviet Karelia in the early 1930s. This correspondence with other immigrants, her personal memories, and later her archival research became the basis for her four half-journalistic, half-autobiographical books on Karelian fever.[43] It is symptomatic, however, that both her works and other book-length memoir accounts were written in either Finnish or English: the traumatic experiences of immigrants in the Soviet Union and their desire to address the communities that they associated themselves with—that is, Finnish, American, and Canadian but not Russian audiences—prevented them from narrating their experiences in Russian.

By the 1970s, emigration policy had been slightly relaxed in the Soviet Union, which let a handful of former North American immigrants leave the USSR, usually under the pretext of a "family reunion." Some of them published memoirs, which became the first accounts of events of the Karelian fever after a long period of silence.[44] Since 1990, the government of Finland launched several repatriation programs encouraging the immigration of people of Finnish descent from the USSR and later post-Soviet states, primarily Russia and Estonia. Among about 20,000 immigrants who came between 1992 and 2001[45] were a number of American and Canadian Finns, who also published their life stories.[46]

These "second wave" memoirs about the exodus to Soviet Karelia were written from fifty to seventy years after the actual events. This raises the question of the degree to which their interpretations were tainted by particular strategies of remembering and coping with the traumas of Stalinist repressions and the Second World War. Nevertheless, these memoirs provide a much more detailed picture of the lives of immigrants in Soviet Karelia and the USSR than the one presented in newspapers. The long silence between the actual experience of American and Canadian immigrants in Soviet Karelia and its representation in memoirs is easy to explain— the experience of repression and, in the case of early re-emigrants of the 1970s and 1980s, the fear for friends and relatives in Soviet Karelia forced them to forget, or at least to avoid remembering, their terrible past. For example, Sylvia and Lawrence Hokkanen, who lived in the USSR for almost eight years and managed to get back to Canada in 1941, decided to talk about their experiences only fifty years later.[47] Almost all memoirs published by re-emigrants between the 1970s and 1990s present vivid descriptions of the cultural shock that they went through after arrival in Soviet Karelia and an equally emotional narrative of ensuing hardships. A significant emphasis in these memoirs is also placed on the Great Terror, which everybody considered to be the most terrible time of their lives.

One example of how narrative strategies changed over time and place is particularly interesting. Olga-Maria Koponen, a Canadian Finnish woman who moved to Finland in the 1990s, published two memoirs with a time lapse between them of thirty-five years. During the Karelian fever, she arrived in Soviet Karelia from Canada with her husband and a young daughter—and with a belief in the bright future of a socialist society. In 1935, her husband died of tuberculosis, and later the same disease claimed the life of her daughter. Koponen was employed in the forest industry, performing physically demanding work such as logging and log driving in different regions of Soviet Karelia. This was what her first memoir account was about, published in Petrozavodsk in 1976 under the title "Women in Forest Harvesting" as part of a memoir collection about Karelian economic development in the 1920s and 1930s.[48] This was a realistic narrative about hard labor that was difficult even for men and, at the same time, an enthusiastic and elevated story of emotionally rewarding work in a friendly collective, a hymn to women who were at the forefront of building Communism. Her book published in 2002 in Finland, after Koponen re-emigrated from Soviet Karelia, is an absolutely different account, depicting life in Soviet Karelia as very difficult, full of loss and hardship and rarely leaving space for enthusiasm or other positive emotions.[49]

Thus, until recently, the main primary sources on the history of the immigration of American and Canadian Finns to Soviet Karelia were contemporary newspaper publications, memoirs, and interviews with re-emigrants in North America or Finland. This explains why most works in this field focused primarily on the Karelian fever from the perspective of Finnish communities in the United States and Canada. A limited empirical basis and the specific character of personal accounts prevented scholars from addressing the immigration of Finns as part of trans-Atlantic history, in which Gylling's visions of ethnicity-based development of Soviet Karelia, the economic depression in the West and the industrialization campaign in the Soviet Union, and the political enthusiasm in Finnish immigrant communities mixed in an amalgam of personal fates and global politics.

"WE CAME HERE TO BUILD SOCIALISM"

In this and the following section, we will try to combine an analysis of personal narratives with an analysis of statistics to reach a better understanding of North American Finns as a distinct sociocultural group. A study of the ways in which immigrants turned their experiences into narratives, the focus of this section, provides insight into the political and cultural categories that were important to them, while statistical research helps to highlight the issues related to the social composition of this immigrant group. By combining these two approaches, we hope to offer a complex answer to an equally complex question: who were these people who decided to change their lives so dramatically and gave everything up to their last cent to immigrate to the USSR?

As we mentioned above, radical views were fairly widespread among North American Finns, and many of them at that time sincerely believed in the future of socialism and in its current progress in the Soviet Union. Memoir accounts of immigrants provide plenty of examples that their authors were confident that a fair society was being built there. For them, the Earth rotated, as Communist propagandists were convincing them, at the will of Bolsheviks.[50] A propaganda campaign of socialist achievements in the USSR was organized on a large scale, and recruiters of the Karelian Technical Aid Committee found a receptive audience. A particularly deep impact was left by a documentary film about life in Soviet Karelia titled *The Old and the New* screened in Finnish clubs in the United States and Canada.[51] It was a dream in which people wanted to believe, and recruiters depicted to the appreciative audience, most likely sincerely, a picture of "equality and brotherhood for all," though most of them had only a vague idea about its actual implementation in the USSR. "In Karelia, you won't find layabouts and idlers. Everybody is equal, and officials don't wear white collars and felt hats, as they do in capitalist countries."[52]

The more absurd the arguments of recruiters were, the deeper their impacts sometimes were, especially on children and youth. In one Finnish school, a Communist propagandist gave a lecture about the future realm of workers, with equality and justice for all. When children asked him where he had got this information from, he responded that he had learned it from Karl Marx, who had come to Finland during the summer vacation of 1930.[53] Of course, such stories and Communist ideals of parents had deep impacts on how children comprehended the surrounding reality. A Finnish immigrant, Kalle Ranta, recollected that his father regularly told him about Karl Marx, Friedrich Engels, Vladimir Lenin, and the new power of workers in Russia, which did not have any crises or unemployment. These stories formed in his young character nearly a phobia of capitalism: "I often sat with a gloomy face feeling that soon a whirlpool of capitalism would engulf all my hopes and plans. This might sound absurd, but it really reflected the attitude to the world."[54] Mayme Sevander, mentioned above, was eleven when her family moved to the USSR. In all her books, she wrote that ideological motivations and the membership of North American Finns in Communist and radical organizations were the main reasons for the Karelian fever.

There is no doubt that, among people who had earlier left Finland because of their radical political beliefs, many had dreams of Communism and the world revolution that would implement it. They saw Soviet Karelia as a place where these dreams could come true. Those immigrants who, upon arrival in Karelia, wrote to Soviet newspapers that "we arrived in the Soviet Union to build socialism together with you"[55] were sincere; they really believed in building a new society—at least in the beginning. An active pro-Soviet campaign in the leftist press that preceded the Karelian recruitment campaign was very successful and formed the symbolic universe of thousands of Americans and Canadians of Finnish descent. Still, our rough calculations show that actual members of the American and Canadian Communist Parties constituted less than 15 percent of the total number of Finnish emigrants to Soviet Karelia.[56] This figure is indirectly confirmed by the politics of both parties. Their leadership introduced maximum quotas for their members willing to emigrate to Soviet Karelia—they could not constitute more than 15 to 20 percent of the emigration flow.[57]

Besides, the pro-Soviet propaganda campaign in the leftist American and Canadian press, even though directed at radical immigrant groups, would never have been as effective without the Great Depression. Political and ideological motivations were important, of course, when people were deciding whether to emigrate, but the economy remained the most critical factor. This was true for almost all Canadian emigrants and for most American emigrants. Many interviews with or memoir accounts of Finnish immigrants to the USSR depicted a nearly identical picture:

> Finland suffered from famine. . . . Then father decided to go to America. He left in 1926, and mother—in 1927. They went to Canada, because people said that there was a need in workers for logging. They fared well there, I mean, in financial terms. Father had two horses, two cows, and a house, they carved huge refrigerators in a rock—we didn't have such refrigerators at that time as now. Finns lived in their own community. They always helped each other and didn't communicate much with locals [Canadians] and other immigrants. Of course, there were difficulties, as we didn't know the [English] language. Well, many didn't want to learn it either. By the time my brother and I were born, [our] parents had got on [their] feet, more or less. They had a good household, father had a regular salary, but still America seemed alien to us. Then, in the early 1930s, unemployment struck. And the radio and newspapers kept on calling to move to the USSR, to build socialism. It was then that [our] parents decided to emigrate to Russia.[58]

> During the crisis, life became very difficult. My husband kept on trying to find a job. If he worked at least for a week in a month, we considered it a big luck.[59]

> Back in America, we lived in Detroit, an automobile city. Father worked at the Ford factory, while mother earned some money in a household of some millionaire. He had his own servants, but mother came twice a week to clean up the house. We lived quite well. Had a Ford of our own—well, almost everybody had a car at that time. Lived in private houses. . . . Then unemployment came to America. It was really hard. Every day father was leaving home to search for a job and came back tired and hungry. At first mother asked him every day: "Any news?" He only sighed. Then she stopped asking him.[60]

Recruiters were convincing people that "it is much better to build socialism with your hands in Karelia than to suffer of hunger and unemployment in the exploiters' country."[61] The leftist press also appealed to a sense of duty—Russian comrades, as it wrote, fought not only for their own freedom but also for the freedom of the world proletariat, and American workers had to return the favor by helping to secure revolutionary progress with their labor.[62] However, people who were depressed by the unemployment and afraid for the future of their children were much more influenced by practical arguments: "In the USSR, everybody has equal opportunities. Here you won't find a beggar, no one goes to bed with an empty stomach, and there are no lines for bread. Medical care is free, old people get pensions, and workers can go to sanatoriums and recreation centers."[63]

The influence of such propaganda was intensified by the stories of eyewitnesses who visited Soviet Karelia as guests, official delegates, and so on. Those who had been to Petrozavodsk spoke of high salaries and low prices and confidence in the future, and their reports had a great impact on people who lived with an uncertain tomorrow. A Finnish immigrant, Aino Streng, remembered that our neighbor Henriksson returned from Karelia. He said: "Salaries in Karelia are very high. A forest worker earns on average twelve and up to twenty rubles a day. And qualified workers earn at the least 600 rubles a month." I asked: "What is the price of life there?" Henriksson replied: "I would answer this way: a bottle of vodka costs seventy kopecks." It looked like a fairy tale! Seventy kopecks! Nobody knew what it would be in the Canadian money, but this comparison implied that it was very cheap.[64]

For Canadian Finns, the main driving force for emigration to Soviet Karelia was job opportunity, which they had no more in Canada. Many believed, as the example above demonstrates, that they would have high salaries and a cheap life in Soviet Karelia. Such dreams were only natural: the main wave of Finnish immigration to Canada occurred in the second half of the 1920s. Many of these immigrants had not had enough time to take root in their new country by the time of the Great Depression, and unemployment ravaged their communities. Immigrants were fired first; besides, Finns worked in industries hardest hit by the crisis: building, forestry, mining, and agriculture.

In the United States, economic hardship was also a primary motivation for most Finns who decided to emigrate to Soviet Karelia. However, the reasons for emigration were less focused on the threat of unemployment. While the emigration flow from Canada was composed mainly of Finns who had lost their jobs during the crisis and were without means to support themselves and their families, the social composition of Finnish emigration from the United States was much more diverse. Many American Finns belonged to fairly wealthy social groups, as proven by their large contributions to the Equipment Fund of Soviet Karelia and the personal possessions that they took with them. Most had their own houses and cars, considered the norm in Finnish immigrant communities in the United States. There were even rich people among these emigrants: personal files of emigrants show such people as "an owner of a legal firm," "an owner of a farm priced at 20,000 dollars," or "an owner of a car repair service priced at 8,000 dollars."[65]

These people who had achieved much in America considered emigration as an opportunity to secure their old age and the future of their children. For many families, the decisive argument in favor of emigration to the USSR was educational opportunity: in Soviet Karelia, their children could get an education in the Finnish language on all levels, from kindergarten to college. Dagny Salo, who went to Petrozavodsk with her parents in 1931 and later became a recipient of the Honorary Teacher of Karelia award, recalled her experience:

> So why did my parents decide to immigrate? Father had been unemployed for two years. I had graduated from high school, and my brother had completed the eighth grade. I was fifteen, soon sixteen, and would hardly find any job without professional education, and we had no money, so I could not get any degree. Brother was in the same situation, because in the village where we lived there was no high school for him. Would he find a place to go to a high school? So the future was empty for me and Toivo. Everything was unclear. That's why, when we arrived in Petrozavodsk, the next day father sent me to a Finnish nine-grade school.[66]

Emigration of many relatively prosperous families to Soviet Karelia can also be partly explained by the ignorance of Finnish Americans and Canadians: quite a few of them had little idea of the true state of affairs in the country to which they were going. Of course, not everyone completely believed recruiters, and they often warned about the hardships that would await emigrants to Soviet Karelia. Potential emigrants were not promised gold in heaps; on the contrary, recruiters told them about problems with food supplies and housing and recommended that they take enough clothes, household goods, and working tools to last a while, for many of these things were unavailable in Soviet Karelia. Matti Tenhunen, often later accused of deception, warned potential emigrants from the beginning: "We need real workers, rather than seekers of luck and well-being. The Soviet Union is not a rest home for the elderly. . . . You will have to get used to eating black bread instead of white. . . . You won't have meat, butter, and many other groceries that you are used to having on your tables here."[67]

Many emigrants realized to varying degrees that life in the Soviet Union would be difficult. Miriam Nousiainen, an eight-year-old girl at the time of emigration to Soviet Karelia, remembered that before departure her father told her to "finish your milk, we are going to a place where you won't see it for quite a long [time]." In an interview many years later, she expressed her opinion of his decisions: "Now, I can't imagine how father could think of going with two little children to a country where, as he perfectly knew, there were no normal living conditions. What was he thinking about? What did he rely on?"[68] Such questions were later asked by many, and we can suggest only one explanation: Finnish Americans either could not imagine what really awaited them or believed that all difficulties they would face in the Soviet Union would be temporary. And then pro-Soviet propaganda emphasized the availability of jobs, high salaries, and eventually a happy future. The promise of stability and confidence in the future in a society where economic crises would be impossible inspired people's imaginations and became important motivations for immigration.

Apart from political and economic reasons, cultural factors were also important. Most Finns, who had left their native land for the New World in search of jobs and a better life, were able to find work across the Atlantic. But America or Canada could not replace Finland in cultural terms, which became particularly clear during the crisis. The ethnic and cultural isolation of Finns, language problems, and suspicious treatment, because of perceived radicalism, of Finnish communities by authorities destroyed immigrants' desire to integrate into American or Canadian society. Such people regarded re-emigration as the best possible solution. Yet for those who had fought on the Red side in the Finnish Civil War and were active in leftist organizations in North America, a return to Finland, where the Communist movement was banned, was barely realistic, and for others who had left Finland to build a better life in the New world it would equal capitulation.

In this situation, Soviet Karelia became even more attractive. It was close to Finland and shared similar nature and climate, and Finnish was its second official language. Moreover, for a large part of the nineteenth century and the first part of the twentieth century, Karelia had been part of an imagined cultural and political space of Finland. In the symbolic world of Finnish emigrants, Soviet Karelia was nearly a native land. As Aino Streng remembered, "we were very glad that we were going to eastern Karelia,[69] where Finnish was spoken. We were satisfied, as we knew that Finland was so close. Only a large forest divided us."[70] Newspaper articles about Soviet Karelia stressed the prominent role of the Finnish language there and emphasized that local authorities supported Finnish settlers in order to spur national development of socialist Finnish culture. Recruiters promised that, unlike in the United States and Canada, in Soviet Karelia Finns would be the first among other immigrants and have a higher social status because of their ethnicity.[71] Many indeed believed in the privileges and affection that they were supposed to receive in a new socialist land. Some Finnish emigrants

Tov. TOIVO JA HIIMA TASASEN

KARJALAAN LÄKSIÄISET

TYÖVÄENYHDISTYKSEN HAALILLA 719 Montana Ave., LAUANTAINA
T.K. 14 päivä, alkaen kello 8 illala.

Kehoitamme kaikkia työläistovereita saapumaan tähän
tilaisuuteen. Tilaisuudessa tullaan suorittamaan hyvä ohjelma.
Ohjelmassa tulee olemaan laulua, soittoa, runoja, puhe
y.m.y.m. ohjelmaa. Toveri Tasanen"saarnaa"tilaisuudessa meille
lähtijäis⁴saarnan". Tämä on viimeinen tilaisuus meillä olla
näiden toverien seurassa. Saapukaamme suurena joukkona jättä-
mään jäähyväisemme näille monivuotisille toimihenkilöillemme,
jotka nyt lähtevät sosialismin rakennustyöhön Neuvosto-Karjalaan.

HUOM! TILAISUUDESSA TANSSITAAN LOPUKSI HYVÄN SOITON
TAHDISSA. - Sisäänpääsy tähän tilaisuuteen on ainoastaan 25 ¢
* * * * * * * * *
TYÖVÄENYHDISTYKSEN JÄRJESTÄMÄ KENTTÄJUHLA
ensi sunnuntaina 15 päivä. Tämä kenttäjuhla tullaan viettämään
TUALATIN PARKISSA

Hyvä ohjelma ja kaikenlaisia "keemejä". Siellä myös tarjotaan
päivällinen,joten saatte huoletta lähteä kotoanne ilman eväitä.
Juhlat aletaan kello 10 a.p. Saapukaa suurena joukkona luonnon
helmaan. Siellä tapaatte myös tuttavanne. Tämä tilaisuus tar-
joa meille kaikille rattoisan päivän luonnon helmassa.

Tov. Portlandin S.T.Yhdistys

FIGURE 8. AN ANNOUNCEMENT OF A FAREWELL CONCERT ORGANIZED IN A LABOR UNION HALL IN PORTLAND, OREGON,
ON THE OCCASION OF TOIVO AND HIIMA TASANEN'S DEPARTURE FOR SOVIET KARELIA, 1932 (NARK, F. R-3631, OP. 1, D. 1,1. 1)
(COURTESY OF THE NATIONAL ARCHIVE OF THE REPUBLIC OF KARELIA).

even mocked a few Swedish emigrants who were going to Soviet Karelia, for they believed that Swedes would be totally helpless there without any knowledge of Finnish.[72]

Communalism was another important cultural value that could influence a decision to emigrate to the Soviet Union. A number of memoirs single it out when they mention that the example of other Finns became critical in making this decision: "There were quite many Finns in Detroit. We all helped each other. There was also a very strong committee of the Communist Party [USA]. A lot of our friends were its members, although not all of them understood its ideas. But it is a common thing for Finns, that if your neighbor advises you to take part in something, why not?"[73]

For many Finns, the fact that everybody around them was on the move became an important argument, and they thought that joining their neighbors and friends would be better than staying in America or Canada—"a gregarious feeling," as one of our respondents characterized it,[74] and another reiterated that "my father wanted to leave for Karelia, he made this decision, and we left. My father was not a member of the [Communist] Party, but a lot of his friends were Communists, and they left for the USSR. The Finns lived together as a family, and they all decided to go and build socialism. Father did the same."[75]

There were also some individuals among Finnish emigrants who hoped to increase their financial capital by launching an enterprise in a new place. There were some adventurers too. The search for El Dorado is, as a rule, a venture for those who have already tried to find it but failed.

All emigrants to Soviet Karelia, including those who did not really believe in Communist propaganda, felt enthusiasm and anticipated great change. When ships were departing from New York or Halifax, people were crying "hurrah!" and singing the "Internationale." A hard voyage that lasted for two weeks was best remembered by most of them for this unprecedented enthusiasm and anticipation of something bright and joyful. "We were going to build socialism; we were going to a free country, where we would be met as best friends!" Yrjö Myllyharju recalled seventy years later.[76] Nobody could imagine what difficulties were awaiting them in the near future.

A SOCIAL PORTRAIT OF NORTH AMERICAN IMMIGRANTS

The question of how many Finns from the United States and Canada emigrated to Soviet Karelia in the early 1930s and how many of them returned is still a matter of debate. Estimates, based on different sources, range from 2,000 to 15,000, with most researchers agreeing that the actual number was somewhere in between.[77] For this book, we used a complex body of documents on the immigration from North America from the National Archive of the Republic of Karelia,[78] which originated from the activities of Karelian organizations responsible for the immigration and arguably represent the most accurate data available on this issue. These materials are abundant, but also contradictory and confusing, and much time and effort were required to process, verify, and analyze data in them. This labor, however, gave us proper compensation by enabling us to draw a social portrait of the Finnish American and Finnish Canadian immigrant groups.

Our analysis in this section is based on several particular collections of documents that more or less accurately represent the changes in the number of North American Finns in Soviet

Karelia. This information comes from the Resettlement Administration and documents of party and security organs that controlled the recruitment and reception of immigrants, their working and living conditions, and the "political and moral" atmosphere in their communities or, in other words, the degree of their reliability. The National Archive also stores a large number of various lists that present data on immigrants as sorted by organizations, years, dates of arrival, or places of living, along with personnel forms from different employment organizations. These archival sources were compiled together to create a single database that now stores information on 5,557 North American Finnish immigrants to Soviet Karelia.[79] Although this figure is by far incomplete,[80] the material from this database helps to create a social portrait of the immigrants. To verify our calculations, we also used data from the 1933 Karelian census.[81]

The main statistical data on North American immigrants in Soviet Karelia as preserved in archival sources are presented in Table 1.

A preliminary note should be made before these data are analyzed. It is not clear who compiled the list and why it was dated January 1934 (left part of the table), but the fact that it was stored in the archival collection of the Karelian *obkom* of the ВКP(b)[82] instead of the collection of the Resettlement Administration is likely evidence that it was made for the top party authorities of Soviet Karelia and that its authors most likely accounted for re-emigration. In other words, only those immigrants who actually lived in Soviet Karelia in January 1934 were counted in the list, while those who had already left, either for other Soviet regions or for North America or Finland, were omitted from the calculations. It explains the difference between the figures in this list and the data of the Resettlement Administration (right part of the table).

As we mentioned in passing in Chapter 2, several pioneer groups of North American Finns arrived in Soviet Karelia already in the 1920s. In 1922, a well-equipped group of nine immigrants from the United States established a fishing commune on the White Sea coast in a place called Kniazhia Guba (Russian for "Prince's Bay"). Soon they were

Table 1. Immigration of American and Canadian Finns by Years

Year of arrival	Summary list of January 1934				Information of the Resettlement Administration of Soviet Karelia			
	Men	*Women*	*Children*	*Total*	*Men*	*Women*	*Children*	*Total*
Unknown	7	4	6	*17*				
1930	59	18	10	*87*				
1931	1,126	483	373	*1,982*	1,387	591	620	*2,598*
1932	1,039	479	340	*1,858*	1,124	535	434	*2,093*
1933	291	172	69	*532*	297	150	95	*542*
1934					114	62	30	*206*
1935 (January–March)					25	22	10	*57*
Total	*2,522*	*1,156*	*798*	*4,476*	*2,947*	*1,360*	*1,189*	*5,496*

Sources: NARK, f. P-3, op. 6, d. 12774, l. 1–79; NARK, f. R-685, op. 1, d. 14/160, l. 21, 64; NARK, f. P-3, op. 5, d. 276, l. 70.

followed by a second group consisting of four families and five single men. The cooperative called Knösäs (Finns changed the original name of the place, which was hard for them to pronounce) was effective during the relatively liberal economic policy of the 1920s, but with the economic reforms of the 1930s Finns abandoned it and dispersed.[83] In 1925, the agricultural commune Säde was founded near a southern Karelian town, Olonets, by Canadian miners from Cobalt, Ontario. Between 1925 and 1927, three groups of Canadian Finns came to this commune, and by 1932 its population reached fifty-two people.[84] During the 1920s, a small number of Finnish Americans and Canadians also came to Soviet Karelia on an individual basis. Their motivation, as one of them, Enok Nelson, wrote in a letter to his family in Fort Bragg, North Carolina, in 1922, was "to make lives more meaningful."[85]

According to the 1933 census of Soviet Karelia, between 1920 and 1929 1,167 Finns, including 314 workers, moved to the republic to become permanently settled.[86] Although the majority of these immigrants were Communist émigrés from Finland, labor immigrants registered in the census as "workers" were mostly from North America. Half of these immigrant workers, or 154 people, arrived in Karelia between 1920 and 1926, when the Soviet government encouraged agricultural immigration. Thus, by 1930, between 100 and 200 American and Canadian Finns already lived and worked in Soviet Karelia.

During 1930, after permission from the Soviet government, at least two organized groups of North American Finns arrived in Soviet Karelia: on 25 September, a group of lumberjacks from Canada mentioned in Chapter 2, and on 14 December, a group of professional workers from the United States. The first group, according to data from the Resettlement Administration, comprised twenty-five men, three women, and one child.[87] The second group was larger and included forty-eight men, nineteen women, and eleven children. Men were industrial workers, motor mechanics, and builders; there was even one engineer.[88] At the same time, those North American Finns who had earlier immigrated to other Soviet regions started to resettle in Soviet Karelia, attracted by the Finnish language and culture supported by the Red Finnish government. Among them were Finnish members of the agricultural commune Kylväjä in southern Russia. This group of early immigrants was left nearly unnoticed in the documents of the Karelian authorities.

Thus, at least several hundred immigrants who arrived prior to 1931 should be added to the figure of 5,496, which the Resettlement Administration claimed as the "ultimate" number (see the right section of Table 1). Still, its information for the period of 1931–35 was also incomplete. First, it compiled data only on "recruited and landed industrial immigrants who became [a] permanent labor force in the period between 1931 and April 10, 1935."[89] So this information took into account only those immigrants who registered at the Resettlement Administration upon arrival and were then allocated to their intended workplaces. However, many examples of unauthorized immigration are also known, for people searched for jobs independently or went to stay with their relatives and friends, who had already arrived in Soviet Karelia, and never actually registered at the Resettlement Administration. For example, according to information from the administration, 2,598 North American Finns arrived in Soviet Karelia in 1931, while entry permits were issued to no fewer than 2,770 people.[90] Some of them, of course, changed their minds after receiving entry permits and stayed home, but for the early stage of emigration to Soviet Karelia this was highly atypical. The situation was actually reversed, for people tried to get to the USSR by any means. Apart from groups organized by the Karelian Technical Aid Committee, many families and individuals applied independently for visas, usually as tourists, and then stayed in Soviet Karelia. In August 1931, a Soviet plenipotentiary in Sweden, Smirnov, wrote a letter to Edvard Gylling in which he criticized KTAC for numerous inaccuracies that it had made in the lists of emigrants. According to Smirnov, ships of the Swedish American Line carried many people heading for Soviet Karelia who were not mentioned in any official documents provided by its government, an indication that the emigration flow of 1931 comprised a fairly large number of people who aspired to move to Soviet Karelia at their own risk.[91] In our biographical searches for American and Canadian emigrants, we often ran across names that were never mentioned in any of the available lists of recruited or actually arrived immigrants to Soviet Karelia. These people somehow evaded the attention of the Resettlement Administration, but their traces are visible in other documents, and in our (incomplete) searches we encountered scores of such "ghost" immigrants.

Second, the information related to 1935 covered only its first quarter, from January to March, while the immigration actually continued as late as September. Between 22 April and 20 September, no fewer than 120 American and Canadian Finns in thirteen small groups arrived in Petrozavodsk.[92]

Finally, in 1935, the GPU of Soviet Karelia submitted to the Karelian *obkom* of the VKP(b) a memorandum in which it summarized the activities of the recently dissolved Resettlement Administration. The memorandum claimed that, during its period of operation, the administration recruited 4,681 people from North America, of whom 3,713 stayed in Soviet Karelia.[93] This figure included only those adult men and women who were employed in the economy of Soviet Karelia. If we take into account that approximately a third of the North American immigrants were children and non-working women (a rate that other archival sources suggest) and were missed in the GPU's memorandum, then the total number of immigrants who arrived during the early 1930s, without the earlier immigrants of the 1920s, would exceed 6,000 people.

In summary, we can argue that the total number of American and Canadian Finns who immigrated to Soviet Karelia is somewhere between 6,000 and 6,500 people, more likely closer to the latter figure.

Sociodemographic analysis of the North American immigrant diaspora is sometimes complicated by the terminology of the 1930s in which all immigrants were often called "Canadian Finns" or "Canadian lumberjacks." This tendency, common for the Soviet press and official documents alike, is hard to explain, especially since the majority of Finnish immigrants arrived from the United States rather than Canada. A possible explanation might be related to media coverage of the first immigrant group in the autumn of 1930, which consisted entirely of Canadian lumberjacks. Once this catchphrase appeared in Soviet media discourse, it was applied to all North American immigrants, disregarding their country of origin or occupation. Besides, most Canadian Finns who came to Soviet Karelia were, unlike the more diverse contingent of American immigrants, indeed lumberjacks or had similar proletarian occupations. Publications and documents of that time also often used the umbrella term "foreign workers." Although most often referring to North American immigrants, it could also describe a much larger variety of ethnic groups, since among foreign nationals who worked in Soviet Karelia during the 1930s there were Swedes, Danes, Norwegians, Germans, Czechs, Brits, and even Chinese. To complicate things even more, most Finnish immigrants from North America, especially in the case of Finnish Canadians, came to Karelia with Finnish passports, since the majority of first-generation immigrants had not received American or Canadian citizenship prior to their move to the USSR.[94]

FIGURES 9, 10, AND 11. INDIVIDUAL FACES OF NORTH AMERICAN FINNISH IMMIGRANTS IN SOVIET KARELIA. CLOCKWISE, FROM TOP LEFT, VASANEN (FIRST NAME UNKNOWN), 1936 (PHOTO BY G. A. ANKUDINOV); ANNA HÄMÄLÄINEN, 1937 (PHOTOGRAPHER UNKNOWN); UKKONEN (FIRST NAME UNKNOWN), 1935 (PHOTO BY V. KOTOV) (COURTESY OF THE NATIONAL ARCHIVE OF THE REPUBLIC OF KARELIA).

Multiple archival sources compiled into a single database created as part of the aforementioned project Missing in Karelia (see the Preface) allows for the identification of the country of origin for 5,309 North American Finns. Of this number, 3,098, or 58 percent, arrived from the United States and 2,211, or 42 percent, from Canada. This selection covers about 80 percent of American and Canadian immigrants in Soviet Karelia, so this proportion should be true for the entire North American immigrant group. Particular places in the United States and Canada from where immigrants came are more difficult to identify, since North American place names were rarely mentioned in Karelian documents. Yet, for American immigrants, there is reliable data provided by Rikhard Laiho, who made a list of Finnish immigrants from the United States in cooperation with Dr. Rudolph Pinola on the basis of sources stored in the Immigrant History Research Center of the University of Minnesota and in Finlandia University.[95] This list provides information on almost 3,000 immigrants, with most records showing the place and state from which they moved to Soviet Karelia. According to it, half of the American immigrants originated from three states: Michigan, New York, and Minnesota, which is only natural, for 50 percent of all American Finns lived in these states in 1930.[96] A graphical presentation of states in the exodus of American Finns is shown in Figure 12. The largest American "donor" cities were New York, Detroit, Chicago, and Cleveland.

Immigration to Soviet Karelia was subject to temporal fluctuations. One reason was the planned nature of the Soviet economy: the recruitment and travel of immigrants were organized in annual plans, which had to be negotiated with and approved by the top Soviet authorities; this explains why the immigration flow dropped by the beginning of each new year, for it was the time when new plans had to be negotiated and approved, and peaked in the autumn, when all necessary consents were received and vetoes were overcome. It is remarkable, however, that, while American Finns dominated the immigration flow during the first peak of the autumn of 1931, Canadian Finns made up the majority of immigrants during the second peak of the autumn of 1932.

To explain this dynamic, it is necessary to compare American and Canadian immigrant groups with each other and both with the preceding emigration from Finland to North

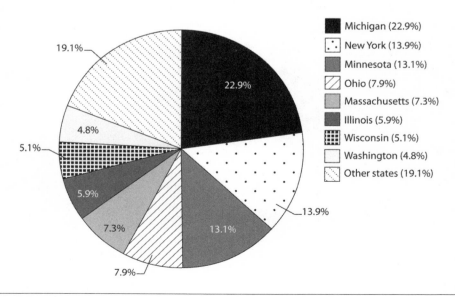

Michigan (22.9%)
New York (13.9%)
Minnesota (13.1%)
Ohio (7.9%)
Massachusetts (7.3%)
Illinois (5.9%)
Wisconsin (5.1%)
Washington (4.8%)
Other states (19.1%)

FIGURE 12. AMERICAN STATES IN THE FINNISH IMMIGRATION FLOW TO SOVIET KARELIA.

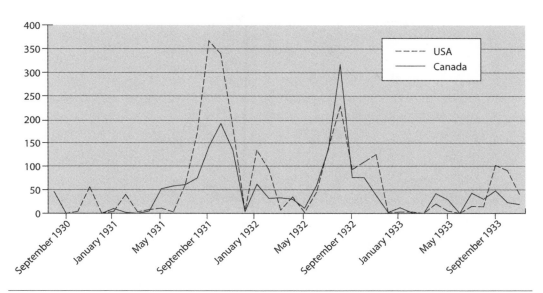

FIGURE 13. TEMPORAL FLUCTUATIONS IN THE IMMIGRATION FLOW, SEPTEMBER 1930 TO DECEMBER 1933.

America. During the American fever in Finland in the late nineteenth century and early twentieth century, approximately 70 percent of Finnish emigrants were between fifteen and thirty-five years of age, and in some years the average age of emigrants was even lower: in 1873 it was twenty-seven, in 1905 only twenty-four. Women constituted about 37 percent of Finnish emigrants to North America and in general were a couple of years younger than men.[97] The leading emigrant group, consequently, was single young men or recently married couples who left for America or Canada in search of better job opportunities.

Finnish Canadian immigrants in Soviet Karelia constituted a group that, in terms of its age and sex composition, was not much different from Finnish immigrants in North America. The average age was thirty-one for men and twenty-seven for women. Children (seventeen and below) made up 17 percent of this immigrant group, with 71 percent of them aged ten and younger, while people between twenty-five and thirty-five constituted 42 percent of Finnish Canadians in Soviet Karelia.

Canadian Finns in general were a recent and young ethnic community, for it formed most actively after the US authorities passed in 1921 the Emergency Quota Act, which redirected Finnish immigration from the United States to Canada. In contrast, most Finns in America arrived there before the First World War. By the time of the Karelian fever, they were typically in middle age and had families with children generally older than those of Canadian Finnish families emigrating to Soviet Karelia. The average age of Finnish American immigrants was thirty-four for men and thirty for women, which can be misleading since it was due to a larger—in comparison with Canadian immigrants—share of children in this group, who constituted 20 percent, with 51 percent of them adolescents aged eleven and older. Adult American immigrants were significantly older than adult Canadian immigrants: 53 percent of them were between thirty-five and fifty-three.

American and Canadian Finnish groups also differed in the proportion of adult men and women: men aged eighteen and older made up 53 percent of American Finns and 59 percent of Canadian Finns, while women aged eighteen and older 27 percent and 24 percent respectively. Canadian Finns had a significantly larger number of single men. In different groups

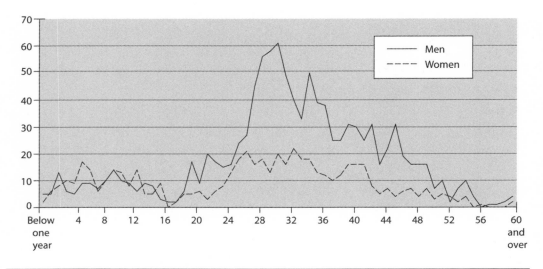

FIGURE 14. AGE AND SEX COMPOSITION OF FINNISH CANADIAN IMMIGRANTS.

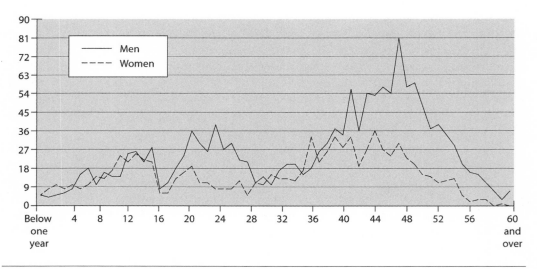

FIGURE 15. AGE AND SEX COMPOSITION OF FINNISH AMERICAN IMMIGRANTS.

of emigrants organized by the Karelian Technical Aid Committee and delivered by ships of the Swedish American Line, single men constituted from 35 percent to 60 percent, while among American emigrants single men were always a minority, making up from 16 percent to 30 percent in groups aboard trans-Atlantic liners. As a result, American emigration was family dominated. The composition of families was more standard and uniform: families with one or two children prevailed in both Canadian and American emigrant groups, while couples and families with three or more children were much rarer.

In Soviet Karelia, most immigrants were employed by large state-owned companies. The largest employer was the Karelian timber industry, in which over 60 percent of all North American immigrants worked, as shown in Figure 16.

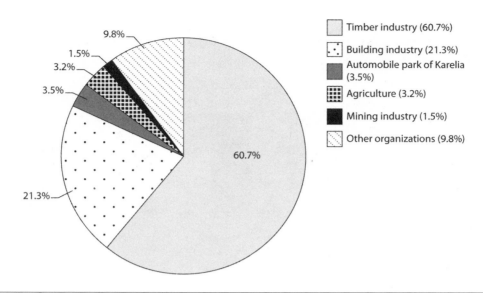

Timber industry (60.7%)
Building industry (21.3%)
Automobile park of Karelia (3.5%)
Agriculture (3.2%)
Mining industry (1.5%)
Other organizations (9.8%)

FIGURE 16. SPHERES OF EMPLOYMENT OF NORTH AMERICAN FINNS IN SOVIET KARELIA AS OF THE AUTUMN OF 1935.

The need of the Karelian timber industry for labor was so urgent and huge that it employed a large number of people without any relevant job experience. Only 50 percent of immigrants sent to logging camps in Segozero and only 15 percent of those sent to logging camps in Tunguda (see map 1) had any relevant experience, though their application forms indicated that logging was a primary occupation of almost all of them.[98] It is difficult to say whether immigrants themselves were so eager to get a job in Soviet Karelia that they provided false information or whether KTAC recruiters did so for them to meet the requirements sent from Soviet Karelia. In any case, Canadian Finns made up the majority of immigrant workers employed in the timber industry, while American Finns dominated in other professional spheres, as shown in Figure 17.

The largest North American immigrant communities arose in Petrozavodsk, Kondopoga, Prionezhskii, and Priazhinskii districts of Soviet Karelia (see maps 1 and 2). The exact number of immigrants in any given settlement in Soviet Karelia, however, is difficult to calculate. Immigrants were permanently on the move, even though a change of job required official permission, which was not easy to obtain. Some organizations pirated skilled personnel from each other: for example, the pulp and paper plant in Kondopoga was known for its unofficial recruiting campaigns among immigrants allocated to other places.[99] Immigrants also tended to move from the periphery to the center as they tried to secure adequate working and living conditions, which were more likely in larger urban centers, such as Petrozavodsk or Kondopoga. Finally, already since the middle of 1931, the number of Americans and Canadians willing to return home from Soviet Karelia kept on growing at a fast pace.

Our calculations of the number of re-emigrants can only be approximate because, unlike recruitment and immigration to the Soviet Union, emigration from it was harder to control. Therefore, documents offer differing and contradictory figures of re-emigrants since they often left without waiting for the expiration dates of their employment contracts, sometimes even without getting their salaries, and not all of them informed the Resettlement Administration of their departures.

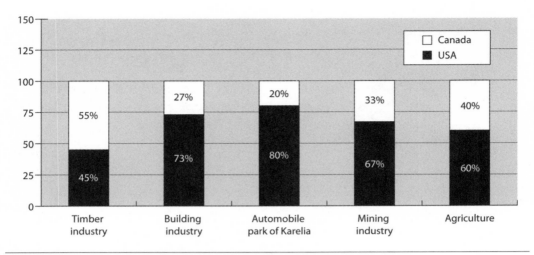

FIGURE 17. DISTRIBUTION OF AMERICAN AND CANADIAN FINNS IN MAJOR ECONOMIC SPHERES.

Table 2. Re-Emigration from Soviet Karelia, 1931–35

	1931	1932	1933	1934	1935 (prior to 15.10)	Total
American immigrants	25	?	533	220	137	
Canadian immigrants	1	?	216	169	70	
Total	26	307	749	389	207	1,678

Sources: NARK, f. R-685, op. 1, d. 3/34, l. 4, 12, 191, 221–26.

According to documents of the Karelian *obkom* of the VKP(b), during 1931 and 1932, 290 adult immigrants left Soviet Karelia, of whom 232 moved abroad and fifty-eight moved to other regions of the USSR.[100] Re-emigration reached its peak in 1933, and by the autumn of 1935, according to the data of the Karelian GPU, the number of re-emigrants reached 968 people (once again the data did not include children).[101] Documents of the Resettlement Administration give an alternative figure: if sources of different years are combined, the resulting figure is 1,678 people (documents differentiate immigrants by the country of origin but do not indicate where they went; see Table 2).

After 1936, it became increasingly difficult to emigrate from the USSR, yet from 1936 to 1938 at least an additional 170 North Americans left Soviet Karelia, seventy-nine of them for the United States or Canada and the rest for Finland.[102] Thus, it can be argued that, in total, over 1,800 American and Canadian Finns left Soviet Karelia between 1931 and 1935. That this estimate is close to the actual figure is evidenced by the number of immigrants who remained there. In 1935, the ethnic Finnish population of Soviet Karelia amounted to about 15,000, of whom two-thirds were immigrants from Finland and one-third—that is, between 4,500 and 5,000 people—immigrants from North America.[103]

CHAPTER 4

The Failure of the Immigration Program

FIRST IMPRESSIONS AND DIFFICULTIES

THE ORGANIZED NATURE OF EMIGRATION TO SOVIET KARELIA GAVE THE KARELIAN Technical Aid Committee the chance to negotiate special terms with trans-Atlantic shipping companies. One of them, the Swedish company Svenska Amerika Linjen (Swedish American Line), became the primary operator responsible for the transportation of emigrants to Soviet Karelia. It operated a passenger service between New York and Gothenburg through Halifax with three liners—MS *Gripsholm*,[1] MS *Drottningholm,* and MS *Kungsholm.* Once in Gothenburg, emigrants took a train to Stockholm and from there sailed by SS *Kastelholm* to Leningrad.[2] The Swedish American Line carried to the Soviet Union in total over two-thirds of all Finnish emigrants from North America. To secure this highly profitable contract, it agreed to pay to KTAC a commission of $11.50 US for an adult and $5.75 US for a child, which became a welcome addition to its budget.[3] Several groups organized their travel independently, sailing from New York to London or Hamburg and from there to Leningrad aboard vessels of the Soviet state company Sovtorgflot.[4] From Leningrad, immigrants travelled to Petrozavodsk, the capital of Soviet Karelia, by train, usually in hard-seated and comfortless carriages. At least one group of American Finns, most likely from the Pacific coast, travelled to Soviet Karelia through Vladivostok and the Trans-Siberian Railroad.[5]

A two-week trans-Atlantic voyage was a difficult experience, but what immigrants saw upon arrival in the USSR often made them forget immediately the difficulties of a long trip. The first reactions to Soviet realities mentioned in nearly all interviews with and memoirs of North American immigrants were feelings of shock, disappointment, and immediate disillusionment:

> We all traveled together. Many passengers were Finns, almost the entire ship. I remember that we passed through Sweden. . . . Adults and children were singing during the whole trip. It was wonderful. I was only seven, but I remember that. My parents were happy, they believed that everything would be excellent. We arrived in Petrozavodsk. The railroad station was dirty. Mother put on a beautiful dress, but there were no stairs, and we had to jump from stone to stone. Mother fell down in dirt and burst into tears. Father said: "This is your Communism." That was my first impression. . . . There were many bunkhouses. It was indeed a town of bunkhouses.[6]

RUOTSIN AMERIKAN LINJA
SUOMALAISTEN SUOSIMA LINJA

14

CANADASTA
SUOMEEN

SUOMESTA
CANADAAN

Matka kestää ainoastaan 10 vuorokautta kumpaankin suuntaan Ruotsin kautta

ITÄ-CANADAN KONTTORI
ARNE RUTQUIST, JOHTAJA

Tammikuun 29 p. 1932.

1410 STANLEY STREET
MONTREAL, CANADA

Mr. Kalle Aronen,
15 West 126th Street,
New York, N.Y.

Mr. Thomas Majander joka saapui meidän "Drottningholm" laivallamme tammikuun 13 p. Halifaxiin kävi konttoorissamme tänäpäivänä ja pyysi meidät kirjoittamaan Teille ja kysyä kuka maksoi hänen pilettinsä jotka lähetettiin hänelle Suomeen.

Hän sanoi että sähkösanoma joka lähetettiin hänelle Suomeen oli luultavasti Teidän allekirjoittama. Pyydämme Teitä hyväntahtoisesti ilmoittamaan meille mitä vastaamme Mr. Majanderille taikka jos tahdotte että hän itse kirjoittaa Teille suoraan.

Jäämme odottamaan vastaustanne ja merkitsemme

kunnioittaen

RUOTSIN AMERIKAN LINJA
per

CW.

FIGURE 18. SCHEME OF THE TRANS-ATLANTIC SHIPPING ROUTE OF THE SWEDISH AMERICAN LINE (NARK, F. R-685, OP. 2, D. 127,1. 14) (COURTESY OF THE NATIONAL ARCHIVE OF THE REPUBLIC OF KARELIA).

We sailed to the USSR aboard a ship, through Leningrad. What amazed me deeply and at once were the first words a man who met us said: "Keep your eyes open on your wallets and bags, or they will be stolen immediately!" My parents were very surprised; mother even asked: "There is no theft in the Soviet Union, is there?" He burst into laughter and did not reply. . . . Petrozavodsk met us cheerlessly. My first thoughts were "it is so dirty here!" Streets had board sidewalks and were very narrow. Mother was silent during the entire trip to our new house, and when she saw it she started to weep.[7]

As soon as we arrived in Leningrad—it was on 27 May 1933—we were instantly warned: "Hold your pockets and suitcases, there is much stealing in Russia." Then we went to Petrozavodsk by train. . . . At first we lived in a bunkhouse. The bunkhouse was very inconvenient. Well, parents were really shocked. At that time [immediately after arrival], many Finnish families constantly quarreled, [and] women cursed husbands for their decisions to bring families to the USSR.[8]

Although such strong negative reactions were typical for adult immigrants, children comprehended their new life in a different manner. Mayme Sevander, a ten-year-old girl at the time, framed her first impression of Petrozavodsk in terms of an adventure:

On 29 April 1934, [our] train was approaching Petrozavodsk. When we approached the town, a strange panorama opened to our eyes: a mostly wooden architecture, a morning sun shining on church domes, a high factory chimney smoking in the midst of the town. But what thrilled me most was a huge lake. It fascinated us, although we used to live near large water bodies, Lake Superior and the Atlantic Ocean. And the town's name was queer and hard to pronounce: Petrozavodsk. Father at once explained to us its meaning—Peter [the Great]'s Factory. In one word, everything promised something new and interesting, except for a terrible railroad station that the train soon arrived at.[9]

A twelve-year-old boy, Kaarlo Ranta, thought—unlike his frightened parents—that "things were not that bad: we had bread and butter from Insnab,[10] spent all day long outdoors—what else could we [children] ask for?"[11]

At the customs office, immigrants had their first experience of dealing with Soviet officials and the Soviet bureaucratic system. For many of them, this experience influenced all their further impressions of the surrounding Soviet reality. During the recruitment campaign, potential emigrants were told that they could take into the USSR tax-free food, clothes, and other everyday consumer goods in amounts sufficient for two years, as well as machines and tools necessary for their work. As a result, emigrants took with them everything that they regarded as necessary for a new life in a new place, including double beds, bureaus, bicycles, typewriters, sewing machines, cameras, gramophones, musical instruments, and baseball bats.

In reality, the question of which goods could be imported tax free by immigrants caused lengthy debates among the Soviet Chief Customs Administration, the People's Commissariat of Foreign Trade, and the government of Soviet Karelia, which were able to settle their differences over this issue only in 1933.[12] Consequently, misunderstanding was common when immigrants passed through Soviet customs. In one case, a large group of Finns who had departed from New York for the USSR on 25 September 1931 spent their last dollars in Gothenburg to buy a batch of bicycles, which were then confiscated in Leningrad and never returned.[13]

Apart from bureaucratic tangles, immigrants were sometimes confronted with illegal actions of Soviet customs officers. Baggage was sometimes confiscated without any explanation or inspected in the absence of its owners, who were given no receipt of confiscation and discovered only upon arrival the loss of many items. The confiscated or stolen goods reflected a shortage of manufactured goods in Soviet trade: immigrants registered complaints for missing shabby shirts, old shoes, stockings, clothes boilers, baskets, and even children's potties.[14] In a few cases, entire baggage was gone, and requests to find it were treated with a uniform response: "The Customs Administration informs that it has not received any baggage registered to the inquirer's name."[15]

Sometimes customs officers engaged in unconcealed blackmail. Aino Otto, who came to Soviet Karelia in May 1933, had almost all of her belongings, including old clothing and linens, confiscated. After she made several attempts to retrieve her baggage, the head of customs openly said to her that she would succeed only after she paid "an additional state levy in foreign currency personally to him."[16] These problems could be solved only after the direct involvement of the Karelian authorities and Edvard Gylling, to whom immigrants appealed for protection in such cases.[17] It is hardly surprising that these first direct contacts with Soviet realities became the point at which North American immigrants started to lose faith in what they had thought was El Dorado found.

In a number of very unfortunate cases, the head of a family died or became disabled, usually by a workplace accident, soon after immigration, before his family took any firm root in the Soviet soil and could rely on local resources to cope with ensuing financial hardships. The Resettlement Administration responded by establishing in May 1931 a special fund from other immigrants' donations and money left after the sale of equipment imported by immigrants;[18] later documents, however, provide evidence that this fund was ineffective, and disabled immigrants complained of a total lack of financial support from official sources.[19]

As immigrants battled through their first negative impressions of Soviet realities, their hosts, the government of Soviet Karelia, were engaged in another struggle—to keep the immigration going. From the beginning, despite official support, the recruitment campaign in North America was hampered by the resistance of numerous Soviet organs that tried to slow down or even stop the immigration to Soviet Karelia. Reasons for this resistance ranged from the competing visions of Soviet regional development, such as those of the OGPU, which objected to the recruitment of foreign nationals to a republic bordering potentially hostile Finland, to sheer inefficiency of the Soviet bureaucratic system, such as in the People's Commissariat of Foreign Affairs, which regularly failed to provide immigration visas to applicants. In September 1931, Gylling had to submit a formal complaint to the Commissariat of Foreign Affairs with a request to normalize the procedures for issuing visas to immigrants. He wrote, in particular, that 141 visa applications had been rejected since May 1931, and among the unsuccessful applicants were wives and children of workers who had been issued entry permits or had already arrived in Soviet Karelia. Such separation of families provoked very negative attitudes among immigrants and further complicated the recruitment of new workers in the United States and Canada.[20]

In 1931, the government of Soviet Karelia planned to bring in 2,846 immigrant workers. In the end, the plan was fulfilled by slightly more than half that number, for only 1,663 workers, of whom 1,387 were from North America and the rest from Finland and Sweden, actually arrived in Soviet Karelia.[21] Gylling complained that obstacles raised by the OGPU and Commissariat of Foreign Affairs resulted in a loss of specialists vitally needed in the Karelian economy.[22] However, Soviet security organs were concerned with issues absolutely different from the economic development of a Soviet region. In January 1932, the Karelian leadership received a letter from Sergey Kirov, the first secretary of the Leningrad *obkom* of the VKP(b) and the second person in the Soviet Communist hierarchy after Stalin. This letter referred to "concerns of the GPU and LVO[23] over Canadian immigrants": namely, while 2,000 Canadian and American citizens had already arrived in Soviet Karelia and about 10,000 were to arrive during 1932, the issue of which territories should be restricted for immigrants had not yet been solved. Military and state security authorities also questioned the very reasonableness of mass recruitment of foreign workers to Soviet Karelia and suggested, "on the ground of state defense needs," that "the settlement of foreigners in certain territories and communities in Karelia . . . should be considered unacceptable." The territories to be closed to immigrants included all those located, first, close to the Finnish border; second, in the vicinity of gulag camps (particularly along the White Sea-Baltic Canal) and gulag-operated timber-harvesting areas; and third, at or near strategic military locations.[24]

The government of Soviet Karelia ignored most of these recommendations, and American and Canadian Finns were employed in many areas designated as restricted. As a result, Soviet security organs had additional reasons to impede immigration to Soviet Karelia. In February 1932, the Commissariat of Foreign Affairs, under an order of the OGPU, stopped processing visa applications of Americans and Canadians recruited to Soviet Karelia. An active correspondence followed between the government of Soviet Karelia and the deputy director of the OGPU, Vsevolod Balitskii, which gives insight into the nature of power relations between authorities of different levels in the early Stalinist period. In response to an inquiry from Karelian leaders regarding why the Soviet government's directives to facilitate North American immigration to Soviet Karelia were violated, which created, in their words, "a politically inadmissible situation," Balitskii sent a telegram cited below:

> To the Chairman of the Karelian SNK [Edvard] Gylling.
> The resolution of the SNK of the USSR of March 5, 1931, allowed you to bring in for forest harvesting in Karelia up to 2,000 qualified forest workers from Canada, and the resolution of the SNK of the USSR of March 30 allowed [you] to use this quota for immigrants from the USA as well. By February 25, 1932, 2,956 entry permits were issued for immigrants to Karelia. Thus, the quota of foreign workers given by the SNK has been fully taken up, and you have to apply to the higher authorities for a new quota of foreign workers to be employed in forest harvesting.[25]

The government of Karelia promptly indicated in its response that these calculations, first, ignored two other resolutions of the Soviet government (the one in autumn 1931 that permitted the recruitment of an additional 785 immigrant workers and the one in spring 1932 that permitted the recruitment of 250 fishermen) and, second, did not take into account that the resolutions allocated quotas for workers—that is, heads of households—while their family members had to be counted separately, which the OGPU failed to do.[26]

When the OGPU refused to waive its veto in the Commissariat of Foreign Affairs, the Karelian leaders appealed to the only authority that could change the situation in its favor—the top Communist leadership. In May 1932, Kustaa Rovio, the first secretary (or head) of the Karelian *obkom* of the VKP(b), sent to the Central Committee of the VKP(b) a memorandum addressed personally to Stalin titled "On the Import of Labor Force from the USA and Canada."[27] It briefly outlined events preceding the immigration and described the current state of affairs. According to the memorandum, by 1 May 1932 the Karelian authorities had recruited in North America 3,734 workers, or 6,435 people including family members. Of this number, only 1,764 workers, or 3,228 people including family members, had actually arrived in Soviet Karelia. The rest had submitted their visa applications and were ready to depart, but, because of the opposition of the OGPU, the Commissariat of Foreign Affairs did not issue them entry visas. The resulting situation, argued Rovio, was disastrous and shameful, for hundreds of recruited workers with families who had sold their properties and packed up for the journey to the USSR had to wait months for visas. As a result, some of them were already unable to travel, for they had spent all their money saved for the trip, and the purchase of tickets was now beyond their means.

To justify his request that the OGPU and Commissariat of Foreign Affairs continue issuing visas immediately, Rovio outlined facts that, in his opinion, proved the necessity and vitality of the Karelian immigration program. He emphasized that immigration incurred no financial obligations for the Soviet authorities because American and Canadian immigrants paid their own travel expenses and brought with them urgently needed tools and machines. By May 1932, these immigrants had imported equipment worth over $130,000 US. And they invested their savings, also in dollars, as loans to the government of Soviet Karelia for the purchase of new equipment and bought Soviet bonds with a total value of over 100,000 rubles. In Petrozavodsk alone, North American immigrants organized a fundraising campaign that raised 60,000 rubles for the construction of two planes, 6,386 rubles for motorization of the Soviet Border Guard, and 4,542 rubles for the construction of a tank. Rovio emphasized that they were efficient workers and highly qualified engineers who made multiple technical innovations and introduced new technologies to Karelian industries. The fact that they brought their families also proved their earnest intentions to settle in Soviet Karelia. He finally accentuated a small share of re-emigration: of 3,228 immigrants, only seventy-three left the Soviet Union during the year and a half that the Karelian immigration program was in force. At the end of the memorandum, Rovio asked Stalin to support the petition of the SNK of Soviet Karelia for an extra quota of 6,000 workers from the United States and Canada.

This appeal had a positive effect. In July 1932, the SNK of the USSR gave permission for the entry of 2,000 workers from the United States, Canada, and Sweden to Soviet Karelia.[28] Altogether, in 1932, the Karelian authorities planned to recruit 5,225 immigrant workers of various professions, including 3,790 workers from the United States, 956 workers from Canada, and the rest from northern Sweden. With their families, the total number of immigrants was announced as about 11,000 people.[29] This figure was calculated on the basis of requests from Karelian industries and organizations and the number of applications submitted to the Karelian Technical Aid Committee by Americans and Canadians willing to emigrate to the Soviet Union. This ambitious plan, however, was soon shattered by Soviet realities.

In the meantime, despite Rovio's lauds intended for Stalin's ears, North American Finns kept on leaving Soviet Karelia. Multiple reasons forced immigrants to leave. Some of them were mentioned explicitly in a letter that an American, Edvard Mason, sent to the Resettlement Administration from Finland en route back to the United States. This letter, dated to March 1932, enumerated motivations shared by the majority of re-emigrants and is worth citing with only minor omissions (it was written in English and is reproduced verbatim):

Dear Comrade,

    I am back from Petroskoi[30] and on the way to USA. When I arrived there with Lehtimäki's group, I found things much different there as was described in New York. We was promised work in the aeroplane shop, but there was nothing of this kind, and nothing under construction, or in the sight, that such shop would be constructed in nearest future. We was promised 3 room apartment, but there was no house of that kind built in all town and we had to put in poorest leaving quarters one could ever think of. Sufficient food was promised, but it was poorest I ever eat in all my life. And wages, which was going to be 300 rubels per month, was little over 200 rubels per month for the time I worked there on the building. And when they wanted me to go to lumber camp, I refused, demanding the work for which I assigned, then they told me I could quit, which I did. I demanded the money back what I paid to you and Lehtimäki, they refused, offering me the rubles, which I couldn't use. . . .[31]

Upon return to their home communities, many re-emigrants wrote articles for the American and Canadian Finnish-language press describing the many hardships in Soviet Karelia. The Soviet press reacted harshly to such publications, calling them "dirty libel against [the] socialist way of life," and printed refutations similar in content to the one cited below:

> Refutation. We, American workers of [logging camp] Lugolambi, strongly reproach people who arrived here [in Soviet Karelia] and were trusted as comrades but got caught, voluntarily or not, in a despised harsh provocation against the working class of the USSR and Karelia. We declare that we are free citizens of the USSR, work enthusiastically and willfully. Here one will never find, as counterrevolutionaries say, alleged forced labor and other unbearable conditions. We declare that housing and other conditions here are fully satisfactory and unanimously reproach those bourgeois accomplices who distribute false rumors and serve fascists and other counterrevolutionaries.
>
> We reproach the actions of the people who had come here to build Soviet Karelia and in a period of several months threw up their jobs, threw up harvested logs, having not floated them to processing facilities. We are convinced that each man and woman should stand on the labor front as sentinels, and desertion is shame. We who stayed here promise to float the logs to processing facilities, to accomplish the tasks set for us, and to work under the guidance of the working class. Approved at the meeting of workers on April 19, 1932.[32]

Such "refutations," published in the regional Soviet press, could hardly make their way to Finnish communities in the United States and Canada. Meanwhile, the stories of re-emigrants sobered the most radical Finns of North America. In 1933, the flow of emigrants to the USSR decreased by four times, and by the summer of 1935 it almost ceased. The number of people willing to go to Soviet Karelia was still surprisingly large, especially in Canada. In two memoranda addressed to the Soviet government in September 1935, Edvard Gylling wrote that more than 3,000 people (2,232 in Canada and 971 in the United States) had sent applications for immigration to the Soviet Union. Although visas were issued to them, they had no money to pay their travel expenses, and Gylling asked Moscow to transport them to Soviet Karelia aboard ships of the Soviet company Sovtorgflot without charging travel costs.[33] This indicates that the emigrant contingent had changed considerably. Applicants in 1935 were much poorer than earlier emigrants and were unable to invest anything in the Equipment Fund. Subsequently, the Karelian Technical Aid Committee lost the main source of its income. Besides, by that time, only the Canadian office of KTAC remained operational. After the departure of Oscar Corgan from the United States in April 1934, recruiting there almost ceased. Most importantly, September 1935 turned out to be the last month of the Red Finnish government of Gylling. His dismissal in October put an end to attempts to resurrect the Karelian immigration program.

CHALLENGES OF EVERYDAY LIFE

The failure of the immigration program of the Karelian authorities was much due to their ultimate inability to create acceptable living and working conditions for immigrants. On a formal level, of course, Karelian authorities put much effort into preparatory activities. The government of Soviet Karelia organized numerous meetings with the management teams of large industrial enterprises and organizations, and the latter submitted lengthy accounts of their efforts to prepare satisfactory living and working conditions for immigrants. Yet what looked good on paper often proved disastrous in execution.

In March 1931, a large meeting was held in the People's Commissariat of Labor of Soviet Karelia with representation from all factories and organizations where foreign workers were employed. At this meeting, new rules regulating the accommodation of immigrant workers were established since the leadership of Soviet Karelia was worried by the high rate of turn-over among North American workers and the first cases of re-emigration from Soviet Karelia. Among the most important agreements reached during the meeting was the one that set new norms for housing conditions for foreign workers—one room for two single men and one or two rooms for one family. Salaries and hourly rates were increased and now included the amortization of tools that immigrants brought with them from North America. Food supply under the conditions of sharply decreased agricultural production, collapsed private trade, and inefficient state distribution was another problem. To address it, the meeting resolved to set special high rates of food rationing for immigrant workers and specialists, to establish a special food fund to supply them, to distribute rations through outlets restricted to other population groups, and to organize special cafeterias in places with large concentrations of immigrant workers. To ease the process of adaptation, the meeting also resolved to keep arriving foreigners together in large groups assigned to factories and logging camps so that they would live in relatively compact and homogeneous communities.[34]

It soon turned out that, in the meager economic realities of Soviet Karelia of the early 1930s, it was barely possible to provide North American workers with the living conditions to which they were accustomed. And, regarding Finnish immigrants themselves, despite their immense enthusiasm for the socialist cause, they were totally unprepared for the Soviet way of life.

Housing was the first thing that shocked immigrants: they were not used to living in bunkhouses, where five to six people shared one room, often without any facilities. In many cases, two or three immigrant families had to share one room. Sometimes accommodations had no electricity or furniture, were swarming with bugs, and were unfit for the winter. A memoir by Christer Boucht recalled a typical reaction to life in such conditions: "A hard night followed. . . . Children were crying because they could not sleep on rigid benches. Twenty-five people were sleeping in one room. There was no bedding at all in this room. A stove was barely smoldering in a corner, [and the room] was faintly illuminated by an electric lamp. The bunkhouse was so dilapidated that we could see the sky through cracks in the roof."[35]

In the emigrants' dreams—and probably in the stories of American and Canadian recruiters—Petrozavodsk was a large and beautiful city with straight and broad streets, multi-story buildings, and many parks and gardens.[36] In reality, in the early 1930s, the capital of Soviet Karelia was a small and dirty town with fewer than a third of its streets paved, cows and goats grazing at the crossroads, and few streetlights. Horses were the major means of transportation. The electric power supply was often cut, and almost a quarter of the population lived without it at all. There was no sewage system or centralized water supply. Over

97 percent of housing in Petrozavodsk consisted of one- or two-unit wooden houses. Much of the housing was old, and few new houses had been built after the First World War, which created a huge shortage in the housing market. Up to six independent households could sometimes share one apartment, having only one room to use.[37] Many families could not even dream of an apartment of their own and had to rent a room or even just part of a room. Extreme overcrowding with poor sanitary conditions led to a high incidence of disease and consequently a high mortality rate.[38]

Under such conditions, local authorities could provide immigrants with no other type of housing than barrack-type bunkhouses. Memoirs of immigrants and archival documents offer similar accounts of the conditions in which people were forced to live for many months. This passage describes the living conditions of foreign workers employed by one of the Petrozavodsk building companies: "The bunkhouses given to the foreign workers are unfit for the winter time (thin walls provide little protection from the cold). The norms [established for living conditions] are rudely violated, [and] the living quarters are overcrowded as several families live in one room. The bunkhouses for workers with families are not equipped with stoves, [and] electric lighting is very weak. As a rule, furniture is not available. Extreme overcrowding of the bunkhouses resulted in the abundance of bugs in them. . . . There are cases of mass diseases, especially among children."[39]

A number of official resolutions in 1931 and 1932 insisted on the need "to oblige all economic organizations responsible for the admission of the immigrants to increase the rate of building of new houses and infrastructure." The building of housing for the immigrants was proclaimed as "overurgent, the first to be provided with funding, building materials, and labor force, so that the deadline of its completion could be met straight in time."[40] Yet change came very slowly. Numerous inspections of the immigrants' living conditions, regularly organized since 1931, revealed that none of the Karelian organizations that employed immigrant workers had completed their projects on time. Most often they lacked building materials and sufficient labor.[41] This and other difficulties were described in detail in the report of a commission appointed in the autumn of 1932 by the Karelian authorities to inspect housing conditions in which North American immigrants had to live:

> Foreign workers employed by Karellesstroi [a building company] live in a house on 97a Lenin Ave. without stoves and with a leaking roof. A similar situation was detected in the house of foreign workers on 108 The First May Ave., where in the last year so many cracks appeared in the roof that during rains it is impossible to stay in rooms, and dwellers have to wait in corridors. Despite multiple petitions from residents to the management of Karelles [the largest timber company of Soviet Karelia], which owns the house, the latter is very slow in solving this problem. Repairing of the roof has been started but then stopped halfway through due to the lack of nails.[42]
>
> Apart from the poor state of houses belonging to Karellesstroi and Karelles, as mentioned above, the bunkhouse at the railroad station of Petrozavodsk, in which foreign workers stay during [their] first days after arrival before they are allocated to their employment organizations, is also in a very inadequate condition. The walls of the bunkhouse have cracks up to five centimeters wide. . . . A house of Karelavto [an automotive company], which is populated entirely by foreign workers, is not yet even completed; its walls are not plastered even inside, to say nothing of the facades, and, as a result, in windy weather sawdust flies through living rooms. Interior plastering is in progress, which is, however, very slow, as only four out of twelve rooms have been plastered during the [last] month, and now due to lack of plaster the work has stopped."[43]

In numerous logging camps where North American Finns worked, the housing question was even worse during the early stage of immigration. People were settled in bunkhouses totally unfit for winter and lacking any facilities. Inspectors from Petrozavodsk reported that, "in the logging camp of Matrosy, twelve families reside in the bunkhouse No. 1. Rooms there do not have stoves and ovens. There are only two stoves in the corridor, but they are too weak to heat the entire house. The corridor is dark, the floor requires urgent repairing. The dining room is dirty and dark, the number of flatware is insufficient, and there are no washing facilities."[44]

In some places, accommodations were simply unavailable. For example, in the village of Shunga, where sixty-one North American miners (along with forty-eight family members) worked during the summer of 1932, the workers had to huddle in houses of local peasants, because the mine had no residential buildings of its own.[45]

Initially, the North American Finns reported their grievances enthusiastically to such inspection committees, hoping that they would bring immediate results. Inspectors, however, had no real power to improve even the worst housing conditions. Without any real leverage to affect the management of organizations employing foreign workers, all inspectors could do was pass formal resolutions: "to purchase water tanks within two weeks" or "to get rid of cockroaches within ten days." [46] Sometimes the recommendations of inspectors were just absurd: "It is suggested that the sewage system must be constructed within three days."[47]

Soon immigrants realized that there was no point in waiting for help from above and started to solve their housing problems themselves. A whole "American Town" emerged in the southern part of Petrozavodsk, comprising eight two-story houses. These houses were divided into four sections, each with eight rooms and a shared kitchen. The toilet was outside, in the yard, but was kept in good sanitary condition. There was also a large playground for children and a sports field between the houses.[48]

Later, immigrants organized building cooperatives, pooling their financial resources and building their own houses. It was in this way that the first three cooperative houses were

FIGURE 19. A GENERAL VIEW OF PETROZAVODSK WITH HOUSES OF THE AMERICAN TOWN (KRASNOARMEISKAIA STREET) IN THE CENTER, BETWEEN 1932 AND 1935 (PHOTOGRAPHER UNKNOWN; COURTESY OF THE NATIONAL ARCHIVE OF THE REPUBLIC OF KARELIA).

erected near Lake Onega in Petrozavodsk, soon followed by one more, immediately dubbed "a foreign currency house" (*valiutnyie doma*) by the local Russian population.[49] Two-room apartments with separate kitchens and premises for bathroom units (not operable yet because of the lack of a water supply system and a sewage system in Petrozavodsk) became objects of envy among other town residents. Once these cooperative houses were built, American and Canadian immigrants gradually moved from the American Town to their new individual apartments. In 1936, across the street from the American Town, a large house with sixteen apartments was built in an "American" fashion, as both its builders and their neighbors claimed. It was called *iskurintalo,* or the "house of superproductive workers." Each apartment had a bathroom and toilet, yet both were still useless because of the lack of corresponding infrastructure in Petrozavodsk.[50] In the mid-1930s, American and Canadian immigrants living in the Finnish communities in Petrozavodsk, Kondopoga, and other logging settlements also built one-family houses.[51]

Food, just like housing, was a painful issue for North American immigrants. According to Bolshevik communal visions, a centralized system of state-owned canteens had to be created during the First Five-Year Plan in order to relieve Soviet women from their domestic burdens. Upon arrival, immigrants who were bound to eat in these state-owned canteens learned what this meant in practice. According to their accounts, the food provided was of poor quality but expensive, as a letter sent home from Kondopoga demonstrates: "We live quite poorly. [The authorities] keep on pressing but don't care about meals. Local lunch is nothing of comparison to what the American unemployed are used to eating: a first course is a soup—a watery skilly,[52] a second course is several vendaces,[53] and the total price is 1.5 rubles."[54] In some places, in order to get this meager lunch, people had to stand in line for an hour or two since the infrastructure was absolutely insufficient (primarily the canteens themselves but also the economic mechanisms in the Soviet-planned economy, such as delivery and distribution of food). One of the numerous Karelian government inspectors, sent in March 1932 to inspect

the food supply services available to immigrant workers employed in Karelstroiob'iedinenie (a state building trust), reported that,

> of two available canteens, one is assigned to cater exclusively to the group of foreign workers and their families, in total 800 people. Meanwhile, the size of this canteen and the number of tables there make it fit for no more than 200 people. Likewise, the capacity of the kitchen is also insufficient for cooking meals for all customers. This condition creates huge queues that usually stretch in several rows from one wall of the canteen to the opposite. People stand in lines for two or three hours. Meals are cooked the same for everyone. There are no dietary meals for the people who need them and no special meals for children, who are forced to stand in long queues together with adults.[55]

American and Canadian immigrants were also shocked by the unsanitary conditions of Soviet public canteens. Huge accommodations in which hundreds of people dined had no separate facilities for cooking, dishwashing, or food storage. In addition, the facilities were infested with rats and cockroaches.[56] Attempts by Finnish Canadians and Americans to change the situation, at least in small ways, resulted in lamentable ends. At some point, foreign workers in Stroiob'iedinenie, at their own expense, rebuilt a canteen intended for their families. Shortly thereafter, it was closed under the guise of reconstruction, but within several days the immigrants learned that the administrators of the canteen had sold most of the furniture.[57]

Because of the low quality and strangeness of the food, many immigrants became ill soon after arrival, and a number died of gastrointestinal diseases.[58] The lack of vegetables and fruits in the diet led to the spread of scurvy: during the summer of 1933, over 100 foreign workers had scurvy in Petrozavodsk alone.[59] Proper medical care was not available everywhere all the time. Lines to the doctors' offices were longer than those in canteens; besides, in some settlements, there were no doctors at all, only nurses who had a very restricted assortment of drugs and did not speak the language of their Finnish patients.[60]

Children were especially vulnerable under such circumstances. Miriam Nousiainen recalled later that, when her family arrived in Karelia in 1932, for the first time in her life she tasted undercooked rye porridge. She refused to eat it. Three days later her father was forced to beat his eight-year-old daughter in an attempt to make her eat Soviet meals.[61] Elsa Balandis had a similar recollection:

> Father's friend who had immigrated from America earlier lived in our bunkhouse. Once he was cooking millet porridge. . . . In America, people cook it only to feed the chickens. We had no food at that time. So he came, sat down, and started to eat—I was sitting next to him, watching him. He asked: "You want some?" Well, a child wanted, of course. So I ate so much that I threw up. Mother started to cry and curse father: "Why have you brought us here, the girl is so hungry that she eats chickens' food!"[62]

Despite difficulties with the food supply, many immigrants, especially those with families, gave up going to the public canteens and instead tried to cook at home.[63] Initially, North American immigrants had substantial support in the form of special shops operated by Insnab. Insnab, a typical Soviet-era abbreviation (from *inostranets*, "foreigner," and *snabzhenie*, "supply"), was a state-owned organization established in 1932 with the goal of distributing food and consumer goods among foreign workers and specialists employed in numerous building sites of the First Five-Year Plan. Organization of a special supply network was necessary for political purposes: the Soviet Union, which declared itself a "state of victorious socialism" and did its best to propagate this image abroad,[64] in reality existed in the harsh conditions of a food-rationing system. Economic reforms of the late 1920s and early 1930s, which included liquidation of the remnants of a market economy that had survived through the 1920s, collectivization of private households in rural areas, and centralized distribution of industrial and agricultural production (in other words, all those measures that the Soviet leadership believed essential for the accelerated industrialization of the Soviet economy), led to huge food and commodity shortages and the introduction of a rationing system. Bread rationing was first registered in the USSR in 1928, and in 1929 food and commodities rationing was enforced in all Soviet urban centers. At the beginning of 1931, the Politburo of the VKP(b) introduced a rationing system that regulated the distribution of food and consumer commodities in the entire USSR on the basis of standardized principles and rates. Ration cards were issued only to those employed in state-owned enterprises and organizations and to their families. This excluded from the state rationing system social groups such as peasants and people deprived of political rights (so-called *lishentsy*), who constituted 80 percent of the Soviet population. Rationing rates for people involved in this system were based on a complicated hierarchy of groups and subgroups and depended on how close they were to the process of industrial production. Since the beginning of 1931, four rationing groups existed in the Soviet Union (special, first, second, and third); the first two, comprised of the populations of the most important industrial centers of the Soviet Union, had the best quotas, while rationing for the second and third groups could barely keep people from starvation. According to this hierarchy, the population of Soviet Karelia belonged to either the second or the third group and received through this centralized rationing system only basic foodstuffs, such as bread, sugar, cereals, and tea, at smaller rates than the populations of the Soviet industrial centers, those in the special and first groups. Regarding all other products, the population of Soviet Karelia had to rely on local resources that were very scarce. In other words, Soviet society—hailed as the only one in the world to avoid the Great Depression—lived in conditions far worse than those that many nations encountered in the 1930s and even during the world wars.[65] It was in this context that foreign workers had to be convinced that, while Western market economies allegedly gave no assurance for the future, a socialist economy, though still characterized by relatively low living standards, guaranteed a moderate subsistence level for today and social security for tomorrow. Insnab became such a guarantee, functioning until 1935, when food rationing in the USSR was finally lifted.

The food supply for foreign workers and specialists organized through Insnab was substantially better than that provided to the local population, though the difference gradually decreased by the mid-1930s. Not only did Canadian and American immigrants have much higher food rations, but also they could buy food at lower prices. The list in Table 3 demonstrates the rationing rates of Insnab for North American Finns in Soviet Karelia in the autumn of 1932. Compare these figures with the rates for the second and third rationing groups in effect for Soviet Karelia, as shown in Table 4.

Shopping in Insnab, very meager by American or Canadian standards, was nevertheless a source of envy among the local population. Yet even with these privileges it was not always possible to purchase food since Insnab's food stocks were in Petrozavodsk, and, because of insufficient quantity or poor logistics, outside the capital town food shortages were common even in the Insnab network. Besides, there was regular theft, substitution of high-quality foods

Table 3. Rationing Lists of Insnab for Foreign Specialists and Foreign Workers, Autumn 1932

Items (monthly rates unless indicated otherwise)	Foreign specialists		Foreign workers	
	For a foreign engineer	*For his family member*	*For a foreign worker*	*For his family member*
Bread (daily)	800 gm	400 gm	800 gm	400 gm
Meat	7 kg	3 kg	5 kg	2 kg
Butter	1.5 kg	1 kg	1 kg	800 gm
Milk (daily)	for both groups, 1.5 liters for adults and 1 liter for children below 14			
Fish	3 kg	2 kg	2 kg	2 kg
Sugar	3 kg	1.5 kg	2 kg	1.5 kg
Cereals	3 kg	2 kg	2 kg	2 kg
Flour	2 kg	2 kg	2 kg	2 kg
Laundry soap	1 kg	1 kg	1 kg	1 kg
Toilet soap	2 pcs	2 pcs	2 pcs	2 pcs
Tea	100 gm	50 gm	100 gm	50 gm
Vegetable oil	0.5 l	0.5 l	0.5 l	0.5 l
Cigarettes (daily)	40 pcs	-	25 pcs	-
Smoked meat	1 kg	0.5 kg	1 kg	0.5 kg
Smoked fish	1 kg	0.5 kg	1 kg	0.5 kg

Source: NARK, f. P-3, op. 2, d. 791, l. 104.

Table 4. Soviet Rationing Rates for the Second and Third Population Groups, 1931

Items (monthly rates unless indicated otherwise)	Second group		Third group	
	Workers	*State employees, members of families of workers and state employees*	*Workers*	*State employees, members of families of workers and state employees*
Bread (daily)	800 gm	400 gm	750 gm	350 gm
Flour	-	-	-	-
Cereals	1.5 kg	850 gm	1 kg	500 gm
Meat	1 kg	1 kg	-	-
Fish	2 kg	1 kg	-	-
Butter	-	-	-	-
Sugar	1 kg	1 kg	800 gm	800 gm
Tea (yearly)	100 gm	50 gm	100 gm	50 gm
Eggs	-	-	-	-

Source: Osokina, *Za fasadom stalinskogo izobiliia*, 251.

with poor-quality foods, and improper storage, as described in the following excerpt from the report of yet another inspector sent to investigate the living conditions of North American immigrants in Soviet Karelia: "There are cases when immigrant workers are provided with bad-quality commodities. The shop No. 1 of Insnab in Petrozavodsk does not have special storage facilities for meat, which often becomes rotten. Because of the bad quality of food, many of the immigrants suffer from intestinal diseases."[66]

Finally, there were lengthy queues in Insnab shops, as in all other Soviet shops of that time, many of its employees did not speak Finnish, and local offices of Insnab were reluctant to establish their own food funds, relying only on central sources of food supply.[67]

In May 1932, all special canteens for foreign workers formerly run directly by companies that employed them were transferred to the management of Insnab. This resulted in a sharp rise in prices by almost 150 percent, which caused outrage among the North American immigrants.[68] In general, their criticism of Insnab's activities—the aim of which was supposedly to decrease social tensions among foreigners—was so harsh that even Soviet security organs were concerned with the discontent:

> The subordination of canteens for foreign workers to Insnab caused much debates, resentment, and questions, which had not been resolved until now. In Matrosy, apart from 300 [North American] foreign workers, there are ten illegal immigrants from Finland who until May [1932] dined with other foreign workers. When Insnab took the management of the canteen in Matrosy, it insisted on the exclusion of these ten illegal immigrants from provision, despite a collective letter of appeal of other foreign workers who announced their will to share their rations with these ten people; [workers also argued that] otherwise a separate canteen had to be organized for [the illegal immigrants]. However, Insnab rejected their appeal, and now there are two canteens in Matrosy (as workers call them, one for "gentlemen" and another for "the common folk"). Besides, during the last winter, hot meals were delivered to all [North American] brigades and to groups of workers employed in logging, directly to their workplaces in the woods. Now Insnab refuses to organize deliveries of hot meals for groups of fewer than sixty people, while an average worker group engaged in logging has between fifteen and twenty and never more than thirty people. This controversy has not been resolved, and it is making the foreign workers nervous. . . . Insnab also poorly delivers food to its remote Karelian offices. For example, in Ukhta [in northern Soviet Karelia], where a population of 250 foreign workers and family members lives, the Insnab shop has food supplies sufficient for only seventy people for the period of four months;[69] moreover, basic foodstuffs such as cereals, pasta, flour, meat, et cetera are not available there at all. . . . Finally, foreign workers are dissatisfied with the bureaucracy and lack of administrative expertise in Insnab. In Ukhta, one person is employed simultaneously as an authorized representative of Insnab, a manager, a storekeeper, and a financial accountant. As a result, he is unable to cope with all his duties, and in order to get food and other products [North American] workers must stand in queues. An unsatisfactory situation also emerged in the shop of Insnab in Petrozavodsk. Its staff treat customers in a rude way.[70]

In January 1933, the management of Insnab decided to revise lists of foreign workers subject to special rationing rates. Only highly qualified specialists were supposed to retain privileges in the food supply system.[71] As a result, approximately a third of American and Canadian Finns were deprived of higher rates. Moreover, since no careful inspection of North American workers had been even attempted, and the Karelian office of Insnab had not consulted the management of factories and organizations where North American Finns worked, many qualified specialists were often left outside Insnab lists because of incorrect translation of their professions from Finnish into Russian.[72] All of this provoked an angry reaction among immigrants, with protest meetings held in all organizations where they were employed. Niilo Vilpus from Detroit, who worked at the Petrozavodsk auto service station, said at one such meeting that, "now, when Insnab rates have been revoked, we pay for meals 300 rubles more than before. It makes workers think about departure. Since I left America, there was no butter on my table. If a man works in a capitalist country, he is never hungry. And here hunger is a matter of everyday life, and we, workers from America, are not used to working hungry."[73]

In the beginning, many immigrants saved themselves from malnutrition thanks to dollars that they had brought to the Soviet Union. There were several foreign currency stores in Soviet Karelia where one could purchase manufactured goods unavailable otherwise. Besides, dollars could be exchanged for rubles. As mentioned above, the exchange rate in these shops (belonging to the network of Torgsin) was several times higher than the official exchange rate; besides, immigrants could sell their dollars on the black market at an even better rate. As one immigrant wrote in a letter to his relatives, "those who have American money can live a more or less decent life. . . . American money is very expensive—here it is possible to get thirty to fifty rubles for one dollar."[74] Yet the problem with insufficient food supply often could not be resolved even with money. American and Canadian Finns, for example, suffered from the lack of coffee, which was impossible to buy: "You're asking if we can buy coffee here for rubles. . . . I don't hope at all that at some point in time it will become available. . . . Of course, many wait, and so do I, but it's fruitless. We should be glad that we receive at least black bread. It is already two years since I tasted coffee the last time, and about what THEY eat and what THEY drink I'd better remain silent."[75]

The organization of labor and Soviet work ethics were yet another stumbling block for many North American immigrants. Although usually they had better job conditions than those of local workers (including higher salaries, better logging sites, and technical equipment), the work that they had come to Soviet Karelia for did not bring them satisfaction. It was hard for immigrants to adapt to a work environment in which the division of labor was much less developed than in North America and in which they had to perform all operations themselves. Initially, even highly qualified immigrant workers had production rates twice as low as those of local workers. As inspection committees reported, the main reason why North American workers were not able to comply with production plans and received lower salaries was that they "were used to working in a highly technological environment."[76]

A number of workers were also transferred to jobs for which they were not qualified, while for some specialists work was simply non-existent. One immigrant complained in a letter of this situation: "I came to Karelia with a hope to find a job of a plumber. I was told that there were plenty of plumbing jobs in Karelia. . . . But I was deceived. In Petrozavodsk, there is no sewage and, of course, no department responsible for its construction—and there won't be any for several years to come, I am sure. . . . I was hired as a plumber to a place where people don't know the word *sewage*. . . . I am aghast."[77]

American and Canadian immigrants were shocked by the negligence and lack of responsibility of their co-workers and the administration. They were irritated by regular downtimes caused by delays in the supply of materials or because of other reasons, which had a direct impact on their salaries. Sometimes immigrant workers got into conflicts with the administration when they refused to fulfill what they considered senseless orders or when managers rejected new forms and methods of labor suggested by immigrants. This is what happened, for example, during the early stage of the Karelian fever, when Canadian lumberjacks complained to the immigration authorities that the director of the logging camp in Matrosy was opposed to the introduction of new technologies in timber harvesting.[78] The management of factories often regarded initiatives, suggestions for improvements, and the independent positions of American and Canadian immigrants as showing a lack of discipline and an unwillingness to recognize authority.[79]

Sometimes it turned out that the work experience of North American immigrants, their expertise, and their equipment were not required at all. In May 1931, a group of American Finns brought with them to Petrozavodsk a brick-making machine that cost, according to archival documents, more than $16,000 us and could produce 17,000 bricks per hour.[80] A year later they complained that the machine had been idle for nine months and that nobody among responsible officials cared about this state of affairs.[81] Suggestions for improvements made by immigrant workers were rarely realized, and when they were their authors received almost no bonuses. Egalitarianism was a common practice at workplaces, for workers received the same wages without regard to their actual contributions. Also, the differences in salaries among the various organizations could be great: for example, a carpenter in the Petrozavodsk ski factory earned seven to eight rubles a day, while a carpenter in the building trust Karellesstroi earned only five rubles.[82] Sometimes salaries were not paid for two or three months. As one American woman expressed her displeasure, "in the United States I received thirty dollars as a monthly unemployment compensation, could buy good sandwiches with butter and meat being unemployed, while here, no matter how hard you work, you won't get anything but just skilly."[83] Life in Soviet Karelia had to be tough if the experience of living on thirty dollars a month in America seemed to her almost like a paradise.

Illusions were also shattered when immigrants discovered how hard it was to change the place of employment. Formally, North American immigrants, unlike illegal Finnish immigrants, were free to leave a job and find another, but in reality things were quite different. Petrozavodsk could not accommodate all those who wished to move there from the faraway territories of Soviet Karelia; besides, because of security regulations, they were not allowed to work in a number of factories and offices. As a result, many immigrants found themselves in the position of "serfs," unable to leave their workplaces. There was only one (radical) option under such circumstances—to leave the Soviet Union. "What kind of democracy is this," one of them wondered, "when you can't take a job of your choice?"[84]

Yet another aspect of life in Soviet Karelia made it unbearable for many North American immigrants: a complete lack of cultural activities. Immigrants were ready to organize leisure activities themselves, but there was no appropriate infrastructure in the form of clubs or stadiums, especially outside Petrozavodsk. There were just a few daycares, and most women were compelled to stay at home with their children. "We can make visits to five places," immigrant women in one of the forest settlements joked bitterly, "to the grocery store, to get firewood, to the [communal] bath, to get water, and to a toilet. How can this satisfy a living person?"[85] Unlike men, who were occupied at their workplaces, women endured the burdens of everyday Soviet life with much less enthusiasm, and in many cases it was they who initiated re-emigration from the USSR. This tendency worried Karelian authorities, as one of the documents shows: "We don't work enough in families. The woman is neglected. . . . In many cases, workers' wives openly express their wish to go to Finland, at least for a short stay."[86]

In general, American and Canadian immigrants had more than enough reasons to leave Soviet Karelia. It is thus surprising that the majority of them never did so. This is harder to explain than the reasons for their immigration to the USSR. Likely, many had nowhere to go and no money to pay for a return ticket. Roy Niskanen, brought by his parents to Petrozavodsk in 1932 as a one-year-old child, recollected in his interview that "everything was sold back there [in the United States], nothing was left there. As far as I remember, they said that the whole land plot, the whole farm, was sold for $1,000—which was almost nothing—to somebody. And there were facilities, cattle, sheep. . . . We were leaving forever. That's why no question was even raised whether we should go back, because how and to where were we supposed to go back? To start everything anew? But there was only emptiness."[87]

Some immigrants eventually adjusted to Soviet conditions, and some married local residents, which removed any chance to leave the USSR, because in the 1930s the Soviet authorities would never permit the emigration of a Soviet citizen. Some immigrants actually found jobs that they had dreamt of in America and now had opportunities to fulfill their dreams. A few stuck to their beliefs in the "bright communist future": "My grandma just couldn't understand the problems with food supply. How was it possible that in the workers' paradise people don't even have enough bread . . . ? However, uncle always had a clear explanation. Food crisis will be over soon, this is just a temporary phenomenon. As soon as people learn to work wholeheartedly, poverty will immediately vanish, and absolute prosperity will come."[88]

Belief in future prosperity helped the immigrants to endure difficulties, and they wrote in letters to relatives—perhaps in an attempt to convince themselves rather than those who stayed in the New World—that "everybody here has a job, has money. . . . Purchasing power here is very high. There are queues in shops. [Consumer] goods are in short supply. Factories are not yet able to satisfy all needs, but it will soon become a matter of the past. After all, we have completed the Five-Year Plan by 100 percent."[89]

Just as the reasons that drove Finns from their communities in North America across the Atlantic to the Soviet Union were complex, so too were their motivations to remain there despite all the difficulties and frustrations that they encountered in Soviet Karelia. Economic motives—the inability to fund one's way back home or a good professional position found in the USSR—were interwoven with educational opportunities in the Finnish language for children, opportunities that were unavailable in North America. Immigrants internalized the political language that Soviet elites used to communicate with the population of the USSR ("we have completed the Five-Year Plan by 100 percent"), and for many of them belief in the socialist cause seemed too essential to their personal identities to "desert from the labor front," as they argued in the newspaper article quoted above. After all, staying in Soviet Karelia gave them hope in building a socialist world, while returning to North America would mean the shattering of their socialist dreams. As one memoir account later claimed, "we lived in terrible conditions, but despite that fact our parents were full of enthusiasm. . . . They were ready to withstand all difficulties for a future happiness."[90]

CHAPTER 5

American and Canadian Immigrants in the Soviet Economy

IMMIGRANTS AND THE SOVIET ECONOMIC SYSTEM OF THE 1930S

THE DIFFICULTIES THAT NORTH AMERICAN IMMIGRANTS ENCOUNTERED IN SOVIET Karelia were just a small portion of the much wider socioeconomic processes of nationalization and centralization in the Soviet Union. During the 1930s, a new system of economic management took shape in the USSR that later would be called the administrative or command economic model. Its most characteristic features were long-term planning, implemented through Five-Year Plans, and a hierarchical structure of management. During the late 1920s and early 1930s, a bulky bureaucratic machine emerged to exercise centralized control over all levels of economic management. It comprised, from top to bottom, several levels of bureaucracy, including the central government, economic ministries (people's commissariats), central offices of industrial management (*glavks*), state trusts, and, finally, individual factories.[1] All economic activities in the Soviet Union were subordinated to Five-Year Plans, which determined in all spheres of industry and agriculture what to produce, at which rates, and in which amounts. The rhetoric of "fulfillment and overfulfillment" (*vypolnenie i perevypolnenie*) of economic plans was widely used to mobilize the Soviet population in the work of constructing socialism. In particular, a purely propagandistic slogan—"The Five-Year Plan in Four Years!"—that would accompany the lives of several generations of Soviet people became a blueprint for practical actions after Stalin's plenary speech at the Sixteenth Congress of the VKP(b) in June 1930.[2] Two and a half years later, in January 1933, Stalin officially declared that the First Five-Year Plan had actually been fulfilled during four years and three months.[3] In reality, the Soviet economy during its accelerated industrialization existed in a permanent state of crisis, and its planned rates of growth in all major industries (electricity, metallurgy, coal, mineral fertilizers, tractors) failed to be achieved, though the overall increase in production was still impressive, especially with the Great Depression in the rest of the world as a background.[4] At the same time, a sharp increase in investments in heavy industry led to a disproportion between its rapid growth and the development of light industry and industrial infrastructure (first of all transportation and energy), to say nothing of social infrastructure, including housing, laundries, public canteens, nurseries, sports facilities, and so on.

Soviet Karelia was part of these nation-wide processes. By the turn of the 1930s, it finally lost its autonomous position within the Soviet economy, and its industries were fully integrated into the system of centralized economic management. The new place of Soviet Karelia in the national economy brought immediate consequences for the immigration program of its Red Finnish leadership. Originally, the Karelian authorities planned to bring to Soviet Karelia as many highly qualified specialists of different occupations as possible. This was part of Edvard Gylling's economic program to create a balanced Karelian economy, in which different industries were supposed to develop relatively evenly, without big disproportions. Now, in the new model of a planned and centralized economy, all local resources were to be strictly subordinated to Moscow in order to achieve the goal of accelerated industrialization. Driven by contemporaneous perceptions of how the effective management of resources should look, on a practical level this new economic strategy led to even more intensive exploitation of the most profitable sectors of peripheral Soviet economies. In Soviet Karelia, the key sector was the forest industry.

Central economic authorities were not interested in the balanced development of the Karelian or any other regional economy that would demand large capital investments. Instead, centralized distribution of resources and consumer products was envisioned as the optimal way to deal with local imbalances. As a result, during the years of the First Five-Year Plan, no factories for either mechanical or chemical processing of timber were built in Soviet Karelia, though initially the plan suggested that five new sawmills, five pulp and paper plants, and four chemical timber-processing factories would be constructed.[5] In practice, all efforts were directed toward achieving a rapid increase in the output of harvested timber, since its export to Europe could secure the inflow of foreign currency, vital for the industrialization of the Soviet economy. Thus, contrary to the economic visions of republican authorities, Moscow reduced Soviet Karelia's role in the Soviet economy to a supplier of raw materials that were used—directly or through exports and the purchase of foreign equipment—for the industrial development of other Soviet regions.[6]

Demands from Moscow to increase the production of timber changed the professional composition of immigrants from North America in favor of forest workers, primarily lumberjacks. Moreover, to satisfy these demands, many North American workers of other occupations were soon after arrival sent to logging camps, sometimes against their wishes. Consequently, over 60 percent of North American Finns became employed in the Karelian forest industry, and it was there that their contribution to the republican economy was the largest.

AGENTS OF TECHNOLOGICAL TRANSFER:
IMMIGRANTS IN THE FOREST INDUSTRY

Traditionally, timber harvesting in Soviet Karelia was a seasonal job carried out during winter and early spring: without roads and trucks or tractors, it was possible to transport harvested wood from logging sites only over short distances on horse-driven sledges to nearby rivers. Since most rivers were shallow with many rapids, logs could be rafted to sawmills, usually located on lakeshores, only during high water: that is, in spring. The labor force was made up almost entirely of local peasants for whom timber harvesting was a side job during time off from their primary agricultural occupations. Work techniques had not changed at all since the nineteenth century—trees were felled with inefficient two-handled saws and ordinary axes that peasants used for other activities in their households.

Large-scale recruiting of seasonal workers from regions south of Soviet Karelia was another obstacle to a more efficient forest economy. Most of them had no or little experience in timber harvesting, and their labor productivity was, as a rule, lower than that of local lumberjacks, sometimes by up to 30 percent.[7] Without professional forest workers and innovations in tools and working methods, it was impossible to bring timber harvesting in Soviet Karelia to the rate of production that the First Five-Year Plan demanded. The skills, experience, and professional tools of North American immigrants became a driving force that brought revolutionary changes to the forest industry of Soviet Karelia and eventually helped to modernize it nation-wide.

Already by the autumn of 1932, 1,049 workers from North America were employed by Kareles, a state trust responsible for timber-harvesting operations in Soviet Karelia. Most of them worked in logging settlements located close to Petrozavodsk (Matrosy, Lososinnoie, Shuia, Vilga), though several groups, totaling 288 workers (473 people with family members), were sent to remote northern logging camps, to the regions of Segozero (Tumcha), Tunguda (Lugolambi), and Ukhta.[8]

There was much to learn from Canadian and American lumberjacks. While an average forest worker in Soviet Karelia harvested 4.3 cubic meters (152 cubic feet) of timber a day, and the daily rate for other Soviet regions was slightly over 3 cubic meters (106 cubic feet), the productivity of a Canadian or American lumberjack reached on average 8.5 cubic meters (300 cubic feet) a day,[9] and "model" workers employed in Matrosy managed to achieve a production rate that was unchallenged in the USSR: 12 cubic meters (424 cubic feet) of harvested wood a day.[10]

This work efficiency among North American immigrants was primarily the result of using specialized instruments that they brought with them—bow saws, cross-cut saws, and so-called Canadian axes. Canadian axes became particularly famous in the entire USSR—their design

FIGURE 20. CANADIAN LUMBERJACKS IN A COMMON ROOM OF A BARRACK IN MATROSY (EARLY 1930S) (COURTESY OF THE NATIONAL ARCHIVE OF THE REPUBLIC OF KARELIA).

(narrow blade and long handle made of durable wood) was a perfect fit for all operations in timber harvesting. Bow saws of a Swedish design gave much narrower saw cuts and enabled fallers to work individually, whereas standard Russian saws for tree cutting were operated by a crew of two; the introduction of Swedish bow saws also dramatically increased labor productivity in timber harvesting. Technical characteristics of American cross-cut saws earned them a proper name in the Russian language, in which they were called *kroskot* or *roskot*—a derivative of the English word *cross-cut*.[11]

Most North American lumberjacks brought to Karelia all the equipment that they needed for work, sometimes even two or three kits. Saws and axes were also purchased in the United States and Canada by the Karelian Technical Aid Committee with the money received through immigrants' contributions (to the Equipment Fund). In June 1932 alone, Karelles purchased tools worth approximately $20,000 us, which had been contributed by immigrants.[12] Once in Soviet Karelia, these tools were compulsorily registered in the offices of Karelles, which issued a special directive demanding that every imported axe and saw be assigned a unique number, given only to qualified workers, and regularly monitored whether it was stored and used properly.[13] Technical specialists of Karelles also studied these tools, ordered samples axes and saws from producers, and insisted that their production be launched locally.[14] Soon axes and saws of the Canadian and Swedish designs were being produced by the factory Onezhskii in Petrozavodsk.[15]

Another important contribution of American and Canadian Finns to modernization of the forest industry in Soviet Karelia in particular, and the ussr in general, was the transfer of their experience in the management and mechanization of work processes. Prior to their immigration, the local forest industry did not have enough qualified mechanics and drivers, which made the horse the only, and quite inefficient, solution to the transportation needs of year-round timber harvesting.[16] Tractors first appeared in some logging camps in Soviet Karelia during the winter of 1929–30, but their use in the forest industry became widespread only with the immigration of a large number of professional mechanics and drivers from America and Canada.[17] Tractors were American Caterpillars and Soviet Fordsons (the latter were assembled in Leningrad under a license from the Ford Motor Company). That American and Canadian Finns became a major factor in mechanization of the timber industry is evidenced by the fact that in 1932 a Pocket Guide of a Tractor Driver was published in Petrozavodsk in the Finnish language for drivers of Leningrad-produced Fordsons.[18] The same year American and Canadian immigrants employed in the logging camp Lososinnoie started using trucks for tree hauling.[19] The first trucks used for tree hauling in Soviet Karelia were twenty-three American Model AA Fords, some of which were brought by immigrants themselves or purchased via their financial contributions.[20] During the first half of the 1930s, nearly the entire automotive fleet of the Karelian timber industry was concentrated in the immigrant settlements of Lososinskii, Matrosy, and Vilga.[21]

Apart from technological innovations, American and Canadian immigrants became actively involved in professional education as a sort of grassroots faculty instructing Soviet workers how to use more efficient methods of labor management and operate new machines. Regular excursions of Soviet forest industry specialists and workers were organized to Finnish North American communities in Matrosy, Lososinnoie, Vilga, and Interposiolok.[22] Matrosy, where the first Canadian team of lumberjacks settled at the end of 1930, earned, in particular, fame throughout the ussr. In 1933, 480 Finns lived in Matrosy (82.5 percent of its population),[23] most of them immigrants from Canada or the United States. To facilitate the transfer of new technologies and methods of work organization, a professional school was established in Matrosy. Forest workers came from the Urals, Siberia, Caucasus, republics of Komi and Chuvashiia, and other Soviet regions to attend courses organized by American and Canadian workers at this school.[24] North American tree-felling teams also traveled across the Soviet Union to share their experience. In one case, two Canadians, Daavid Järvis and Aarne Lehtinen, made several trips to different logging camps in the Urals and Arkhangelsk region, where they organized special courses to teach modern technologies and principles of labor management to local forest workers.[25] The recently established Karelian Research Institute studied the organization of labor in logging teams of North American immigrants to create a scientific model of effective timber-harvesting methods, and many of them were employed in its experimental site in Padozero.[26]

FIGURE 21. A CANADIAN WORKER CROSS-CUTTING A TREE WITH A BOW SAW, PRIONEZHSKII *RAION* (DISTRICT), 1931 (PHOTO BY YA. M. ROSKIN; COURTESY OF THE NATIONAL ARCHIVE OF THE REPUBLIC OF KARELIA).

In the first half of the 1930s, the Karelian press published numerous articles and brochures in Russian and Finnish popularizing methods of labor management and innovations that North American immigrants brought to the forest industry of Soviet Karelia. Newspapers and magazines of that time often carried headlines such as "To Borrow American Experience," "Canadian Workers in Karelian Forests," "We Must Actually Start to Transfer the Canadian Experience," and "Battle for Timber."[27] Articles were followed by more practical brochures that tried to summarize principles and methods of work used by immigrants from North America.[28] One author, Iosif Tonkell, was particularly prolific on this theme, publishing numerous articles and several books in Russian and Finnish in Petrozavodsk, Leningrad, and Moscow.[29] The main message of his and other publications was that the experience and work methods of American and Canadian forest workers achieved excellent results in Soviet Karelia and "deserve[d] . . . a most rapid practical introduction [in the Soviet forest industry] on the widest possible basis."[30] Indeed, new methods of labor management, cutting, transportation, and storage of timber, first introduced in Soviet Karelia by American and Canadian Finns, were soon applied elsewhere in the USSR.

PATCHING THE SOCIALIST ECONOMY

The rhetorical nature of the First Five-Year Plan created an economy of mobilization driven by tensions between unrealistic production plans and actual economic possibilities. Soviet economic life of the early 1930s, to use a metaphor, was a never-ending patching of ruptures created less by economic hardship than by the aggressive rhetoric of accelerated industrialization, which demanded that major tasks of economic modernization be accomplished in ridiculous time periods ranging from several months to several years. Soviet political and economic authorities of all ranks were obliged to report regularly increases in industrial output, and failure to do so led to dismissals and even repressions.[31] North American immigrants, most of whom were skilled workers and specialists, represented a vital if somewhat scarce resource that the Karelian authorities were eager to use to patch their regional economy, in which new ruptures appeared almost daily caused by unrealistic planning, a highly ineffective bureaucratic management system, and populist campaigning in the Soviet press.

By the turn of the 1930s, Soviet Karelia was a mostly agrarian region with a poorly developed industry. According to the Karelian census of 1926, professional workers constituted only 7.2 percent (10,400 people) of the working population; the share of people employed in areas other than agriculture, including office work and a nascent service sector, was 25.7 percent (37,500 people). During the First Five-Year Plan, the absolute number of the working class and its share in the active population of Soviet Karelia significantly increased: by early 1933, Karelian factories and mines employed over 17,000 people; moreover, about 20,000 workers were employed on a regular basis in timber harvesting, 12,500 worked at construction sites, and more than 10,000 worked in transportation.[32] Yet Soviet Karelia still confronted a severe shortage of qualified workers, and Finnish immigrants who had obtained work experience in various industries in North America became the most qualified and demanded group of the Karelian proletariat.

Forest workers, the most common occupation among North American Finns, constituted about 45 percent of all immigrants, and the second largest professional sphere was related to construction: carpenters, joiners, painters, plasterers, roofers, concrete workers, plumbers, and electricians made up about 30 percent of all immigrants.[33] Most of them worked in the Karelian trust Stroiob'iedineniie building domestic housing and public facilities in Petrozavodsk and Kondopoga. Additionally, because of a chronic shortage of domestic housing and state funding for it, American and Canadian workers joined building cooperatives, trying to provide decent accommodations for their families and later neighboring communities. The most successful experiment of cooperative building in Petrozavodsk was Rakentaja (Finnish for "builder"). By 1932, it had 1,500 members, of whom 56 percent were Finns. In a manner typical for the time, the cooperative used its resources not only for the original purpose of building domestic housing but also to organize food supply for its members by establishing commercial relations with agricultural producers.[34]

Needs of the building industry for equipment and tools were also satisfied first when the Karelian authorities planned how to use financial contributions of American and Canadian immigrants to the Equipment Fund of the Karelian Technical Aid Committee. The building trust Stroiob'iedineniie received tools and machines that cost more than those purchased for any other Karelian state trust, including Karelles, the largest employer of immigrants. As of June 1932, KTAC had purchased for Stroiob'iedineniie tools and machines worth $40,000 US. To reduce transportation expenses, purchased items travelled along with the immigrants, who thus brought to Soviet Karelia nearly everything ranging from nails to equipment for entire factories. In 1931, they imported, among other things, 100 tons of nails worth $8,000 US and equipment for a brick factory, and in 1932 they brought equipment for a wood-processing factory.[35]

The skills and labor of American and Canadian immigrants also proved critical for the fulfillment of production plans in the pulp and paper plant in Kondopoga and the ski factory in Petrozavodsk. Kondopoga, a town located fifty kilometers north of Petrozavodsk, was an important industrial center, and because of its job opportunities and proximity to the capital of the republic it had the second largest Finnish immigrant community after Petrozavodsk. The first plans for building a hydropower station and a paper factory in Kondopoga dated back to 1921 as part of the famous GOELRO plan,[36] and two years later construction started. In January 1929, the hydropower station commenced operation, followed by the launch of a paper factory with modern Swedish and German equipment in June 1932. In 1935, construction of a pulp factory in Kondopoga was completed, and the combination of the two was then called the Kondopoga pulp and paper plant.[37]

Red Finns played an important role in the construction and operation of the Kondopoga factory during the 1920s. Many of them were qualified workers, and some had special technical education that let them occupy high-ranking positions during construction. The first director of the Kondopoga paper factory, who worked at this position from 1929 to 1937, was Hannes Järvimäki, a prominent leader of the Finnish Social Democratic Party. His deputy was Kalle Ekman, another Red Finn and an engineer of the pulp and paper industry by education. The deputy director of the Kondopoga pulp factory was Eero Antonen, who had a professional education in the pulp industry; the deputy director of the Kondopoga brick factory was Anselmi Mäkinen; the deputy head of the Kondopoga Construction Company was Edvard Kalske; the chief electrician of the Kondopoga paper factory was Eino Lintunen; and its personnel director was Simo Susi.[38] By 1933, there were 744 Finns in Kondopoga (19.4 percent of its population).[39]

Since the late 1920s, large groups of Canadian and American immigrants had arrived in Kondopoga despite protests from Soviet security organs, which regarded the factory and its power plant as strategically important production facilities to which foreign nationals were not supposed to have access. Ignoring these protests, the Finnish leadership of Soviet Karelia tried to recruit to Kondopoga as many qualified workers as possible, since the operation of expensive Western equipment installed in the pulp and paper plant required professional technical skills. The recruitment campaign to Kondopoga was carried out under the slogan "to make the Kondopoga paper factory a school for ethnic Karelian and Finnish proletariat."[40] By 1 October 1932, 150 North American immigrants were employed in Kondopoga's factories and building sites, and the total number of American and Canadian Finns living in Kondopoga increased to 278.[41]

The Petrozavodsk ski factory was another prominent industrial project in Soviet Karelia during the First Five-Year Plan where North American immigrants played an important role in construction and subsequent operation. It had modern equipment and produced skis for both the civilian population and the Red Army. Here the contributions of Finnish American specialists were instrumental already during construction of the factory since its original design proved to be unrealizable, and the experience and skills of American immigrants were widely applied for multiple alterations to and optimization of the technological process.[42] Red Finns occupied positions in the top management of the factory: its director was Elias Tuomainen, an engineer with solid experience in industrial management.[43] The position of technical director was held by Vihtori Snellman, an experienced specialist of ski production who, prior to his employment in Soviet Karelia, studied the organization of work in ski factories in Finland.[44]

As in the case of the Kondopoga pulp and paper factory, the Petrozavodsk ski factory was supposed to become a forge of ethnic Karelian and Finnish proletariat. The People's Commissariat of Labor demanded that 75 percent of employees of the ski factory be representatives of the Finno-Ugric people of Soviet Karelia,[45] a directive that was fulfilled by 1934, when Karelians constituted 15 percent of the total labor force of the factory and Finns made up 60 percent.[46] Of over 300 Finnish workers, half were immigrants from the United States and Canada.[47] A technical school was affiliated with the factory and trained from twenty-five to thirty qualified workers annually.[48] The transfer of technology and the training of qualified personnel brought positive results, for production output grew from 93,000 pairs of skis in 1932 to 115,000 pairs in 1933. Skis produced in Petrozavodsk were praised as the best in the USSR and competed on the European market.[49]

Finally, North American immigrants became actively involved in a number of infrastructure projects in Soviet Karelia. The first water supply and sewage system in Petrozavodsk was constructed to a great extent by their efforts. In the autumn of 1932, a special team consisting mainly of American and Canadian workers was assembled for this work, headed by foremen Lauri Luoma and Yrjö Salmi. The team had to build a wooden pipeline one kilometer long, starting from the bottom of Lake Onega. The pipeline was constructed during a harsh winter simultaneously on the ice and on the bottom of the lake. The underwater part of this work was completed entirely by two Finnish Americans, a diver, Viljo Seppä, who brought his diving equipment from Detroit, and his assistant, Väinö Heimola.[50]

This engineering accomplishment of the Finnish American team was widely hailed in the Karelian press. However, the rest of the construction—the laying of pipes in the town, the building of pumping facilities, and so on—took three years because of a lack of cement, pipes, and other materials. On Saturdays, many residents of Petrozavodsk went to work voluntarily to accelerate construction of the water supply system. American specialists headed by Kustaa Julen became responsible for making changes to the original design of the system when it had

FIGURE 22. CONSTRUCTION OF THE WATER SUPPLY SYSTEM IN PETROZAVODSK, 20 APRIL 1934 (PHOTOGRAPHER UNKNOWN; COURTESY OF THE NATIONAL ARCHIVE OF THE REPUBLIC OF KARELIA).

to be adapted to the local landscape or when chronic shortages of metal required an increased use of wood for certain elements. On 5 November 1935, the water supply system of Petro-zavodsk was finally completed and put into operation. To celebrate the occasion, a fountain was opened in the main square.[51] This wooden water supply and sewage system, designed and built mostly by American immigrants, was in use for the next forty years.

American and Canadian immigrants also worked in transportation—about 7 percent of immigrants were truck drivers, tractor drivers, and motor mechanics—and mechanical engineering and mining, in which about 6 percent had jobs as mechanics, founders, turners, metalworkers, miners, and crusher operators.[52] The mining industry in particular was, according to the original recruitment plans of Edvard Gylling's government, one of the economic areas to be modernized by a large influx of immigrants from North America. Unlike in the forest industry, however, attempts to modernize the Karelian mining industry with immigrants' skills and hands were a story of failure, which is nevertheless interesting to examine because it offers another perspective on the Soviet economy in the early 1930s.

Since the Karelian authorities had to submit their immigration plans for approval to Moscow every year, composition of the recruited labor force was planned long in advance on the basis of applications sent in by Karelian economic organizations. The latter, consequently, had only one chance a year to satisfy their needs for a qualified labor force, and local managers often rushed to ask for as many specialists as possible. As a result, recruited specialists sometimes found themselves in situations in which the Karelian organizations that had invited them could not actually give them jobs. Such was the case with North American immigrants recruited by requests from the Karelian state trust Karelshungit in 1932. Karelshungit was founded in April 1932 by the Karelian government to mine shungite, a

FIGURE 23. GARAGE OF THE KARELIAN STATE AUTOMOTIVE TRUST KARELAVTO, PETROZAVODSK, 1930S (PHOTOGRAPHER UKNOWN; COURTESY OF THE NATIONAL ARCHIVE OF THE REPUBLIC OF KARELIA).

combustible mineral intended to be used instead of coal in a number of factories in Leningrad. With these plans in mind, the management of Karelshungit signed a contract with the Resettlement Administration to recruit mining specialists from the United States and Canada. The administration fulfilled its part of the contract, and during 1932 seventy-six people moved from North America to Soviet Karelia to work in the mines of Karelshungit. By that time, however, none of the factories in Leningrad wanted to risk replacing coal with shungite in their manufacturing processes, which left the recruited miners (both North American and local) without work.[53]

Moreover, North American Finns and the management of their employment enterprises and organizations often became involved in conflicts when the local administration refused to accept new forms of labor organization that immigrants brought with them and tried to introduce to increase productivity. In 1932, a scandal erupted between foreign workers and the management of a mine belonging to the Karelian state trust Karelgranit and located in Shoksha, a village approximately fifty kilometers south of Petrozavodsk. Apart from a typical list of complaints related to everyday matters (lack of housing, improper medical treatment, insufficient food rations, etc.), immigrants openly accused the management of the mine of sabotage. They informed the top management of Karelgranit that they had to quarry granite with crowbars, the most primitive tools possible, without work boots or even gloves, while the mining equipment that they had brought from the United States stood idle in the mine's storehouse and some of it had already become irreparable.[54] Despite these open accusations, bureaucratic management of the Soviet economy was so inefficient that the administration of Karelgranit found itself unable to force the management of its mine in Shoksha to satisfy any of the immigrants' everyday needs or to meet their professional demands. Correspondence between the head office and the mine lasted for half a year and did not result in any particular measures.

FIGURE 24. MINING OF SHUNGITE, SHUNGA, 1930S (PHOTOGRAPHER UNKNOWN; COURTESY OF THE NATIONAL ARCHIVE OF THE REPUBLIC OF KARELIA).

It is hardly surprising that in such conditions the rational and emotional reactions of immigrants, and not only those employed in mining, were strongly negative, and many Karelian organizations often could not keep qualified specialists from the United States and Canada, who changed jobs, left Soviet Karelia for other regions of the USSR, or re-emigrated to Finland or North America. Yet it would be simplistic to emphasize only negative work experiences: in Soviet Karelia, immigrants also encountered, and themselves contributed to the making of, a different attitude to labor that actually helped them to materialize or reinforce their socialist identities.

THE MAKING OF SOCIALIST LABOR

Despite obvious successes in the accelerated industrialization, many (if not most) achievements of the first two Five-Year Plans were the results of a severe intensification of labor, or, as Leon Trotsky wrote, they were "largely due to people's muscles and nerves" rather than effective industrial management.[55] The Soviet press did its best to mobilize workers by constructing and then appealing to the feeling of enthusiasm and by creating an atmosphere of labor as military effort; it published headlines and articles that resembled wartime summaries with metaphors such as "feat of labor" and "breaches on the labor front." Mobilization speeches were delivered by decision makers of all ranks, and Stalin's phrase "the workforce determines everything" (Russian "КАДРЫ РЕШАЮТ ВСЕ") became one of the slogans of Soviet industrialization.[56]

Yet enthusiasm and self-sacrifice during the years of the First Five-Year Plan were far from being just discursive constructs of Soviet propaganda: they were embodied in millions of Soviet people. The atmosphere of mass enthusiasm of the First Five-Year Plan is often mentioned in primary sources, such as letters, diaries, and memoirs. The delight of creation, the expectations of happiness, justice, and brotherly love, those were the emotions of that time, culturally constructed but also lived through as personal experiences. The Bolshevik leadership regarded people's enthusiasm as a valuable labor resource and appealed to it by promoting the concepts of "shock-working" (*udarnichestvo*) and "socialist competition," which during the Second Five-Year Plan were complemented by the new concept "Stakhanovite movement."[57] Yet there were elements of a social contract in this utter strain of human resources, and not only those related to material reward and tacit rehabilitation of consumption as a means of social differentiation, as expressed in another of Stalin's catchphrases, "life became better, life became merrier," at the First All-Soviet Meeting of Stakhanovite Workers.[58] For ordinary Soviet people—at least for the most "conscious" of them, who internalized and embodied socialist visions of culture and progress—enthusiasm was the emotion that let them overcome the "temporary difficulties" that, according to Stalin and his ideologists, were part of the immense task of socialist construction.

Although American and Canadian Finns often considered Soviet methods of organizing work strange, once they had immigrated to Russia they also became the audience of this socialist spectacle and reproduced in their work, everyday practice, and narratives the cultural categories that surrounded them. A later memoir by Viljo Nurminen, an immigrant from Canada and a former worker at the ski factory in Petrozavodsk, offers insight into how North American immigrants absorbed new socialist values and ideas:

> We, the workers who came to the Soviet Union from capitalist states, were under a strong and dignifying influence of Soviet people who worked selflessly for the common good of the socialist future. After the ordeal that life in capitalist states like Finland, the United States, or Canada had been, we realized the delight of a free creative labor for the first time only here in the USSR. It is impossible to forget the enthusiasm of socialist competition of those years: all workshops and departments of the [ski] factory were aching to achieve the highest level of production. This passionate labor atmosphere that we had never experienced earlier consumed us completely.[59]

This account published in 1976 was written in the genre of socialist memoir, and the author could not publicly offer any other interpretation of his own personal experience of the 1930s other than from the perspective of enthusiastic labor and socialist superiority. Yet the personal experience underlying this narrative was likely real. The Petrozavodsk ski factory, of which Nurminen speaks in his memoir, was indeed famous in Soviet Karelia for its "shock-workers," "front-rank workers," and Stakhanovites, many of whom were North American Finns.[60] The selflessness and industriousness of American and Canadian workers in the first half of the 1930s was frequently described in the Karelian press and in memoir accounts. Finally, poems and songs that North American immigrants composed in Soviet Karelia reflected their vision of labor as a pathway to socialism. In this vision, enthusiasm was a much better investment in the future than dollars or material possessions:

> We got down to business, the axe flashed at once.
> The trees never saw work of such brilliance.

The thunder of hammers and roar of anvils:
In mines and in forges the work's in full swing.
New steel keeps on boiling in a melting furnace,
The workers' republic's increasing its pace!
The future's still hiding much hardship ahead,
The road is winding, but we see its end!
The day of our victory will soon be at hand!
Workers will forge their future in the Soviet land![61]

In the Karelian press, North American immigrants became the personification of labor enthusiasm and international solidarity of the proletariat. It is hardly surprising, therefore, that qualified American workers were given the responsibility of building a monument to Vladimir Lenin in the center of Petrozavodsk. After his death in 1924, monuments to the "leader of the world proletariat" were erected all over the Soviet Union, and Soviet regions were even engaged in an informal competition to see which one would have "a higher Lenin." As for the 1930s, Soviet Karelia was ahead of many of them: the sculpture of Lenin designed by Matvei Manizer, a sculptor from Leningrad, was six and a half meters (twenty-one feet) high, and the overall height of the monument (which depicts Lenin orating from a platform) was eleven meters (thirty-six feet) high, while its weight exceeded 140 tons.[62]

FIGURE 25. MONUMENT TO LENIN ON THE SQUARE OF 25 OCTOBER (NOW LENIN SQUARE), PETROZAVODSK, 25 FEBRUARY 1937 (COURTESY OF THE NATIONAL ARCHIVE OF THE REPUBLIC OF KARELIA).

In the spring of 1933, a fundraising campaign was launched in Soviet Karelia to collect money to build a monument to Lenin. Simultaneously, prisoners from the fledgling gulag quarried granite plates and blocks that were later shipped by barge to the harbor of Petrozavodsk. When in the harbor, these enormous blocks of stone (each weighing over ten tons) were put on wooden sledges and dragged by tractors to the central square. Some particularly massive blocks were carried for several days. Supervision of this heavy job was delegated to Eino Tuomi, a Michigan-born Finn who had moved to Soviet Karelia in 1932.[63] The granite blocks were pecked and trimmed by experienced masons, of whom at least three were from North America: Johan Hautamäki, August Rautio, and Vihtori Rimpilä.[64] The opening celebration was held during the anniversary of the Bolshevik Revolution on 7 November 1933. The accuracy of the monument and its huge size made it outstanding even on the Soviet scale, and Soviet newspapers reported that "it is the first time when the monument to Lenin is erected with a regard to all details."[65] In many ways, the monument to Lenin in Petrozavodsk became an embodiment of early Soviet dreams of a grandiose future that would be achieved through enthusiastic labor—dreams that American and Canadian immigrants shared and worked hard to realize.

AMERICAN AND CANADIAN AGRICULTURAL COMMUNES

Only slightly over 3 percent of North American immigrants were employed in the agricultural sector of Soviet Karelia. Their role in its development, however, was out of proportion to their number, and they became pioneers in the establishment of collective forms of agriculture in Soviet Karelia.

The meaning of a commune underwent a number of transformations in the Soviet Union before its social usage was mostly restricted to daily life ("communal apartment" as quintessentially Soviet housing in which one apartment was shared by several families who had only one room or sometimes part of a room).[66] Immediately after the revolution of 1917, communes were established as large ethnic autonomies (Karelian Workers' Commune, Volga German Workers' Commune) and on a smaller scale as a specific form of organized work and life of more limited groups of people (e.g., communes of fishermen). In this sense, communes were regarded as a symbol of common people's power, when everyone had equal rights and possibilities to participate in emancipated labor, in industrial management, and in the organization of everyday life. People from many countries expressed their desire to take part in this new social experiment, and in the early 1920s the Soviet government encouraged and stimulated industrial and agricultural immigration of foreign workers and farmers, who were supposed to facilitate the building of a new socialist economy with their professional working skills and new efficient tools and machines.

In June 1921, the Council of Labor and Defense issued a decree on American industrial immigration. Its first paragraph read thus: "It is desirable to develop certain industrial enterprises or groups of enterprises by leasing them to groups of American workers and industrially advanced [*industrialno razvitym*] peasants on a contractual basis, which would give them a certain degree of economic autonomy."[67] Soon a number of contracts with foreign workers were signed, the most prominent of them with American representatives of the international union Industrial Workers of the World, to whom concession rights were granted for a number of factories in Siberia (Kuzbass, Tomsk) and the Urals (Nadezhdinski). This was how, for instance, the Autonomous Industrial Colony Kuzbass was established in January 1922 (it existed until 1926).[68] In October 1922, Finns from the United States founded in the Northern Caucasus (Rostov region) an international agricultural commune named Seiatel (Russian for "sower") after their American hometown of Seattle.[69]

Setting up an agricultural commune in Soviet Karelia, however, was a much more problematic issue. Its harsh climate—the southern border lay at the sixtieth parallel and the northern border at the sixty-eighth parallel—was the main reason why agriculture had never been the main economic activity of the local population. Approximately half of the peasants' income was earned in seasonal work in other parts of Russia or in Finland.[70] In such unfavorable conditions, local peasants, especially in northern Soviet Karelia, were not interested in investing capital and labor in their fields, and new methods and crops were slow to win recognition in Karelian agriculture. During the 1920s, it was still based on small rural households that cultivated small plots of land and used outdated farming technologies (slash and burn clearing, a three-field system) and primitive tools (wooden plows, scythes, sickles). Local cattle were also underproductive, with cows producing on average as low as 700 liters (185 gallons) of milk a year.[71]

The first efforts to introduce collective forms of labor and property in rural areas of Soviet Karelia were made during and right after the Russian Civil War, long before the total collectivization in the USSR. The first communes and state-owned farms (*sovkhozes*) were established in Soviet Karelia in 1919 on the basis of former monastic or church farms. For example, the commune Imeni Lenina (Lenin Commune) was founded on lands that had been the property of the local bishop, while Sovkhoz No. 1 occupied the former Petrozavodsk municipal farm.[72] These new forms of socialist agriculture were encouraged and supported by the state, but despite all efforts they were very slow to adapt to the limited market economy of the 1920s and could not compete against private producers. Consequently, all communes in Soviet Karelia collapsed just several months after they were established (the only exception was Imeni Lenina, which existed until 1926), while four state farms set up in the early 1920s barely made ends meet because of a lack of financial assets, low efficiency, and the high cost of labor. In 1926, the net profit of Sovkhoz No. 1, the most efficient of the four, amounted to a ridiculous forty-one rubles.[73]

Successful communes and collective farms organized by Finnish immigrants served as a striking contrast. In the mid-1920s, they founded Pohjan pojat (Sons of the North) in the Ukhta district and Raataja (Laborer) in the Kondopoga district. But the most famous of all was Säde (Sun Ray) established by Finns from the Canadian province of Ontario.

Finnish miners from Cobalt, Ontario, formed an agricultural commune as early as 1922, but negotiations with the government of Soviet Karelia took three years, and only in 1925 was the commune granted ninety-one hectares (225 acres) of land near the town of Olonets in southern Soviet Karelia. By that time, the commune had collected $14,000 US, part of which was spent to purchase a Fordson tractor, a power saw bench, and other equipment. In the autumn of 1925, the first three commune members arrived in Soviet Karelia. In June 1926, the second group of nine people arrived, bringing another tractor and more equipment. By that autumn, Finns from Cobalt had cleared and plowed up eleven hectares of abandoned land, built a mansion, a bath, a stockyard, storage and power saw facilities, and a road to Olonets. In the spring of 1927, five more families arrived from Canada. That year an additional twelve hectares were cleared, the cattle herd grew to eleven cows, and the first pigs were acquired.[74] These were the early days of the commune Säde.

By 1930, the building of the commune was largely completed. Communards even constructed a water supply system that provided water to all of the commune's facilities—something unheard of in Soviet Karelia before. The commune had a forge, a sawmill, a rick barn, a vegetable store, a grain dryer, and other facilities.[75] This was by all measures one of the most modern and innovative farms in Soviet Karelia.

The commune's activities focused mainly on livestock farming. Initially, the Canadians in Säde had cows of local breeds, and later they imported more productive cattle from Finland. By 1930, the commune had fifteen dairy cows, seven heifers, and eight calves. The cattle were kept in excellent condition, and it is hardly surprising that the milk yields of Säde were the highest in all of Soviet Karelia—reaching an astonishing (for that time) twenty-five liters (6.6 gallons) a day compared with the average of eight liters (2.1 gallons) a day. The communards found that the local Karelian breed of cattle, which had been considered low yield, could produce similar amounts of milk if provided with adequate care and food. In Säde during 1928–29, cows imported from Finland gave an average of 2,560 liters (676 gallons) a year and cows of the local Karelian breed 2,250 liters (594 gallons) a year, whereas the average figure for Soviet Karelia was 700 to 800 liters (190 to 210 gallons).[76] Sales of milk brought considerable profits to the commune, as did purebred calves ordered by the People's Commissariat of Agriculture of Soviet Karelia or sales of pigs and pork. In 1933, Säde was announced the best stock breeder in Soviet Karelia.[77]

FIGURE 26. CANTEEN OF THE COMMUNE SÄDE, OLONETSKII *RAION* (DISTRICT), 1932 (PHOTOGRAPHER UNKNOWN; COURTESY OF THE NATIONAL ARCHIVE OF THE REPUBLIC OF KARELIA).

In 1929, Säde planted its fields with wheat for the first time. The seeds were received from the agricultural experimental station in the Leningrad region as part of an experiment to grow wheat in northern Russia. The experiment was successful, and for several years after 1930 Säde supplied neighboring *kolkhozes* with seed grain.[78] In the commune itself, wheat harvests were 40 to 50 percent higher than the average in Soviet Russia, and these yields were the result of the large-scale mechanization of all farming operations: apart from tractors that Säde was the first to introduce in southern Soviet Karelia, communards used a threshing machine and other agricultural machines.[79] The commune represented Soviet Karelia in several agricultural exhibitions in Moscow, and in 1934 it received the first award from one of them: the gold medal and a car.[80]

During the first years of the commune, its members did not receive salaries for their work: only free accommodation and meals were provided. When the period of formation was over, the management of Säde began paying to communards monthly salaries of ten rubles and annual child benefits of twenty to forty rubles, depending on the age of the child. According to the socialist vision of emancipated gender, women were freed from many household duties: the social canteen provided the population of Säde with four meals daily, and the commune employed a laundress and a charwoman. The first chairman of Säde was Kalle Lahti; in 1929, this position was taken by Kalle Siikanen. A special emphasis was placed on cultural activities: the commune had a library, which subscribed to eleven newspapers and magazines, and a club that had a radio receiver, a billiard table, and different board games. Säde also had an amateur theater and an amateur orchestra that organized dances on Saturday nights.[81]

The commune aroused much interest both among the local population and everywhere else in Soviet Karelia. Local peasants started joining Säde, and delegations from Soviet Karelia and neighboring Soviet regions became frequent visitors to it, attempting to learn and imitate the technological processes used in its agricultural activities. During 1931 alone, ninety-two excursions to the commune were organized for groups from the Leningrad region and Soviet Karelia.[82] Experimental plots of Säde served as the basis for practical training of students of the Leningrad Agricultural Academy and of young specialists from different Karelian *kolkhozes*. The Soviet press widely publicized the achievements of Säde. Publications grew in number particularly at the turn of the 1930s, when collectivization of the Soviet peasantry began in the USSR. The lives and labor of the commune's members demonstrated the advantages of *kolkhozes* over individual farms. Writers Eemeli Parras and Lauri Luoto praised the commune in their works,[83] and it welcomed as its guests a famous Danish writer, Martin Andersen Nexø, and German socialist painter Heinrich Vogeler.[84]

However, acceleration of agricultural collectivization soon changed the atmosphere in Säde and the basic principles of its work as economic autonomy gave way to plans imposed from above. Original members started to leave the commune, and by February 1935, among its fifty-four members, only six were from Canada and three from the United States, while others were either immigrants from Finland or local peasants.[85] In the autumn of 1935, with the start of an anti-Finnish campaign in Soviet Karelia, several leaders of Säde were arrested, including Kalle Siikanen, its founding member, while the commune itself was reorganized into a *kolkhoz*, which since 1939 was called Kolkhoz Imeni Ivana Papanina (Ivan Papanin's Kolkhoz). Its new leader, Eino Stenfors, was soon arrested as well.[86]

Although the Finnish leadership of Soviet Karelia had to follow orders from Moscow to collectivize all individual farms into *kolkhozes*, initially it avoided a wide-scale campaign of total collectivization. In 1930, the share of collectivized farms reached only 15 percent, four times lower than the average level in the USSR.[87] The central authorities had to press Edvard Gylling's government, and only then did Soviet Karelia begin to catch up with other regions. Total collectivization of rural areas was important as a method of organizing the labor force not only in agriculture, which was of secondary importance in Soviet Karelia, but also in the forest industry, which brought much more profit to the national and republican budgets. Members of Karelian *kolkhozes* were obliged to work at timber harvesting and floating, and those who avoided this work were brought to legal responsibility.[88] In this respect, *kolkhozes* in Soviet Karelia became a convenient way to mobilize cheap labor for the forest industry. Most able-bodied men and horses were employed for various forestry jobs, while the main burden of agricultural activities now lay on women. As a result, members of most *kolkhozes* in Soviet Karelia often did not have enough time for field work, and the level of agricultural production was decreasing, which reduced the supply of food to urban areas.

When the system of centralized food supply started to fail, the administrations of many logging settlements, which started to experience irregularities and shortages in the food supply, established their own small farms to provide workers with extra food. The popularity of such farms was also sparked by Finnish immigrants, and almost every forest settlement in Soviet Karelia with a large Finnish community had such a farm serving the needs of its inhabitants. One of the best examples of this initiative was forest settlement Internatsional.

This settlement was founded by twenty-five American and Canadian lumberjacks in 1931 on the territory of the abandoned and dilapidated monastery Vazheozerskii located in the Olonets district, 120 kilometers south of Petrozavodsk.[89] The settlement was named Internatsional since the majority of its population were immigrants from the United States, Canada, and Finland (the contemporary name is Interposiolok, meaning "international settlement" in Russian). By 1933, 185 Finns lived in Internatsional, making up 83.7 percent of its population.[90] Although the inhabitants of Internatsional were mostly employed

FIGURE 27. FINNISH CANADIAN IMMIGRANTS IN THE COLLECTIVE FARM (*SOVKHOZ*) OF ILIINSKII, EARLY 1930S (GOLUBEV AND TAKALA, *USTNAIA ISTORIIA*, 42).

in the forest industry, from the beginning its administration intended to create an auxiliary farm that would supply the workers with locally produced food. In 1932, a *forest sovkhoz,* as this new type of economic organization combining agricultural and industrial elements was called, had 16.5 hectares (forty-one acres) of land planted with forage herbs, potatoes, and vegetables, a herd of twenty cows and fifty pigs, and an established fishery in the local lake of Vazhozero.[91]

The problem of food shortage during the early 1930s forced other North American communities in Soviet Karelia, including building brigades and large groups of industrial workers, to establish similar farms as well. In the winter of 1932, American workers employed in the Kondopoga factory addressed a request to the Karelian leadership to provide them with a plot of land, where they could establish a farm to provide food for their families. They were ready to invest their own money deposited in foreign bank accounts (approximately $6,000 US and 10,000 Finnish marks) in the purchase of cattle and necessary equipment.[92] By that time, a similar agricultural collective farm, Mullistaja, existed in the logging settlement Siurgi,[93] where Finns comprised 100 percent of the population.[94] In the *sovkhoz* Sunskii, which supplied agricultural products to construction sites in Kondopoga, 84 percent of the *sovkhoz's* inhabitants were Finns as of 1933.[95]

Attempts to expand the network of state farms (*sovkhozes*) were made simultaneously with collectivization. In 1929, the state trust Sovkhoztrest was founded, and by 1932 it operated nine *sovkhozes,* most of them located in dense forests or wetlands where large investments were needed to launch effective agricultural production. The trust was unable to find these investments, and its *sovkhozes* languished in poverty.[96] Sovkhoz No. 1, responsible for the provision of vegetables and dairy products to Petrozavodsk, had no mechanical equipment and was unable to satisfy the needs of Soviet Karelia's capital city. As a result, the Karelian leadership decided to establish near Petrozavodsk Sovkhoz No. 2 and to invite American Finns from the southern Russian commune Seattle/Kylväjä.[97]

Sovkhoz No. 2 was founded in 1930 on a so-called Coal Swamp located nine kilometers from Petrozavodsk. The place gave the *sovkhoz* its informal Finnish name Hiilisuo (*hiili* meaning "coal" and *suo* meaning "swamp"). It received over 100 acres of land for initial production and almost 2,500 acres more for prospective development. Up to a third of the land was not arable, while the rest, mostly wetland, required a lot of effort to start agricultural production.[98] Yet Finnish American farmers from Seiatel-Seattle had a lot of experience in collective agricultural work that helped to overcome these challenges; besides, new settlers came from the United States and Canada with their own equipment, and by the autumn of 1932 sixty-nine immigrants (167 people with family members) were employed in Hiilisuo.[99]

The first two years of the *sovkhoz's* development were very hard. The reclamation of wetlands had just started, and there was a disastrous shortage of forage for purchased cattle that came to Hiilisuo already weakened by disease. In July 1931, the *sovkhoz* purchased 167 cows, but the entire herd was in a famished state, most of the dairy cows were old and gave too little milk to raise calves, and soon the *sovkhoz* farmers were forced to slaughter all the calves. By December 1931, almost the entire herd had perished because of disease and malnutrition. To make things worse, the tractors that immigrants had brought from the United States were unfit for work on the local wetlands: a Caterpillar was too heavy, while a Cletrack had too narrow tracks to be used on bogs.[100]

Nevertheless, enthusiasm and persistent work, as well as personal investments of American and Canadian settlers, soon brought positive results. In the autumn of 1931, an American farmer, Joonas Harju, came to Hiilisuo, and his contribution proved instrumental for the further development of the *sovkhoz*. He purchased, using his private funds, a large herd of thoroughbred cattle, a tractor, two cars, and a radio station.[101] From 1933, Karelian newspapers published articles on Hiilisuo describing it as an advanced and model farm, the level of which other collective and state farms had to attain.[102] For the leadership of Soviet Karelia, in particular Gylling, Sovkhoz No. 2 likely had much importance as a model for agricultural development under total collectivization. There were plans to open an agricultural school on its basis, which, according to Gylling, would become "a forge that would train skilled specialists for the socialist agriculture."[103] The school was opened in the summer of 1935, when the destiny of his government was already determined. By that time, Hiilisuo employed 308 workers, including fifty-six American Finns and 160 illegal Finnish immigrants. This ethnic composition of the *sovkhoz*, as well as the personal sympathies of Gylling, proved fatal for both Hiilisuo itself and its founding members from the United States once the anti-Finnish campaign was launched as part of the Great Terror.

To summarize, in Soviet Karelia during collectivization of the early 1930s, the only successful working collective or state farms were those that were established on a voluntary basis, that had qualified management and experienced and motivated workers, and that were able to purchase necessary equipment, cattle, and seeds. The majority of these successful farms were established by immigrants from the United States, Canada, and Finland. In the second half of the 1930s, when the Finnish period in the history of Soviet Karelia was over and Finns turned from being a local elite into the group most severely affected by the Great Terror, all former achievements of Finnish agricultural communities were first discredited and later consigned to oblivion.

In the broader context, political opposition from Moscow and unpreparedness of local economic authorities to provide normal working and living conditions to American and Canadian immigrants did not allow them to become a mass labor force in Soviet Karelia, which was possible considering the number of applications sent to the Karelian Technical Aid Committees in New York and Toronto. But even the relatively small North American immigrant group that settled in Soviet Karelia during the early 1930s made a significant contribution to the development of Karelian industry and agriculture.

CHAPTER 6

North American
Finns in Soviet Culture

WHICH LANGUAGE SHOULD THE EMANCIPATED SPEAK?

FROM THE FIRST DAYS OF THE BOLSHEVIK REVOLUTION, THE NEW GOVERNMENT excessively used a rhetoric of emancipation to legitimize its power. The political agenda of Bolsheviks included the emancipation of workers and peasants from capitalist exploitation, the emancipation of women from domestic oppression, and the emancipation of colonial peoples from colonizers' rule. Armed with Marxist conceptions of ideology as false consciousness, Bolshevik leaders also attacked prerevolutionary bourgeois culture as an instrument that served to reinforce the ideology of exploiting classes and to convince exploited classes that the interests of the exploiters were their own. Genuine emancipation of workers and peasants, therefore, demanded that an entirely new culture be constructed; only then could socialism be achieved.[1]

Thus, Bolshevik revolutionary reforms in economy and sociopolitical life were immediately followed by attacks on old cultural forms, which presumably served as agents of bourgeois influence preventing the Soviet population from realizing their true class interests. A new, class-based culture had to be implemented, armed with Marxist dialectics and inculcated through Communist education. Main objectives on the cultural front (military rhetoric was widely used in Soviet narratives of the 1920s and 1930s) were to eradicate illiteracy among workers and peasants, to reorganize the management of educational and cultural institutions, to create a new Soviet way of life (*novyi byt*), and to form a new social group of intellectuals: the Soviet intelligentsia. Underlying all these objectives was a question that Bolsheviks did not explicitly pose but that, in a form inspired by Gayatri Chakravorty Spivak's writing,[2] can be addressed to the theory and practice of early Soviet cultural policies: which language could (and should) the emancipated Soviet subject speak?

For contemporary academic scholarship on early Soviet cultural policies, the relationship among language, state, and society is at the forefront of research. The main questions that this body of research poses are the following. Which new language and literary forms were created in the course of Soviet revolutionary transformations? How were Soviet people supposed to use, and how did they actually use, these new forms? What kind of new Soviet subjectivity emerged as a result of "speaking and writing Bolshevik"? How did new language forms reinforce state control and discipline in Soviet society?[3] These questions were particularly pressing in the Soviet ethnic periphery, where "language building" (*iazykovoie stroitelstvo*) was not simply a metaphor for the emergence of new forms or meanings but a real process of creation of new literary languages and, through them, new national cultures. As Stalin put it as early as 1925, in the multinational Soviet state under the dictatorship of the proletariat, national cultures had to be "socialist in their contents, national in form."[4] Throughout the 1920s and much of the 1930s, there was intense political struggle over the question of who defined which cultural forms and meanings were indeed class based and which were relics of capitalist ideology or foreign influence—or, to put it another way, who held the right of cultural production in the Soviet Union, since sharp increases in literacy, egalitarian cultural practices, and establishment of a wide network of schools, universities, and clubs contributed to an unprecedented rise in the number of people and institutions claiming the right of agency in cultural production. Finnish political immigrants who played a decisive role in establishing Soviet Karelia in 1920 were very active in this struggle.

Although Finns comprised a small minority among predominantly Russian and Karelian populations of Soviet Karelia, it was Finnish and not Karelian that from 1920 to 1937 was its second official language. Finnish literary culture flourished in the republic, which had its Finnish-language press and book publishers, theaters, a radio channel, as well as school, professional, and even higher education. This situation was made possible by a combination of political factors that had brought Red Finns to the summit of political power in Soviet Karelia. Also important was the fact that, among Karelians, who were perceived by Soviet and Red Finnish leaders as an ethnic entity, large dialectical differences and territorial segregation hindered the formation of a normative literary language. Finally, in spite of all regional peculiarities, the language policy of Red Finns in Soviet Karelia had to take into account the "general line" in the nation-wide cultural and language policies of the VKP(b).

Contemporary scholarship on early Soviet language policies distinguishes three main stages or periods through the 1920s and 1930s. Initially, during a relatively liberal period in the 1920s, Soviet authorities encouraged local cultural elites to participate and even take the initiative in cultural mobilization of their ethnic groups, provided that they demonstrated loyalty to the socialist cause. It was a heyday for literary languages of large ethnic groups, especially those that had existed during the imperial period; at the same time, many smaller ethnic groups that had not produced enough intellectuals before the Bolshevik Revolution still had neither a literary tradition nor sometimes even a national alphabet.

The second period of Soviet language policies was ignited by the launch of the First Five-Year Plan in 1928 and characterized by accelerated construction, in the spirit of the time, of new written languages on the basis of almost all existing vernaculars in the USSR. Latin script became a de facto standard writing system for new written languages, and their realm of application was significantly expanded to make Soviet ethnic groups more active and enthusiastic participants in building the socialist state. At the same time, Soviet authorities became more radical on the question of who could be in charge of cultural production in ethnic regions. The time for compromise with prerevolutionary intellectuals was over, and the Bolshevik leadership now relied on a new generation of Soviet intellectuals regarded as politically more loyal to Soviet power and allegedly less rooted in prerevolutionary bourgeois ideology.

Finally, since approximately 1934, Soviet authorities started to reinstate the dominant position of the Russian language in ethnic regions. In the second half of the 1930s, most written languages, especially those recently created, were transferred to the Cyrillic alphabet, and their vocabularies and grammars were increasingly Russified, while some of these new written languages were even fully abandoned in favor of languages of their larger neighbors.[5] The transition from one stage to another followed changes in the vкр(b)'s "general political line,"[6] which firmly tied language production to changes in Soviet political and ideological order.

Although nation-wide political changes had immediate effects on language policies in Soviet Karelia, their effective course was determined by regional factors, including the historical trajectory of the Karelian language and the political and cultural agenda of the republic's Red Finnish government.

Before the Bolshevik Revolution, the Karelian vernacular existed as oral dialects, whereas Russian functioned as the language of education and "high" culture for those Karelians who moved from rural areas to urban centers of Arkhangelsk or Olonets provinces. There were attempts at the turn of the twentieth century to develop and popularize a Karelian alphabet and literature, but these attempts were restricted nearly entirely to religious texts. The Karelian population of the territories along the Finnish border was actively involved in migrant labor or petty trade in Finland, which facilitated dissemination of the Finnish language and writing in these areas, especially in northern Karelia. Yet, for the majority of the Karelian population, there was no pressing need to learn a second language, either Russian or Finnish, and bilingualism thus remained a relatively marginal phenomenon in prerevolutionary Karelian communities: only a small share of men regularly employed as seasonal workers or peddlers could speak languages of their neighbors.[7]

When plans were drafted in 1920 to establish an ethnic Karelian autonomous region, Finnish Communists were commissioned by the Soviet government to address the question of which languages were to be the official languages of Soviet Karelia. Finnish linguistics of the early twentieth century, which developed in the context of the Finnish nationalist movement, regarded Karelian dialects as dialects of the Finnish language, and this provided Red Finns with an argument that Finnish would function well as the written language of the Karelian vernaculars. Creation of a proper written Karelian language, it was also argued, would require too much time and effort.[8] A new term was coined to justify this perceived community of Karelian and Finnish languages, the "Karelian-Finnish language." The term was used in the 1923 decree that upgraded the status of Soviet Karelia from a workers' commune to an autonomous republic.[9] Edvard Gylling argued that official bilingualism in Soviet Karelia, which implied the equal use of Russian and Karelian-Finnish languages in administration and education, would make its population more favorable to Soviet power and accelerate the adoption of literacy and revolutionary culture.[10] The first two All-Karelian Congresses of Soviets (February and October 1921), the supreme body of power in the newly established Karelian autonomy, provided a legislative basis for this decision.[11] In March 1922, it was confirmed by the Central Committee of the rкр(b), which decreed that both Russian and Finnish could be used as languages of school education.[12]

At the same time, in order to avoid a negative public reaction among the Karelian population, the political leadership of Soviet Karelia emphasized that introduction of the Finnish written language as official would not encroach on the rights of Karelian dialects, supposed to acquire at some future point their own systems of writing. For the present moment, however, functions of the Karelian dialects were limited to everyday oral communication, while literary Finnish was designated as their normative written form, a scheme elaborated in a 1924 resolution of the Central Executive Committee of Soviet Karelia.[13] The concept of the Karelian-Finnish language, in this respect, was a justification of attempts at soft Finnicization of Karelians in the sphere of writing and literary culture. The Finnish leadership of Soviet Karelia argued that the literary Finnish language served as "a natural extension of Karelian dialects" and thus would help to consolidate the Karelian language and eliminate the borders that restricted it to a narrow sphere of everyday oral communication.[14]

During the first half of the 1920s, the use of Finnish in administration and school education was limited to northern Karelian communities that spoke a dialect most closely resembling the literary Finnish language. As for southern (Olonets) Karelians, the dominant written language remained Russian. Since the mid-1920s, however, the practical application of Finnish expanded following the official policy of indigenization (*korenizatsiia*), which encompassed all ethnic territories of the Soviet Union. Through this policy, formulated at the Twelfth Congress of the RKP(b) in 1923, the Communist Party proclaimed its intention to overcome the de facto existing inequality among ethnic groups in the USSR. One of its principles was that title ethnicities had to have proportional representation in local bodies of administration and in the party apparatuses of their autonomous territories, and their languages had to be used more actively in education and administration. The main message of this policy was voiced by Stalin, then the people's commissar for nationalities: "In order for non-Russian peasants [*inonatsionalnoie krestiianstvo*] to perceive Soviet power as their own power, it is necessary that it becomes comprehensible for them, that it speaks in their native languages, that schools and organs of government are built from local people who know languages, customs, and life of non-Russian nationalities."[15] These concessions to Soviet ethnic groups in the spheres of language, culture, and manpower policy were intended to circumvent separatist sentiments and activities and to create the basis for the formation of new ethnic elites loyal to the Soviet regime.[16]

In Soviet Karelia, the policy of indigenization was called "karelization" but actually involved an active expansion of Finnish, especially in education, and even further promotion of Finns (at the expense of Karelians) to official positions, even though Finns in Soviet Karelia were a small minority and their resulting share of authority hardly reflected ethnic composition of the republic. Under the facade of the Karelian-Finnish language, Finnish became the language of education in the majority of schools in ethnic Karelian regions. In the academic year of 1929–30, of 250 schools located in Karelian, Vepsian, or Finnish communities, teaching was held in Finnish in 191 and in Russian in the rest (fifty-nine), whereas none officially operated in Karelian or Vepsian languages, though they could still be used in oral form for communication between teachers and students. In six border regions of Soviet Karelia where 80 to 90 percent of the population was Karelian or Vepsian, all schools operated in Finnish.[17] This situation was reflected in the system of teacher education: in 1920, a Finnish teaching college was established in Petrozavodsk in addition to the already existing Russian teaching college. They coexisted through the 1920s and first half of the 1930s.[18] At the same time, no attempt was made to start training Karelian-speaking teachers.

This policy met with mixed reactions among the local population. Although in northern Karelian areas teaching in Finnish was more successful, in southern Soviet Karelia, where differences among local dialects and the literary Finnish language were significant, most Karelians commonly preferred Russian as the language of education for their children.[19] Practical considerations also imposed constraints on the implementation of language policy in Soviet Karelia: during the second half of the 1920s, for example, in more than half of Karelian primary schools, first graders started to study in local dialects, and teaching was switched to the primary language of education only gradually in the course of the school year.[20] The possibility of choosing Russian or Finnish in education, as well as using local dialects for oral communication in schools, administration, or juridical practice, softened, for the time being, public opposition to the imposition of Finnish.

FIGURE 28. FACULTY AND STAFF OF THE FINNISH PEDAGOGICAL COLLEGE, PETROZAVODSK, 1934 (PHOTOGRAPHER UNKNOWN, COURTESY OF THE NATIONAL ARCHIVE OF THE REPUBLIC OF KARELIA).

This status quo satisfied Finnish Communist leaders of Soviet Karelia as long as nobody challenged the position of Finnish as the second official language. At the end of the 1920s, however, the national context changed when Soviet authorities launched a campaign aimed at the accelerated development of minority languages. This meant that the Karelian written language was again on the political agenda, and Finnish leaders of Soviet Karelia reacted promptly. In August 1929, a flexible language policy encapsulated in the concept Karelian-Finnish language was replaced by more uncompromising principles formulated by the Karelian *obkom* of the vкр(b). Ethnic Karelians no longer had the right to choose between Russian and Finnish as the language of education: instead, Finnish was declared the only written language of Karelian culture.[21] This abrupt change in language policy in favor of accelerated and forced Finnicization of Soviet Karelia was a reaction of Red Finnish leaders to a new public debate about the question of Karelian writing. The turn of the 1930s was when a number of small Finno-Ugric ethnic groups acquired systems of writing; most importantly, in 1930, a writing system was introduced for the dialect of Tver Karelians, a subethnic Karelian group residing in central Russia.[22] This questioned the validity of the use of Finnish as the written language for Karelian dialects in Soviet Karelia and sparked a "language war" between Finnish immigrants and supporters of the Karelian written language. The most active and influential advocate of the rights of Karelians for their own written language was Professor Dmitry Bubrikh of Leningrad State University. A prominent disciple of Nicholas Marr, a Lysenko of Soviet linguistics,[23] and a leading specialist in Finno-Ugric philology, Bubrikh implemented in his practical activities the principles of Marr's sociolinguistic theory, according to which a language was a phenomenon of the social superstructure and consequently reflected the class nature of the society in which it had been formed and functioned. In light of this allegedly Marxist perspective on languages, the "bourgeois" Finnish language could not be used as the official language of proletarian Soviet Karelia. Bubrikh drew a sharp distinction between Finnish and Karelian languages as languages, correspondingly, of the exploiters and the exploited and went as far as accusing Soviet supporters of the

Finnish literary language of promoting the theory of a common Finno-Ugric protolanguage developed by "fascist" Finnish linguists. By doing so, he argued, Red Finns played into the hands of Finnish nationalists who dreamt of a "reunification" of all Finno-Ugric people of the Soviet Union into a "greater Finland."[24] His arguments found support among a certain part of the Soviet state apparatus, and on 25 April 1931 the Presidium of the Nationalities Board of the Central Executive Committee, the supreme Soviet body responsible for national questions, issued a decree obliging the government of Soviet Karelia to create the Karelian writing system and, once that task was completed, to transfer all education in the ethnic region of Soviet Karelia from Finnish to Karelian.[25]

Yet, for Red Finns, this debate was too essential to surrender without a fight, for at stake were their culture and political authority. Through connections in the vKP(b), they convinced the party leadership that Finnish was actually a revolutionizing force in Karelian communities, and in June 1931 the Politburo of the Central Committee of the vKP(b) repealed the decree of 25 April, a decision later confirmed by the Presidium of the Central Executive Committee of the USSR.[26] We hypothesize that this support reflected strategic plans of Soviet leaders related to possible revolutionary developments in Finland, for the Communist cadre trained in Soviet Karelia could quickly satisfy the demand in a new revolutionary authority for, finally, Red Finland. Confirming this success in the autumn of 1931, the Karelian authorities passed another resolution, according to which Finnish was reinstated as the primary language of education and administration in ethnic Karelian territories.[27] In reaction to this struggle with advocates of Karelian literacy, Red Finnish authorities in Soviet Karelia moved to solve the language question in an accelerated and forcible manner. Already by 1932, 99.6 percent of children of Karelian ethnicity were educated in the Finnish language.[28] In a similarly coercive manner, it was used in the adult literacy campaign. While in 1929 Finnish was taught only to 21 percent of Karelians attending adult literacy schools, in 1932 this figure rose to 70 percent.[29]

This story highlights that Soviet politics of the early Stalinist period developed as a struggle between different power groups that used revolutionary transformations and rhetoric to pursue their goals, build alliances, discredit and eliminate enemies, and realize their visions of the socialist future. The supreme party leadership regulated this struggle on the lower level of the Soviet bureaucratic hierarchy by giving its support to groups able to demonstrate a higher degree of loyalty than their opponents. For the time being, Red Finns managed to convince the party leadership that their language and nationality policies were worth this supreme support. However, negative attitudes among Karelians toward forced Finnicization increased tensions between the Karelian population and authorities, which gave Moscow a rationale to start, from 1933, criticizing Red Finns for their "blunders" in cultural policy. This was also an indication that the period of open dialog between the vKP(b) leadership in Moscow and regional elites was drawing to its end, a process that concluded with the Great Terror, which ultimately suppressed the center-periphery relationships in the USSR from the sphere of the political into the sphere of the bureaucratic. After all, popular protest against the Finnicization of Karelians was particularly strong at the turn of the 1930s, whereas by the mid-1930s it was pushed aside by more pressing problems, such as famine and commodity shortages. Yet it was the cultural and language policy of Red Finns that the Soviet leadership used to justify the dismissal of Gylling and his supporters from authoritative positions in Soviet Karelia in 1935.

By the mid-1930s, however, fifteen years of enlightening efforts of Finnish Communists had radically transformed the cultural landscape of Soviet Karelia. For Red Finns, a small minority that, because of a concurrence of circumstances and politics, found themselves at the head of a much larger but mainly illiterate Karelian nation, language and cultural policies were means to secure their political dominance and social superiority in a new revolutionary society. Not surprisingly, the government of Soviet Karelia, making use of its economic autonomy, invested more in culture and education than most other Soviet regions: in 1929, for example, these costs constituted 12 percent of the Karelian budget, twice as much as the national average.[30] Professional training of educators capable of teaching in Finnish was another area in which Red Finns concentrated their efforts. As mentioned above, in 1920 a Finnish teaching college was established in Petrozavodsk that attracted Finnish- and Karelian-speaking students from all over Soviet Karelia. The faculty of the college included prominent Red Finnish politicians and intellectuals, among them Heino Rautio, principal between 1921 and 1930; Lauri Letonmäki, a former member of the Finnish Diet and commissar of justice in the short-lived government of Red Finland; and Hannes Pulkinen, another former Finnish mp. In 1930, the second Finnish teaching college was established in northern Soviet Karelia in Ukhta for the training of primary schoolteachers.[31] Graduates of both colleges joined the ranks of fast-growing national intelligentsia of Soviet Karelia, securing the position of Finnish language and culture in the republic.

During the 1920s and early 1930s, the government of Soviet Karelia built a system of education that encompassed all levels. By 1933, more than 500 schools (half of them Finnish), fifteen professional schools, one agricultural and two teaching colleges, and a teaching university functioned in Soviet Karelia.[32] In 1931, the educational system was complemented by the Karelian Research Institute, the first research-oriented institution established in Soviet Karelia.[33]

FIGURE 29. BUILDING OF THE FINNISH PEDAGOGICAL COLLEGE IN PETROZAVODSK, 1930S (PHOTOGRAPHER UNKNOWN; COURTESY OF THE NATIONAL ARCHIVE OF THE REPUBLIC OF KARELIA).

The Karelian Research Institute, the creation of which was inspired and facilitated by the head of the Karelian government, Edvard Gylling, initially enlisted only eight full-time staff members. Its early research activities focused on the history of Finland and Karelia and on studies of Finno-Ugric languages. Historical research was coordinated by Eero Haapalainen, a prominent member of the Finnish labor movement, and linguistic studies were supervised by another Red Finnish intellectual, Viktor Salo, who, among other things, pioneered Soviet research on Karelian and Vepsian folklore and dialects.[34]

Scholarly knowledge produced by the Karelian Research Institute had important political implications, for it was supposed to legitimize Red Finnish visions of history and language development. Salo's call for the "purification" of the Soviet Finnish language from "bourgeois" forms was a response to Marrist (language-as-superstructure) criticism of Finnish as a language that reflected the capitalist structure of contemporaneous Finland and was not suitable for revolutionizing Soviet Karelia. Salo and other Red Finnish linguists developed a counter-theory that, in the Soviet society of emancipated labor, Finnish would start reflecting a new socialist basis and would undergo necessary revolutionary transformations.[35] Similarly, historical research produced in the Karelian Research Institute described Soviet Karelia in terms of ethnic and cultural community between Karelians and Finns and functioned as a counter-narrative to alternative versions of Karelian history. The latter, written by Russian-language historians, involved different chronologies and geographies that drew on perceptions of Soviet Karelia as part of Russia and emphasized the borderline between it and Finland, a perspective that undermined the legitimacy of the Red Finnish government.[36]

The results of the language policy of Red Finns in Soviet Karelia were, to say the least, contradictory. On the one hand, it was fairly successful in quantitative terms. In 1920, only 24 percent of inhabitants of Soviet Karelia were literate, and, since Russians as a more urbanized population had a generally higher level of literacy, among ethnic Karelians this figure was even lower.[37] In 1933, the share of literate people among Karelians reached 46 percent, of whom nearly half (48 percent) used Finnish or both Finnish and Russian writing systems.[38] We can also speculate that the spread of Finnish literacy among ethnic Karelians slowed down their de facto Russification, which happened to a number of similarly small ethnic groups in the Soviet Union. On the other hand, the attempts of Red Finns to consolidate Karelians into an ethnic community took the shape of a civilizing mission, in which Finnish Communists imposed and, in the early 1930s, enforced their language and culture on the Karelian population. In fact, while their political writing remained committed to socialist and internationalist ideas, their political practice in a whimsical way attempted to realize ideas that they obviously borrowed from the nationalist context of Finnish culture: that is, ideas of re-educating "backward" Karelians into "progressive" Finns, even though their concepts of backwardness and progress were expressed in revolutionary rather than nationalist terms. This process was additionally accelerated by the VKP(b) leadership, which encouraged similar language and cultural policies in other Soviet ethnic peripheries (e.g., in Soviet Moldavia, where the Romanian literary language was de facto the standard written language between 1932 and 1938).

In his research on the Soviet nationalities policy, Terry Martin developed Miroslav Hroch's three-phase model of the development of nations by adding a fourth phase, "phase D."[39] He argued that at phase D the Soviet state controlled nationalist sentiment in its ethnic regions by establishing national languages and local elites—that it, by pushing the process of nationalist development to its logical end, beyond which political or social conflicts caused by national mobilization were no longer possible. The language policy in Soviet Karelia can be interpreted as part of this process, when the Soviet leadership used Red Finns to build a national region and to construct Karelians as a Soviet ethnic group and as subjects loyal to and enthusiastically working for the socialist cause. American and Canadian immigrants arrived in Soviet Karelia when the language policy of Red Finns was at its height. Their immediate inclusion in the literary process became an important part of the making of a new Soviet Karelian writer and a new Soviet Karelian reader.

AMERICAN AND CANADIAN IMMIGRANTS AS WRITERS

The language question was one of the decisive factors of the Karelian fever. Recruiters of the Karelian Technical Aid Committee eloquently addressed Canadian and American Finns, describing how their native language was used in all spheres of life in Soviet Karelia, and many biographical narratives incorporated this argument in the representation of immigrant experience.[40] Attracted to Soviet Karelia by the possibility of using Finnish in everyday communication and education, once there North American immigrants found themselves in the role of producers of a new culture, socialist in content but national in form, to use Stalin's famous formula once again.

The stage for their literary activities was well prepared, for the national literature of Soviet Karelia was yet another sphere of cultural and symbolic production that Red Finns strove to claim as their own to secure an additional resource for political struggle with other groups claiming authority in Soviet Karelia. First they created a solid material basis for Finnish-language writing there. In 1927, the Finnish-language press Kirja (Book) established four years earlier by Finnish immigrants in Petrograd opened its Karelian branch in Petrozavodsk, and in 1931 it became the head office of Kirja. Its scale of production was fairly large, taking into account the fact that Finns were a minority in both the Leningrad region and Soviet Karelia: during the operating year of 1932–33, Kirja published thirty Finnish-language fiction books plus a number of technical and political titles.[41] Petrozavodsk was also home to a diverse Finnish-language press. A regional newspaper, *Karjalan kommuni* (Karelian Commune), was published as early as November 1920, which, after the Karelian Workers' Commune was reorganized into an autonomous republic, was also renamed as *Punainen Karjala* (Red Karelia). Its circulation grew steadily from 1,350 copies in 1923 to 3,000 in 1928 to 14,500 in 1931. The first Karelian literary magazine was established in the Finnish language in 1928; its original title, *Punakantele* (Red Kantele), was changed in 1932 to *Rintama* (Front). A number of Finnish-language periodicals in a mixed political and literary genre were also published targeting specific audiences, including *Isku* (Strike), *Lokakuu* (October), *Illankuluksi tukkikämpässä* (Spending an Evening in a Loggers' Barrack), *Valtatielle* (To the Highway), and a youth magazine titled *Nuoret iskurit* (Young Shock-Workers). In 1934, Kirja was the fourth largest non-Russian publisher in the RSFSR: that is, in Soviet Russia proper, without other national republics of the USSR.[42] In the mid-1930s, Finnish-language books constituted 13 percent of all library collections in Soviet Karelia, while in libraries in northern Soviet Karelia, where most people could read Finnish, this figure sometimes reached 85 percent.[43] All material preconditions for a boom in Finnish-language literature in Soviet Karelia were thus met.

In 1926, the first professional organization of writers was established in Soviet Karelia under the name of Karelian Association of Proletarian Writers. Like other fields and agencies of cultural

FIGURE 30. ANOKHIN PRESS IN PETROZAVODSK, WHICH SPECIALIZED IN FINNISH-LANGUAGE PRINTING, 1930S (PHOTO BY YA. M. ROSKIN; COURTESY OF THE NATIONAL ARCHIVE OF THE REPUBLIC OF KARELIA).

production in Soviet Karelia, this association was dominated by Finns. Of its forty-four members as of 1931, only nine wrote in Russian and thirty-five in Finnish; affiliated membership through literary circles in Karelian towns and villages added forty-six more members, of whom thirty-one were Finnish, fourteen Karelian, and one Estonian.[44] For over a decade, the professional organization of Karelian writers (in 1934 it was reorganized into the Karelian branch of the Soviet Writers' Union) was headed by Jalmari Virtanen, a Red Finnish poet.

The choice of the name of the Karelian writers' organization was symptomatic: it referred to the Russian Association of Proletarian Writers (RAPP, as it is usually referred to in scholarly literature, using its Russian acronym,) chosen as a patron of Karelian literature among multiple competing writers' organizations and unions of the 1920s. RAPP defined itself as a "weapon" of the cultural policy of the VKP(b) in its struggle against all deviations from the party's "general line"; by taking a similar name, professional writers of Soviet Karelia did not just emphasize their loyalty to policies of the VKP(b) but also adopted a certain aesthetic program. The making of a new Soviet literature included a call for working-class people to become writers; it was the proletariat itself that had to create a new socialist literature, "the literature of readers."[45] American and Canadian immigrants had to become these rank-and-file workers of the literary front in the national literature of Soviet Karelia.

As discussed above, Finnish Americans and Canadians had been recruited to Soviet Karelia as workers and technical specialists; some of them, however, had come with impressive portfolios of published literary work. Santeri Mäkelä (1870–1937 or 1938) published his first poems in Finland in the late 1880s. In 1890, he emigrated to the United States and found a job in the Michigan iron mines. There he published a novel, *Life in Eternal Darkness,* based on his work experience.[46] His 1903 poem "A Pitman's Song" ("Kaivantomiehen laulu"), in which lyrical symbolism was built on Marxist rhetoric of class struggle, became a popular song among American Finns.[47] In 1907, he returned to Finland, where he became a Social Democrat member of the Finnish Diet (1910–14, 1917–18), but he had to flee to Soviet Russia in the aftermath of the Red Guard's defeat in the Finnish Civil War.[48] His literary trajectory finally brought him to political journalism, and throughout the 1920s and the first half of the 1930s he published articles and occasionally poems on revolutionary themes in Soviet Finnish-language journals.[49]

If Mäkelä created and used new literary forms to interpret revolutionary events in Marxist terms—a path that eventually made him primarily a journalist and only then a poet, another American Finnish immigrant, Lauri Luoto (pseudonym of Väinö Sjögren, 1886–1938), wrote in the genre of revolutionary adventure novel. Luoto emigrated to the United States in his youth, where he worked as a lumberjack and miner, but later he returned to Finland and participated in the Finnish Civil War on the Red side. Forced to flee to Soviet Russia after the defeat of the Red Finnish cause, he attempted once again to emigrate to America through Siberia and the Far East, but the Trans-Siberian Railroad at that time was controlled by the White Russian forces of Admiral Kolchak, and Luoto had to stay in Russia. Sometime in the 1920s, he moved to Soviet Karelia. His first novel, *A Refugee,* about the Russian Civil War in Siberia, was published in 1925 by a Finnish American socialist publisher in Superior, Wisconsin, which also published three of his other novels in the same genre of revolutionary adventure, this time about the Finnish Civil War.[50] Luoto was a prolific writer: his four novels totalled over 1,400 pages (each was about 350 pages long), which, in the era of commercial publishing and paper shortages in the USSR of the 1920s, was perhaps too expensive for Soviet Finnish-language publishers, who simply would not have been able to sell enough copies to cover their expenses. There was another reason why his books were published in America: the genre of adventure novel was associated in Soviet literature of the 1920s with petty bourgeois literature since it indulged rather than educated readers.[51] Luoto's entry in the 1932 *Soviet Literary Encyclopedia* was fairly critical of his writing style, arguing that his American novels were characterized by "ideological fallacies (underestimation of the leading role of the proletariat, exaggeration of peasant initiative in a number of local uprisings). . . . [His] language is slipshod and suffers from a romantic pretentiousness."[52] Luoto found his way into Soviet Finnish literature through small literary forms. He published articles and short stories in Soviet Finnish-language newspapers and literary magazines, and in the early 1930s he published two collections of essays on the life of a Finnish American fishing commune in the White Sea and the life of the Finnish Canadian agricultural commune Säde.[53] His three plays written between 1931 and 1935 were staged by the National Finnish Theater of Soviet Karelia.[54]

Mikael Rutanen (1883–1932), the son of a poor peasant from central Finland, had worked in the Finnish forest industry since childhood and emigrated to the United States at the age of fifteen, in 1898. There he became known as a Finnish proletarian poet who romanticized hard manual work in an esthetic close to the European Romantic tradition.[55] It was through this perspective that he perceived Soviet Karelia, to which he emigrated in 1931. There was hardly another Finnish-language poet of the 1930s who wrote of Soviet Karelia in equally enthusiastic terms rooted in Finnish Karelianism of the nineteenth century. His participation in the organized labor movement made the theme of work, especially hard manual toil, central in his poetry, but on a symbolic level it was expressed in Romantic rather than Marxist terms.[56] Rutanen died in a work accident in 1932, less than two years after his immigration, and his Karelian poems were published posthumously.[57]

The fourth prominent Karelian author of North American origin was Eemeli Parras (1884–1939), whose writing was probably the first in the Finnish language to be associated with the canon of socialist realism. He emigrated to Canada from Finland in 1902 at the age of eighteen in search of utopian socialist ideals. A year earlier a group of Finnish socialists under the guidance of Matti Kurikka, a famous partisan of utopian socialism, founded the Finnish commune Sointula (Place of Harmony) on Malcolm Island north of Vancouver Island in British Columbia. The commune boasted the first Finnish Canadian newspaper, *Aika* (Time).[58] Parras joined the commune, but after it was disbanded in 1905 because of financial difficulties he moved to work in copper mines. He joined the Socialist Party of Canada and as a party agitator disseminated socialist ideas in Finnish communities in the United States and Canada. In 1907, Parras returned to Finland to work as a journalist, but three years later he returned to the New World, this time to the United States, where he became an active member of the labor movement. He lectured in workers' clubs and published articles in the Finnish-language socialist newspapers *Työmies* (Worker) and *Toveri* (Comrade).[59] His first book of socialist poetry, *From the Bottom,* was published in 1910.[60] His desire to emphasize social and political tensions in his writing brought him from poetry to the prosaic genres of theater drama and novel: his play *Wild Mountains,* about American miners, was published in 1911,[61] and his novel *Warm Blood and Cold Sweat,* about the life trajectories of three Finns in America, came out three years later.[62] The radicalism of his political views and activities irritated American authorities, and in 1932, after Parras joined the Communist Party USA, he was arrested and deported to Finland. En route to Helsinki, he managed to change his travel itinerary for Leningrad, from where he moved to Petrozavodsk.

In Soviet Karelia, Parras was appointed fiction editor of the Finnish-language press Kirja. He kept on writing prolifically; some of his poems, essays, and short stories dating from the Soviet period were published in his last book, *On Both Sides of the Ocean.*[63] More importantly, his 1933 novel *People of Jymyvaara* was the first Finnish-language novel written in the canon of socialist realism, a system of literary and artistic representations that aimed at no less than the production of socialist reality through literature and art.[64] *People of Jymyvaara,* printed simultaneously in the USSR[65] and America[66] (perhaps the first socialist realist novel to be published in the New World), was an epic novel that traced the history of the Finnish family Jymyvaara from the 1860s to the Finnish Civil War of 1918, framing it in terms and symbols of the collapse of the old patriarchal way of life, class exploitation, the teleological course of history, and revolutionary changes promising the birth of a new society. It set standards of the socialist realist novel as a genre in Soviet Finnish-language and later Karelian-language literatures,[67] and it became an entrance ticket for Parras to the summit of Soviet literature: in 1934, he became a member of the Soviet Writers' Union and represented Soviet Karelia at the First Soviet Writers' Congress. In 1937, he completed another historical novel titled *Maura.* It was never published since, after his arrest in 1938, the manuscript was confiscated and later destroyed.[68]

The call for mass participation in the making of new Soviet literature drew into the ranks of Soviet writers a number of immigrants without previous publishing experience, among them Finnish Americans Sakarias Kankaanpää[69] and Eemeli Rautiainen[70] and Finnish Canadians Salli Lund[71] (pseudonym of Salli Hill) and Ilmari Saarinen,[72] who became renowned after the Second World War. Vieno Levänen from Hancock, Michigan, became a prominent translator of Russian literature into Finnish.[73]

The literature of North American Finnish immigrants in Soviet Karelia was in no way a monolithic cultural phenomenon, but it still involved common patterns and, more importantly, a common direction of its stylistic and semantic evolution. The works outlined above allow for a certain delineation of these patterns and evolution in order to understand how Finnish-speaking authors with American and Canadian life experiences and socialist identities joined the process of the formation of new Soviet socialist literature. North American Finnish writers came to Karelian literature with their specific cultural baggage, which included, in a rather contradictory manner, Finnish neo-Romanticism, for which Soviet Karelia was an important symbolic space, and the experience of socialist writing in which Marxist terminology and revolutionary rhetoric became symbolic images and interpretive frameworks. In Soviet Karelia, these Finnish American and Finnish Canadian authors became actively involved in the making of new socialist realist literature, because its esthetic and political program promised a radical transformation in the future. Both neo-Romanticism and proletarian symbolism of Finnish writers became, despite their seeming contradictoriness, building blocks of socialist realism as a system that aspired to appropriate even stylistically mutually exclusive forms and meanings as long as they could be qualified as proletarian literature, art, or music; this inclusiveness of socialist realism gave Boris Groys, one of its most prominent interpreters, the basis to call it metaphorically "a style and a half."[74]

To a certain degree, Soviet Finnish-language literature retained its own place in this universal system of socialist realism because of specific material and language: the very fact of choosing Finnish for writing made their works part of a different intertextuality in which Elias Lönnrot, Jean Sibelius, or Akseli Gallen-Kallela were more important than Ivan Turgenev, Peter Chaikovsky, or Viktor Vasnetsov. Symptomatically, the main Finnish-language literary magazine published since 1928 in the Soviet Union was called until 1932 *Punakantele* (Red Kantele[75]), which merged in a syncretic manner proletarian and nationalist symbols.[76]

Yet, as American and Canadian immigrant writers were making the new Soviet literature, the new ways of writing, new symbolic interpretations of reality, and new relations between the state and literature were in a dialectical process of making them into Soviet writers. Finnish-language writers helped to create the canon of socialist realism by providing their national symbolism, their individual texts, and, most importantly, their voluntary consent to adapt to its requirements, to put one's individual style and skills at the service of the "common good." In a metaphorical way, they were active builders of the cage of socialist realism that, once completed, would contain them in a narrow field in which one could indeed be "national in form" but express only those meanings loyal to party policies. This can explain, among other things, why Lauri Luoto stopped writing his revolutionary adventure novels at the turn of the 1930s or why in 1937 the head of the Karelian writers' organization, Jalmari Virtanen, wrote a poetic panegyric to Stalin and the Great Terror,[77] in which he would eventually perish, and kept on sending letters even from prison expressing his absolute belief in Stalin and the socialist cause.[78] The participation, however provincial and minuscule, of Soviet Finnish-language writers in the symbolic construction and legitimization of Soviet reality gave them no other way than support of the regime that eventually turned against them.

Repression of Finns and the Finnish language in Soviet Karelia began in the autumn of 1935, at the same time that the written Karelian language was finally created. In June 1937, the Constitution of Soviet Karelia established Karelian as the third official language together with Russian and Finnish. By the end of 1937, the official use of Finnish became de facto prohibited on the national scale, and in April 1938 the Karelian *obkom* of the VKP(b) appealed to Stalin asking him to amend the constitution by removing Finnish from the official languages of the republic.[79] Most of the Finnish-language writers, including Americans and Canadians Luoto, Parras, Mäkelä, and Rautiainen, perished in the Great Terror.

STAGING, PERFORMING, AND EXERCISING NEW IDENTITIES

Despite all the efforts that Soviet elites put into the development of public education, they could not boast about universal literacy throughout the 1930s. In Soviet Karelia, the level of literacy rose from 61.9 percent in 1926 to 76.0 percent in 1932 and kept on rising,[80] but this increase was largely due to adult literacy courses in which people were taught only basic reading and writing skills. New forms and practices of writing and reading were appropriate as instruments to reforge intellectuals, but less educated Soviet masses had to be targeted in a more comprehensible manner. More powerful and effective means of disseminating Soviet ideas among them were required, such as professional and amateur theater, and other forms of performance, as well as radio and eventually cinematography, "the most mass-scale of the arts" in Lenin's words. On the one hand, they mobilized audiences to the Soviet cause, be it enlistment in the Red Army, completion of labor feats, or, more globally, inclusion in the new symbolic order. On the other, they also allowed for the party's control over esthetic and political self-expression of revolutionary masses, especially among youth. Performing arts as a form of cultural production and consumption, as well as workers,' peasants,' and youth clubs as their locus, became a vital part of Soviet cultural policy.[81]

The cultural practices of North American Finns were a perfect fit for the objectives that Soviet authorities set for performance genres. Finnish communities in the United States and Canada were split along political lines: the Finnish Lutheran Church served as the central organizing force of social life for Finns who leaned toward conservative political views, while the social activities of politically radical Finnish communities were organized around workers' clubs, in which numerous amateur theaters, orchestras, and dance bands functioned.[82] Since emigrants to the Soviet Union were recruited entirely from the latter group, upon arrival there they discovered that their experience on the amateur stage was claimed for making a new socialist national culture in Soviet Karelia, in exactly this combination of international and ethnic rhetoric. Within a few years, many of those who came to work as lumberjacks or construction workers changed their primary employment for theaters, music bands, or local radio, attracted by the new possibility of realizing their identities through cultural production.

Theater was the first performing art totally transformed by a large influx of American and Canadian immigrants. Finnish-language amateur theaters existed in Soviet Karelia throughout the 1920s, but only in the autumn of 1932, after an entire amateur theater troupe headed by Kuuno Sevander arrived from America, did a professional Finnish theater, officially named National Theater of the Karelian ASSR, begin its first season in Petrozavodsk. Ragnar Nyström (literary pseudonym Ragnar Rusko), a prominent Red Finnish writer and dramatist, was its first manager and artistic director until his arrest in 1937.[83]

Together with works by prominent Finnish and Russian authors, the National Theater of Soviet Karelia staged multiple plays written by Finnish immigrants. Most of them, including all plays by Nyström, were thematically built around the Finnish Civil War, hardly surprising given that both actors and their audience were either its former participants or sympathizers on the Red side. Estheticization through theatrical performance of their personal experiences of revolutionary events, subsequent defeat in the struggle against the White side, and finding a new home in Soviet Russia allowed for repeated restoration of the starting point at which their sociopolitical group emerged. Theater was thereby an important way of reinforcing their identities in the Soviet cultural milieu, which, during the 1930s, was actually becoming increasingly less revolutionary. American cultural influences that immigrants brought with them provided additional imagery for this estheticization of revolution. In 1935, the National Theater staged a musical play titled *Herra Melperi lähtee sotaan* (Malbrouck Goes Off to the War) about a failed White Finnish raid on Soviet Karelia during the summer of 1919. Kalle Rautio, one of its two composers and a graduate of the Department of Music at the University of California, brought into the play elements of a Broadway musical, which made *Herra Melperi lähtee sotaan,* according to contemporary accounts, a hit among the Karelian public.[84]

Similar professionalization of amateur performance happened in folk singing and dancing in the USSR. In the 1930s, under the auspices of the state, numerous professional singing and dancing ensembles emerged that performed what was defined as "folk" performance forms. As recent research suggests, while the repertoires of these ensembles were built on the use of authentic forms of folk singing and dancing, they actually contributed to the evisceration of ethnic cultures and the dissemination of Soviet meanings under their disguise,[85] acting in a way analogous to mechanisms of the modern myth as described by Roland Barthes.[86]

American and Canadian Finns were perfect executors of these Soviet cultural policies

FIGURE 31. FINNISH AMATEUR BALLET TROUPE FROM KONDOPOGA PERFORMING *ICE HOUSE* IN THE SUMMER PARK OF PETROZAVODSK, 6 JULY 1935 (PHOTOGRAPHER UNKNOWN; COURTESY OF THE NATIONAL ARCHIVE OF THE REPUBLIC OF KARELIA).

in Soviet Karelia. Combining Finnish ethnicity and socialist views, they literally embodied Stalin's formula of cultures national in form but socialist in content, while their previous experience in amateur performance in their home communities in North America gave them necessary skills to fill the demand for the professional performance of folk art. It was only natural that their contribution was instrumental in the professionalization of folk singing and dancing culture in Soviet Karelia. In particular, they played a crucial role in the formative period of the state dancing and singing ensemble Kantele, established in 1936. Kalle Rautio adapted Karelian and Finnish folk melodies into scenic music that could be performed by the Kantele's orchestra of folk stringed instruments. Sirkka Rikka, whose singing career started in a Finnish workers' club in Detroit, was the leading singer of the ensemble from its early years well into the 1960s. Similarly, Chicago-born Kerttu Viljanen was one of the ensemble's core musicians from its establishment to the 1960s, whereas the career of Canadian-born dancer Elsa Balandis (née Lehtonen) in Kantele spanned 1942 to 1962. There were a number of other American and Canadian immigrants whose careers were less brilliant or lasting, but they all, nevertheless, constituted the core of the first generation of professional performers of folk singing and dancing in Soviet Karelia.[87]

Symphonic music was yet another cultural sphere in Soviet Karelia transformed by North American immigrants. Some of them had professional music education, while many more had experience in playing in amateur bands in American and Canadian workers' clubs. Kalle Rautio, mentioned above in the context of Karelian theater and folk music, was one of the most prominent figures in the history of symphonic music in Soviet Karelia. He emigrated from the United States in 1922 with a degree in music from the University of California, and

FIGURE 32. SIRKKA RIKKA, PEOPLE'S ACTRESS OF SOVIET KARELIA, AT A CONCERT DURING THE KARELIAN-FINNISH MUSIC AND DANCE WEEK IN MOSCOW, OCTOBER 1951 (COURTESY OF THE NATIONAL ARCHIVE OF THE REPUBLIC OF KARELIA).

in 1931 he became the founder of the first professional symphonic orchestra in Petrozavodsk. Of its fifteen musicians, eleven were Canadian or American. In 1933, it became affiliated with the republican radio broadcasting service and became de facto the national symphonic orchestra of Soviet Karelia. Rautio was made its second conductor, while its staff numbered already fifteen musicians from North America.[88]

American Finns also brought to Soviet Karelia jazz, which became a prominent phenomenon of its cultural life, especially in Petrozavodsk. Finnish musicians organized a jazz band that regularly played in the town park during much of the 1930s. Although initially the audience was made up entirely of other immigrants, this American jazz band gradually attracted more Russian fans, to the degree that it was a noticeable factor in the modernization of urban life in Petrozavodsk—until 1937, when nearly all of its members were arrested and sentenced to forced labor in gulag camps.[89]

Together with literature and performing arts as important means of making a modern subject, all visions of modernity—capitalist and socialist alike—dictated that not only should people's souls and minds be educated through language and culture but also that their bodies should be disciplined and improved through newly created institutions of sport and physical culture. Just as Bolsheviks regarded the Soviet population as illiterate and uncultured, needing to be educated and inculcated into proper high culture, so too were they equally disappointed with the insufficient readiness of Soviet people's bodies to become involved in the process of socialist construction.[90] In 1935, the official republican newspaper *Red Karelia* wrote regarding the state and development of physical culture (*fizkultura*) in Soviet Karelia:

> Who are our enthusiasts of physical culture?
> Karelia has a tiny group of old [prerevolutionary] enthusiasts. There are thousands of young athletes, the majority of whom don't have yet either good technique or sufficient practical experience and skills. There is the third group of enthusiasts of physical culture, and a rather big one. It is Finnish comrades who moved to Karelia from Finland and America. All of them are good sportsmen who have since early childhood been involved in athletics, gymnastics, skiing, wrestling, and other kinds of sports.
> These [Finnish] activists of physical culture currently occupy top ranks in almost all kinds of sports in Karelia. It is from them that we form first-class teams of skiers, wrestlers, and athletes to participate in different all-Soviet sports competitions.[91]

Soviet authorities and press readily admitted that in terms of fitness Finnish immigrants stood much closer to ideals of physical development than the Soviet population, who were just learning ("don't have yet either good technique or sufficient practical experience") ways to embody—literally through sports—the socialist image of modern men and women. Finnish Americans and Canadians fit Bolshevik visions of how the modern body should look, because their participation in sports and recreational activities was the result of Western modernity, which during the 1920s and first half of the 1930s remained a point of reference for Soviet authorities and rank-and-file builders of socialism alike.[92]

As for immigrants themselves, participation in sports activities became an important means to maintain their distinctive American or Canadian identity. The most popular sport in their communities prior to the Great Terror was, characteristically, baseball. It was not a purely Karelian phenomenon: as mentioned in Chapter 1, Finns were just one group among

FIGURE 33. A GYMNASTIC PERFORMANCE OF STUDENTS FROM FINNISH SECONDARY SCHOOL NO. 2 OF PETROZAVODSK, 1933 (PHOTOGRAPHER UNKNOWN; COURTESY OF THE NATIONAL ARCHIVE OF THE REPUBLIC OF KARELIA).

FIGURE 34. ATHLETES OF THE FINNISH SECONDARY SCHOOL NO. 2 OF PETROZAVODSK IN A STADIUM, PETROZAVODSK, 1933 (PHOTO BY I. BELOV; COURTESY OF THE NATIONAL ARCHIVE OF THE REPUBLIC OF KARELIA).

immigrants from North America to the Soviet Union in the 1920s and 1930s, and baseball was extremely popular among youth in American communities in the USSR. The largest of them, based in Moscow and Nizhny Novgorod, boasted several baseball teams. In June 1934, the Soviet English-language newspaper the *Moscow News* helped to organize an amateur baseball tournament that pitted teams from Moscow and Nizhny Novgorod against each other; the team of the Moscow Foreign Workers' Club easily defeated its opponents.[93]

Baseball fever among Finnish Americans in Soviet Karelia was so high by that time that in 1933 they had five men's and two women's teams.[94] By 1934, an amateur league had been organized in Petrozavodsk, and the league's statistics were occasionally published in the *Moscow News*.[95] It was also through this newspaper that Finnish American baseball players from Petrozavodsk challenged the team of the Moscow Foreign Workers' Club, which had just defeated its opponents from Nizhny Novgorod; Muscovite Americans accepted the challenge and in July 1934 came to Soviet Karelia for a two-game series. The Karelian team headed by Albert Long from Detroit won both games (12–7 and 12–2). A return match was held in Moscow the next month, which also ended with the victory of the Karelian team 14–9.[96]

Despite its distinct, even conspicuous, Americanness, Soviet authorities initially encouraged and popularized baseball as part of their efforts to modernize physical culture in the USSR.[97] This tolerance, however, was short lived, ending with the onslaught of the Great Terror, which claimed many Finnish American amateur players, including the Karelian captain Long, arrested in July 1938 and sentenced to three years in gulag camps.[98]

The phenomena discussed in this chapter are a good example of the crooked line of cultural modernization that Bolshevik ideologists envisioned for the Soviet population in the 1920s and the first half of the 1930s, which they implemented in Soviet Karelia with the help of American and Canadian immigrants, who acted as agents of this modernization, and which they seemingly abruptly abandoned in the period between 1935 and 1937. Enchanted by visions of technical and cultural progress in the West, Soviet elites extensively appealed to Western technological knowledge and cultural models as instruments to promote their own socialist version of the modern state and population. Such a small group as American and Canadian immigrants were in Soviet Karelia could become so prominent in its cultural life during the first half of the 1930s only because their cultural competence from experience in modern Western societies was an exact fit with reformist visions of Soviet leaders.

And then in the middle of the 1930s came a changed attitude to everything foreign, including the role of immigrants in the making of Soviet culture. As Sergey Zhuravliov, a historian of Western immigration to the USSR, framed it in contemporary terms, the principal question in which all forms of interaction between Soviet society and immigrants were rooted changed from "what should we learn from foreign workers?" to "what should foreigners learn in the USSR?"[99]; Michael David-Fox metaphorically called this shift "the Stalinist superiority complex."[100] In this changed national context of the latter half of the 1930s, North American immigrants were no longer perceived as Communist *kulturtragers*, whose cultural patterns should be mastered by the Karelian population, while those North American cultural forms that had implanted in Soviet Karelia became increasingly criticized as "petty bourgeois" and "harmful."

FIGURE 35. AN ATHLETIC PERFORMANCE IN THE STADIUM DINAMO IN PETROZAVODSK, 1935 (PHOTOGRAPHER UNKNOWN; COURTESY OF THE NATIONAL ARCHIVE OF THE REPUBLIC OF KARELIA).

FIGURE 36. IMMIGRANT WORKERS OF THE PETROZAVODSK SKI FACTORY DURING THEIR LEISURE TIME, 1930S (COURTESY OF THE NATIONAL ARCHIVE OF THE REPUBLIC OF KARELIA).

CHAPTER 7

Challenges of Cross-Cultural Communication

IN RECONSTRUCTING THE NATURE OF CROSS-CULTURAL COMMUNICATION BETWEEN the population of Soviet Karelia and North American immigrants, the main problem is that of source criticism. The largest group of documentary sources is comprised of Soviet official documents, including reports of the OGPU and later NKVD, which encompassed public sentiment among Soviet people. These reports reproduced opinions, complaints, and occasional enunciations, which could be submitted as letters or anonymous reports, but informants presented certain information and omitted other information, and nearly always they removed the original contexts in which the statements were made. Private sources, such as letters, diaries, interviews, and memoirs, complement the information from official documents and allow for its verification. However, the social background of opinions reflected in these two groups of documents was, as a rule, different: VKP(b) organizations and the OGPU/NKVD were more interested in rumors and sentiments among workers and the rural population, while authors of diaries or memoirs were commonly intellectuals who sought to retain their voices in history. Besides, an interpretation of private writing also needs to take into account the time, place, and conditions of the writing, its purpose, censorship (including inspection of private mail), ideological and personal biases, traumatic syndrome of repressions, war, and many other factors.

Criticism of sources is complicated by the problem of hermeneutical circle: namely, how to combine, evaluate, and use evidence from various, often contradictory, and always biased sources on the practices of communication between cultural groups, if this communication itself was based on a combination of cultural values, stereotypes, and biases. The perception of North American (and, more broadly, all Finnish) immigrants by the inhabitants of Soviet Karelia formed and changed under the influence of economic considerations of everyday life, which, in a whimsical manner, were intertwined with ethnic stereotypes, some of which had long existed in Russian-Finnish cultural interaction, while some were a recent invention of the Soviet modernist project. American and Canadian immigrants, in turn, confronted a society that was drastically different from their ideas of a "socialist paradise."

FROM THE IMAGE OF NEIGHBOR TO THE IMAGE OF ENEMY

By the early twentieth century, Russian society had a generally positive image of Finns constructed mainly through numerous itineraries and travelogues published in abundance by Russian travelers, officials, journalists, and writers. Even a tsarist assault on Finland's autonomy at the turn of the twentieth century and a subsequent wave of publications that was highly critical of Finland could not change much this ethnic image constructed since incorporation of Finland into the Russian Empire in 1809. Most descriptions of the Finnish national character represented Finns as hard-working people who were resolute, silent, slow, reliable, honest, and law abiding.[1]

As for the population of Russian Karelia, close economic ties between Karelians and Finns and the end of military conflicts on the Russian-Finnish border after 1809 also contributed to a generally positive image of the Finn among the Karelian population, which in many ways coincided with a stereotyped image of the Finn in Russian literature and press. The centuries-old confrontation between Russia and Sweden, of which Finland was part prior to 1809, had, of course, a strong effect on the mutual perception of people living on both sides of the border. It is symptomatic, however, that in Karelian villages enemies coming from across the border were called Ruočči, Swedes, even if they spoke Finnish.[2] Large-scale Finnish immigration to Olonets province in the second half of the nineteenth century also did not lead to ethnic conflict with or resentment among the local population: in sparsely populated Karelia, there were work opportunities for all, and Karelian peasants living in border areas could, in turn, make good money by selling to Finland fish or game or by harvesting timber for Finnish contractors. It is hardly surprising that after the Bolshevik Revolution, especially in the years of hunger, inhabitants of Karelian villages long remembered these opportunities with nostalgia.[3]

The rise of the Bolsheviks to power, the emergence of independent Finland in the political landscape, and military confrontations on the Soviet-Finnish border, which between 1918 and 1922 turned into several conflicts when Finnish volunteer and regular detachments made incursions into Russian Karelia, had negative impacts on mutual images of the neighbors. In addition, Soviet propaganda of the 1920s and 1930s constructed bourgeois Finland as an open enemy that desired to crush the young Soviet state. Political slogans and stereotypes of the first two Soviet decades redefined the laborious Finn as a class enemy, a "white bandit," or a "bloodthirsty butcher."

From the beginning, Soviet propaganda created and disseminated through the press two images of Finland and Finns. Together with attacks on white bourgeois Finland, the Soviet press published articles that constructed an image of "tormented red Finland," "a brother and closest ally" of Soviet Karelia that would get up off its knees assisted by "the brawny hand of Red Finns."[4] Yet verbal imagery associated with Finland as an enemy was much stronger and more frequent. During the years of early Soviet-Finnish conflicts, Soviet newspapers unceremoniously described Finland with metaphors such as "a cat in a tiger costume" or "a shark that encroaches on somebody else's property" and wrote of "impudent shamelessness of the government in Helsingfors," which tried to reach its hands into the resources and riches of its neighbor and aspired to make Russian Karelia a Finnish colony.[5]

In the late 1920s, Finland was increasingly characterized as "fascist,"[6] but after a failed Mäntsälä rebellion of 1932 (Soviet Karelian newspapers called it a "fascist coup,"[7] which it basically was) and the ensuing collapse of the Lapua movement, a major radical right-wing organization behind the coup, the more established concept of "white Finland" once again became dominant in Soviet newspapers. During the 1930s, after ideas of a world revolution silently disappeared from the Soviet political agenda and the Soviet leadership concentrated on "building socialism in one country," the number of articles related to Finland in the Karelian press gradually decreased and were thematically reduced to anniversary articles (celebration of the fifteen-year anniversary of the Finnish Revolution) or reprints of publications from the central Soviet press on Finnish war preparations or certain aspects of Soviet-Finnish relations.[8]

The inhabitants of Soviet Karelia had mixed feelings about these black-and-white stereotypes dictated to them by Bolshevik propaganda. In the first years after the Bolshevik Revolution and Russian Civil War, the population of Soviet Karelia, especially of its border areas, which were directly affected by Soviet-Finnish conflicts, could easily be influenced by reports of "Finnish danger" and felt animosity toward "white Finnish bandits." At the same time, the closer people lived to the border, which in the 1920s remained easy to cross illegally, the easier it was for them to compare lifestyles and policies on both Finnish and Soviet sides. This comparison often was not in favor of the latter, which, to a certain degree, negated the efforts of Soviet propaganda to convince people that Finnish neighbors were their main enemy. Quite the contrary, the Karelian population increasingly tended to blame their misfortunes on the new power that, as they believed, had brought only hunger and unemployment. In this context, anti-Soviet propaganda from Finland in the early 1920s had a much stronger effect than Bolshevik agitation. This was evidenced by thousands of Karelian refugees who saw the main danger for their families not in white Finnish incursions but in the Bolsheviks in power and who sought refuge in white Finland so much hated by Soviet leaders.[9]

When the Civil War was over, the Soviet government set a goal to "distract attention of Karelians from Finland,"[10] which had to be implemented, in particular, by émigré Finnish Communists. The government of Edvard Gylling sent Red Finns to establish Soviet power in ethnic Karelian regions, for it believed that they would find a common language with people who barely spoke Russian easier than Bolshevik activists. Most Red Finns, however, were former industrial workers full of revolutionary enthusiasm, but hardly aware of the peculiarities of rural life, which caused additional problems when they communicated with Karelian peasants. Finnish Communist émigrés readily condemned the "white bourgeois regime" of Finland but had no means to effectively fight hunger and unemployment, so their arguments deflated; moreover, because of very poor infrastructure on the Russian side, provisions to certain remote Karelian areas could be delivered in winter and spring months only from Finland, which strengthened the sympathies of Karelians for their neighbors.[11]

Since Red Finns were the immediate authority that represented the Bolshevik power in Karelian areas, local inhabitants started to blame them as the people responsible for their misfortunes. Economic hardships among the Karelian population resulted in images of white Finnish aggressors, which they adopted from Soviet narratives, superimposed onto Soviet Finnish leaders. Soviet security organs kept a close eye on this tendency. In its report for May 1928, the GPU of Soviet Karelia informed the Soviet government that

> there is widespread antagonistic sentiment among the Karelian population toward Finns, which is caused, on the one hand, by the introduction of school teaching in Finnish and, on the other hand, by a large number of Finns in the central administrative bodies of Karelia. This also leads to talks of a possible incorporation of Karelia into Finland: "Finns are at the head of our government, Finnish is taught in schools, and what if we will be annexed by Finland?" Kulaks and the well-to-do element of the Karelian population try to intensify this sentiment using agitation: "While we have Finns at

power, we will live poor, because they issue wrong laws," and in a number of cases they claimed: "We should create our own organization and expel all Finns from the government."[12]

However, anti-Finnish feelings among the local population were seldom addressed to the Karelian government. Instead, their grievances were aimed first at local officials and managers, who were always in the public eye. People were dissatisfied with the current state of affairs in management: "Why [do] Finns keep on occupying leading positions in the [state timber trust] Karelles, while Karelians are not allowed to them?" Such sentiments were sometimes generalized to the entire Finnish leadership of Soviet Karelia, and this was perceived by Soviet authorities as a real threat. Some Karelian returnees who fled to Finland during the Civil War, for example, argued that in Finland they were treated much better than back home, where "[Red] Finns control everything and life is miserable," and they called for the "expulsion of red scoundrels from Karelia."[13] Similar complaints were made by workers of factories in which the top management consisted of Finns: complaints included wage discrimination of Russians compared with Finns and Karelians as well as the reserve and self-restraint of Finns and their tendency to keep their distance from others, to "stick to their nationality." Workers of the Kondopoga pulp and paper plant complained that "there are two classes in Karelia: exploiting Finns and exploited Russians and Karelians, [and] this should be eliminated before it is too late."[14]

This confrontation between Red Finns and the local population embodied, in fact, a much larger conflict between Soviet authorities and this population. Similar antagonism could be observed in places and organizations where Karelians, Russians, or Jews occupied authoritative positions. Inhabitants of northern Karelia were reported to say that "there was one revolution in Karelia, but we will have to make a second one, for too many Russian administrators came to us," while workers of a lumber mill in Medvezhyegorsk complained of a "Jewish stranglehold" because "managerial positions were all occupied by Jews."[15]

Thus, by the late 1920s, the image of Finland and Finns formed in Karelian society was quite discrepant. Bourgeois Finland and its revolutionary proletariat, which "suffered under the yoke of white terror," as newspapers wrote, were somewhere far away, while Red Finns were nearby, and among the local population they were perceived as "masters" (*khoziaeva*) dreaming of taking over their native land or sometimes even as a "fifth column": "Now, under Soviet power, there are many Finns working as Soviet bureaucrats, but if a war breaks out they would betray, as [Russian] Germans betrayed in old times under Nicolas [II]."[16] During the 1920s, this image of an internal alien clearly dominated images of hostile Finnish bourgeoisie and friendly Finnish proletariat imposed by Soviet propaganda.

To make things even more complicated, the Finnish influence on Karelian territories was still strong in the 1920s, and idealized memories of prerevolutionary life accentuated current economic hardships and provoked accusations: "If we had been annexed to Finland, we would have lived much better. If Finns hadn't given away Karelia in 1920, we would have lived like barons."[17] At the end of the 1920s, the population of border regions listened almost exclusively to Finnish radio stations, which, as Soviet party documents worrisomely noted, would have a negative impact on "politically undeveloped listeners."[18]

The situation gradually changed during the 1930s. A new generation came of age, for which prerevolutionary cross-border contacts were only stories and which was educated into a new Soviet symbolic order. Soviet people became more literate and read newspapers more, and a network of propagandists was expanding, as was the number of schools, clubs, libraries, radio sets, and cinemas. Higher literacy rates and new methods of ideological influence entailed a larger degree of propaganda absorption among the Soviet population.

Still, old problems remained, and new ones appeared: the same low wages and an insufficient supply of provisions and merchandise were now augmented by forced collectivization, increased taxation, and intensified repression. With all this in the background, ethnic conflicts were pushed to the sidelines; besides, after 1935, when the Red Finnish government of Gylling was removed from power, Finns were no longer associated with the Soviet order. Criticism was now directed more at the supreme Soviet leadership, which "reigned to the degree when workers starve or have to eat horses" and "torture[d] peasants, forcing them into *kolkhozes* as if they were slaves."[19] At the same time, people increasingly tended to accept official propaganda, which convinced them that foreign capital and domestic enemies were the main culprits of the difficulties that Soviet people had to overcome. In this situation, the image of Finland as a hostile state became an increasingly dominant social stereotype among the Karelian population.

Two new groups of Finnish immigrants who arrived in the early 1930s—labor immigrants from North America and illegal immigrants from Finland—created new problems in interethnic relations in Soviet Karelia. This time, however, ethnic tensions between newcomers from the United States and Canada and local inhabitants arose on a different, more pragmatic, level, since they were now caused by economic and quotidian, rather than political, grievances.

"BOURGEOISIE HAS COME TO US IN BIG NUMBERS . . ."

American and Canadian immigrants of the early 1930s found themselves in a society in which the concepts of red and white, proletarian and bourgeois, socialism and capitalism had become cultural categories and were internalized within a rigid dichotomy of self and other. Adaptation to this society for immigrants from the North American world of Finnish socialism, which was also politicized, but in a very different manner, turned out to be a difficult process.

With the beginning of immigration from North America, the Karelian press launched a campaign to shape a positive image of immigrants among the local population. Central and regional newspapers published numerous enthusiastic responses of immigrants regarding Soviet realities and described in detail their "labor feats and achievements." Newspapers carried headlines such as "To Borrow the Experience of Americans," "Canadian Workers in Karelian Forests," "Canadian Lumberjacks Greet the Address of the [Karelian] *Obkom,*" "None of Us Will Return to America," "Masters, Not Slaves," and "We Came to Help."[20] Yet the image of North American immigrants actually forming among the local population was drastically different from the one imposed through the press. Partly, it was caused by cultural differences in cultural categories and values of the mostly urbanized immigrant group from North America and the predominantly rural population in Soviet Karelia. But the main reason, once again, was economic: American and Canadian Finns were perceived by the half-starved people of Soviet Karelia not as a separate ethnic group but as "foreigners," "spongers," and "bourgeoisie" who had arrived to take away their rights and workplaces.

Leaving the New World, emigrants idealistically believed that they were headed for a country where true equality had been achieved, where there were no crises or unemployment, and where all people lived like one big family, working and recreating together.[21] Upon arrival, they found themselves in a stratified society based on the political and economic inequality of different social groups. But here, unlike in North America, they occupied one of the highest positions in the social hierarchy. Immigrants were exempted from agricultural taxation for ten years and from income tax for three years, had special food rationing, had a first right to housing and entry into universities, and were exempted from military conscription.[22]

North American immigrants were well aware of the peculiarities of their social position: "We were not some sort of border hoppers but legal immigrants who came upon invitation and had contract jobs. We had special rights and special privileges."[23] Immigrants took these privileges for granted: "We occupied a special position, as we had our own food rationing. . . . If it hadn't been for it, none of us would have lived here in Karelia even one day."[24] And they could hardly understand how the local population could survive on such meager wages without any additional rationing: "Only American Finns purchased food in Insnab[25] shops. . . . Besides, our norms of rationing were special, larger than average. But how could Russian people survive, without any benefits of this kind, I cannot understand even now."[26]

It was natural that privileges that American and Canadian immigrants enjoyed caused envy and hatred among the local population. People were reported to have said that "Americans came here to eat our bread!"; and "Bourgeoisie has come to us in big numbers, they are fed, while Russian workers can starve to death, and nobody will care."[27]

The salaries of North American immigrants as a rule were significantly higher than those of local workers and were not always justified by their higher qualifications. Differences in wages could reach an astonishing 80 percent, as in the factory Onezhskii in Petrozavodsk, where immigrant workers earned 180 rubles a month and local workers earned only 100 rubles.[28] In the building trust Stroiob'iedinenie, a Russian worker earned on average 45 percent less than an American or Canadian worker (median salaries were 143.30 and 207.45 rubles respectively).[29] Russian workers were outraged that immigrants were given higher salaries for similar work and that they were often appointed to better-paid positions at the expense of local workers: "[The management] of our workshop doesn't like Russians, Americans are placed to all good positions, while we are transferred to day work, but on the other hand we work accordingly: in canteen, smoking room, and toilet."[30]

Competition over limited economic resources was not the only factor to determine difficult and often conflicted relations between immigrants and the local population. Cultural factors were of equal importance because of huge differences in social values, norms, and visions of the proper order of things.

Immigrants could not understand or refused to accept many things in the surrounding reality. In workplaces, they were particularly sensitive to unjust distribution of wages, poor organization of labor, long idle times and regular shock-work, as well as bureaucratization and inertia of Soviet industrial management. Unlike Russian workers, who took much of this for granted, immigrants demanded from factory managers effective organization of work, timely and just payments, regular vacations, and good housing. In cases of conflict, they tended to use the same methods as they had in America or Canada: stoppages, walkouts, ultimatums.[31] Such actions often caused irritation among local workers, who saw in them violations of Soviet work ethics, while authorities assessed them as a complete failure to understand "practical questions of [socialist] building, difficulties of the transition period, and especially the tactics of our party."[32]

Heavy-handed dealing with immigration by local authorities also contributed to escalations of conflict between the population of Soviet Karelia and North American immigrants. Resolutions of the VKP(b) and the Karelian government adopted to ensure proper conditions of life and work for immigrants were sometimes implemented in absurd ways. Local inhabitants were already indignant about immigrants' higher salaries and priority in the distribution of housing and food; yet, according to documents of the 1930s, many conflicts were sparked not because of concrete actions but by the contemptuous manner in which Soviet officials explained these privileges: "Food is not for you, but for Americans, and you will get along without it";[33] "You need housing? I know it. I have normal housing, but I won't give it to you. We expect qualified foreign workers to arrive and spare housing for them. And who are you? Unskilled workers. Do you think we can provide housing to unskilled workers?"[34]

The great attention that the Karelian press paid to American and Canadian immigrants sometimes also irritated local people. Some publications even sparked new outbreaks of hostility. For example, in August 1932, ten Russian and Finnish workers went by boat to a summer cottage across a small bay of Lake Onega. The boat capsized, and six men—including four Finns and two Russians—drowned. The government of Soviet Karelia expressed condolences to the families of the immigrants who had died through obituaries published in the leading Karelian newspaper, *Krasnaia Karelia,* and provided allocated funds for their funerals. Families additionally received accident benefits of 1,000 rubles each. No word was mentioned of the two dead Russians, however.[35]

Finally, American and Canadian immigrants themselves stirred up interethnic tensions. Educated in cultural categories based on Western progressivism—which was only reinforced by their allegiance to socialist ideas—many of them, especially initially, demonstrated rather cynical and contemptuous attitudes toward the population of Soviet Karelia, regarding Russians as backward people who were barely capable of order and progress.[36] If appointed to managerial positions, they tended to promote their compatriots at the expense of other workers. In April 1932, Russian workers employed at the October Revolution logging factory refused to work as a protest against preferences that the manager of the machine shop, Peterson, and his deputy, Mäki, gave to other Finns, sometimes to the detriment of the production process. Peterson, in particular, dismissed a Russian foreman to appoint his son to the position, even though the latter had no experience in this kind of work. Moreover, his salary was increased to forty-seven rubles a day, a fantastic sum for the time.[37] American and Canadian managers were also sometimes involved in a cover-up of disciplinary violations of their compatriots.[38]

Workplace conflicts sometimes led to serious accidents that endangered people's lives. According to a report written by the master mechanic of the factory Onezhskii in Petrozavodsk, during just ten days in April 1933, four accidents occurred in which enough evidence was collected to prove that they had been orchestrated. The most serious was when a Russian mechanic, knowing that an American shift would follow, drained hot water from a tank before leaving. In the ensuing accident, several people were burned.[39]

Interethnic relations were equally complicated on the level of everyday life, at which cultural differences sharply revealed themselves. Back in North America, Finnish immigrants were a socially disadvantaged group, especially in Canada, where most Finns were recent arrivals and living standards in Finnish communities were below average. Emigration to Soviet Karelia turned out to be an ascent in the social order, and local people immediately labeled American and Canadian immigrants as "moneybags" and "bourgeoisie." But immigrants thought that their increased social position did not bring any economic benefits but rather the reverse. Used to higher living standards, in Soviet Karelia they found themselves without things that they regarded as vital. In letters to relatives in the United States and

Canada, they asked them to send certain "must-haves," which were not limited to clothes (sweaters, underwear, socks, shoes) and foodstuffs (coffee, biscuits, candies). Immigrants complained that they lacked things that were parts of their lives in North America: alarm clocks, cameras, typewriters, calendars, notebooks, musical instruments. Young immigrants longed for chewing gum.[40] For immigrants, especially younger ones, these things were needed to materialize their American or Canadian identity, but for local people all these things were exotic curiosities that enlarged the gap between the two social groups. American and Canadian clothes, at least at the initial stage of immigration, also marked a drastic difference between immigrants and local inhabitants. This difference was one of the clearest recollections in an interview with a Canadian, Elsa Balandis, who had arrived in Soviet Karelia with her parents in 1933:

> We lived in a barrack of the pulp and paper plant in Kondopoga. People walked to work—and there was a lot of dirt there and other—so they walked in bast sandals [*lapti*]! Shoes made of bast. There were nails in barrack walls, and I was always curious what they were for. So bast sandals get wet, and they hung them on nails so that they would dry up, and everybody had his own nail. And I once gathered all these bast sandals, brought to the barrack, and said to mother: "Look what I've found!" She immediately answered: "Well, of all things, what have you done—these are shoes!" "What shoes? These things are shoes?" "Go and put them back in place immediately, people will be searching for them, they need them to go tomorrow to work."[41]

The desire of Finnish immigrants to create comfort and maintain cleanness, or at least their surrogates, even in the crowded communal life of Soviet barracks, was often interpreted by their neighbors as petty-bourgeois. Immigrants, in opposition, could not conceal their disdain for their neighbors for their untidiness. Even seventy years later one of them remembered that the "houses of Russians and Finns could be distinguished from afar. They [Russians] never cleaned their yards, piled garbage just outside their doors, and during the time we shared one roof with them they never even painted their window frames."[42] These cultural differences were especially visible and important to women. Both in Finland itself and in Finnish communities in the New World, married women typically left the labor force when their children were born to take on the role of full-time housewives, and they tended to retain this social role during the early years of immigration in Soviet Karelia. Soviet women, on the other hand, were loaded with a double burden of industrial and domestic labor and could not invest the same amount of time and effort in maintaining their homes. Finnish women, in the spirit of progressivism typical among Finnish immigrant communities of the early twentieth century, expressed disdain for dirty floors, "uncultured" children, and neglected yards of their Russian neighbors. The latter, in response, stuck to Soviet ideological clichés in accusing Finnish women of being "spongers" and "idlers" who had learned in their bourgeois home countries how to live at somebody else's expense.[43] Both sides, then, used cultural clichés to dress up everyday antagonism toward each other. The Soviet authorities registered these conflicts together with those in workplaces: "Wives of foreign workers who are disconnected from labor and don't know the [Russian] language lead a secluded way of life and are often subject to unhealthy moods caused by daily problems."[44] Similar situations in which women tended to evaluate Soviet realities much more skeptically than their husbands because of their deeper immersion in quotidian activities were typical of other immigrant communities all over the Soviet Union.[45]

Cultural activities of North American immigrants—amateur theaters, choirs, sports groups, orchestras, outings—also produced misunderstandings. Their neighbors sometimes refused to believe that in half-starved Soviet Karelia of the early 1930s, without proper means of subsistence, one could become involved in such recreational activities. Sometimes this misunderstanding developed into rumors that Americans and Canadians, apart from special Insnab rationing rates for foreign specialists, received additional rations from the Red Finnish authorities of Soviet Karelia. These rumors appealed to the logic of how, otherwise, immigrants could sing, play, or compete in sports while people around them were hungry most of the time.[46]

The language barrier was another important reason that slowed integration processes and provoked tensions. In the first years after immigration, Americans and Canadians, especially women who stayed at home, expressed little desire to learn Russian, which Soviet official documents interpreted as a disturbing reluctance. According to data of Petrozavodsk professional unions, at the end of 1932, 821 immigrants were members of different sports groups, while only twenty-one attended a group of Russian-language learners.[47] Wide use of Finnish in the first half of the 1930s in Soviet Karelia was only one reason for this reluctance to learn Russian. Another was unwillingness to accept the surrounding social and cultural reality as one's own, often revealed in the rejection of Russian language and culture. Mayme Sevander recalled in her memoir that "many people, just like mother, didn't learn the Russian language. In all her time in the United States, my mother had never mastered English, and Russian was impossible for her; when she saw the alphabet, she just shook her head."[48] In a way, American/Canadian and Soviet linguistic experiences of older first-generation immigrants were similar. Unable—or unwilling—to accommodate their identities to new sociocultural realities, they stuck to their ethnic communities, where they could reproduce cultural models brought from Finland.

Most interethnic conflicts between immigrants and the local population in workplaces or at home cannot be explained through simple causal logic: seemingly simple events occurred because of a complex network of social and cultural factors, and what one can take as a cause was actually a trigger unleashing a much deeper process. So, underlying a conflict between Finnish and Russian workers when, after a loss in a chess match, the latter nearly provoked a fight[49] could be diverse factors such as a particular workplace or domestic conflict, immigrants' specific perceptions of Soviet realities, or fundamental differences in cultural practice. What Canadian and American immigrants regarded as prerequisite to materializing, through things, or embodying, through bodily practices, their identities was perceived by the population of Soviet Karelia as strange and alien: their manner of work, tools, way of life, clothes, behavior, and so on. It is hardly surprising that, when immigrants sincerely complained of what they thought were serious problems, they often received an equally sincere response: "Go back to your Finland or America, the bourgeoisie has nothing to do here!"[50]

Thus, the desire of North American immigrants to settle in compact groups was driven by both internal and external factors: to ensure reproduction of their sociocultural models in an ethnically homogeneous environment and to bring to a minimum communication with Russian culture and society, which they often comprehended as backward or hostile. Immigrants preferred to work in Finnish collectives and to have Finnish neighbors, and recreational activities were mostly limited to their ethnic community. Their isolationism was, in a way, an attempt at cultural self-preservation.

CHALLENGES OF SELF-IDENTIFICATION AND INTEGRATION

Isolation from the local population was characteristic of all Finnish immigrant groups in Soviet Karelia, both from Finland and North America. But at the same time the three immigrant groups did not always get along with each other. Political immigrants—Red Finns—often considered American and Canadian Finns as apolitical and wealth-seeking individuals who had left their original homeland in search of an easy fortune. On the other hand, North American immigrants who had their own social illusions were sometimes suspicious of the political activism of Red Finns. And both socially privileged groups treated with neglect illegal Finnish immigrants, who lived in much harsher conditions, arguing that they themselves were responsible for their current misfortunes.

At the same time, once in Soviet Karelia, immigrants started undergoing immediate identity transformations. First to change were priorities in choosing cultural models of self-identification: instead of political orientation (Finnish identity in North America was built upon socialism and radicalism[51]), ethnic factors came to the fore. Although Red Finns who occupied the political heights of Soviet Karelia still identified themselves primarily as Communists and proletarian internationalists, political enthusiasm for building a new society among rank-and-file political immigrants from Finland died out rather soon. The Karelian leadership was concerned with this situation, especially because a gradual loss of socialist ideals, growing despair, disappointment in the socialist project, and desire to distance themselves from strange Soviet realities led to increasing alcohol addiction among Red Finns.[52] Similarly, when American and Canadian emigrants were leaving the New World, they fancied themselves part of the "international proletariat" rather than representatives of the Finnish nation.[53] Appeals to national pride and nostalgia were an important part of recruiting strategies of the Karelian Technical Aid Committee in the United States and Canada,[54] but political and economic motivations still dominated when decisions to emigrate to Soviet Karelia were made. Yet, soon after immigration, socialist ideals and enthusiasm among builders of a new world were pushed to the sidelines, and feelings of ethnic belonging and traditional cultural practices became main determinants of the self-identification of immigrants.

This transformation of the identities of Finnish immigrants was perhaps inevitable. As a rather typical European nation-state, Finland underwent a period of national mobilization in the nineteenth century and early twentieth century. As in the case of other nationalist projects, Finnish nationalism was constructed through new cultural forms and education; in addition, Russia as the other was an important part of nation building in Finland. Finnish ethnic identity created in this project could temporarily give way to socialist ideas, though even in the United States and Canada Finnish immigrants tended to stick to their Finnish-language organizations. But a move to Soviet Karelia, where immigrants were confronted with hardships and difficulties of all kinds, shattered their beliefs in socialism and actualized ethnic identities.

In a new political and sociocultural environment, under the scrutiny of local inhabitants who were not used to ethnic and cultural diversity, the self-perceptions of immigrants were bound to change. Only a few of them retained their socialist ideals and adapted to Soviet ways of life, identifying themselves first as proletarian internationalists and then as Soviet people. Even among youth, who tended to assimilate faster, many were not ready to abandon their self-identification as Finns. The majority of older immigrants who were socialized into the ethnosymbolic world of Finnish nationalism and could compare Soviet living standards with those in North America were less inclined to feel pride in socialist achievements, regarded Russian culture and language as part of a different and strange world, and—once the tide turned against Soviet Finnish communities in the mid- and especially late 1930s—sought defense in reducing to a minimum contacts with those outside their communities. A feeling of ethnic affinity became a strategy that helped people to navigate their life trajectories through a social reality that, after the end of the Finnish period in the history of Soviet Karelia, had to be mapped anew.

The population of Soviet Karelia had its own perceptions of immigrants that were very different from their self-identifications. Initially, as mentioned above, local inhabitants perceived North American Finns not as an ethnic group but as alien outsiders who supposedly represented a threat to their well-being. Ethnic markedness of this image was minimal, but it was richly fed by stereotypes of luxurious bourgeois life.

Simultaneously, as documentary and private sources demonstrate, grassroots tolerance and respect were already appearing during the first years of immigration. International nights, coordinated actions of North American and Soviet workers against the arbitrariness of factory administration, neighborly help, repairs to shared housing[55]—all of this was evidence that social and cultural rapprochement between the local population and immigrants had begun. It became particularly obvious when somebody was seriously ill or a family lost its breadwinner. In these cases, help to immigrants often came first from neighbors or even strangers rather than the state or employment organization.[56]

North American immigrants also gradually arrived at awareness of how much more difficult the lives of the local population were compared with theirs: "Of course, they don't fulfil their [production] quotas. If we, Finns, had to work on such food, with such tools and in such conditions, we would have harvested even less timber and would succumb several weeks later."[57] Immigrants started to appreciate the ability of their Russian colleagues and neighbors to maintain good temper: "They have such poor food and such wretched housing, and still not only they work, but are also good-natured. They are friendly and even hospitable."[58] Women found a common language when it came to fashion: some American immigrants became known as excellent dressmakers whose clientele included both Finnish and Russian women.[59] Thus, in a curious manner, national stereotypes constructed by the nationalist master narrative and learned through school or socialization in home communities turned out to be stronger than socialist activism and radicalism, another product of Western modernity, but both succumbed to everyday practices of communication that challenged established images of the other and forced both immigrants and the local population to re-evaluate their stereotypes and mutually adapt their cultural values.

American and Canadian youth were building their own relations with the surrounding sociocultural reality, and Soviet youth political organizations (Young Pioneers or Komsomol, the Communist Youth) were only one channel through which Finnish youth were socialized into Soviet culture.[60] Amateur performances, sports, cinema, dance evenings, dating, and sexual relations were all important parts of the youth culture of North American immigrants in Soviet Karelia[61] and, consequently, expanded for them the possibilities for adaptation and socialization. Their previous socialization into American or Canadian culture also made them less receptive to cultural values and strategies of their families: although their parents spoke to each other in Finnish, immigrant children often used English for communication within their group. Finally, they were the first to pick up the Russian language in situations of daily communication, such as studies, recreational activities, and communal life. This communication, in turn, made American and Canadian youth part of new communities that broke borders between ethnic groups.[62]

Children of school age adapted to new conditions even faster. In many cases, they served as the only mediators between their parents and the Russian-speaking world around them. Although there were Finnish schools in Petrozavodsk and other places with large Finnish populations, and initially American and Canadian children had very limited contacts with their Russian peers, day-to-day communication outside the immigrant community slowly did its work. As Toini Pränny recollected seventy years later, "at that time we felt that we started understanding each other. Although our knowledge of the [Russian] language was still very poor, we could somehow reach an agreement on something or discuss something. We, kids, often translated what Russian people said."[63]

Throughout the 1930s, as the situation for North American immigrants gradually changed, including the cancellation of privileged food rations, the return of the most dissatisfied immigrants back to America or Canada, and joint work activities or improved standards of living in the USSR, so did—for the better—communication between immigrants and the local population. After the late 1930s, official documents no longer mentioned conflicts between these two groups. Paradoxically, this change coincided with the intensification of a campaign against Finnish bourgeois nationalism, which would lead to the dismissal of the Red Finnish government of Soviet Karelia. Since the mid-1930s and especially during the Great Terror, Soviet Finns turned into the most targeted group in Soviet Karelia, and reports of party or state security organs, as well as memoirs and interviews with immigrants themselves, registered numerous cases of sympathy for Finns among the local population.[64] A changed attitude toward Finnish immigrants was revealed in a return to old ethnic terms to refer to them: "Finns," "Americans," "Finno-Americans," "Canadians," and "Finno-Canadians" were used instead of the previous derogatory term "bourgeoisie," and a new concept appeared in speech in Soviet Karelia that encapsulated these meanings in one word, *kolopaika*. Etymologically, this word possibly reflected how Russian speakers comprehended characteristic phonetic features of the Finnish language; since morphologically it resembled Russian words of the feminine gender, a masculine form was also used, *kolopaets*.[65] In the Karelian context of the mid-1930s, this concept referred to an industrious, meticulous, but slow-working and slow-speaking Finn.

The years of the Great Terror and the Second World War once again radically changed self-identifications of American and Canadian immigrants: those who survived this dreadful time preferred for many years not to remember, or at least not to remind others of, their origins. For most of them, later life in the USSR became the time of final assimilation into Soviet society. The Cold War, which pitted the United States and, to a lesser degree, Canada against the socialist world, also did not facilitate the use of personal histories by immigrants for identity building. Only in the late 1980s and 1990s did many immigrants decide to bring their personal or family histories back into public spotlights. In a final struggle for the determination of ethnic loyalties, Finnish identity had the upper hand, for most American or Canadian immigrants who left Russia at that time chose Finland, rather than the United States or Canada, as their destination. Those who stayed behind either already regarded themselves as Russians or just could not negotiate a coherent identity in a patchwork of allegiances and loyalties that they had assembled throughout their lives. One of them, Kalle Ranta, who came to Soviet Karelia at the age of eleven, when asked a question about his self-identification, could not give any definitive answer: "I don't know myself who I am. Parents were Finns, I was born in America, was a US citizen, and lived my whole life in Russia. Try to answer yourself."[66]

CHAPTER 8

American and Canadian Finns in the Great Terror

PRELUDE TO THE GREAT TERROR

HUNDREDS OF BOOKS HAVE BEEN WRITTEN ABOUT THE GREAT TERROR IN THE SOVIET Union that reveal, in varying degrees, the horrors of political purges and mass repressions carried out in 1937 and 1938. Unlike earlier campaigns of arrests or mass deportations conducted in the Soviet Union and aimed at specific social groups, the Great Terror encompassed all population groups without exception, from the highest levels of the Communist Party hierarchy to ordinary citizens. Another feature was that, while staged from above, by the highest level of the Soviet leadership, it was equally driven from below, by regional and local authorities as well as the "masses" themselves.

The mass repressions of 1937–38 were carried out in two major directions, along "kulak" and "national" lines. Together with the extermination of internal enemies—"kulaks, criminals, and other anti-Soviet elements," wide-scale ethnic cleansings were carried out against "external enem[ies], equally dangerous for the state."[1] Many years later Vyacheslav Molotov, who served as chairman of the Council of People's Commissars at that time, attempted to justify this policy in the following way: "1937 was necessary. . . . Thanks to 1937 there was no fifth column in our country during the [Second World W]ar."[2] It was inevitable, taking such logic into account, that most victims of the repression were from ethnic minorities that represented "bourgeois-fascist" (in the contemporary Soviet terminology) states located on or near the Soviet border, such as Germans, Poles, Latvians, Estonians, and Finns.

The two lines of the Great Purge explain the character and scale of repressive actions in Soviet regions. In Soviet Karelia, the lines were determined by the proximity of Finland to the Soviet Union and by the significant number of Finnish immigrants in Soviet Karelia. The share of people repressed under the "national line" in 1937 and 1938 amounted to 55 percent. Although the share of Finns in the population of Soviet Karelia in the mid-1930s barely exceeded 3 percent, more than 40 percent of all victims of the Stalinist terror in Soviet Karelia were Finns: in comparison, Russians and Karelians, the two largest ethnic groups of Karelia, which together made up about 85 percent of its population, comprised 25 percent and 27 percent respectively of the total number of victims.[3]

The Great Terror was prepared by the long struggle against "external and internal counterrevolution," which dated back to the Bolshevik Revolution. From the first years of Soviet rule, political police carried out surveillance of the population and penetrated into all aspects of political, economic, and cultural life of the nation. The repressive policy against "alien elements" and "class enemies" reached a mass scale in the late 1920s, after Stalin at the July 1928 Plenum of the Central Committee of VKP(b) expressed his vision that class struggle would only intensify as the Soviet Union approached socialism. Together with political groups that openly challenged Stalin's power, such as Socialist-Revolutionaries, Mensheviks, Trotskyites, Zinovyevists, and other oppositional forces, hundreds of thousands of peasants became victims of the repression when, in the course of "struggle for the collectivization," they were labeled as kulaks and slated to be "liquidated as a class." The year 1929 marked the beginning of forced relocation of kulaks (*spetspereselenchestvo*), also known as the "kulak exile." During 1930 and 1931, 1,803,392 people, or 381,026 peasant families, were deported as part of this "dekulakization" program to remote areas of northern Russia, Siberia, the Far East, and Central Asia.[4]

At the turn of the 1930s, another wave of repressions—the struggle against so-called national deviationism—swept over the Soviet Union. The national question in the Soviet Union had always been part of larger politics, since Bolsheviks never regarded national building as an end in itself. In the future socialist world, as they believed, all ethnic and national distinctions would disappear, and eventually humanity would become one whole. Soviet ethnic and national politics, therefore, never had an independent basis, being part of the larger project of socialist building, and lacked structural laws of its own. Therefore, national building during the policy of indigenization (*korenizatsiya*)[5] inevitably led to contradictions between economic and political interests of Soviet regions and centralizing tendencies emanating from Moscow.[6] This conflict on the domestic front was aggravated by looming international conflicts that threatened to involve the Soviet Union. This afforded an opportunity for Stalin to announce that, under the conditions of intensifying class struggle, ethnic and national contradictions inevitably arose as deviations from the approved line of local bourgeois nationalisms. "National deviationists" were accused of attempts to support a new international campaign aimed at partitioning the USSR. After Stalin's summary report presented at the Sixteenth Congress of the VKP(b) in 1930, its delegates adopted a resolution that identified the struggle against deviations from the Soviet national line as one of the party's priorities.[7] This created a regulatory basis for the actions taken by the Soviet authorities after the congress that are sometimes called a "dress rehearsal" to 1937.[8] Resolutions of the congress were used to accuse many prominent regional leaders of nationalism, both in autonomous and in union republics. The OGPU fabricated a number of cases against "national deviationists": counterrevolutionary organizations of Ukrainian nationalists, the Union for the Liberation of Belarus, the Union for the Liberation of Finnic Peoples (SOFIN), the anti-Soviet organization Turkmen Azatlygy (Turkmen Freedom), and others. Most of the victims of these "cases" were scholars, teachers, and cultural workers of ethnic republics.[9]

In Soviet Karelia, as everywhere else in Soviet Russia, operations involving "wiping out all kinds of counterrevolutionary elements"[10] were launched by Soviet security organs immediately after the Bolshevik Revolution. Because of its border location, the emphasis was on counterespionage, caused not only by intensive activities of the Finnish intelligence in Soviet Karelia[11] but also by regular cross-border contacts between residents of Karelian and Finnish border territories, which were deeply rooted in the prerevolutionary past and lasted, despite Soviet repressive measures, until the late 1920s.

For a long time, the OGPU in Soviet Karelia concentrated its work on so-called Karelian refugees, also known as Karelian adventurists—residents of border regions, mostly ethnic

Karelians, who fled to Finland during the Russian Civil War and gradually returned home after the amnesty of 1923. Soviet authorities presumed that a large part of them had been recruited by the Finnish intelligence. The OGPU's information reports of the mid-1920s show that political police regularly organized roundups in many border Karelian settlements to catch "enemy agents." Most of these roundups were not successful; reports usually concluded that "the spies fled" and that only local residents were arrested.[12] Vast quantities of smuggled goods were confiscated, as a rule, during such raids, which indicates that unlawful activities between border Karelian and Finnish territories mostly involved cross-border trade rather than espionage. With the growth of the Finnish population of Soviet Karelia, security organs paid more and more attention to Finnish immigrants, most of whom were regarded by the OGPU as "an unreliable element that should be kept under constant surveillance," which particularly affected "border hoppers" from Finland.[13]

Equally carefully, Soviet political police watched Finnish political immigrants, especially senior officials in the Karelian political hierarchy whose almost every step was meticulously recorded.[14] The OGPU's information reports of the 1920s compulsorily included a section titled "Nationalism," in which all occurrences of interethnic conflicts between political immigrants and the local population were scrupulously registered. As a rule, such conflicts occurred between Russian workers and Finnish managers and administrators. OGPU agents also registered discrimination against Russians compared with Finns and Karelians in terms of wages as well as a general tendency of Finns to maintain social distance, to "stay within the borders of their ethnic group."[15] These reports often concluded with a standard phrase: "Interethnic strife does not take sharp forms." Indeed, all these conflicts were of a social, rather than an ethnic, nature, since workers in Soviet Karelia had confrontations with administrations at most factories, disregarding the ethnicity of the latter.[16] In this context, contradictions between Red Finns and the population of Soviet Karelia were just part of a much larger conflict between Soviet power and Soviet people.

By the late 1920s, the section on "Nationalism" had almost completely disappeared from the OGPU's information reports because of a changed model of relations between the Soviet center and its regions. Economic and nationalities policies of Edvard Gylling's government and, in particular, its efforts to accelerate development of border regions with predominantly Karelian populations came more and more into conflict with the general line of the VKP(b) aimed at total centralization. Already in 1929, a year after the First Five-Year Plan was launched, Soviet Karelia lost its economic autonomy, while its Communist Party organization was subordinated to the Leningrad *obkom* of the VKP(b). Reflecting these changes, the focus of the OGPU's information reports shifted to popular dissatisfaction with the expanding campaigns of collectivization and dekulakization as well as concerns with famine that was gradually overcoming Soviet Karelia. Part of the mass famine of the early 1930s, it affected Soviet Karelia as severely as most other Soviet regions. Security organs registered terrible cases, as documented by one of these reports:

1. In Ukhta district [*raion*]: In December 1932 and January 1933, the population added tree bark to bread.
2. In Medvezhiegorsk *raion:* In February of this year [1933], a significant number of women engaged in prostitution in exchange for bread, which they got from the prisoners of the [gulag] camp of the White Sea-Baltic Canal.
3. In Kem *raion:* In March of this year, swelling caused by starvation was registered.

4. In Priazha *raion:* In January of 1933, a large part of the population was consuming almost nothing but tree bark with insignificant addition of flour.[17]

As everywhere else in the USSR, the Karelian leaders of the OGPU claimed that "counter-revolutionary activities of rebellious and subversive elements" accounted for this situation, an explanation that allowed them to initiate wide-scale operations aimed at "bourgeois national-ist counterrevolution."[18] The apogee of this "struggle" was the "case of the conspiracy of the Finnish General Staff."

The GPU of the Leningrad Military District carried out the laborious task of fabricating this case from October 1932 to May 1933. Its executive officers were Karp Shershevskii, the head of the GPU of Soviet Karelia, and Ivan Zaporozhets, the deputy plenipotentiary for the OGPU in the Leningrad Military District.[19] The prosecution claimed that all counterrevolutionary and espionage activities in Soviet Karelia were directly supervised by the Second Department of the Finnish General Staff, which allegedly created an elaborate network of agents in the entire territory of Soviet Karelia and those territories of the Leningrad region populated by Ingrian Finns.[20] Realistically, its most likely aim was to intimidate those inhabitants of these territories who openly resisted the policy of collectivization and negative effects of the acceler-ated industrialization. In terms of the number of repressed people, the "case of the conspiracy of the Finnish General Staff" was among the largest repressive campaigns of the early 1930s. In the memorandum to Stalin titled "On the Most Important Counterrevolutionary Organi-zations in the USSR Liquidated from 1930 to 1933" (25 December 1933), Genrikh Yagoda, then deputy head of the OGPU, wrote that the two largest of these organizations were the counterrevolutionary organization People's Commissariat of Agriculture (6,000 people) and the so-called Industrial Party (2,000 people). The third largest was the "counterrevolutionary subversive organization created by the Finnish General Staff that covered fifteen districts of Karelia and eight districts of Leningrad region (*oblast*) liquidated in 1933. This organization was particularly active in detachments of the Special Karelian Jaeger Brigade."[21]

Altogether 1,358 people were repressed under this case, including 1,048 in Soviet Kare-lia and 310 in the Ingrian territories of Leningrad region. Of these, 577 were sentenced as "active spies" (resident or field agents, commandos, spies, and informants of the Finnish intel-ligence).[22] The social background of the accused demonstrates that peasants were the main victims of this operation. The prosecution did not bother itself with the search for hard facts and proofs of guilt. The "concentration" of Karelians in border regions, the "clogging" of these regions with "former Karelian adventurers" (*karavantiuristy,* a term denoting partici-pants of the anti-Soviet rebellion in northern Soviet Karelia during the winter of 1921–22), the systematic lagging behind deadlines imposed by economic planning—all of this served for the GPU as an unquestionable proof that Soviet Karelia was brimming with counterrevo-lutionary ferment. The indictment concluded that "agents of the Finnish General Staff had penetrated [in]to all key sections of the Soviet party and military apparatus," and its liquida-tion "prevented a military uprising in Karelia and border regions of Leningrad region."[23] In May 1933, people tried in this case were sentenced to different terms of imprisonment, nearly half of them were sentenced to five to ten years of gulag camps, and at least 10 percent were sentenced to capital punishment.[24]

From 1956 to 1962, the Military Tribunal of the North Military District reviewed the "case of the conspiracy of the Finnish General Staff" and established that all accusations were completely falsified and not supported by any comprehensive evidence. Most people repressed during this trial were rehabilitated.[25] Yet, in the early 1930s, this first large-scale OGPU operation in the northwest region of the USSR proved that espionage was the best possible pretext for mass political repression. The security organs of Soviet Karelia also demonstrated that they now acted independently of the republican authorities and followed orders only from their immediate superiors in Moscow and Leningrad.

In 1933, the first serious criticism of the Finnish authorities of Soviet Karelia came with accusations that their politics favored bourgeois Finland and that the implementation of nationalities policy there was flawed by "a deviation from the Leninist-Stalinist line."[26] The VKP(b) organization of Soviet Karelia was blamed for nourishing "local nationalism, which served as a coverup for the bourgeois-nationalist counterrevolution and called for [foreign military] intervention."[27] This defined the enemy, and after that the struggle against local nationalism marked the beginning of Moscow's undeclared war against the Finns of Soviet Karelia.

CALM BEFORE THE STORM

The "case of the conspiracy of the Finnish General Staff" and early accusations that Red Finns connived at local nationalism were followed by a period of relative calm. On 8 May 1933, the Central Committee of the VKP(b) and the SNK of the USSR issued a law that temporarily suspended mass deportations and arrests.[28] Indeed, many events of 1934—refusal of a "great leap forward to socialism," abolition of bread rationing, minor political reforms in rural areas (reorganization of political departments of machine and tractor stations)—were interpreted by contemporaries as a prelude to a more liberal political course. From 1935 to 1936, political repression was dispensed in relatively small "portions" that alternated with temporary periods of calm: supporters of harsh measures were restrained by the economically unstable situation of the Soviet Union as well as by moderate forces in the VKP(b).[29] There was, however, no change in the party's general line. Stalin's famous saying, "NKVD is four years late,"[30] can be interpreted as a reference to the potential of the Great Terror to be triggered in any of these four years of relative calm. For the Soviet leadership en masse, repression of the "socially alien element" seemed a way to solve real economic problems haunting their visions of the development and security of the USSR and to overcome contradictions that characterized its social model. For Stalin personally, purges swept away his old party comrades, who had challenged his power in the past, and brought to power a new generation of party bureaucrats loyal to him. For rank-and-file Communist functionaries, the Great Terror became a resource for building careers, securing high positions, and getting access to material gains in the deficit economy of the 1930s. Finally, purges that followed one another during the 1930s and intense propaganda campaigns that accompanied them can be interpreted as part of a more general tendency to discipline, in the Foucauldian sense of the word, Soviet subjects by imposing on them the idea of the absolute priority of state interests over individual moral norms. In many ways, this project of making a new Soviet subject was successful: most Soviet people did not challenge the authority of the political leadership and were ready to attribute numerous failures and glaring problems in the socioeconomic development of the Soviet Union to its enemies. To condense the atmosphere of fear and suspicion, full use was also made of the deteriorating international situation in Europe and of the growing threats of a global war. The machinery of repression engulfed more and more social groups, gathering momentum, and at some point state terror turned from being selective into being total and nearly unstoppable. In this respect, the role of resolutions of the February–March 1937 Plenum of the Central Committee of the VKP(b) was that they officially confirmed the course of intensification of mass repression.

In Soviet Karelia as a border region, the "thaw" of the mid-1930s was even shorter than those in most other Soviet regions. Particularly for the Finns of Soviet Karelia, including American and Canadian immigrants, the starting point of the Great Terror was 1935. After the "case of the conspiracy of the Finnish General Staff," Karelian security organs continued careful surveillance of the political situation in the republic. Reports boasting of the elimination of new espionage groups were regularly presented at meetings of the Bureau of the Karelian Regional Committee of the VKP(b).[31] Industrial accidents increasingly became a pretext for political and criminal accusations against innocent people. In April 1934, after an accident at the construction site of the Petrozavodsk water supply system, the first criminal case was opened against American Finns.

This case, code-named Pipe in the investigation materials, was rooted in a conflict between American workers and Soviet engineers of the Karelian Construction Trust who designed a system of gravity water supply consisting of two wooden pipes (each 765 yards long and nineteen inches in diameter) that ran parallel to each other to the bottom of Lake Onega. American technical specialists openly expressed their doubts about the workability of this system and offered their own variant, which they claimed would be more effective. It was rejected, and Americans refused to work on this project, which they deemed dubious. Construction was started nevertheless, but soon an accident followed, as predicted by the American specialists. Yet, contrary to logic, those four American specialists who had done their best to prevent it by criticizing the failed design and developing an alternative one were accused of this failure. The management of the Construction Trust accused them of breaking "labor discipline" and the principle of undivided authority, while investigation materials qualified this accusation as "sabotage of American Finns at the construction site of the town water supply."[32] Arrests were avoided only after Kustaa Rovio, the first secretary of the Karelian Regional Committee of the VKP(b), personally rose to defend the immigrant workers.

The assassination of Sergey Kirov on 1 December 1934 launched another campaign of political terror. After the Moscow Center trial in January 1935, when several former Bolshevik leaders were sentenced to imprisonment, a wave of arrests of former party opposition members swamped the Soviet Union. In Soviet Karelia, the hunt for former members of the party opposed to Stalin was combined with renewed efforts to cleanse border territories of "counterrevolutionary elements" and to counter envisioned espionage activities of the Finnish intelligence. In February 1935, Karp Shershevskii, the head of the Karelian NKVD, reported to the Karelian Party Committee of the VKP(b) that "the Finnish intelligence revives insurgent organizations that had been revealed and liquidated during 1933–1934" and demanded that harsh measures be implemented to ultimately destroy them.[33]

At the insistence of the NKVD at both national and republican levels, in the spring of 1935, the Karelian Regional Committee of the VKP(b) approved plans of operations "on the deportation of class aliens from Petrozavodsk" (March) and "on the cleansing of the twenty-two-kilometer border zone from kulaks and anti-Soviet elements" (April). These cleansing operations were followed by the compulsory issuing of passports to all residents of the fifty-kilometer border zone.[34] As a result of these measures, the population of the border territories decreased considerably, and many *kolkhozes* of Kalevala, Reboly, and Olonets districts of Soviet Karelia started to experience labor shortages.[35]

Drastic changes were also under way in the VKP(b) organization of Soviet Karelia. The party cleansings were followed by a thorough inspection and updating of party membership documents. A special directive of the Bureau of the Karelian Regional Committee of the VKP(b) instructed that "particular care and all available measures" be applied to the inspection of Finnish political immigrants and border hoppers, of former participants in the uprising in northern Karelia in 1921 and 1922, and only then of "members of Trotskyite-Zinovievite opposition."[36] In comparison, while during the party purge of 1933–34 about 73 percent of people who lost membership in the VKP(b) were Russians, 20 percent Karelians, and only 3 percent Finns (i.e., Russians bore the main burden of party purges), in the four following years the number of Finns who were members of the VKP(b) organization of Soviet Karelia decreased by four times.[37]

The beginning of 1935 did not promise any radical turmoil in the political life of Soviet Karelia. In January, Gylling was re-elected as head of the Karelian Council of People's Commissars.[38] The Fourth Plenum of the Karelian *obkom* of the VKP(b) in August 1935 also proceeded in a peaceful manner. A representative of the Leningrad *obkom*, Mikhail Chudov, announced that the Central Committee of the VKP(b) decided to transfer Kustaa Rovio, the party leader of Soviet Karelia, to Moscow, but no political accusation was made against him. The plenum did discuss some "mistakes" that had been made by the VKP(b) organization of Soviet Karelia, including enforcement of the Finnish language, a disproportionate (compared with their share of the population) number of Finns in administrative and managerial positions, and the admission of "unreliable" people to the VKP(b). At the same time, recruitment of foreign specialists to Soviet Karelia and recognition of the Finnish language as the second official language of the republic were not questioned. "We must make people learn Finnish," Chudov argued in the debates. Gylling was even franker when he declared that education of professional specialists with expert knowledge of both Russian and Finnish would be relevant "after the revolution in Finland."[39]

Yet the transfer of Kustaa Rovio to Moscow and the appointment of a Leningrad Latvian, Pyotr Irklis, as the first secretary of the Karelian Regional Committee of the VKP(b) deprived Finnish communities of Soviet Karelia of a vital political resource—control over the most important authoritative body in the republic. From then on, Soviet security bodies had no major obstacles in their attacks against the Finns of Soviet Karelia. In the same summer (1935), they launched an attack on political immigrants. The first to fall prey were "groups in support of the Finnish Communist Party."

Since 1918, when the Finnish Communist Party (FCP) was established in Moscow, and until 1944, it was banned in Finland and could act there only underground, while its leadership and head office remained in the USSR. Unable to raise finances from Finnish sources, it was funded by the Communist International (Comintern). In 1931, the Executive Committee of the Comintern cut subsidies to the Finnish Communist Party and suggested that its Central Committee organize a fundraising campaign among Soviet Finns to compensate lost funding.[40] The decision to decrease funding of the Finnish Communist Party was likely the result of general criticism of its activities that the Executive Committee of the Comintern voiced in 1930.[41] The background of this decision was the "class against class" tactics developed by the Ninth Plenum of the Executive Committee of the Comintern and approved by the resolutions of the Sixth Comintern Congress (1928): the Finnish section of the Comintern seemed too moderate for this ultra-left political course and became its victim. Cuts in the financial support of the Finnish Communist Party also occurred during a very difficult period when the Communist underground and leftist worker organizations in Finland were eliminated, and likely this decision of the Comintern leadership was caused by its intention to redirect the activities of Finnish Communists from their native country to the Soviet northwestern regions, where the Finnish diaspora was growing quickly at that time. Before 1931, the majority of Soviet Finns were political immigrants, and since most of them had joined the VKP(b) they could be controlled and guided by local party organizations. The situation changed in the early 1930s as new immigrants recruited in North America or arriving illegally from Finland remained outside the VKP(b) system and had to be controlled otherwise. "Educational work" among Finnish immigrant communities was entrusted to the Finnish Communist Party (in particular its Foreign Bureau). One form of this work was fundraising in support of the Finnish Communist Party, and special bureaus were established in Leningrad and Petrozavodsk for this purpose.[42] It was soon clear, however, that irregular fundraising activities brought a meager income. The solution to this problem was seen in the form of permanent groups in support of the party.

Groups in support of the Finnish Communist Party were established in Soviet Karelia in 1932 and 1933 following directions of the Comintern and a resolution of the Foreign Bureau of the Finnish Communist Party.[43] These groups acted under the auspices of the Karelian Regional Committee of the VKP(b) and were headed by people who occupied prominent positions in the official hierarchy. Their work was coordinated by Otto Vilmi, a former underground activist of the Finnish Communist Party and the Comintern in Finland, Sweden, and Norway, who now represented it in the Karelian Regional Committee of the VKP(b).[44] The majority of their members were Red Finns who directly participated in the Finnish Civil War as well as their younger comrades: that is, members of Communist and left socialist organizations of Finland and North America. Most of them were also members of the VKP(b). Apart from fundraising for the Finnish Communist Party, the main tasks of these groups were propaganda among the Finnish population of Soviet Karelia and training of administrative and political staff for future socialist Finland.[45]

The Soviet leadership, for the time being, encouraged the activities of the Finnish Communist Party in Soviet Karelia and blessed the groups in its support. After all, groups in support of Finnish Communists were also obliged to "actively implement and protect the political line of the Central Committee of the VKP(b)" among the Finnish population of the USSR. They had to "keep track of qualified specialists who in case of a war could become of use for the Finnish Communist Party and Soviet organizations." Besides, group leaders were obliged to "assist Soviet authorities in revealing active counterrevolutionary elements and enemies of the Finnish Communist Party among [Soviet] Finns."[46] Ironically, as later charges against activists of the Finnish Communist Party demonstrated, it was the NKVD that was the main beneficiary of this information.

Although groups in support of the Finnish Communist Party were rather small (usually from three to five people, rarely fifteen or more) and their activities were restricted to certain places with significant Finnish communities (Petrozavodsk, Kondopoga, Interposiolok, Lososinnoie, Ukhta),[47] their very existence was used by Soviet authorities as a pretext for the anti-Finnish campaign. Documents of state security agencies characterized them as "illegal, subversive," and "counterrevolutionary" organizations as early as 1935. The signal for the beginning of the anti-Finnish campaign was given in the summer of 1935 when the "Moscow opposition group of the Finnish Communist Party" was allegedly revealed and its leaders, Kullervo Manner, the chairman of the Finnish Communist Party from 1920 to 1935 and a member of the Comintern's Executive Committee,[48] and Hanna Malm, were arrested under accusations of "counterrevolutionary nationalist propaganda and struggle against the Comintern and the Central Committee of the Finnish Communist Party."[49] In July and August, arrests continued in Soviet Karelia among members of local groups in support of the Finnish Communist Party. In autumn, it was the turn of the Red Finnish leadership of Soviet Karelia.

The opening of the Fifth Plenum of the Karelian Regional Committee of the VKP(b) on 29 September 1935 marked the beginning of a wide-scale witch hunt in which Finns were the main victims. The plenum announced serious political accusations against Finns who occupied high positions in Soviet Karelia and declared that the struggle against "Finnish bourgeois nationalism" had commenced.[50] Pyotr Irklis, the new first secretary of the Karelian Regional Committee of the VKP(b), collected in a record-breaking manner "compromising materials" against Finnish Communists, consulting both Soviet power centers: Moscow (Nikolai Ezhov and Vyacheslav Molotov) and Leningrad (Mikhail Chudov).[51] The existence of groups in support of the Finnish Communist Party in Soviet Karelia was characterized as an "exclusively Karelian and very indecent phenomenon."[52] Timid attempts by Matti Stein (born Hannes Mäkinen), then head of the Finnish Section of the Comintern and head of the Finnish Communist Party from 1935 to 1937,[53] to defend, albeit cautiously, Finnish Communists aroused a negative reaction among plenum delegates. His speech was repeatedly interrupted by the audience, especially when he tried to prove that unfair and unfounded accusations against Finns could only add fuel to the fire of Finnish nationalism. In the end, Stein succumbed to audience pressure and finished his speech with a eulogy to proletarian internationalism. He even told a joke about a slow-witted Finn who needed to feel a knife at the back of his neck in order to understand what was wanted of him. "Now, at least, words seem to be enough," concluded Stein, and the audience applauded.[54]

After the plenum, the Central Committee of the VKP(b) decided to relieve Edvard Gylling from the post of chairman of the Karelian Council of People's Commissars. He was transferred from Soviet Karelia to Moscow, and a Tver Karelian, Pavel Bushuev, was appointed as the new republican leader.[55] All the Karelian newspapers were filled with articles unmasking the bourgeois nationalists, and many local party committees underwent thorough inspections and sometimes were completely reorganized. Many Finns were expelled from the VKP(b) and lost their positions; every region of Soviet Karelia, especially Petrozavodsk and the border areas, endured a wave of arrests. In October and November 1935, many activists of groups in support of the Finnish Communist Party were arrested, including Otto Vilmi.[56] Once expelled, most Finns faced repression by the NKVD: during 1935, it arrested over forty people, while fifty more were officially wanted, and the other fifty were to be deported from the territory of Soviet Karelia.[57]

This changed attitude toward Finns in Soviet Karelia was immediately noticed in Finland,[58] yet arrests of Finnish Communists in Soviet Karelia seemed to arouse little concern among the leadership of the Finnish Communist Party. In early December, Pyotr Irklis received two letters from Matti Stein that mentioned nothing of events in Soviet Karelia. The letter dated 3 December, however, had the following lines: "Since now, the Finnish Communist Party will not have an official representative in Soviet Karelia. Our activities in Karelia in form of [support] groups or an official representative have been liquidated forever. We will only carry out that kind of activity that we have earlier discussed with you and

Comrade Shershevskii."[59] In this letter, Stein referred to an earlier discussion with Irklis, the first secretary of the Karelian Regional Committee of the vKP(b), and Shershevskii, the head of the Soviet Karelian NKVD, in which they most likely negotiated a deal: Finnish Communists in Soviet Karelia were sacrificed to prove the loyalty of the Moscow-based leadership of the Finnish Communist Party to Soviet authorities. The position of Finnish Communists in Moscow had its internal logic: by sacrificing their Karelian comrades, they tried to secure themselves as well as the future of the party in general. Ongoing purges in the vKP(b) at that time made everyone a potential victim, and in the pursuit of survival rank-and-file Communists became involved, voluntarily or not, in the process of mutual extermination. For the time being, the Finnish Communist Party secured its existence, even though Irklis and Chudov made clear accusations when they wrote to Moscow about "intolerable methods of illegal work on behalf of the Finnish Section of the Comintern."[60] The uncompromising struggle against opposition in its own ranks helped the Central Committee of the Finnish Communist Party to regain the trust of the Stalinist leadership. In this logic, Finns in Soviet Karelia, including American and Canadian immigrants, were expendable.

In 1936, there were no large-scale public campaigns against Finns, but people continued to disappear. Without any commentary in the press, most Finns occupying top-level positions were relieved of them and expelled from the vKP(b). Pyotr Irklis, as the new leader of the Karelian party organization, repeatedly sent memoranda to Moscow reporting on the progress of the ongoing struggle against "nationalist, espionage, and interventionist elements."[61]

The campaign of 1935–36 affected North American Finns only in passing. The Resettlement Administration was dissolved, and the NKVD started to build files on them. However, the authorities still avoided open attacks against American and Canadian immigrants; moreover, they even publicly demonstrated goodwill toward them. Irklis, in his scathing speech against the Finnish leaders of Soviet Karelia, which he delivered at the plenum of the Karelian Regional Committee of the vKP(b) in October 1935, criticized the recruitment policy of the former Finnish leadership but added that "we, of course, never objected and will never object to the workers who came to us, we are sincerely glad that they are together with us, under the guidance of our party, to advance the great cause of socialism."[62] Yet some precautionary measures were taken against North American immigrants as well.

American and Canadian members of the Karelian groups in support of the Finnish Communist Party became the first North American victims of Stalinist repression. One of them was Toivo Uitti, the leader of a support group in Lososinnoie. During the 1920s, while still in Finland, he was an underground member of the Finnish Communist Party and emigrated to Canada only under a threat of disclosure. After half a year of life in Canada, he moved to the USSR. In 1934, he was entrusted by the Finnish Communist Party to become the head of its support group in Lososinoie, but already in the summer of 1935 he was accused of espionage for "fascist Finland" and arrested. Matti Torplund, the chairman of the vKP(b) cell in Lososinnoie and a member of the group in support of the Finnish Communist Party, a former member of the American Communist Party, was expelled from the vKP(b) for "class blindness": that is, for failure to recognize that his friend Uitti was a "spy."[63]

In the autumn of 1935, three members of the agricultural commune Säde were arrested, including Kalle Siikanen, the commune chairman; Eelis Ahokas; and Juho Niemi. Siikanen and Ahokas had come to Soviet Karelia from Canada in 1926 to found the commune, and Niemi had immigrated from the United States in 1932. The men were accused of sabotage and participation in a counterrevolutionary group. Siikanen was also charged with "being the right hand of Edvard Gylling in questions of agriculture."[64] The families of the arrested men were exiled to northern Soviet Karelia and forbidden to come to Petrozavodsk.

By the mid-1930s, the ethnic composition of Säde had substantially changed, for only six commune members out of fifty-four were immigrants from Canada and three more from the United States.[65] The fact that it was North American Finns who became the victims can be explained by their contacts with groups in support of the Finnish Communist Party, though the commune itself did not have such a group. One such group functioned in the Olonets battalion of the Karelian Jaeger Brigade, but its activities were largely restricted to the battalion itself. Another group was created in Olonets by Finnish students of the Higher Communist School of Agriculture who came to Säde for internship in 1934. These groups were small and rather passive, but later the NKVD accused nearly the entire Finnish population of Olonets of being directly involved in their activities.[66]

Attacks on the Karelian groups in support of the Finnish Communist Party were not consistent. The largest group that functioned in Kondopoga enlisted fifty members of whom sixteen were former members of the Canadian and American Communist Parties,[67] yet they were not affected by the repressions of the mid-1930s. Most of them (at least nine) were repressed later, during 1937 and 1938.[68]

In general, during 1935, the arrests of American and Canadian immigrants were preventive, intended to intimidate them. Toivo Uitti was released soon after his arrest, and Matti Torplund was reinstated as a VKP(b) member. Besides, in the mid-1930s, the fates of people were still decided by courts. In the spring of 1936, Juho Niemi and Kalle Siikanen were acquitted and released, and they returned to the commune Säde with their families. Eelis Ahokas was sentenced under Article 58/10[69] of the Soviet Criminal Code to one year of compulsory labor and, after serving it, returned to the commune too. The years of 1937 and 1938, however, spared none of them.

In October 1935, the Finnish diaspora in Soviet Karelia suffered another blow when the VKP(b) cell in Sovkhoz No. 2 (Hiilisuo) was completely reorganized. This farm, the brainchild of Gylling, was established in 1930 by American Finns who had come to Soviet Karelia from the commune Seattle/Seiatel in the North Caucasus. It was intended to act as a model farm and a forge of agricultural specialists. By the autumn of 1935, Sovkhoz No. 2 employed about 300 Finns, mostly illegal immigrants from Finland, while the number of Russians and Karelians was no more than ten.[70] The number of North American Finns was about forty, including sixteen former communards from Seattle/Seiatel plus nine family members.[71]

The repression of Finns in Hiilisuo was triggered by a tragic occurrence, the mass poisoning of the collective's cattle on 18 October 1935 because of negligence or carelessness of cattlemen.[72] It was immediately called sabotage, a favorite label of Soviet propaganda to explain any economic failure, and the chairman of the *sovkhoz*, Aaro Holopainen, who had come from the United States in 1931, was arrested the same day. The poisoning of the cattle was actually timely because archival documents show that the NKVD started to monitor the work of Hiilisuo long before 18 October: the first arrests of illegal Finnish immigrants employed in the *sovkhoz* were carried out already in 1934, and between 1 January and 1 August 1935 140 people were fired from the *sovkhoz,* of whom 131 were Finns.[73]

The poisoning presented a pretext to complete the purge of Hiilisuo. On 30 October 1935, the Petrozavodsk committee of the VKP(b) passed a resolution on the liquidation of the VKP(b) cell in Sovkhoz No. 2. Its management—chairperson Aaro Holopainen and secretary Ida Terho—were accused of "implementation of bourgeois and nationalist policies and illegal contacts with bourgeois Finland" that "resulted in mass poisoning of pedigree cows." New management was instructed to inspect, at breakneck speed, all employees of the *sovkhoz* and to purge from it "class aliens and nationalistic elements."[74] This work was actually under way already by the NKVD. Illegal immigrants from Finland bore the brunt of this repression: several people were arrested, while more were forcefully transferred to another place of work. Finally, according to instructions from the NKVD, twenty Finns were to be fired.[75]

Among them was a former American farmer, Joonas Harju, who had invested his own capital in the development of Hiilisuo. He funded, in particular, the purchase of pedigree cattle and farming equipment from Finland. His dismissal from the *sovkhoz* in February 1936 aroused such serious protests on behalf of other Finnish workers that the new director of the *sovkhoz,* who in his official correspondence labelled Harju a "capitalist" and the "owner of the *sovkhoz,*" was forced to annul the dismissal order. Harju, however, did not return to work, though he regularly visited his friends who stayed in the *sovkhoz.*[76] His later fate is unknown.[77]

Aaro Holopainen and the cattleman Simo Kivonen, made scapegoats during the investigation, were sentenced to long prison terms (ten and seven years). An additional inspection carried out after the sentences resulted in the withdrawal of charges of sabotage for Holopainen and a reduced term. However, in September 1938, a new verdict was issued that condemned him to death, and on 1 October he was executed near Petrozavodsk. A week later his twenty-three-year-old son Toivo, born in the United States, was executed at the same place. Simo Kivonen was executed on 14 October 1938.

Documents of 1935 and 1936 also often mentioned "anti-Soviet activities of Finns in the region of Kestenga." According to the Karelian NKVD, there, in lumber camps near the Finnish border, "counterrevolutionary nationalist elements assembled that incited terrorist sentiment against the party leaders."[78] Such accusations were always based on the drunken talk of scared people. In particular, they arrested a former Red Guard soldier, a participant in the Finnish and Russian Civil Wars, Juho Koponen, who said during a drinking party that "Stalin conducts a wrong nationalities policy, torments Finns. Rovio and Gylling are gone, but our forces are growing. We will show them. Communists have to be hanged; they are bloodsuckers."[79] This expression gave Soviet security organs a pretext to fabricate a whole criminal case, and both rank-and-file lumberjacks and regional bosses of the Red Finnish background became their victims. It is likely that the arrests of four North American immigrants on 19 February 1936 in Sofporog, or Sohjanankoski (the Kestengskii, now Louhskii, district in northern Soviet Karelia), were related to this case. Two of them, Canadian immigrants Johan Heiniemi and Jalmari Randell, were soon released, while two American immigrants, Reino Numminen and Kaarlo Sipilä, were sentenced under Article 58/10 of the Soviet Criminal Code to three years of imprisonment. Their later fates are unknown, but the fact that they were rehabilitated only in 1992[80] likely means that they perished in the gulag camps and nobody ever searched for them.

Organizers of the recruitment efforts to resettle North American Finns in Soviet Karelia—Matti Tenhunen, Kalle Aronen, and Oscar Corgan—were not affected by the repressions of the mid-1930s, apart from changes to their employment status. It is possible that someone removed them from the line of fire. Among Finns arrested during the autumn of 1935 was Heino Rautio, director of the publishing house Kirja. After his arrest, its entire VKP(b) cell was reorganized. In one day, 13 November 1935, at the session of the Karelian Regional Committee of the VKP(b), fourteen employees of Kirja were expelled from the party, including Teemu Törmälä, Kosti Klemola, Felix Kellosalmi, Victor Paju, and Lauri Letonmäki.[81] But just before these events, Tenhunen and Corgan, who had worked at Kirja, were transferred to different jobs: Corgan was appointed to work as the director of a bookstore in Ukhta (Kalevala, a border territory),[82] while Tenhunen became head of the Karelian Regional vkp(b) Press.[83] Aronen worked as a driver in Petrozavodsk after the Resettlement Administration was liquidated.

Yet the witch hunt targeting Soviet Finns could not pass by the people who had been key figures in the recruitment campaign in North America. Archival documents show that the nkvd had thoroughly collected compromising materials against Tenhunen, Aronen, and Corgan since the establishment of the Resettlement Administration. According to this archival evidence, there were multiple informants in the North American communities in Soviet Karelia who provided the necessary materials for the nkvd. Particularly interesting are reports of 1934 from an agent whose code name was Veteran and who gave detailed accounts of Finnish organizations in North America, of the interest of the Finnish government in them, and of the activities of the Karelian Technical Aid Committee in the United States. Most compromising materials were related to the activities of Tenhunen and Aronen, who would later become the main accused in the "case of the Karelian Technical Aid Committee and the Resettlement Administration."[84]

In September 1935, when the central office of the nkvd demanded a summary of American and Canadian immigration to Soviet Karelia, Karp Shershevskii, head of the nkvd of Soviet Karelia, wrote a memorandum on the activities of the Resettlement Administration that summarized all materials and drew appropriate conclusions. This document emphasized the "commercial implications of the activities of Tenhunen and Aronen" expressed by the fact that the agency had recruited in the first place people who could contribute financially to the Equipment Fund. Because of these "speculative activities," immigrants to Soviet Karelia were, "instead of lumberjacks, bankrupt pub keepers, kulaks, smugglers, evident adventure hunters, and crooks." This situation was allegedly exploited by foreign intelligence services, which recruited spies from the ranks of immigrants.[85] This document completely reframed all earlier positive assessments in the domain of internal and external threats.

Shershevskii's materials formed the basis of the decision to liquidate the Resettlement Administration in October 1935. Shershevskii was ordered to inspect the work of the Resettlement Administration's staff for "possible political crimes."[86] Two years later the results of this "inspection" were put to an appropriate use. Tenhunen and Korgan were arrested in the autumn of 1937 and executed in Medvezhiegorsk in central Soviet Karelia, while Aronen was caught in the last wave of arrests in the summer of 1938 and executed in Petrozavodsk in September. All three were rehabilitated between 1956 and 1958.

The reaction of Finns to what happened after the Fifth Plenum of the Karelian Regional Committee of the vkp(b) and the change of the republican authorities was diverse. Already in the autumn of 1935, Petrozavodsk was full of rumors that the Soviet nationalities policy was about to change, that mass repression was about to be launched against Finns, and that they had to escape from Soviet Karelia at all costs.[87] Some people did leave, while others sought asylum in remote forest settlements, and still others refused to believe the rumors, seeing the first campaign as a nightmare that would soon end. As the anti-Finnish measures grew in scale, so did fear, and the opinion became increasingly popular among Finnish Communists that they were abandoned to the mercy of fate. Many repeated a phrase attributed to Eino Rahja, a veteran member of the Finnish Communist Party, that its Central Committee did not lift a finger to prevent the anti-Finnish campaign in Soviet Karelia.[88] But there were people who rose up in opposition to these policies. Teemu Törmälä, a top manager of the publishing house

Kirja expelled from the vkp(b) and fired from his job, went to Moscow to search for the truth. He visited the Central Committee of the vkp(b), the Central Committee of the Finnish Communist Party, and the editorial office of the newspaper *Pravda,* and he was assured by everyone that the anti-Finnish repression would soon end and that justice would be restored.[89] The end of 1936 and the beginning of 1937 indeed became a short break in the struggle against Finnish bourgeois nationalists. But it was only the calm before the storm.

THE FINNISH OPERATION OF 1937–38

The February–March 1937 Plenum of the Central Committee of the vkp(b) opened a new and most traumatic period in the history of Soviet repressive policies. By the end of the summer, when Nikolai Ezhov, the people's commissar of internal affairs of the ussr, signed Operative Order No. 00447, "the operation for repression of former kulaks, criminals, and other anti-Soviet elements" (30 July 1937), based on the resolution of the Politburo of the Central Committee of the vkp(b), the terror had become total. The operation was ordered to start on 5 August 1937 (in some southern and eastern regions on 10 and 15 August) and to be completed within four months. For its implementation, the Soviet People's Commissars of the ussr allocated 75 million rubles from its reserve fund. All republics and regions were assigned target figures for the number of arrests: for Soviet Karelia, the initial target was 1,000 people, of whom 300 were of the "first category" (execution). In full, Order No. 00447 dictated that 268,950 people had to be repressed in the Soviet Union. Of them, 75,950 were to be executed.[90]

Two weeks later, on 15 August 1937, Ezhov signed Order No. 00486, "the operation for repression of wives of traitors of the motherland," which became the basis of repression of relatives of "enemies of the people," including "socially dangerous children of convicts."[91] By early 1938, 27,114 wives and 36,795 children of "enemies of the people" had been repressed in the Soviet Union.[92]

Simultaneously, "national orders" of the nkvd were issued. The most important were Orders No. 00439, "the operation for repression of German citizens suspected of espionage against the ussr" (25 July 1937); No. 00485, "the operation for repression of members of the Polska Organizacja Wojskowa (pow), Polish illegal immigrants, political immigrants from Poland, former members of the Polish Socialist Party, and other Polish political parties" (11 August 1937); and No. 00593, "the operation for repression of former employees of the China Far East Railroad and re-emigrants from Manzhouguo (Harbinites)" (20 September 1937).[93] Of course, these orders, particularly the latter, can be called "national" only by a long stretch of the imagination, yet they became the basis for the mass repression of many ethnic minorities in the Soviet Union, including Finns.

These documents introduced simplified orders for procedure of investigation and execution of sentence. The execution of sentence was commissioned to a specially created extrajudicial institution, *troika,* established within the nkvd offices in all Soviet regions (republics, districts [*krais*], regions [*oblasts*]) and comprising the first secretary of the regional committee of the vkp(b), the head of the local nkvd office, and the regional prosecutor. In Soviet Karelia, as everywhere else, composition of the republican *troika* would change several times since, during the Great Purge, judges could easily become victims. During the year-and-a-half-long campaign, four first secretaries (Irklis, Nikolskii, Ivanov, Kuprianov) and two people's commissars of internal affairs (Tenison, Matuzenko) served in the Karelian *troika*. Only the prosecutor Mikhailovich managed to remain in his office—and, consequently, in *troika*—until November 1938. The "Polish" and "Harbinite" orders further simplified the procedure of trial and execution by introducing a new practice, so-called *dvoikas* ("twosome" or "NKVD and the prosecutor of the USSR commission"). People who were repressed in the national operation of the NKVD were registered in special lists (which included a short biography for each victim), so that one signature could decide the fate of several dozen people at once. The "national" line of the Great Purge was supervised by the Third Department of the NKVD (struggle against espionage), while the "kulak" line was supervised by the Fourth Department (struggle against internal counterrevolution).

In Soviet Karelia, the work of "liquidation of anti-Soviet elements" was launched immediately after the February–March 1937 plenum, and it is possible to date the large-scale operation in Soviet Karelia to as early as March 1937, nearly five months before the issue of Order No. 00447. Beginning in the second half of March 1937, numerous reports were sent from Petrozavodsk to the Central Committee of the VKP(b) regarding the reorganization of party work as well as facts demonstrating the "revival of bourgeois nationalism." Within a month of the plenum, the new Karelian leadership uncovered and destroyed "fascist nationalist groups of Finnish terrorists" and "counterespionage and subversive rebellious organizations" in all border areas of Soviet Karelia, in the republican trust of the timber industry, Karelles, and in the People's Commissariat of Land.[94] Gylling, the former chairman of the Karelian government, still lived and worked in Moscow when a special resolution of the Karelian Regional Committee of the VKP(b), adopted on 26 March, renamed all *kolkhozes* and streets bearing his name.[95]

In general, it is difficult to differentiate the "kulak" and "national" operations: in many cases, "internal and external counterrevolution" were presented as one united threat, most evident in the case of the "counterrevolutionary nationalist organization in Karelia," code-named the "case of Gylling-Rovio."[96] The first report on this case was sent to Moscow at the end of July 1937. The membership list of this organization comprised fifty people, of whom forty-seven were Finns, two were Karelians, and one was Vepsian, all three ethnicities belonging to closely related Finno-Ugric peoples. Karl Tenison, the people's commissar of internal affairs of Soviet Karelia, identified Edvard Gylling and Kustaa Rovio as the leaders of the organization and asked his superiors to sanction their arrest in Moscow and "their subsequent transfer to our jurisdiction."[97] It is interesting that this initiative had clear local roots, for the Karelian leaders in Petrozavodsk did not know that Rovio had already been under arrest for three weeks and Gylling for two.

Officially, the mass operation in Soviet Karelia started on 5 August 1937. Each fifth day a telegram was sent from Petrozavodsk to Moscow, to the Eighth (Archival) Department of the Glavnoe Upravlenie Gosudarstvennoi Bezopasnosti (GUGB) (Main Directorate of State Security) of the NKVD, with information regarding the number of people arrested and convicted by the *troika*. During the first month of the operation (5 August–5 September 1937), 728 people were arrested.[98]

On 26 September, the chairperson of the Karelian *troika* and the head of the Karelian NKVD, Karl Tenison, delivered at the Plenum of the Karelian Regional Committee of the VKP(b) a report on the operation of liquidation of the "counterrevolutionary bourgeois nationalist organization." According to Tenison, this organization was one of the most elaborate and had existed since 1920, when Gylling and other Red Finns arrived in Soviet Karelia. They allegedly became the founders of a "nationalist center," and later, when Rovio, the first secretary of the Karelian vkp(b) between 1929 and 1935, joined it, "the alignment of forces in the republic was completely centralized in the hands of nationalists." Gylling and Rovio sought to intensify the recruitment of immigrant workers and insisted that illegal immigrants from Finland concentrated in nkvd camps were allowed to settle in Soviet Karelia. As for North American Finns, "they had a decent life over the ocean working as contractors, and here they agreed to work as rank-and-file workers. . . . It is clear that they had come with a clear mission: to establish, through their wives, legal connections with foreign countries." The report argued that the main objective of the "center" was annexation of Soviet Karelia by Finland and "restoration of capitalism by way of military intervention." To achieve this objective, operational bases were established in different places (Kondopoga pulp and paper plant, Petrozavodsk ski factory, Matrosy, Vilga) where anti-Soviet elements were concentrated, mostly illegal Finnish immigrants and North American Finns. The main operational base was located in Kondopoga, but in total insurgent bases were revealed in eleven Karelian districts. The Karelian Jäger Brigade was to serve as "the nucleus" of the planned rebellion, and special paramilitary detachments were allegedly created in certain places. The largest of these detachments was, according to Tenison, stationed secretly near Petrozavodsk. In the case of military actions, its task was to seize control of the road that linked Petrozavodsk and the Soviet-Finnish border (*Vokhtozerskii trakt*) in order to cut off Petrozavodsk from reinforcements and provide safe access for the Finnish army. Insurgent organizations were also involved in nationalist propaganda, espionage, sabotage "in the entire economy of Karelia," and terrorist acts such as "sending to Moscow terrorists who, disguised as *stakhanovites,* attempted to be accepted by Comrades Stalin and Molotov." In the end, Tenison assured the audience that there was still a lot of work to be done to eliminate all sprouts of the "nationalist center."[99]

All measures for the extermination of internal and external counterrevolution were planned to be completed within three or, at the latest, four months, but the first weeks proved that many local bureaucrats were satisfied neither with deadlines nor with the quotas for arrests as given in Ezhov's orders. The Central Committee of the vkp(b) and the nkvd of the ussr received numerous telegrams with requests to increase the quotas for arrests, especially for capital punishment. Soviet Karelia was part of this "initiative," and the central leadership eagerly satisfied the local requests.[100] As a result, by 20 November, the date initially given as the deadline for completion of the operation, the Karelian *troika* had sentenced to death 1,690 people (72 percent of its convictions), far more than its original quota of 300.[101]

In general, however, after the main nkvd orders were issued, the Karelian leadership found itself in a relatively difficult situation. The local office of the nkvd directed efforts mostly toward the repression of Finns and Karelians, though the orders dictated that it search as well for counterrevolutionaries among Germans, Poles, Latvians, and Estonians (to say nothing of "Harbinites"), all of whom were tiny minorities in Soviet Karelia.[102] In his directives to the Karelian districts, Karl Tenison demanded that his subordinates keep "a thorough register of all Finnish nationalist elements, primarily among political immigrants, former Social Democrats, former members of the Finnish Communist Party and the vkp(b), illegal immigrants from Finland, American Finns, and Swedes."[103] He continued to complain to Moscow that his work was complicated by the lack of official directives on the "Finnish line." Some sources allow us to suppose that a draft nkvd order on the Finnish operation was indeed prepared and that its author—Corps Commander Mikhail Frinovskii—suggested that repressive measures be taken not only against Finns but also against the "Karelian and, in general, Finno-Ugric population."[104] The order was never issued, but the Karelian leadership was granted permission for the Finnish operation: it was based on NKVD Orders No. 00485 (Polish) and No. 00693, "operation for repression of illegal crossers of the border of the USSR" (23 October 1937).

In December 1937, the first register lists were compiled with the names of people from "groups accused of espionage and subversive activities," and the Karelian *dvoika* started its work. The scale of its work is incomparable with previous repressions: the first nine register lists (4–30 December) included 900 people, of whom 727, or 80.8 percent, were sentenced to death. The ethnic composition of the victims also underwent a significant change: now Finns constituted 64.2 percent of the executions.[105]

The first results were summarized in a long memorandum that Tenison sent to Ezhov and Frinovskii on 10 January 1938. As of 1 January, 5,340 people had been arrested in Soviet Karelia, including "70 residents and 1,267 agents of foreign intelligence services." Of the 874 people arrested as part of the anti-Finnish campaign, 59 were claimed to be "resident agents" of the Finnish intelligence service and 283 its "illegal agents." An additional 480 were claimed to be "participants in counterrevolutionary nationalist insurgent or subversive organizations."[106]

In early January, the arrests by and activities of the extrajudicial bodies were suspended: the formal deadlines for all operations had passed, though previously issued sentences were still executed. Yet it was only a brief respite before the decisive assault. Although it was 1937 that came to embody the terror of that time, in many places, including Soviet Karelia, the bloodiest events were to take place in 1938.

On 31 January, new instructions were issued to extend national operations and the functioning of the extrajudicial bodies until 15 April. At the same time, for nine Soviet republics, twelve districts (*krais*) and regions (*oblasts*), and one autonomous republic (i.e., Soviet Karelia), the operation under Order No. 00447 was extended until 15 March, and new quotas for arrests were established. Soviet Karelia could repress an additional 700 people, of whom 500 could be executed.[107]

According to archival evidence, arrests and the activities of the republican *troika* were suspended for only two weeks, between 5 and 20 January, while in several districts the anti-Finnish campaign was carried out without any break.[108] Since late January, new directives ordering that "elimination of spy-diversionist organizations" had to be intensified were sent in large numbers from Petrozavodsk to Karelian regions. Initially, they caused serious confusion among the commanding officers of frontier guard detachments and of district departments of the NKVD. They were sending back inquiries asking for clarification of the situation—who had to be arrested and who not—and complaining that "there is not enough [human] material to work with."[109]

Their nervousness was likely explained by changes in the apparatus of the NKVD: a new round of mass repressions entailed purges in the political police itself. In Soviet Karelia, only senior NKVD officers were thus far affected. In January, the deputy commissar of internal affairs, the right-hand man of Karl Tenison, Captain Alexander Solonitsyn, was withdrawn from the republic. Tenison himself was withdrawn in early February. Of Latvian ethnicity, he was obviously regarded as unfit to continue effectively the execution of national operations. In April 1938, Tenison was arrested under charges of "right Trotskyism" and of serving as an agent of Latvian intelligence. A month later, before the trial, he died in the hospital of the Butyrka prison in Moscow.[110] A new commissar of internal affairs of Soviet Karelia was appointed, Colonel Stepan Matuzenko, a former Ukrainian peasant and psalm singer whose education combined a parish school and an OGPU school of frontier guards.[111]

Order was quickly imposed. The new commissar clarified how the "final elimination of all presence of foreign intelligence services among the Finnish colony" was to be carried out and gave clear instructions who had to be arrested (almost all Finns), how trials had to be carried out (with increased speed), and how trial documents had to be filled out. A separate file was created for each convicted person, which included (in two copies) a short biographical note based on a preset pattern. Completed files were sent with special military messengers to the Third Department of the Karelian NKVD in Petrozavodsk.[112]

Below is a biographical note sent from Petrozavodsk to all district departments of the NKVD as a model for composing similar notes for convicted persons. Combining real and fabricated data, these notes represented an Orwellian rewriting of history, reinterpreting people's biographies from the perspective of Soviet security bodies that, from the beginning of Finnish immigration from North America, regarded immigrant communities in Soviet Karelia as swarming with spies, saboteurs, and other "unreliable elements." The discursive construction of people's biographies gave security bodies grounds to determine their fates, in most cases condemning them to death.[113]

Huuki
Kalle Karlovich, born 1898
> United States, Mexico,
> lived in Finland, of Finnish ethnicity
> nationality: USSR, w/o party affiliation, in [the Civil War of] 1918
> was a volunteer on the White side.
> Before the arrest had worked as a carpenter of the tractor base.

Petrozavodsk
In 1926, Kalle Huuki was recruited by the Finnish intelligence and was assigned to reveal underground workers' organizations.

In 1927, Huuki was transferred to America, where he continued to work for the Finnish intelligence.

In 1931, Huuki was transferred to the USSR.

In 1936, Huuki established contact with an insurgent organization in the Kestenga region, where he carried out counterrevolutionary nationalist propaganda by lauding Finland. While working in the regional woodworking enterprise, Huuki committed acts of sabotage.

In 1937, he changed the place of work for Interposiolok of the Priazha region, where he established connections with an espionage-nationalist organization and participated in discussions on the preparation of a military uprising against the USSR.

Admitted his guilt, also proved guilty by the evidence of accused Harju.[114]

Classify as the first category.[115]
NKVD   Prosecutor of the Karelian Republic
(Tenison)   (Mikhailovich)

For "a more accurate record of the progress and results of the operation," special reporting forms were developed that included detailed charts comprising all ethnicities mentioned in

NKVD orders. These filled-in forms were to be sent from Karelian regions to Petrozavodsk on the first and fifteenth of each month.[116] Since late February, there had been an avalanche-like growth of Finnish names in these forms sent by regional offices of the NKVD along with requests to approve the arrests of these "suspects." Arrests were sanctioned immediately, sometimes even on the telephone. In order to fulfill the directions "to enlarge the number of interrogated up to thirty people at once,"[117] many regional NKVD offices involved the VKP(b) and Komsomol activists in interrogations and arrests.

To reduce time lags between arrests and trials, a special investigating brigade was formed that became known in Soviet Karelia as the "iron" or "steel" brigade. It was created in Medvezhiegorsk in December 1937 specifically for the Finnish operation under the command of a state security lieutenant, N.F. Tidor. Arrested Finns who refused to testify against themselves were transported to Medvezhiegorsk, where Tidor was responsible for completing investigations of their cases and obtaining the necessary testimonies. Documents delicately labeled this process as "investigation procedures" (*sledstvennaia obrabotka*). Acting on the principle of "any means to an end," the "steel brigade" achieved incredible results—accused people signed all the documents given to them.[118] Medvezhiegorsk also became the chief place of execution for non-judicial trials in Soviet Karelia.[119] One can only be terrified by the pace of the firing squad headed by A.F. Shondysh, head of the Third Department of the NKVD at the White Sea-Baltic Canal: on 28 December 1937, at 4 a.m., 138 people were shot, including 89 Finns; on 2 January 1938, at the same time, 60 people were shot, of whom 59 were Finns; on 10 January, 148 people (83 Finns); on 20 January, 150 people (82 Finns); and on 21 January, 104 people (62 Finns).[120]

Of course, "special methods" of investigation and interrogation were kept away from the public eye and became known only much later from those victims who survived in prisons and gulag camps. Some information has also been preserved in archival documents. An example of such terrifying evidence is presented below.[121]

> **Top Secret. Series "K"**
> To the Head of the 72nd Border Guard Detachment of the NKVD
> > Major Comrade Dolmatov
> > Village Kniazhaia of the Kandalaksha Region
> > Attached find the investigative case No. 46359 of accused Hill, Viktor Ienosovich, in order to investigate the cause of his death during the interrogation and to identify those guilty of giving and carrying out the order of drowning his corpse without a proper postmortem forensic medical examination.
> > Order to investigate the case to the Plenipotentiary Officer of the Special Department.
> > Attach the materials of the investigation to the case of Hill and send them back to the NKVD of Soviet Karelia by 27.03.38.
> > Matuzenko, Antonov,
> > 16.3.38

We have been unable to find any other evidence related to this case. It is likely that the victim was Victor Joonas Hill, born in 1888, who had arrived in Petrozavodsk from the United States on 27 December 1931.[122] This is all that we know about him. His name is not mentioned in any of the lists of repressed or rehabilitated people. In the spring of 1938, he disappeared, and everybody forgot about him. It is highly probable that this case was far from unique, and we do not know of many similar stories of American and Canadian Finns who disappeared without a trace during the Great Terror.

As time passed, local security organs took the initiative in the Finnish operation. While in February the head office of the Karelian NKVD in Petrozavodsk had to urge on its regional offices, in March and early April (the deadline was initially set as 15 April) the latter kept on sending new lists of suspects requiring sanctions for their arrests and urging not to delay the sanctions "because the deadline is fast approaching."[123] Explanatory notes attached to these lists demonstrated the logic behind the arrests, according to which people with any deviations in their biographies were regarded as a priori guilty: "[The regional department of the NKVD] requests a sanction to arrest nine illegal Finnish immigrants who live in Matrosy under special surveillance of the NKVD. We do not have evidence against the aforementioned Finns, but they are interesting people. They have to be immediately isolated."[124] Soon, however, there was no need to rush: the Finnish operation was extended, initially for one month, and then the NKVD of the USSR issued a new order, No. 1160 (28 May), which once again extended national operations until 1 August.[125] In Soviet Karelia, mass arrests continued until 10 August, and individual cases continued even after this deadline.

The final results of the operation were summed up in mid-August. They clearly demonstrate how much "more effectively" the secret police bodies worked in 1938: in comparison with 1937, the number of repressed Finns more than tripled, from 743 to 2,446 people.[126] According to the reports, the intelligence services of ten states (Japan, Germany, England, France, Poland, Latvia, Estonia, Turkey, Norway, and, of course, Finland) "operated" in Soviet Karelia.[127] Altogether between 1 January and 10 August 1938, 5,164 people were repressed, including 1,903 (33 percent) within the "kulak" line and 3,208 (55 percent) within "national" operations.[128]

These data, based on materials of the Karelian NKVD from 1938 to 1939, cannot be characterized as complete. For instance, they do not include the results of operations involving the resettlement of families of "enemies of the people" carried out in Soviet Karelia during the summer of 1938. On the whole, we have only a general picture of what was happening there. In areas where Finns formed visible minorities—Prionezhskii, Kondopozhskii, Kalevalskii, and Priazhinskii regions and, of course, Petrozavodsk—arrests were made daily. People were seized on the streets in broad daylight in full view of shocked passersby. There were "hot" days when lorries full of people were driven away from large factories, including the Kondopoga pulp and paper plant and the Petrozavodsk ski factory.[129] At the same time, large-scale operations were carried out to resettle families of repressed Finns from Petrozavodsk and the border areas.

On 9 June 1938, Stepan Matuzenko, a new people's commissar of internal affairs of Soviet Karelia, sent to Moscow, "personally to Comrade Ezhov," a memorandum "on the resettlement of Finnish Americans and families of repressed Finns from the Karelian ASSR." This document is worth a lengthy quotation, for it framed and expressed a new official interpretation of North American immigration to Soviet Karelia.

> An anti-Soviet organization of Finnish bourgeois nationalists was revealed and destroyed on the territory of the Karelian ASSR. Ringleaders of this counterrevolutionary organization, its chairmen Gylling and Rovio, did not find support for their vile intentions among the working Karelian population and used illegal immigrants from Finland, remaining unconquered [sic] kulaks and members of the Karelian rebellion [of 1921–22].

Apart from that, Gylling reinforced the enemy lines by recruiting [North] American Finns from Canada through the specially organized Resettlement Administration. This measure was justified by the insufficient labor force in the Karelian timber industry. Finns arrived from Canada with private cars, typewriters, foreign currency, and instructions from foreign intelligence services. . . . Among the Finns arrested during 1937–38, there were 2,100 spies, or 20 percent of all Finns living in Karelia. Bourgeois-nationalist Finnish organization placed in responsible and leading positions only its supporters, i.e., Finns. Consequently, they concentrated in their hands the most important party, administrative, and public organizations, as well as industrial enterprises, agriculture, and transportation. . . . Their measures to frustrate plans set by the party and the government led to the current complicated situation in Karelia, which struggles hard against the consequences of their subversive activities.

The nationality policy in Karelia, because of Gylling, Rovio, and their henchmen, became totally distorted. Workers of Karelia had to read newspapers and books, listen to radio programs, educate their children in the language foreign to them. Ethnic tensions and hostility were cultivated in all possible ways.

The staff of the NKVD of the KASSR carried out special work to register remaining Finnish Americans. Personal records were made for 1,416 people, of whom 81 are foreign nationals. Most Finnish Americans live in border areas and a certain part in Petrozavodsk.

I am asking for your order to resettle from the border areas of the Karelian republic 1,416 Finnish Americans to Omsk or Arkhangelsk regions where they should be employed exclusively in timber harvesting. Besides, I am asking for sanction to resettle 1,500 families of repressed Finns living in border areas and Petrozavodsk to outside of Karelia.[130]

In the historical context of the search for internal and external enemies, all biographic facts that deviated from more or less typical Soviet biographies were interpreted as proof of disloyalty to Soviet power. Possession of private cars, typewriters, and foreign currency was automatically equated with "instructions from foreign intelligence services." The concentration of Finns, who constituted a large portion of the Karelian proletariat, in important industrial sites and their large share in the regional bureaucracy were reinterpreted as attempts to put industries and the administration of Soviet Karelia under "Finnish" control. The cultural policy of Gylling's government, in the new interpretation of Karelian security organs, was allegedly aimed at "cultivation of ethnic tensions and hostility." In other words, all categories of Gylling's immigration policy were reverted from positive to negative, which led to a logical conclusion: all American and Canadian immigrants remaining in Soviet Karelia had to be deported to internal areas of the Soviet Union, namely Siberia or the northern territories.

Moscow did not grant the required sanctions, and in late August Matuzenko once again appealed to Nikolai Ezhov with a similar request: "In order to destroy the favorable soil in which foreign intelligence services can implant new espionage organizations on the territory of Karelia, particularly in border areas, it is necessary to hasten the issuing of sanctions to resettle from Karelia all Finnish Americans who arrived from Canada [sic], as well as families of repressed Finns, Estonians, Latvians, Germans, and Poles."[131]

This appeal was also left without a formal response, and American and Canadian immigrants as a group did not become victims of total deportation, which happened to a number of other ethnic groups in the Soviet Union. Yet, despite the lack of formal approval, the cleansing of border areas and Petrozavodsk was carried out during the summer of 1938. People were resettled from Petrozavodsk, Uhtinskii, and Rebolskii regions to "rear" regions of Karelia, including Kemskii, Pudozhskii, and Zaonezhskii. According to instructions, resettlement was enforced on "families of enemies of the people, repressed Finns, Swedes, Estonians, Latvians, and ethnicities that live outside the Soviet Union."[132] People were usually given twenty-four hours, and sometimes as little as two hours, to pack. The scale of the operation can be estimated only on the basis of indirect data. For example, it is known that between 20 July and 23 August 395 families, or 922 people, including 417 children, were resettled from Petrozavodsk.[133] In October, Matuzenko reported to Ezhov that, after the resettlement operation, 1,350 Finns (including families of the repressed) still lived in border areas of Soviet Karelia, and he asked for permission to complete the operation.[134]

The last chords of the mass operations sounded in the autumn of 1938. On 17 September, Ezhov signed Order No. 00606 to create special *troikas* "for trial of cases of the people arrested under the NKVD of the USSR Order No. 00485 and others." This meant the immediate massacre of those who had been arrested during the spring and summer of 1938 under the national orders. During two incomplete months of the work of Soviet Karelia's special *troikas* (Kuprianov, Matuzenko, Mikhailovich), 1,805 people were convicted, including 1,499 Finns, and of those convicted 1,708 people (94.6 percent) were sentenced to execution.[135] Consequently, if we admit, on the basis of presumably incomplete data, that by 10 August 9,536 people were arrested and convicted in Soviet Karelia, including 3,189 Finns,[136] then the total number of Finns repressed there in 1937 and 1938 was at least 4,688, with a third of them becoming victims of the Great Terror in its last two months.

The joint resolution of the SNK of the USSR and the Central Committee of the VKP(b), "on arrests, procurator control, and investigation" (17 November 1938), suspended mass repressions. The peak of the Great Purge had passed.

TRAGIC STATISTICS

Since the early 1990s, national governments, public organizations, and individual scholars have been involved in research projects aimed at identifying personal information of victims of Stalinist terror. Searches conducted by the Karelian office of the Memorial, a Russian civil rights society, and by researchers Mayme Sevander and Eila Lahti-Argutina produced reliable data on 739 North American Finns who became victims of the Great Terror during 1937 and 1938.[137] But this list is far from complete. Lahti-Argutina's register of Finnish victims of the Great Terror, in particular, indicates the country of birth but does not mention the country of origin for many Finnish immigrants. Only from other archival documents can we learn that, to take just one case, Arho Erola, a worker for the Karelian Building Trust, repressed and executed in April 1938,[138] had arrived in Soviet Karelia from the United States in one of the first immigrant groups in December 1930.[139] For some people, however, archival documents do not provide any information related to their repression. Fredrik Lindholm, the art director of the Finnish National Theater during the 1940s and 1950s, arrived in Soviet Karelia from Canada in 1931. In the spring of 1938, he was arrested along with an entire building crew of twelve Finns when they were finishing a pavilion on the Petrozavodsk railroad station. Imprisonment followed, then the gulag camp in Solikamsk, where his hands were broken. Yet he was lucky: he was among very few Finns released before the Soviet-Finnish War (the Winter War of 1939–40), and he was able to return to Soviet Karelia and even completed his education in art school in 1941.[140] His name is not mentioned in any official list of repressed or rehabilitated people.

There can be many such examples. Still, the current data provide a general idea of the state terror deployed against North American Finns and allow us to identify certain tendencies and patterns of terror.

Among 739 North American Finns who were, according to the victim list of Lahti-Argutina, repressed during 1937 and 1938, 323 people had arrived in Soviet Karelia from Canada (seventeen had been born there) and 416 from the United States (ninety-four had been born there). This is roughly proportionate to the number of Americans and Canadians in the North American immigrant group in Soviet Karelia, where 58 percent of the immigrants were from the United States and 42 percent from Canada. If we assume that by the late 1930s approximately 4,500 to 5,000 immigrants still lived in Soviet Karelia (this figure takes into account a likely number of re-emigrants), the share of the repressed among them was likely 15 percent.

The proportion of men and women among the repressed is almost equal among both American and Canadian groups of immigrants: 384 men (92 percent) among American Finns and 311 men (96 percent) among Canadian Finns. Men thus bore the brunt of the Great Terror, while women remained relatively unaffected by direct repression. Of course, they still suffered immensely because of the loss of breadwinners or as relatives of "enemies of the people," which automatically made them the most socially disadvantaged group.

To better understand the impact of the Great Terror on North American immigrants, we compared the demographic composition of repressed immigrants vis-à-vis the overall demographic composition of the North American diaspora in Soviet Karelia. In two charts below (Figures 37 and 38), we have superimposed two lines: the dashed line represents the age composition of American and Canadian men in the immigrant community in Soviet Karelia as of 1937–38, and the solid line represents the age composition of victims of the Great Terror, so it is possible to see graphically how large the impact of anti-Finnish repression was on the immigrant communities.

These data give a general idea of losses that Finnish American communities in Soviet Karelia suffered during the Great Terror. We assume that by 1937 between 1,300 and 1,400 Finnish American men still lived in Soviet Karelia, which means that the share of the repressed among them was about 28 percent, roughly each fifth male immigrant. The age distribution of victims generally coincided with the age composition of the Finnish American immigrant group, as the chart above demonstrates. There were, of course, deviations: among young men born in 1917 and 1918, nearly all were repressed (seventeen of nineteen), while the share of repressed among men born in 1898 was 15 percent, much below the average. American immigrants suffered major losses in the age group of forty-five to fifty-five: in total, 160 people, or 42 percent of repressed American men.

The age composition of Canadians repressed during the Great Terror mirrors the age composition of the entire Canadian immigrant group. As in the case of American immigrants, less affected by repression was the generation between twenty and thirty years of age—those who had grown up and received education in the Soviet Union and in any case were too young before immigration to the USSR to be accused of espionage in large numbers (though such accusations were still regularly applied to this age group). We assume that by 1937 the approximate number of Finnish Canadian men in the USSR was about 1,100, which means that the share of the repressed among them was roughly 28 percent, similar

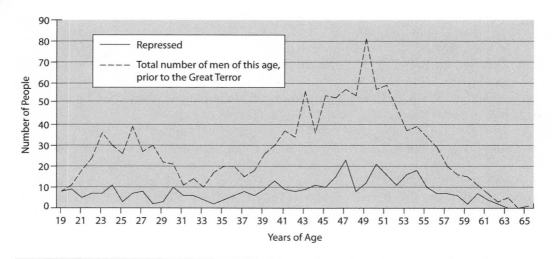

FIGURE 37. AGE DISTRIBUTION OF FINNISH AMERICAN MEN REPRESSED DURING 1937 AND 1938 COMPARED WITH THEIR TOTAL NUMBER PER AGE GROUPS.

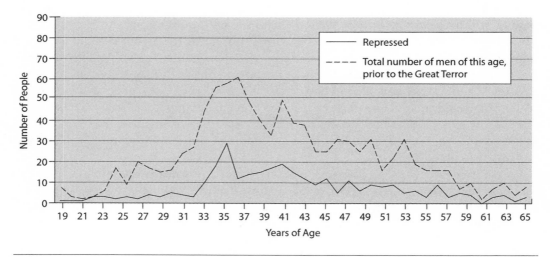

FIGURE 38. AGE DISTRIBUTION OF FINNISH CANADIAN MEN REPRESSED DURING 1937 AND 1938 COMPARED WITH THEIR TOTAL NUMBER PER AGE GROUPS.

to the percentage of Finnish American victims of the Great Terror. The most affected age group of Canadian Finns was men between thirty and forty: 156 men, or 50 percent of the repressed.

The most elderly of repressed Americans was Juho Paavo Niemi, born in 1873 in Finland. In 1932, he emigrated to Soviet Karelia from the United States, worked in the commune Säde, was arrested in July 1938, convicted as a spy, and executed on 12 October in Olonets at the age of sixty-five. Among the repressed, there were also eleven very young men of eighteen and nineteen. All had been born in 1919 and arrested in Petrozavodsk in the summer of 1938. One of them had moved to Soviet Karelia with his parents from Canada, the rest from the United States (nine of the ten were American born, including two from Michigan). Three of these young men worked at the factory Onezhskii, while six others were musicians of the Petrozavodsk Folk House and students of the Petrozavodsk Music College. Seven of them were executed as spies in September 1938; two others were sentenced to ten years in gulag camps, and only two whose cases were investigated in January 1939 were ultimately released.[141]

The arrests of North American Finns peaked during two periods: between December 1937 and February 1938 and then between July and August 1938. The first peak corresponded with official sanctions granted for the implementation of the Finnish operation, while the second occurred just before the end of the Great Purge. This is particularly clear if the dates of arrests of Canadian Finns are represented as in Figure 39. Although both peaks affected American immigrants as well, the summer months of 1938 turned out to be the most devastating for them (see Figure 40). The total impact of the Great Terror can also be seen from the perspective of immigrant flows of different years. Table 5 and Figure 41 demonstrate which share of each yearly flow (from 1930 to 1935) fell victim to Soviet repressive policies several years later.

Almost all arrested Finns were accused under one or several paragraphs of Article 58, "Counterrevolutionary Crimes," of the Criminal Code of the RSFSR, most commonly under paragraphs 58/2 (counterrevolutionary rebellion), 58/6 (espionage), 58/7 (sabotage), 58/10 (anti-Soviet propaganda), and 58/11 (counterrevolutionary crime). Most often sentences used paragraph 58/6, alone or in combination with others. Of those victims whose sentences are known, 61 percent of the accused were charged with espionage, and almost all of them (91 percent) were sentenced to death. In total, 84 percent of Canadian Finns and 71 percent of American Finns were sentenced to execution. Most were shot near Petrozavodsk or Medvezhiegorsk.

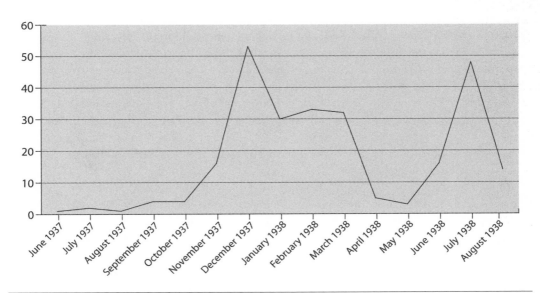

FIGURE 39. MASS ARRESTS OF CANADIAN IMMIGRANTS.

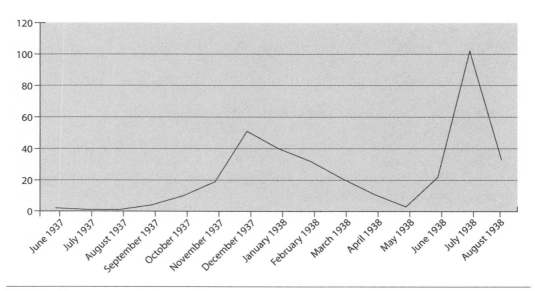

FIGURE 40. MASS ARRESTS OF AMERICAN IMMIGRANTS.

REHABILITATION, FORGETTING, REMEMBRANCE

Single rehabilitations began to occur immediately after the end of the Great Terror: in 1939, one North American immigrant was rehabilitated, in 1940 three more. The mass rehabilitation of innocent victims of the 1930s began only in the mid-1950s, after the death of Stalin, triggered particularly by the decision of the Central Committee of the KPSS of 4 May 1954 on the establishment of central and regional commissions for the review of criminal cases of people convicted of counter-revolutionary crimes. A Karelian commission was established among others.[142] Cases were reviewed on the basis of an official request from either a victim or his or her relatives. During the period from 1955 to 1965, 311 Canadian and American Finns were rehabilitated, 42 percent of the overall number of repressed immigrants. Often relatives were informed that the convicted person had died of a natural cause, and only when the second wave of rehabilitations started during perestroika would they learn of the real cause of death. Relatives were also misinformed of the real dates of deaths in order to conceal the scale of repression in 1937 and 1938. In the case of Oscar Corgan, a former head of the Karelian Technical Aid Committee from 1932 to 1934, relatives were first notified in 1956 that he had died of stomach cancer on 18 July 1940, and only thirty-five years later, in 1991, did they learn that he had been shot on 9 January 1938 (see Figures 42 and 43).

Then a lengthy pause followed, and only in the late 1980s did the process of rehabilitation of illegally convicted people resume. The decree of the Presidium of the Supreme Soviet of the USSR of 16 January 1989 rehabilitated those who had been sentenced by non-judicial bodies. The law of the Russian Federation "on the rehabilitation of victims of political repression" (No. 1761–1 of 18 October 1991) significantly enlarged the number of victims eligible for official rehabilitation by including all convicted under the so-called counterrevolutionary articles. This time cases were reviewed on the basis of documents of security organs, without official requests or complaints from the formerly repressed people or their relatives. As a

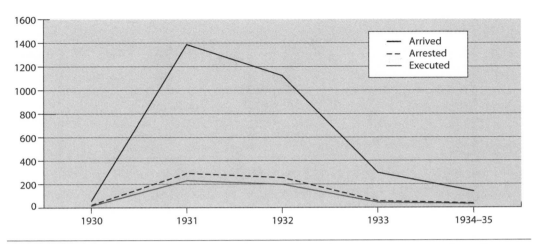

FIGURE 41. THE SHARE OF REPRESSED IN THE MALE POPULATION OF NORTH AMERICAN COMMUNITIES IN SOVIET KARELIA, ANALYZED PER YEAR OF ARRIVAL.

Table 5. The Share of Repressed People among the Population of North American Immigrants to Soviet Karelia, Analyzed Per Year of Arrival

| Year of arrival | Men | | | Women | | |
	Arrived	Arrested (absolute/in percentage)	Executed (absolute/in percentage)	Arrived	Arrested	Executed
1930	59	23 (39%)	16 (27%)	18	0	0
1931	1,387	292 (21%)	230 (17%)	591	11	4
1932	1,124	255 (23%)	198 (18%)	535	20	10
1933	297	55 (19%)	44 (15%)	150	4	2
1934–35	139	36 (26%)	31 (22%)	84	6	3

result, during this period, 326 North American Finns were rehabilitated, 44 percent of the total number of repressed immigrants. We still do not have any data on the rehabilitations of eighty-three people (11 percent).

The fact that over half of Finnish Americans and Canadians were rehabilitated only during and after perestroika, or have not been rehabilitated, means that many of the immigrants who perished in Soviet prisons and camps were not searched for. Several explanations can account for this. After the years of the Great Terror and the Second World War, many repressed immigrants simply had no relatives in the USSR who would have submitted after 1954 formal requests for rehabilitations. This was partly because single people constituted a large share of the immigrant community and partly because whole families were sometimes repressed. Children left without parents were sent to orphanages, some were adopted and their names changed, and many learned of their ancestry only decades later.[143]

There was yet another reason why many innocent victims were forgotten, even repressed from individual and public memory for many decades. The fear that people experienced during the Great Purge was so great that some of them changed their names

Karjalais-Suomalainen Sosialistinen Neuvostotasavalta
Карело-Финская Советская Социалистическая Республика

KUOLINTODISTUS
СВИДЕТЕЛЬСТВО О СМЕРТИ

ЦЮ № 084835

Kansalainen
Гр.   *Корган*

(sukunimi—фамилия)

Оскар-Федерик   Карлович

(nimi ja isännimi—имя и отчество)

on kuollut *(18/VII —1940) восемнадцатого июля*
умер(ла)

(vuosi, kuukausi ja päivä kirjoituksella ja numeroilla—

тысяча девятьсот   сорокового года

прописью и цифрами год, месяц и число)

kuoleman syynä on ollut   *рак желудка*
причина смерти
josta siviiliasian kuolinrekisteriin
о чем в книге записей актов гражданского состояния о смерти

1956 vuonna   *ноября*   kuun *21* päivänä
года   месяца   числа

on tehty vastaava merkintä   № *53*
произведена соответствующая запись за

Kuolinpaikka: Karjalais-Suomalaisen SNT:a   kaupunki
Место смерти: Карело-Финская ССР, город

piiri   kylä
район   селение

Rekisteröintipaikka   *Сухта   районное бюро*
Место регистрации
ЗАГС

(siviilirekisteritoimiston nimi ja paikka—

наименование и местонахождение бюро ЗАГС)

ноября   v. 19 *56* г.

Siviilirekisteritoimiston johtaja
Заведующий бюро записей актов   *Корган*
гражданского состояния

Финский (Карельский) из. Гознак. 1947.

FIGURES 42 AND 43. TWO OFFICIAL DEATH CERTIFICATES THAT RELATIVES OF OSCAR CORGAN RECEIVED AFTER HIS REHABILITATION. THE FIRST, ISSUED IN 1956 (*LEFT*), CLAIMED THAT HE DIED OF STOMACH CANCER ON 18 JULY 1940; THE SECOND, ISSUED IN 1991, CONFIRMED THAT HE WAS EXECUTED ON 9 JANUARY 1938 (COURTESY OF STELLA SEVANDER).

СВИДЕТЕЛЬСТВО О СМЕРТИ
KUOLINTODISTUS

Гражданин (ка)
Kansalainen *Корган*

Оскар-Фредерик Карлович

sukunimi
nimi, otsesto – etu- ja isännimi

умер(ла)
on kuollut *9. 01. 1938 года   Девятого января*
число, месяц, год – päivä, kuukausi, vuosi

Одна тисела двемсот тридцать

(цифрами и прописью – numeroilla ja kirjoittamalla)

восимого года

в возрасте *51* лет, о чем в книге регистрации актов о смерти
vuoden ikäisenä, mistä siviilirekisterin kuolinluetteloon

19 *56* года
vuoden   *ноября* месяца *21* числа
kuun   päivänä

произведена запись за № *53*
on tehty merkintö   n:o

Причина смерти
Kuoleman aiheutti   *Расстрелян*

Место смерти: город, седение
Kuolinpaikka: kaupunki, kylä   *Не установлено*

район
piiri

область, край
alue, aluepiiri

республика
tasavalta

Место регистрации
Rekister...   *Райотдел Калевальского*
наименование и местонахождение органа ЗАГСа –
siviilirekisteritoimiston nimi ja sijaintipaikka

16 "   *августа*   19 *91* г.
v.

Заведующий отделом (бюро)
актов гражданского состояния
...irekisteriosaston (toimiston)
johtaja   *Хейнонен*

...ГИ   № 390096

and did not want to remember their pasts and disappeared relatives. One case serves as a good illustration of the complex interrelation between processes of rehabilitation, forgetting, and remembering. Mayme Sevander's book *The Wanderers* (*Skitaltsy*) mentions the Salo family from Cleveland, Ohio. At the height of the Great Terror, Henry and Emilia Salo made a desperate attempt to flee to Finland. Their plan failed, they were arrested, and their son Taisto remained alone. The further fate of the entire family remained unknown for many years.[144]

Only recently discovered data shed light on this case. Henry and Emilia arrived in Soviet Karelia from the United States in 1931 and were arrested in Kondopoga on 27 August 1938, after the end of the mass anti-Finnish operation. In October 1938, they were sentenced to five years of imprisonment under Article 19–84,[145] which proves that they indeed tried to escape across the border. We do not have any data on whether they survived imprisonment, but they were rehabilitated only fifty-one years later, in 1989, according to a decree of the chief prosecutor of Soviet Karelia.[146] As for their son, Taisto, he was brought up in orphanages where he changed his last name to Likhachev. Since 1958, he lived in the Murmansk region, worked as a geologist, and never, even to his family members, mentioned his ancestry. Only after his death in 1991 did his son accidentally learn of his father's original name as well as the fact that his father had been a Finn from the United States.[147]

This case is far from unique. Many of those who survived the Great Terror refused to remember their experience of repression even in the 1990s. Forgetting sometimes dominates over remembering and even official rehabilitation, as evidenced by the fact that at least eighty-three repressed American and Canadian immigrants have never been rehabilitated and, consequently, are officially regarded as guilty of crimes that they never committed. In this case, forgetting still legitimates the regime responsible for their deaths.

The tragedy of North American Finns was accompanied by intentional efforts of Soviet authorities to erase memories of them and their contributions to the economic, social, and cultural development of Soviet Karelia. Because of these efforts, all official histories of Soviet Karelia long remained silent about the story of North American immigrants.

Official documents stopped mentioning North American immigrants already in 1936. If one examines newspapers or official materials of the second half of the 1930s, one might get the impression that there had never been American or Canadian Finns in Soviet Karelia. Even reports of the NKVD rarely mention them and then only with a specific label, "Finnish Americans from Canada" (*finnamerikantsy, pribyvshiie iz Kanady*). But, as a rule, NKVD materials that characterized the political situation in Soviet Karelia ignored the specificity of this group, generally mentioning instead "hostile activities of Finnish fascists" or "bourgeois nationalists of Finnish origins." The situation could be different in personal criminal cases that made all kinds of allegations about a person's life in North America, including "connections with American Trotskyites" or, as in the case of Matti Tenhunen, implementation, while in the United States, of "activities hostile to the Soviet Union."[148] But Canadian or American Finns were never mentioned as a separate "suspicious" group, and no case was fabricated against them that would have accused them of espionage or other subversive activities beneficial to American or Canadian intelligence (as typically happened with immigrants from Finland, Germany, and most other European nations). Canada and the United States were among the few states that the Karelian NKVD did not suspect of sending spies to Soviet Karelia. In all criminal cases that involved North American immigrants, they were indicated as Finns or people "of Finnish origin." When American or Canadian immigrants were accused of espionage, it was always allegedly for the Finnish intelligence, even if an accused person had been born in the United States or Canada and had never even visited Finland.

The last time that North American Finns were mentioned in the Soviet press was in 1939 when the 24 April issue of *Pravda,* the central Soviet newspaper, published an article written by Gennady Kupriianov, first secretary of the Karelian *obkom* of the VKP(b), titled "In the Karelian Forests." Describing the progress of the Karelian forest industry, Kupriianov mentioned three front-rank workers (*peredoviki*) who were immigrants from Canada. Only their last names were given: Partonen, Vuorela, and Santanen. This publication had obviously been ordered by the central Soviet authorities (no article would have appeared in *Pravda* otherwise), who, as well as the Executive Committee of the Comintern, could no longer ignore rumors and problems related to the Karelian fever accumulating in left-wing organizations of North American Finns, primarily in the Communist Party of Canada. After the end of the recruitment campaign in 1935, the leadership of the Communist Party of Canada sent several inquiries to the Comintern asking its Executive Committee to settle financial issues related to the activities of the Karelian Technical Aid Committee in Canada. The problem was that the Soviet travel agency Inturist, which, according to its contract with KTAC, took over transportation of Finnish emigrants to Soviet Karelia during later stages of the immigration process, owed $3,695, a significant sum at that time, to KTAC. This created a predicament for organizers of the recruitment when dissatisfied Finnish re-emigrants started to demand that the money that they had invested in KTAC be returned to them.[149] The new authorities of Soviet Karelia, who came to power in 1935, after the dismissal of Gylling, ignored the contract terms or expressed doubts about their validity.

The complicated situation that emerged in the Finnish organization of the Communist Party of Canada was described in detail in several letters that the secretary of the Finnish organization of the CPC, Gustav Sundquist, the general secretary of the CPC, Tim Buck, and the representative of the CPC in the Comintern, Tom Ewen, sent to the Executive Committee of the Comintern between 1936 and 1939.[150] They complained that John Latva, head of the Canadian office of KTAC, was under the threat of legal prosecution because of lost investments and that by 1939 the question of investments lost during the emigration to and re-emigration from Soviet Karelia had grown to such a degree that the entire Finnish organization of the CPC was on the verge of collapse. Moreover, Finnish Communist leaders were unable to resist intense anti-Soviet campaigning organized by returnees who spoke of "harsh persecutions of Finns" in Soviet Karelia. Canadian Communists who had no information on what was happening in the Soviet Union asked for an explanation of how to answer anxious questions regarding "our miserable comrades who suffer of tortures and persecutions."[151]

The apogee of these complaints from Canadian Communists was a letter sent by Tom Ewen to Georgi Dimitrov, the general secretary of the Comintern, on 4 April 1939:

Dear Comrade Dimitrov!

In accordance with the directives from the Communist Party of Canada, I have written during the past seven months a number of letters and memoranda to members of the Executive Committee of the Comintern in which I insisted that something had to be done to assist the Communist Party of Canada in settling a difficult situation that emerged when a large number of dissatisfied Canadian Finns returned to Canada from Soviet Karelia. Recently I have submitted to you and Comrade Kuusinen [head of the Finnish Communist Party] a number of documents, applications, letters and other documents encompassing the period of four years during which former representatives of the Communist Party of Canada and I have tried to achieve a somewhat satisfactory settlement of our question. These efforts had brought no results so far. . . . Apart from financial difficulties for the Finnish organization of Canada . . . this is related to an even larger political question. Those Finns who have returned back home from Soviet Karelia are writing slanderous fabrications in Fascist and Trotskyite [sic] newspapers of Canada. Their articles are in turn reprinted verbally by Fascist press in Finland. Our Canadian party and our Finnish Canadian comrades cannot respond with concrete facts to this slander and accusations. . . . I believe that both questions could have been settled, if not completely then at least partly, several years ago and that further delays will only accelerate demoralization and complete liquidation of a valuable part of the Canadian workers' movement—the Finnish organization of Canada.[152]

Dimitrov, who seemed to have finally understood the complicated character of this situation, sent a memorandum to Andrei Zhdanov, secretary of the Central Committee of the VKP(b) and chairman of the RSFSR Supreme Soviet. The memorandum "on the anti-Soviet activities of the Finnish population in Canada" was promptly redirected to the leadership of Soviet Karelia. Forced to react quickly, the Karelian authorities broke all bureaucratic records, for it took them only one week to examine and summarize all materials related to the history of North American Finnish immigration to Soviet Karelia.[153] The documents gathered by the deputy head of the Karelian NKVD, Dmitri Nefiodov, and his summary written for Kupriianov referred to all North American immigrants, with more emphasis on American than Canadian Finns, particularly on the already executed Matti Tenhunen and Kalle Aronen. Still, the material that Kupriianov prepared for Moscow was titled, in response to Dimitrov's letter, "On Finnish Immigrants from Canada."

The fifteen-page memorandum sent to the secretary of the Central Committee of the VKP(b), Andrei Andreev, on 14 April 1939 narrated the story of North American immigrants in such a way as to meet the expectations of the authorities in Moscow. Political assessments, facts, and statistics (some of which were changed compared with Dmitri Nefiodov's data) were recompiled to finally discredit the recruitment campaign among North American Finns and bring oblivion to this page of Karelian history. Below is a summary of the main theses of Kupriianov's memorandum, which gives an idea of silences and biases used to construct a new story—the one of treachery and subversion.

The memorandum argued that immigrants—their total number was deflated to 4,681—resettled in Soviet Karelia only from Canada, and the United States was not mentioned at all. To discredit the campaign, the document claimed that only between 20 percent and 25 percent of immigrants went to work in the forest industry, while the rest became employed in "Soviet administration, trade, theaters, cinematography, et cetera," exploiting a cultural division between the primary sector, in which work was regarded as prestigious and socially important, and less "important" sectors such as services and administration. The rest of the document represented a similar game with numbers and interpretations to picture the recruitment activities of the Red Finnish leadership of Soviet Karelia as subversive.

In 1930–1939, 3,580 people[154] were naturalized in the USSR. During 1936–1939, 474 Finnish Canadians [sic] returned to Canada and the United States, of whom 215 were expelled under the

NKVD orders (Circular No. 68)[155] and 259 left voluntarily. Between October 1937 and April 1939, 139 applications were also submitted to renounce from the Soviet citizenship. . . .

[The Resettlement Administration] was liquidated as a completely useless organization that was engaged in commercial activities rather than in recruitment of lumberjacks. But what is most important, it has been documentally proven that it was used by the Finnish, American, and German intelligences to send spies, saboteurs, and diversionists to the USSR.

[The document claimed that all activities were coordinated by Matti Tenhunen and Kalle Aronen]. During the recruitment of Finnish Canadians, Tenhunen and Aronen pursued only one goal: to flood Karelia with Finns in order to Finnicize the Karelian population and thus to prepare the ground for the seizure of Karelia from the Soviet Union. All this work was implemented in the name of a "Greater Finland."

Bourgeois nationalists did their best to stir up ethnic tensions, inciting Finns to attack Russians and Karelians, [and] in 1937–38 it was found out that many Canadian immigrants to Karelia turned out to be agents of capitalist intelligence agencies, and a number of others were arrested for anti-Soviet propaganda. . . .

All this led to a rise of emigration sentiment among Finns, but they have no ground, and currently the Regional Committee of the VKP(b) struggles successfully with excesses of 1937.[156]

By failing to mention any contribution of North American immigrants to the development of Soviet Karelia during the 1930s, and by reiterating accusations of the anti-Finnish campaign, Kupriianov's memorandum turned the Karelian fever into a phantom of the past that could easily be disregarded. It achieved its desired effect, for upon receiving it the Organizational Bureau of the VKP(b), the second most important body of the party hierarchy after the Politburo, adopted a resolution:

1. To instruct the VKP(b) delegation in the Executive Committee of the Comintern to raise the question of liquidation of the Karelian Technical Aid in Canada. Motivation: Karelia does not need aid.
2. To distribute the memorandum of the Karelian Regional Committee of the VKP(b) on the activities of the Karelian Technical Aid and the Resettlement Administration, as well as on the situation of Finnish Canadians in Karelia, among the Executive Committee of the Comintern in order to refute insinuations and slander disseminated by anti-Soviet agents in Canada and America.
3. To instruct the Karelian Regional Committee of the VKP(b) to organize immediately public speeches of Finnish Canadian immigrants to shed light on their genuine situation and to counter anti-Soviet propaganda against the Karelian republic. . . .
5. To instruct *Pravda* and *Izvestiia* to publish promptly several articles to refute anti-Soviet slander of [the] bourgeois press.
6. To circulate in the Executive Committee of the Comintern a memorandum of Comrade Krutikov[157] that provides data on [the] invalidity of financial claims that the Karelian Technical Aid asserts to Inturist.[158]

Thus, the power of the Soviet propaganda machine was directed not only at rewriting history at home but also at changes to the histories of Canadian and American Finnish communities. This strategy proved to be effective, as evidenced by another letter that Tom Ewen wrote to Kuusinen in October 1939, this time in a style and tone very different from his earlier letters:

Oct. 23rd 1939

Dear Comrade Kuusinen,

The following articles have been prepared and forwarded to the Canadian and USA Party press on the Karelia issue:

May 23rd—"Socialist Builders in Soviet Karelia"; this was published in the enclosed copy of The Daily Clarion—and also distributed in mimeograph press form by the C[ommunist] P[arty] USA.

July 15th—"Canada's Contribution to Soviet Karelia."

Aug. 6th—"Socialist Rulers in Soviet Karelia."

Sep. 29th—"In Soviet Karelia Tomorrow is Ours."

I have not seen the issue but from a letter from comrade Carr I was advised that the second article appeared in "Vapaus," the Canadian Finnish Daily.

The last two articles of which I am not aware of whether they have been published or not, were constructed upon materials received from the committee of the C[ommunist] P[arty] of Soviet Karelia under instructions from the C[entral] C[ommittee] of the CPSU.

Along about June and August I also wrote two radio broadcasts on Soviet Karelia for Radio Centre. I have no copies of these but I presume these can be found in the files of Radio Centre. I understand that you have copies of the other articles and materials referred to.

During the summer I have written a number of letters to our Canadian comrades on the Karelian issue, some of these went forward by mail, and others by trusted comrades returning to the USA. A Canadian comrade Salsberg was in Moscow during August of this year. I discussed the whole question with him and advised on the basis of the materials available from the CPSU, that the claims made by our comrades of the Finnish Organization and others in Canada re the winding up of the affairs of the "Technical Aid to Soviet Karelia" committee would not be honored by the Karelian comrades, who described it as a form of "blackmail."

Also, upon the basis of some of the materials received from the CPSU it was clear that John Latva and others associated with the case were not only agents of the Finnish police, but were utilizing these so called claims to slander the Soviet Union and to split the Finnish Organization of Canada. Our comrade returned to Canada with a clear understanding of what had to be done; (1) to consider the claims for money invalid; (2) to begin an intensive struggle against these Trotskyist elements in the Finnish Organization and in the CP and to clean them out; (3) to develop in our press, and particularly in the Finnish press, a campaign popularizing the great achievements of socialist construction and cultural development in Soviet Karelia. My materials were prepared with this latter view in mind, and the materials received from the Karelian CP and the CPSU have been of great value.

The matter of financial claims [is] considered finished, but on the progress or combating [of] these elements in Canada and the USA who have returned and are carrying on disruptive work among the Finnish people in those countries, I have no concrete information.

Comradely yours, Tom Ewen.[159]

Canadian Communists who, because of their secondary positions in the international Communist movement, had to follow directions from the Comintern and VKP(b) thus became a tool of Soviet propaganda in obscuring the history of American and Canadian immigrants to Soviet Karelia in their home communities. The outbreak of the Second World War further removed all these questions from the agenda of Canadian and Soviet Communist organizations.

In Soviet Karelia, the propaganda campaign of 1939 was hardly noticed by anyone other than its leadership and did not entail any repressive measures among North American immigrants who still lived in the republic. The Great Terror, after all, was over by that time. But major results had been achieved: the inhabitants of Soviet Karelia forgot about North American Finns for fifty years. There is little wonder that even now many of them do not suspect that there live among them children and grandchildren of people who, in the first half of the twentieth century, twice crossed the Atlantic in search of their El Dorado.

CHAPTER 9

Wartime and After

THE SOVIET-FINNISH WAR

AFTER THE END OF MASS ARRESTS IN AUGUST 1938, THE LIVES OF NORTH AMERICAN immigrants gradually started to return to a more normal state. Immigrants were no longer a privileged group, but the food shortages of the first half of the 1930s were also over, and deprivation of privileges and mass arrests removed the causes of ethnic hostility toward immigrants, for whom the local population now had sympathy.[1] What is more important, in 1939 the American and Canadian Finns first arrested started to return to their communities. As a rule, they had been arrested in August 1938 and, consequently, avoided investigations of their cases in a "simplified" manner. And, though these instances were singular (according to Eila Lahti-Argutina's data, only twenty-three people were released before June 1941), the return of repressed compatriots created hope that the Soviet authorities realized that they had committed an injustice and that all victims would soon return home.

Yet 1939 did not become the first year of normal life again for inhabitants of Soviet Karelia, including North American Finns. The militarization of Europe, particularly of Nazi Germany, and its approach to Soviet borders through the Anschluss of Austria (1938), annexation of the Sudetenland (1938) and Bohemia and Moravia (1939), and satellitization of Eastern European states increased fears among the Soviet leadership of anti-Soviet aggression from the west. Apart from dangers, territorial and political changes in Europe also created new possibilities that the Soviet leadership was eager to exploit the expansion of its influence. In the summer of 1939, sluggish negotiations between Great Britain, France, and the USSR over collective security in Europe came to a dead end, and on 23 August 1939 the Soviet leadership concluded a non-aggression pact with Germany (the Molotov-Ribbentrop Pact).[2] Secret protocols of this pact included, among other terms, a provision according to which Finland was attributed to the Soviet "sphere of influence."

The outbreak of the Second World War on 1 September 1939, which pitted Nazi Germany against Great Britain and France, created a window of opportunity for Soviet territorial expansion westward. After the Red Army occupied eastern Polish territories in the second half of September, which led to the partition of Poland between Germany and the USSR, Finland became the next target. On 30 November 1939, after Finland refused—during several rounds of negotiations—to satisfy Soviet demands regarding security of the Soviet northwestern border (particularly areas adjacent to Leningrad), the Soviet Union launched a war against Finland, known as the Winter War.

Without going into detail on the causes and course of the conflict between the USSR and Finland, a subject of extensive scholarship, we would like to emphasize that the beginning of hostilities once again changed the status of the Finnish diaspora in the USSR. Soviet foreign policy had always been legitimated through the rhetoric of proletarian internationalism, which implied that the Soviet state never waged wars against "people" but only against "exploiting classes." The Soviet leadership could not therefore publicly announce the real strategic goals that it pursued in the war against Finland. As a result, just prior to the Winter War, a propaganda campaign was launched that had to convince, if not the international community, then at least the Soviet population that the Red Army crossed the Soviet-Finnish border upon "invitation" from the Finnish people rather than as an act of aggression.[3] Among other means to accomplish this, on 1 December a puppet government of the so-called Finnish Democratic Republic was formed from those Finnish Communist émigrés who had survived the Great Terror. Based in Terijoki, the first Finnish town seized (or "liberated" in the Soviet rhetoric of those days) by the Red Army, and headed by Otto Kuusinen, a prominent leader of the Comintern, the puppet government called on the Finnish people to assist Soviet troops and overthrow the "oppressive" and "bourgeois" government of Finland. In addition, a treaty was concluded between the Soviet government and the Finnish people's government. Its provisions included what Finnish nationalists had only dreamt of: in exchange for small territorial secessions in southern Finland that moved the border away from Leningrad, Finland received Russian Karelia west of the Murmansk Railroad. Explained in terms of the "reunification of brotherly Karelian and Finnish people," it was obviously a step to incorporate Finland, in the form of a Soviet republic, into the USSR.[4]

These political maneuvers allowed for representation of the Soviet-Finnish War not as an act of aggression against a sovereign state but as assistance to the Finnish proletariat in their efforts to implement a socialist revolution. Legitimation of the war among Soviet people was one thing; securing Finnish sympathies for a new Communist government that acted from territories conquered by the enemy was quite another. The Soviet leadership obviously foresaw that Kuusinen could hardly rally substantial support among the Finnish population, so already since mid-November, before the war actually broke out, detachments of the so-called Finnish People's Army were raised from Soviet Finns and Karelians. The Finnish People's Army was a military unit but also (or even primarily) a propaganda tool: plans were designed that, after the Red Army quickly smashed Finnish defenses, the government of the Finnish Democratic Republic would have a triumphal entry into Helsinki accompanied by the Finnish People's Army, which was supposed to create the illusion of a legitimate change of political regimes.[5]

American and Canadian immigrants of fighting age—all of them by that time had been naturalized into the Soviet citizenship—made up a noticeable part of the Finnish People's Army, though it is hard to estimate their exact number in this military unit. It was kept away from the front line and participated in combat only in the last few days of fighting, which made losses among American and Canadian combatants of the Winter War minimal. According to Mayme Sevander, only one American, Robert Kivikoski, and two Canadians, Yrjö Päätalo and Matti Kananen, were killed during the war.[6]

Stubborn resistance of the Finnish Army thwarted plans of the Soviet leadership. Although Finland suffered a military defeat and, according to provisions of the Moscow Peace Treaty of 12 March 1940, had to cede significant territories, immediate Sovietization of Finland was out of the question. To save face, the Soviet leadership changed the federal structure of the Soviet Union. On 31 March 1940, the Karelian Autonomous Soviet

Socialist Republic and territories seized from Finland were merged to form a new republic of the union: the Karelian-Finnish Soviet Socialist Republic. Thereby, though the number of Finns in Soviet Karelia, according to the 1939 census, was only 8,322 people, or less than 2 percent of the 470,000 population of Soviet Karelia,[7] and was nearly invisible in the scale of the USSR, Finns became a title nation, together with Karelians, of one of the principal constituent republics of the USSR.[8]

By that time, the policy of accelerated development of the Karelian literary language, carried out since 1937, had failed.[9] The return of Finns to "elite" Soviet nationalities automatically put an end to these sociolinguistic experiments, and Finnish once again received the status of the second official language of the newly created Karelian-Finnish SSR. This was justified by the arguments of linguistic and cultural commonality of Finns and Karelians that had been used by the previous leaders of Soviet Karelia who had perished in 1937: that Finnish was a highly developed literary language, could easily be comprehended by Karelians, and therefore was best suited to development of the culture of Soviet Karelia ("national in form and socialist in content") as well as development of "national" science and education. Foreign policy importance of the Finnish language was also emphasized since it had to contribute to "convergence of Karelian and Finnish peoples" and to "attainment of close cooperation" among them.[10]

In 1940, Finnish became a compulsory subject in all schools of Soviet Karelia, and Karelian-Finnish State University (now Petrozavodsk State University) was established in Petrozavodsk, in which teaching was also planned (though never implemented) in Finnish. The Finnish Theater of Petrozavodsk was created anew; a republican newspaper, *Totuus* (Finnish for "Truth"), and a journal, *Punalippu* (Finnish for "Red Banner"), were established, as well as a number of small regional Finnish-language newspapers in the areas of Soviet Karelia with large ethnic Karelian populations. Symptomatically, the Finnish language returned to Soviet Karelia in the same linguistic form as it had existed in Finland (i.e., as Finnish immigrants in Soviet Karelia knew it prior to their move there): there were no discussions of the development of "proletarian," or "Soviet," Finnish despite the unchallenged dominance of Marrism in Soviet linguistics (see Chapter 6). Simultaneously, the concepts of "Karelian-Finnish language" and "Karelian-Finnish people" were revived. For American and Canadian Finns, the result of all this was that once again they became specialists in demand in the market of education and culture.

This renaissance of Soviet Finnish culture, however, lasted for only slightly over a year, and even during this time the threat of further repression of Finns did not disappear from the Soviet political landscape. After Germany occupied Norway, the Soviet government intensified measures aimed at cleansing northern Soviet border areas of "disloyal subjects." On 23 June 1940, People's Commissar of Internal Affairs (Head of the NKVD) Lavrentiy Beria signed Order No. 00761, which liquidated all Finnish communities in the Kola Peninsula north of Soviet Karelia. Together with Norwegians, Swedes, Lithuanians, Latvians, and other "foreign nationals," Finns were forcibly deported from the Kola Peninsula first to Soviet Karelia and then to Siberia.[11]

Then, on 22 June 1941, Germany attacked the Soviet Union. Three days later, on 25 June, Finland joined the war as a co-belligerent on the German side. Finland's entry into war brought about another change in the status of the Finnish diaspora in the USSR. The Soviet leadership, which had always been suspicious of it as a potential fifth column, now launched a new round of repression against Soviet Finns.

THE ORDEAL OF WARTIME

Mass wartime deportations in the Soviet Union were launched with relocation of Soviet Germans from European Russia to Siberia and Kazakhstan starting in August 1941. By the beginning of 1942, about 905,000 Soviet Germans were deported from their communities, and by the end of the war this number had grown to 950,000. Apart from civilians, on 8 September 1941, the People's Commissariat for Defense issued Order No. 35105, which withdrew all soldiers and officers of German ethnicity from the acting army, about 33,500 people.[12]

German soldiers and officers demobilized from the Red Army became the basis of the so-called labor armies of the NKVD built on the model of gulag camps: with armed guards, harsh camp regimes, extreme conditions of labor, and low food rations. The formation of labor armies was supposed to solve the problem of acute labor shortages on the home front. In 1942, the State Defense Committee (a supreme organ of state power in wartime) passed several decrees that mobilized into labor armies practically the entire German population of the Soviet Union.[13] The mortality rate in labor armies of the NKVD was comparable to that of gulag camps: during 1942 and 1943, it exceeded 10 percent, and only by 1945 had it dropped to 2.5 percent.[14]

Deportations of Germans became a context of and legislative basis for further ethnic deportations during the war, including the deportation of Soviet Finns. First affected were Ingrian Finns, who had populated territories around Leningrad since the seventeenth century. In August 1941, a decree was passed ordering their immediate relocation from the Leningrad region. The blockade of Leningrad frustrated these plans, but from 1942 deportations of Ingrian Finns continued. In total, about 45,000 Finns were relocated in this operation.[15]

The turn of American and Canadian immigrants came in the autumn of 1941, when, after the "German" order of 8 September, security organs in the Red Army started to clean its ranks of other "suspicious elements." Although a special "Finnish" order had not yet been issued, many Finnish immigrants, according to their later memoirs, were demobilized from the Red Army and transferred to labor armies of the NKVD already in late September and early October 1941.[16] Most likely in such cases commanders of those detachments in which Finnish immigrants served simply played extra safe and rushed to get rid of potentially disloyal soldiers and officers under their command. Memories of the repressions of 1937 and 1938, which ravaged the officer corps of the Red Army, were still too fresh. Just like "purged" Germans, Finnish immigrants were demobilized from the acting army only to become part of the system of compulsory labor supervised by the NKVD with all the ensuing consequences: harsh labor conditions, low food rations, and, as a result, high mortality rates.

At the same time, during the first year of war, a significant number of American and Canadian Finns remained in active service, especially on the Karelian front, where Soviet troops were pitted against the Finnish Army and where Soviet command was eager to use saboteurs behind the enemy's front line, which demanded an excellent knowledge of the Finnish language. It was in this role that Soviet Finns, including American and Canadian immigrants, were most often used at the beginning of the war. Saboteurs and agents were trained in a special school of the NKVD in Belomorsk, a town that became the capital of Soviet Karelia after the Finnish Army seized Petrozavodsk in the autumn of 1941. However, the fact that Finnish immigrants spoke a variant of Finnish that was significantly different from contemporary

Finnish of the early 1940s, as well as blunders in the planning of operations and effective work of Finnish counterintelligence, led to the failure of nearly all these operations.[17]

Each of these failures ended in human tragedy. Aate Pitkänen, who was born in Canada and in 1931, at the age of eighteen, moved from Kivikoski, Ontario, to Petrozavodsk, in the first months of the war left his pregnant wife in evacuation far away in southern Russia to become trained as a spy in Belomorsk. He then tried to infiltrate Petrozavodsk, only to be immediately caught by Finns. A court martial sentenced him to death as a spy.[18] While the trial was still under way, he wrote a letter from a Finnish prison in Petrozavodsk to his parents in Canada in which he attempted to stitch together his Canadian and Soviet experiences and which he finished after news came of his death sentence:

> Petrozavodsk
>> June 10, 1942
>> Dear parents, Father and Mother!
>> First, thanks for the letter, which I received the last autumn. . . . I received it in Medvezhyegorsk already after Petrozavodsk was surrendered. It was a great joy for me, because I didn't expect a letter from you. I also received photos which prove your good being. Your photos are my only current possessions, other than some personal garbage and memories. The rest was engulfed by the war. Only a couple of suitcases are left which travel with Lilia [his wife]. . . .
>> [My] charge is serious, and there are few hopes to come out of this situation alive. I'm only feeling uneasy that I can't write to or help my family and that they don't know anything about my fate.
>> Father, you were right that you moved from here to Canada, as you didn't suffer from the war and weren't taken away from home and family, as I. I hope that this damned war will soon be over, and if I stay alive I hope I will still be able to meet my family and you. . . .
>> With my best regards,
>> Remembering you, your son
>> Aate.
>> P.S. June 12, 1942. Now everything is clear, and you don't need to respond to me. Tomorrow I will lie in the molds. With a farewell greeting,
>> Aate.[19]

Pitkänen's fate was tragic but not exceptional. Those American and Canadian Finns who served in or were conscripted to the Red Army during the first months of the war became enthusiastic fighters for the Soviet cause. It might seem strange that the same people who several years earlier witnessed the destruction of their communities and families by the Stalinist regime became its voluntary and active defenders in wartime, all the more so since they were usually engaged in combat against the Finnish Army rather than the Wehrmacht.

Two factors contributed to this enthusiasm. Paavo Alatalo, who was born in 1920 in the United States and moved with his parents to Soviet Karelia in 1931, described in a recent interview his own reaction and the reactions of his father and his adult Finnish American friends to the news of the beginning of the Soviet-Finnish War as positive. He explained that the social split caused by the Finnish Civil War of 1918 was still alive in their immigrant community and that American and Canadian immigrants still believed (or pretended to believe) that the establishment of Soviet power in Finland would contribute to the elimination of social injustice there.[20] The same logic was likely still valid two years later, in 1941.

Even more important was the factor of Soviet prewar and wartime propaganda. Prewar Soviet ideology emphasized voluntary military training of young Soviet citizens (men and women alike) through paramilitary organizations, such as OSOAVIKHIM (the abbreviation stands for the Society for Assistance to Defence, Aviation. and Chemical Development), so younger generations of American and Canadian immigrants who went through the system of Soviet education during the 1930s were educated to participate in future wars as combatants, even if their professions and occupations were purely civilian in nature. When a real war broke out, they were ready to realize their new social roles, volunteering with the acting army and often sacrificing their lives. Raymond Niskanen, who emigrated with his parents from Minnesota to Soviet Karelia in 1932, was conscripted in the first days of the war to the Red Army artillery troops. When he was surrounded by the enemy during a combat, instead of surrendering, he committed suicide by exploding his own grenade,[21] thus fulfilling Soviet rhetoric of "die but do not surrender" that had become an internal part of his Soviet personality to the degree that he had no other choice but to sacrifice his life.

Altogether, according to calculations of Mayme Sevander, thirty-four Finnish immigrants from the United States and Canada died in the ranks of the Red Army.[22] Those who were lucky to avoid death on the battlefield were often taken as prisoners. Yrjö Mykkänen, one of our interviewees, fought during the first year of the war in a partisan detachment, and in the spring of 1942 he participated in a raid deep into enemy lines. Upon returning from the raid, he was ordered to infiltrate occupied territories as a spy but was arrested immediately after crossing the front line.[23] As in his case, during combat or sabotage activities, sixty-eight American and Canadian immigrants were taken as prisoners by Finns or Germans. According to Sevander, twenty-four of them—usually those who, prior to immigration to the USSR, had Finnish citizenship—were executed by the decisions of Finnish courts martial, since possession of Finnish citizenship qualified them as traitors rather than combatants on the enemy side. The rest, American or Canadian nationals, were sentenced to imprisonment. After the ceasefire was signed between Finland and the Allies, these nationals had to be transferred to the USSR, but ten of them managed to escape to Sweden and from there to the United States or Canada. Thirty-four American and Canadian Finns who had been taken as prisoners of war returned to the USSR, where most of them were immediately sent to gulag camps.[24] This was the fate of Mykkänen, among others, who escaped from captivity in the summer of 1944 only to be immediately imprisoned as a German spy.[25]

The life stories of American and Canadian Finns during the war often reflected the complexity of their prewar life trajectories. Such was the story of the family of Santeri Nuorteva, a prominent member of the Finnish socialist movement in America from 1911 to 1920 and chairman of the Central Executive Committee of Soviet Karelia from 1924 to 1927 (technically its supreme body of power, though its power was more ceremonial than real). Santeri and his wife, Sanni, had two sons and a daughter; all three volunteered at the beginning of the war to act as agents in Finland or areas occupied by the Finnish Army. Pentti and Matti, the two brothers, crossed the front line on 4 February 1942 only to be immediately seized by the Finnish counterintelligence and executed less than three months later, on 20 April. In the meantime, on 30 March, Kerttu, the daughter, was parachuted into Finnish territory and worked for several months as an undercover agent in Helsinki. She was arrested on 7 September and interrogated for several months by Finnish counterintelligence. Only half a year later, in March 1943, did she finally surrender and give away information on Soviet intelligence activities in Finland. Kerttu was sentenced to the death penalty, but its execution was delayed until a ceasefire was signed between Finland and the Allies, after which she returned to the USSR. In 1947, she was sentenced to ten years of imprisonment in Kazakhstan and was released in 1954, the year after Stalin's death.[26]

The final purge of Finns from the Red Army, including Finnish Americans and Canadians (even though both nations by that time had become allies of the Soviet Union), occurred after 3 April 1942 when the State Defense Committee issued an order that all ethnic Finns had to be transferred from field forces to labor armies of the NKVD.[27] Consequently, the use of Soviet Finns for sabotage and espionage activities in territories controlled by the Finnish Army also ceased. By 1 November 1942, the special diversionary detachment of the NKVD on the Karelian front numbered only two Finns among its 100 combatants.[28]

Finally, in the autumn of 1942, during the time of harsh defeats preceding the Battle of Stalingrad, the Soviet leadership decided to isolate, once and for all, Soviet citizens of those ethnicities whose nation-states fought on the German side against the USSR. On 14 October 1942, the State Defense Committee passed Order No. 2409cc, according to which Soviet Romanians, Hungarians, Italians, and Finns were subject to immediate compulsory mobilization to labor armies of the NKVD.[29] It was on this basis that the last Ingrian Finns remaining in the Leningrad region were forcibly deported to internal areas of the USSR.[30] Although this decree was also applicable to Finnish immigrants from the United States and Canada, it affected them to a lesser degree, because during evacuation in the first year of war they became scattered all around the USSR, and in wartime conditions the Soviet leadership simply lacked resources for a large-scale campaign to find and relocate them. Veikko Lekander, for instance, mentioned in his interview that during the war a large group of American and Canadian Finns lived in Komi Republic east of Soviet Karelia who were not affected by this operation.[31] Roy Niskanen, a younger brother of Raymond Niskanen mentioned above, described in his interview the trajectory of evacuation of his family during wartime: from Petrozavodsk through Vologda they moved first to the Chelyabinsk region, then to Omsk, and finally to the Tyumen region.[32] Families became divided and then reunited; people sought any possible employment and were always ready to move when better opportunities arose; in other words, disorderly and sometimes chaotic conditions on the home front disguised immigrants in the common mass of other evacuated Soviet citizens.

At the same time, American and Canadian Finns who served in the Red Army and were not killed or taken prisoner, as well as immigrants of working age on the home front who did not manage to avoid attention of the NKVD, were mobilized into its labor armies. The size of this group can be estimated only approximately. According to Eila Lahti-Argutina's martyrology, in the labor army in Chelyabinsk (which, though, was the largest of all the labor armies of the NKVD), thirty-five American-born Finns and eight Canadian-born Finns perished during the war.[33] Unfortunately, Lahti-Argutina's sources provide only the birthplaces of victims of labor armies and do not mention their country of emigration. If we take into account that second-generation Americans and Canadians were minorities in both immigrant groups, particularly in the latter, we can speculate that the number of American and Canadian immigrants who died in the labor army in Chelyabinsk was several times larger. During 1942 and 1943, the annual mortality rate in the NKVD labor armies reached 10 percent (mortality rates in 1944 and 1945 were significantly lower), which means that at least a fifth of these "servicemen" died during the war. So the total number of American and Canadian immigrants mobilized in labor armies of the NKVD was, according to modest calculations,[34] at least 500 people, of whom at least 100 died because of harsh work conditions and hunger.[35]

After the war ended, most North American Finns returned to Soviet Karelia. Those who had evacuated in 1941 and avoided mobilization to labor armies started coming back already in the autumn of 1944, after Soviet Karelia was freed from the Finnish Army. For others, the return home became delayed for years or even a decade, until Stalin's death in 1953 and the ensuing release of gulag prisoners. One way or another most American and Canadian Finns ultimately came back to Soviet Karelia, the place of so many frustrated hopes, the place that in the end, after the ordeals of the Great Terror and Second World War, finally became their home.

POSTWAR YEARS

The Great Purge and the Second World War did not simply eliminate a significant part of the Finnish population of Soviet Karelia. Their impact was more profound, for they destroyed the pattern of compact settlement of Canadian and American immigrants. During 1937 and 1938, in order to avoid arrest, many of them tried to escape from Finnish settlements that seemed to be plagued by night visits of the NKVD's black cars.[36] The Second World War brought this process to a logical conclusion. Evacuation and re-evacuation scattered people all over the Soviet Union, and those who came back after the war found themselves in the heart of the largest migration in Karelian history. New migration policies of the Karelian authorities were aimed at a sharp population increase, and to achieve it they stimulated migration from Soviet regions devastated by the warfare, particularly central Russia, Belorussia, and Ukraine.[37] Formerly monoethnic and homogeneous communities quickly became ethnically heterogeneous, dominated by a Slavic population, and due to the influx of new migration, from 1939 to 1959, the share of Finno-Ugric peoples (including Karelians, Ingrian Finns, and Vepsians, among whom North American Finns were a small fraction) in the population of Soviet Karelia decreased from 27.0 percent to 18.5 percent and dropped further to 15.8 percent by 1970.[38] As a result, after 1945, there were no more settlements in Soviet Karelia in which Finnish immigrants from North America formed a relative majority or at least a considerable minority.

In absolute numbers, in 1947, the number of Finns living in Soviet Karelia was 4,999, of whom 1,958 lived in Petrozavodsk.[39] A later report identified that approximately a third of them, just as during the prewar time, were immigrants from North America.[40]

This process was coupled with an equally important one. For North American Finnish communities, the late 1930s and 1940s were a time when the generation that had arrived in Soviet Karelia as children or youth became active. In many respects, this generation was quite different from the generation of their parents. Their free knowledge of Russian allowed for much easier communication with the local population, and when compact settling of American Finns was destroyed the number of cross-ethnic marriages, usually between a North American Finn and a Russian increased.[41] Because of the cultural and linguistic situation in Soviet Karelia, the language used in these families was Russian, and one of the most important factors contributing to the preservation of ethnic identity—that is, home language—was gradually lost. Children of these marriages usually spoke poor Finnish, if they communicated with their Finnish grandparents, or no Finnish at all. This downgraded Finnish to the language of oral communication, mostly with parents and grandparents. Cross-ethnic marriages also created a situation in which parents represented various and to a certain degree even

FIGURE 44. FINNISH CANADIANS VALTER LEKANDER (*LEFT*) AND ERVIN NIVA IN PADOZERO, SOVIET KARELIA, CA. 1950 (GOL-UBEV AND TAKALA, *USTNAIA ISTORIIA*, 132).

competing cultures, since both Russian and Finnish languages and cultures were maintained as "official" in Soviet Karelia. Children in these marriages tended to grasp that culture and identity, which were supported by the surrounding reality—that is, Soviet culture—gradually abandoning Finnish or American cultural patterns.[42]

This tendency nevertheless developed differently among different groups of Soviet Finns. Among Ingrian Finns or Finnish immigrants who had moved to the Soviet Union directly from Finland, loss of the native language progressed faster, while North American immigrants tended to speak Finnish and English in their families as late as the 1960s and 1970s.[43] An explanation of these differing dynamics might be that the first two groups were more affected by the Great Terror and wartime repressions, so the loss of language and cultural identity helped them to cope with their traumatic experiences, while North American Finns, as a less affected group, could afford the social luxury of maintaining distinct ethnocultural features. Intellectuals sometimes consciously tried to maintain language skills and Finnish American or Finnish Canadian identities among their children.[44]

Soviet education was another important force that brought cultural transformations in North American Finnish communities. Up to 1937, the system of education in Soviet Karelia provided the option of going through all stages of education (from preschool to higher education) in the Finnish language.[45] It was nevertheless characterized by the strong ideological influence common in Soviet education in general, and this influence intensified after 1937, when the system of Finnish-language education in Soviet Karelia was largely destroyed and the children of North American immigrants were transferred to Russian schools. The experience of younger generations of North American immigrants in the Soviet educational system implied that they tended to take Soviet values shared by their peers and teachers or absorbed from books or other ideological sources. This was also promoted by membership in Octobrist, Young Pioneer, and Komsomol (Communist Union of Youth) organizations and participation in various hobby groups—activities that in many ways served to replace the family as the ground for the construction of identity.

The impact of the Soviet system of education can be illustrated by the example of the Finnish Canadian family of Lekanders. The children (born in 1929, 1930, 1932, and 1934) were all native Finnish speakers who attended a Russian-language school. The elder brother, with whom we conducted an interview, was very fond of reading: during the wartime evacuation to the Komi region (1941–44), he read, as he metonymically said, "the entire regional children's library."[46] However, by the time of the interview (2006), he was unable to read in Finnish. In case his language expertise was required, members of his family who knew the Latin alphabet read aloud, and he translated orally. Everything that he had ever read was in Russian, and the ideological principle of book publishing and the presentation of information in the Soviet press meant that he, along with his entire generation of Canadian and American immigrants, was under the deep influence of official Soviet discourses.

Meanwhile, destruction of compact settling of North American Finnish communities and permanent overtime work of parents during wartime and postwar years often left these young Finnish Canadian and American immigrants without an alternative to official Soviet master narratives. Communities and even families as sites for the cross-generational transfer of ethnocultural values and norms were much eroded during the great social upheaval of the 1930s to

FIGURE 45. VILJO LEKANDER, THE SON OF A FINNISH CANADIAN IMMIGRANT COUPLE, AS A FRESH UNIVERSITY GRADUATE IN PADOZERO, SOVIET KARELIA, CA. 1950 (GOLUBEV AND TAKALA, *USTNAIA ISTORIIA*, 130).

the 1950s. The results of this situation were predictable: ethnic identity gradually gave way to all-unifying Soviet identity. An interview with Dagny Salo, a Finnish American woman born in 1920 in Michigan, revealed astonishing shifts in the worldview of this younger generation of North American immigrants:

Q.: Did you like people in Karelia?

A.: I liked people in Karelia more than in America. . . . I went to America in 1970. I came back disappointed. I am very angry when people reprimand me that I don't pity I had come to the USSR. I have several cousins there [in America], and I wouldn't change places with any of them. . . . All this money, money. I remember a dialog between [my relatives]. Martin is talking about the firm he works in and mentions his boss. Arvid asks: "How much is he worth?" Asked in such a manner, directly! Martin answers: "Around $300,000." "Is that all? I thought he is a millionaire!" Then it slipped into my mind: "[In these terms,] I am worth nothing. I don't even have a bank account."[47]

This first Soviet generation of North American Finns was perhaps most influenced by the ideals of early Soviet society. The generation of their parents lost their idealism in the hardships of everyday Soviet life in the early 1930s and during the purges of 1937 and 1938. The generation of their children would become the products of postwar Soviet education and culture that were gradually affected by negative social processes undermining the Soviet Union from within. Only the generation that was young in the 1930s internalized early Soviet revolutionary discourse so deeply that their belief in a bright socialist future could not be shattered even by the tragedy of Stalin's purges. This is clearly seen in the final sections of Mayme Sevander's first book, *They Took My Father,* where Sevander expresses her personal political and social views: "Though the breakup [of the Soviet Union] clearly was inevitable, it is still hard for me to admit that the country my parents believed in so fervently and sacrificed so much for has failed. It did not fail because socialism is a bad idea, though; it failed because socialism was never practiced there. I still believe that socialism could work, given the right circumstances and the proper foundation."[48]

Everyday activities of American immigrants in the postwar period were also becoming closer to those of the Soviet population. In postwar Soviet Karelia, as in the entire USSR, sports played outdoors, such as football or volleyball, became extremely popular, and engagement in sports activities stopped being a specific phenomenon of North American Finnish communities, as it had been prior to the Second World War. The same situation occurred with cultural activities. Clubs (usually called "houses of culture") emerged in all major settlements through centralized efforts of the state. Participation in amateur theater, various groups of folk dancing, and choir singing ceased to be markers of Canadian or American Finnishness, as these activities were in the 1930s. The general development of Soviet culture in the postwar period resulted in participation in sports and cultural activities that became a social norm, shared by the whole society rather than being a social distinction of one ethnocultural group of North American immigrants.

The role of cuisine in ethnic identity also became less important. This was partly because of a lack of resources, for it was very hard to cook using American or Finnish recipes under food rationing or in distant villages, where often the populations could only buy a restricted number of food products. In the village of Chalna, for example, where several families of North American Finns lived after the war, only bread and frozen fish were available on a regular basis in the local grocery store throughout the late 1940s and early 1950s.[49] With such meager food supplies, it is hardly surprising that, even in families in which both parents were American Finns, few or no specific American or Finnish recipes were used either on a daily basis or on special occasions. In larger towns, such as Petrozavodsk, where more resources were available, these traditions survived better but also stopped being a factor in identity. The only exception was coffee, which always distinguished Finns, even when resources were scarce. When coffee was not available, American and Canadian Finns made surrogate coffee from roasted barley.[50]

Thus, while North American immigrants were perhaps the most culturally distinct population in Soviet Karelia during the 1930s, by the 1950s their cultural practices were not much different from the cultural norms of Soviet society. As a result, in the postwar period, culture as a factor in the construction of the ethnic identity of North American Finnish immigrants generally lost its importance. Some exceptions (e.g., the consumption of coffee) remained, and in everyday life North American Finns preserved some specific habits that differentiated them from the local inhabitants, but these habits were few. The identities of immigrants and especially of their children could no longer rely on their everyday cultural practices. The most important factors in the preservation of a distinct identity became the traumatic experience of the anti-Finnish repressions and family memories.

Despite all these factors, Canadian and American immigrants played a prominent role in the cultural landscape of Soviet Karelia during the postwar period. The Finnish Theater of Petrozavodsk was mostly shaped by American Finns. Kalle Rautio, the most important figure in the musical life of prewar Soviet Karelia, became the music director of the theater after the war. Actors from the prewar company of Kuuno Sevander, another American immigrant, formed the core cast of the theater.[51] American immigrants occupied prominent positions in the Symphony Orchestra of Karelia,[52] as well as in the folk music ensemble Kantele, which became the face of Soviet Karelia in the postwar USSR.[53]

Despite their low numbers in postwar Soviet Karelia, American and Canadian immigrants were also influential in the development of secondary and university education. In 1967, a school was established in Petrozavodsk in which a number of subjects were taught in English. In the egalitarian landscape of Soviet education, nearly immediately it became an elite school that promised higher than average standards of learning. Over twenty-nine years, its principal was Pavel Corgan, a son of Oscar Corgan, one of the main organizers of the Karelian fever emigration.[54] It was mainly because of his efforts that School No. 17 of Petrozavodsk became a flagship school of Karelian secondary education by setting high learning standards for other schools to follow. His older sister, Mayme Sevander, played an important role in organizing the Faculty of Foreign Languages at the Karelian State Pedagogical College in Petrozavodsk and was its dean for many years. In a time when many university students who majored in English had no opportunity for direct contact with an English-language environment, Sevander and other North American immigrants who spoke English as their native language made Petrozavodsk a prominent center of English-language teaching in the USSR.[55]

The years of perestroika became a period of ethnic mobilization for many ethnic groups in the Soviet Union. Unlike indigenous ethnic groups, Soviet Finns as recent immigrants had no chance to establish any kind of territorial autonomy either in late-Soviet or in post-Soviet territory. The revival of their ethnic identities coupled with harsh economic hardships of the late 1980s and early 1990s resulted in another phase of emigration, when both first-generation American and Canadian Finns and their children and grandchildren once again changed their homeland, moving from the Russian Federation to Finland.

FIGURE 46. DAVID MYKKÄNEN, A CANADIAN FINNISH IMMIGRANT FROM PORT MOODY, BRITISH COLUMBIA, AT HIS HOME WITH GRANDCHILDREN. CHALNA, SOVIET KARELIA, 1950S (GOLUBEV AND TAKALA, *USTNAIA ISTORIIA*, 113).

Conclusion

Throughout this book, starting with the title, we regularly used the metaphor of a search to interpret the life trajectories of our protagonists—approximately 6,500 American and Canadian emigrants of Finnish ethnicity who, in the early 1930s, moved across the Atlantic to the Soviet Union. The perspective that this metaphor gave us seemed particularly well suited to an analysis of our material. American and Canadian Finns themselves often used it to describe their experiences of immigration to the Soviet Union as a search for jobs, a search for a more just social order, or a search for a better future for their children. The economic and cultural policies of the Red Finnish government of Soviet Karelia, which initiated the Karelian fever in Finnish American and Canadian communities, can also be interpreted as a search for a specific regional model of development. Finally, interpretation of the policies of Soviet leaders during the 1930s as a search for new ways of constructing the socialist state and the socialist subject expands and deepens our understanding of interwar Soviet history, for it challenges teleological and stalinocentric explanatory models that are still common, despite the revisionist challenge, in studies of this period.

If this metaphor is pursued further, all these searches were indeed searches for mythical El Dorado, in the end an unattainable goal. Yet it changed individual biographies by setting large masses of people in motion, it created new regions, and it completely transformed the huge Soviet nation. In this respect, the fates of North American immigrants, the rise and fall of Red Finns who attempted to build in Soviet Karelia a new socialist society based on Finnish culture and ideas of internationalism, and the ultimate failure of the Soviet project—all of this resembles the symbolism of one of Edgar Allan Poe's last poems, "Eldorado":

> Gaily bedight,
> A gallant knight,
> In sunshine and in shadow,
> Had journeyed long,
> Singing a song,
> In search of Eldorado.
> But he grew old—This knight so bold—And o'er his heart a shadow
> Fell as he found
> No spot of ground
> That looked like Eldorado.
> And, as his strength
> Failed him at length,
> He met a pilgrim shadow—"Shadow," said he,
> "Where can it be—This land of Eldorado?"
> "Over the Mountains

Of the Moon,
Down the Valley of the Shadow,
Ride, boldly ride,"
The shade replied—"If you seek for Eldorado!"[1]

Written in 1849 as a reaction to the California Gold Rush, this poem encapsulated meanings that Western culture associated with goals that were utopian, in the sense that their ultimate realization was a priori impossible, but still worth trying to realize. Our research position was shaped, to a significant degree, by a perspective on the emigration of North American Finns to Soviet Karelia as a search for El Dorado that failed as well as by our desire to understand why it all happened this way. For even seemingly successful immigrants who stayed in the USSR and fulfilled themselves in professional, social, or family roles eventually ended up being disappointed by Soviet Karelia—to say nothing of those who perished in the Great Terror or during the Second World War. Mass re-emigration to Finland of those who were still alive in the 1990s, as well as their children and grandchildren, was evidence that they admitted, consciously or unconsciously, the failure of their life trajectories within the borders of the Soviet Union or those of post-Soviet Russia. Moreover, the stories of American and Canadian Finns in Soviet Karelia are evidence of the failure not only of personal experiences but also of the collapse of Soviet multiculturalism ("we all are Soviet people"). For North American immigrants and their children and grandchildren, the fragmentation and then collapse of Soviet society hailed the beginning of a new search—a search for a new identity and eventually a new homeland. In this respect, it is symbolic that, for those immigrants who moved to Finland after 1990, their search for El Dorado transformed into an odyssey, at the end of which they found no mythical treasure but had returned home.

Yet the metaphor of El Dorado, productive as it might be, is also misleading to a certain degree. By using it, we occupy the position of critics who know the final outcomes of analyzed events but who, because of this knowledge, are also tempted to explain them teleologically, forgetting the diversity of historical experience and agency. Our goal was not only to write a comprehensive account of Finnish emigration from North America to the USSR but also to explain the meanings that people created in this emigration and to understand what kind of reality they aspired to create by selling all their American and Canadian property and settling in Soviet Karelia. Doing this in terms of ultimate failure would be ahistorical: after all, immigrants such as Mikael Rutanen, whose life ended at the height of socialist enthusiasm of the early 1930s (see Chapter 6), or those who died after the Khrushchev-era revitalization of the Soviet project but before it became discredited in the 1980s, were often successful people who happily struggled through immense difficulties and were proud of their contributions to the socialist cause. We tried our best not to narrow this "space of experience and horizon of expectation,"[2] which we encountered in our material, to a narrative in which every development inevitably and logically led to Stalinist repression.

To represent this diversity of historical experience in interwar Soviet society is perhaps the ultimate aim of our research. Finnish emigration from the United States and Canada to Soviet Karelia is interesting not only in itself but also as that drop of water that reflected the whole world of Soviet social, political, and cultural development in the 1920s and 1930s, with all its grievances and joys, losses and victories, successes and tragedies. In the various potential developments that Soviet society of this period contained but failed to realize, the case of Soviet Karelia as a zone of contact and competition between Soviet and Western visions of sociopolitical order seems unfairly forgotten, first by Soviet decision makers and then by historians. Because of large-scale immigration from Finland, America, and Canada, Soviet Karelia of the 1920s and 1930s was a venue where new forms of political, economic, social, and cultural life emerged and developed. This contact zone was shut down in the late 1930s and again after the Second World War, which means that it worked efficiently enough to challenge the specific visions of sociopolitical and -cultural development that the Stalinist leadership deemed mainstream for the Soviet state. Yet, despite all the repressions, the contact zone created by immigrants kept on transforming Soviet Karelia until the very collapse of the USSR.

The fact that most North American immigrants, who probably realized upon arrival in Soviet Karelia that it could be anything but El Dorado, remained there and accepted all the difficulties associated with the construction of a new world is hard to overemphasize. They were not seeking an easy solution to the Great Depression; instead, they were prepared to build a new world with their own hands. And indeed they became actively involved in this process, building Soviet Karelia literally on multiple construction sites and figuratively in new cultural forms that reflected their understanding of the socialist project. This adds another perspective on Soviet history of the 1930s: for the VKP(b) elite to secure their vision of an appropriate sociopolitical order, it was necessary to eliminate all other visions that could lead to successful developments other than the bureaucratic party-state. Finnish immigrants, including Americans and Canadians, unwillingly stood in the way of construction of this party-state by being too effective in their transformation of Soviet Karelia. From this perspective, the tragedy of the Great Terror in their communities was not only that it brought death and suffering to thousands of families but also that it destroyed a whole world where Finnish, American, Canadian, Karelian, Russian, and Soviet cultures met to form a new socialist reality, a world that was sacrificed to satisfy the political ambitions of the Soviet bureaucracy.

Notes

INTRODUCTION

1. Dudley Baines, *Emigration from Europe, 1815–1930* (Cambridge, UK: Cambridge University Press, 1995), 2.

2. Herman Lindquist, *A History of Sweden: From Ice Age to Our Age* (Stockholm: Norstedts, 2006), 592–93.

3. Rolf Danielsen, *Norway: A History from the Vikings to Our Own Times* (Oslo: Scandinavian University Press, 1995), 274.

4. Reino Kero, *Suuren Länteen: Siirtolaisuus Suomesta Yhdysvaltoihin ja Kanadaan* [To the Great West: Immigration from Finland to the United States and Canada] (Turku: Siirtolaisuusinstituutti, 1996), 58.

5. See the Russian-language historiography of foreign immigration to the Soviet Union in Sergei Zhuravliov, *Malenkiie liudi i bolshaia istoriia: Inostrantsy moskovskogo Elektrozavoda v sovetskom obshchestve 1920-kh-1930-kh gg.* [Little People and Big History: Foreigners from Moscow's Elektrozavod in the Soviet Society of the 1920s and 1930s] (Moscow: ROSSPEN, 2000), 31–36.

6. Reino Kero, *Neuvosto-Karjalaa rakentamassa: Pohjois-Amerikan suomalaiset tekniikan tuojina 1930-luvun Neuvosto-Karjalassa* [Building Soviet Karelia: North American Finns as the Introducers of New Technologies in Soviet Karelia in the 1930s] (Helsinki: SHS, 1983).

7. Reino Kero, "Emigration of Finns from North America to Soviet Karelia in the Early 1930's," in *The Finnish Experience in the Western Great Lakes Region: New Perspectives,* ed. Michael G. Karni et al. (Turku: Institute of Migration, 1975), 213.

8. Christer Boucht, *Onnea etsimässä: Punaisesta Karjalasta Kaukoitään* [The Search for Luck: From Red Karelia to the Far East] (Helsinki: Kirjayhtymä, 1973); Kaarlo Tuomi, "The Karelian Fever of the Early 1930s: A Personal Memoir," *Finnish Americana* 3 (1980): 61–75; Christer Boucht, *Karjala kutsuu* [Karelia Calls] (Helsinki: Kirjayhtymä, 1988); Sylvia Hokkanen and Laurence Hokkanen, with Anita Middleton, *Karelia: A Finnish-American Couple in Stalin's Russia, 1934–1941* (St. Cloud: North Star Press, 1991); Ernesti Komulainen, *A Grave in Karelia* (New York: Braun Brumfield, 1995).

9. Michael Gelb, "'Karelian Fever': The Finnish Immigrant Community during Stalin's Purges," *Europe-Asia Studies* 45, 6 (1993): 1091–1116; Varpu Lindström and Börje Vähämäki, "Ethnicity Twice Removed: North American Finns in Soviet Karelia," *Finnish Americana* 9 (1992): 14–20; Alexis Pogorelskin, "New Perspectives on Karelian Fever: The Recruitment of North American Finns to Karelia in the Early 1930s," *Journal of Finnish Studies* 1, 3 (1997): 165–78.

10. Irina Takala and Timo Vihavainen, eds., *V semie edinoi: Natsionalnaia politika partii bolshevikov i eio osushchestvleniie na Severo-Zapade Rossii v 1920–1950-e gody* [One United Family: The Nationalities Policy of CPSU from the 1920s to the 1950s and Its Implementation in Northwestern Russia] (Petrozavodsk: Petrozavodsk State University Press, 1998), with a Finnish

translation published two years later; Markku Kangaspuro, *Neuvosto-Karjalan taistelu itsehallinnosta* [The Struggle of Soviet Karelia for Autonomy] (Helsinki: SKS, 2000); Antti Laine and Mikko Ylikangas, eds., *Rise and Fall of Soviet Karelia: People and Power* (Helsinki: Kikimora Publications, 2002); Mikko Ylikangas, *Rivit suoriksi! Kaunokirjallisuuden poliittinen valvonta Neuvosto-Karjalassa 1917–1940* [Straighten Your Ranks! Political Control over Literary Writing in Soviet Karelia during 1917–1940] (Helsinki: Kikimora Publications, 2004).

11. Andrei Andriainen, "Zamechatelnyi primer internatsionalnoi solidarnosti [A Formidable Example of International Solidarity]," in *Voprosy istorii KPSS* [Problems of History of the CPSU] (Petrozavodsk: Petrozavodsk State University Press, 1968), 87–101; Andrei Andriainen, "Dvizheniie proletarskoi solidarnosti zarubezhnykh finskikh trudiashchikhsia s Sovetskoi Kareliei [Movement of Proletarian Solidarity between Finnish Workers Abroad and Soviet Karelia]," in *50 let Sovetskoi Karelii* [Fifty Years of Soviet Karelia] (Petrozavodsk: Karelia, 1969), 180–98.

12. Natalia Lavrushina, "Iz istorii poiavleniia severoamerikanskikh finnov v Karelii v nachale 1930-kh godov [From the History of Immigration of North American Finns to Karelia in the Early 1930s]," in *Karely. Finny. Problemy etnicheskoi istorii* [Karelians. Finns. Problems of Ethnic History] (Moscow: Russian Academy of Sciences, 1992), 176–89; Irina Takala, "Eldoradoa etsimässä. Tarina ennen sotia Neuvosto-Karjalaan valtavesien takaa saapuneista amerikansuomalaista [The Search for El Dorado: A Story of American Finnish Immigrants to Soviet Karelia in the Interwar Period]," *Carelia* 3 (1993): 4–25; Irina Takala, *Finny v Karelii i Rossii: Istoriia vozniknoveniia i gibeli diaspory* [Finns in Karelia: The History of Birth and Death of the Diaspora] (St. Petersburg: Izdatelstvo Zhurnal Neva, 2002).

13. Mayme Sevander, *They Took My Father: A Story of Idealism and Betrayal* (Duluth: Pfeiffer-Hamilton, 1991; reprinted, Minneapolis: University of Minnesota Press, 2004); Mayme Sevander, *Red Exodus: Finnish-American Emigration to Russia* (Duluth: OSCAT, 1993); Mayme Sevander, *Of Soviet Bondage* (Duluth: OSCAT, 1996); Mayme Sevander, *Skitaltsy: O sudbakh amerikanskikh finnov v Karelii* [Wanderers: Fates of American Finns in Karelia] (Petrozavodsk: Petrozavodsk State University Press, 2006; first Finnish-language edition, Turku: Siirtolaisuusinstituutti, 2000); Alexey Golubev and Irina Takala, eds., *Ustnaia istoriia v Karelii. Sbornik nauchnykh statei i istochnikov. Vypusk 2. Severoamerikanskiie finny v Sovetskoi Karelii 1930-kh gg.* [Oral History in Karelia. A Collection of Articles and Sources. Issue 2. North American Finns in Soviet Karelia in the 1930s] (Petrozavodsk: Petrozavodsk State University Press, 2007).

14. Eila Lahti-Argutina, *Olimme joukko vieras vaan: Venäjänsuomalaiset vainonuhrit Neuvostoliitossa 1930-luvun alusta 1950-luvun alkuun* [We Were Just a Group of Visitors: Russian Finnish Victims of Soviet Repression from the 1930s to the Early 1950s] (Turku: Siirtolaisuusinstituutti, 2001).

15. Ronald Harpelle, Varpu Lindström, and Alexis Pogorelskin, eds., *Karelian Exodus: Finnish Communities in North America and Soviet Karelia during the Depression Era* (Beaverton, ON: Aspasia Books, 2004); Ilya Solomeshch and Irina Takala, eds., *North American Finns in Soviet Karelia in the 1930s* (Petrozavodsk: Petrozavodsk State University Press, 2008); Markku Kangaspuro and Samira Saramo, eds., *Victims and Survivors of Karelia,* a special double issue of *Journal of Finnish Studies* 15, 1–2 (2011).

16. Most of them were published in Russian in Golubev and Takala, eds., *Ustnaia istoriia v Karelii.*

17. See, among the most prominent works, Moshe Lewin, *The Making of the Soviet System: Essays in the Social History of Interwar Russia* (New York: Pantheon, 1985); Steven Kotkin, *Magnetic Mountain: Stalinism as a Civilization* (Berkeley: University of California Press, 1995); Sheila Fitzpatrick, *Everyday Stalinism: Ordinary Life in Extraordinary Times: Soviet Russia in the 1930s* (New York:

Oxford University Press, 1999); and Sheila Fitzpatrick, ed., *Stalinism: New Directions* (New York: Routledge, 2000).

CHAPTER 1. FINNISH IMMIGRANTS IN NORTH AMERICA AND RUSSIA

1. Kero, *Suuren Länteen,* 16–31.
2. Viljo Rasila, *Istoriia Finlandii* [History of Finland] (Petrozavodsk: Petrozavodsk State University Press, 2006), 116.
3. Henrik Meinander, *Istoriia Finlandii* [History of Finland] (Moscow: Ves' Mir, 2008), 116.
4. Russian imperial authorities retained the use of Swedish place names after the conquest of Finland in 1809 (*Uleaborgskaia guberniia* and *Vazskaia guberniia*). Modern names of these Finnish towns and their regions are Oulu and Vaasa respectively.
5. Kero, *Suureen Länteen,* 58.
6. Arthur W. Hoglund, "Finnish Immigrant Letter Writers: Reporting from the US to Finland, 1870s to World War I," in *Finnish Diaspora II: United States,* ed. Michael G. Karni (Toronto: Multicultural History Society of Ontario, 1981), 14.
7. Seppo Zetterberg, ed., *Suomen historian pikkujättiläinen* [A Small Giant of the Finnish History] (Helsinki: WSOY, 2003), 495.
8. Elois Engle, *Finns in North America* (Minneapolis: Lerner Publications Company, 1975), 32.
9. A new law on compulsory conscription passed in 1901 without consent of the Diet of Finland, coupled with the earlier February Manifesto of 1899, which significantly restricted the constitutional rights of Finland, caused a resistance movement in the Grand Duchy, at first passive and then active. See Osmo Jussila, Seppo Hentilä, and Jukka Nevakivi, *From Grand Duchy to a Modern State: A Political History of Finland since 1809* (London: C. Hurst and Company Publishers, 1999), 77.
10. Meinander, *Istoriia Finlandii,* 117.
11. Kero, *Suureen Länteen,* 76.
12. Varpu Lindström, "The Finnish Canadian Communities during the Decade of Depression," in *Karelian Exodus: Finnish Communities in North America and Soviet Karelia during the Depression Era,* ed. Ronald Harpelle, Varpu Lindström, and Alexis E. Pogorelskin (Beaverton, ON: Aspasia Books, 2004), 16–17.
13. Kero, *Suureen Länteen,* 103–07.
14. Ibid., 131.
15. Ibid.
16. Interview with Dagne Salo, in *Ustnaia istoriia,* ed. Golubev and Takala, 54.
17. Liisa A. Liedes and Uuno Vesanen, *Suomalainen helluntaiherätys Pohjois-Amerikassa* [The Awakening of the Pentecostal Movement in North America] (Vancouver: Mission Press Society, 1994), 12.
18. Kero, "Emigration of Finns," 212. The metaphor drew on the perception in Finnish culture of the rhinoceros as an animal that takes care only of itself; see also the later play *Rhinoceros* (1959) by famous French Romanian playwright Eugène Ionesco.
19. Douglas J. Ollila, "From Socialism to Industrial Unionism (IWW): Social Factors in the Emergence of Left-Labor Radicalism among Finnish Workers on the Mesabe, 1911–19," in *The Finnish Experience in the Western Great Lakes Region,* ed. Karni et al., 157.

20. See Arthur W. Hoglund, *Finnish Immigrants in America, 1880–1920* (Madison: University of Wisconsin Press, 1960); Auvo Kostiainen, *The Forging of Finnish-American Communism, 1917–1924: A Study of Ethnic Radicalism* (Turku: Turun yliopisto, 1978); Peter Kivisto, *Immigrant Socialists in the United States: The Case of Finns and the Left* (Rutherford, NJ: Fairleigh Dickinson University Press, 1984); and Reino Kero, *Suomalaisina Pohjois-Amerikassa: Siirtolaiselämää Yhdysvalloissa ja Kanadassa* [Finns in North America: Life of Immigrants in the United States and Canada] (Turku: Siirtolaisuusinstituutti, 1997).

21. Oiva W. Saarinen, *Between a Rock and a Hard Place: A Historical Geography of the Finns in the Sudbury Area* (Waterloo, ON: Wilfrid Laurier University Press, 1999), esp. 109–54.

22. Max Engman and Sune Jungar, "Pereselencheskoiie dvizheniie iz Finlandii v Rossiiu v 1809–1917 gg. [Resettlement Movement from Finland to Russia in 1809–1917]," in *Materialy VI Sovetsko-finliandskogo simposiuma istorikov: Rossiia i Finliandiia 1700–1917* [Materials of the Sixth Soviet-Finnish Symposium of Historians: Russia and Finland in 1700–1917], ed. S. Iu. Kukushkin and I. P. Shaskolskii (Leningrad: Nauka, 1980), 116–17; Takala, *Finny v Karelii,* 8.

23. Sankt-Peterburgskaia *guberniia,* now Leningrad region (Leningradskaia *oblast*). Unlike its capital city, Leningrad, in 1991 renamed St. Petersburg, its namesake region retained the Soviet-era name.

24. Engman and Jungar, "Pereselencheskoiie dvizheniie," 119; Sune Jungar, *Från Åbo till Ryssland: En studie i urban befolkningsrörlighet 1850–1890* [From Åbo to Russia: A Study of Urban Population Mobility] (Åbo: Åbo Akademi, 1974), 85–89.

25. Engman and Jungar, "Pereselencheskoiie dvizheniie," 119. This statistic is available in more detail in Natalia Iukhneva, *Etnicheskii sostav i etnosotsialnaia struktura naseleniia Petersburga, vtoraia polovina XIX—nachalo XX v.* [Ethnic Composition and Ethnosocial Structure of the Population of St. Petersburg in the Second Half of the Nineteenth and Early Twentieth Centuries] (Leningrad: Nauka, 1984), 165–69.

26. Sune Jungar, "Finliandskiie remeslenniki v Sankt-Peterburge [Finnish Artisans in St. Petersburg]," in *Remeslo i manufaktura v Rossii, Finliandii, Pribaltike* [Artisanship and Manufactory in Russian, Finland, and Baltic States] (Leningrad: Nauka, 1975), 93.

27. Engman and Jungar, "Pereselencheskoiie dvizheniie," 121; Iukhneva, *Etnicheskii sostav,* 175.

28. For more information, see Engman and Jungar, "Pereselencheskoiie dvizheniie," 115–38; Alpo Juntunen, *Suomalaista kulttuuria Nevan rannoilla: Piirteitä Pietarin suomalaisen siirtokunnan kulttuurielämästä 1900-luvun alussa* [Finnish Culture on the Banks of the Neva River: Features of Cultural Life of Finnish Immigrants in St. Petersburg in the Early Twentieth Century] (Turku: Turun yliopisto, 1970); Max Engman, *Petersburgska vägar* [Roads to St. Petersburg] (Esbo: Schildt, 1995); Max Engman, *Förvaltningen och utvandringen till Ryssland, 1809–1917* [Administration of Finland and Finnish Immigration to Russia, 1809–1917] (Helsingfors: Tryckericentralen, 1995); and Jarmo Nironen, *Suomalainen Pietari* [Finnish St. Petersburg] (Vantaa: Novomedia, 1999).

29. The territory of Olonets province (Olonetskaia *guberniia*), non-existent since 1922, mostly overlapped the contemporary territory of the Republic of Karelia. Arkhangelsk province (Arkhangelskaia *guberniia*) still exists (though within somewhat different borders) under the name of Arkhangelsk region (Arkhangelskaia *oblast*). Both provinces donated their territories to the newly formed Soviet Karelia in 1920 as an autonomous ethnic republic within Soviet Russia. Olonets province became de facto defunct with the foundation of autonomous Karelia, and in two years (in 1922) it was officially dissolved.

30. Viktor Birin and Irina Takala, "Finny [Finns]," in *Narody Rossii: Entsiklopediia* [Peoples of Russia:

An Encyclopedia], ed. Valerii Tishkov (Moscow: Bolshaia Rossiiskaia Entsiklopediia, 1994), 370; Viktor Birin, *Finny Olonetskoi gubernii* [Finns of Olonets province] (Petrozavodsk: KarNTS RAN, 1991), 4–5, 27–29.

31. Irina Takala, "Finskiie pereselentsy v Karelii i na Kolskom poluostrove [Finnish Settlers in Karelia and in the Kola Peninsula]," in *Pribaltiisko-finskiie narody Rossii* [Baltic and Finnic Peoples of Russia], ed. Evgenii Klementiev and Natalia Shlygina (Moscow: Nauka, 2003), 522.

32. Takala, *Finny v Karelii,* 11.

33. Calculations based on *Pervaia Vseobshchaia perepis naseleniia Rossiiskoi imperii. 1897 g. T. I. Arkhangelskaia guberniia. Tetrad 1* [First General Census of the Population of the Russian Empire. Vol. 1. Arkhangelsk Province. Book 1] (Moscow: Tsentralnyi statisticheskii komitet MVD, 1899), 42–43; and *Pervaia Vseobshchaia perepis naseleniia Rossiiskoi imperii. 1897 g. T. I. Arkhangelskaia guberniia. Tetrad 3* [First General Census of the Population of the Russian Empire. Vol. 1. Arkhangelsk Province. Book 3] (Moscow: Tsentralnyi statisticheskii komitet MVD, 1904), 2–3, 20–21, 52, 64–67.

34. Takala, *Finny v Karelii,* 12.

35. Calculations based on "Liitteenä V. Keynään laatima ja sovittama kansallisuuskartta Itä-Karjalasta ja Kuollan Niemimaasta [Attached Ethnic Map of Eastern Karelia and Kola Peninsula, Prepared and Arranged by V. Keynäs]," in *Karjalan oikeus* [The Right to Karelia] (Helsinki: Otava, 1921), appendix (*liitenä*).

36. Jussila et al., *From Grand Duchy,* 112.

37. Matvei Koronen, *Finskiie internatsionalisty v borbe za vlast Sovetov* [Finnish Internationalists in the Struggle for Soviet Power] (Leningrad: Lenizdat, 1969), 103. Petrograd was the name of St. Petersburg given after the outbreak of the First World War since the original name sounded too German. It was changed to Leningrad in 1924 after the death of Lenin.

38. Takala, *Finny v Karelii,* 20; Tauno Saarela, *Suomalaisten kommunismin synty 1918–1923* [Birth of Finnish Communism] (Tampere: KSL, 1996), 27.

39. Auvo Kostiainen, *Loikkarit: Suuren lamakauden laiton siirtolaisuus Neuvostoliittoon* [Border Hoppers: Illegal Immigration to the Soviet Union during the Great Depression] (Helsinki: Otava, 1988), 57–64, 83; Irina Takala, "Finskoie naseleniie Sovetskoi Karelii v 1930-e gg. [Finnish Population of Soviet Karelia in the 1930s]," in *Karely. Finny. Problemy etnicheskoi istorii,* 158.

40. OGPU, an abbreviation of *Ob'iedinennoie gosudarstvennoie politicheskoie upravleniie,* or United State Political Administration, was a Soviet national security body from 1923 to 1934. It was also referred to as GPU after its predecessor in 1922–1923. Both terms—OGPU and GPU—will be used often in this book.

41. For more information, see Kostiainen, *Loikkarit;* Irina Takala, "Loikkareiden kohtalo Neuvosto-Karjalassa asiakirjojen kuvaamana [The Fate of Border Hoppers in Soviet Karelia as Described in Archival Documents]," in *Kahden Karjalan välillä. Kahden Riikin riitamaalla* [Between two Karelias. On the Land Disputed by Two Powers], ed. Tapio Hämynen (Joensuu: Joensuun yliopisto, 1994), 173–80.

42. A. S. Zherbin, ed., *Karely Karelskoi ASSR* [Karelians of the Karelian ASSR] (Petrozavodsk: Karelia, 1983), 26–29.

43. Unelma Konkka, ed., *Puteshestviia Eliasa Lönnrota: Putevyie zametki, dnevniki, pisma 1828–1842 gg.* [Elias Lönnrot's Travels: Travel Notes, Diaries, Letters from 1828 to 1842] (Petrozavodsk: Karelia, 1985), 8–12.

44. Hannes Sihvo, *Karjalan kuva: Karelianismin taustaa ja vaiheita autonomian aikana* [The Picture

of Karelia: The Background and Stages of Karelianism during the Autonomous Time] (Helsinki: SKS, 1973).

45. Heikki Kirkinen, Pekka Nevalainen, and Hannes Sihvo, *Karjalan kansan historia* [History of the Karelian People] (Porvoo: WSOY, 1994), 255.

46. On the complex relationship among nationalism, history, and geography, see Benedict Anderson, *Imagined Communities: Reflections on the Origin and Spread of Nationalism* (London: Verso, 1983); Eric Hobsbawm, *Nations and Nationalism since 1780: Programme, Myth, Reality* (Cambridge, UK: Cambridge University Press, 1990); and Rogers Brubaker, *Nationalism Reframed: Nationhood and the National Question in the New Europe* (Cambridge, UK: Cambridge University Press, 1996).

47. Stacy Churchill, *Itä-Karjalan kohtalo 1917–1922: Itä-Karjalan itsehallintokysymys Suomen ja Neuvosto-Venäjän välisissä suhteissa 1917–1922* [The Fate of Eastern Karelia, 1917–1922: The Question of Self-Government in Eastern Karelia in the Finnish-Soviet Relations, 1917–1922] (Porvoo: WSOY, 1970); Jussi Niinistö, *Heimosotien historia 1918–1922* [The History of "Kindred Wars," 1918–1922] (Helsinki: SKS, 2005).

48. Article 232, in *Sobraniie uzakonenii i rasporiazhenii rabochego i krestiianskogo pravitelstva* [Collection of Legal Acts and Decrees of the Workers' and Peasants' Government], 1920, no. 53; Ya. A. Balagurov and V. I. Mashezerskii, eds., *Kareliia v period grazhdanskoi voiny i inostrannoi interventsii, 1918–1920* [Karelia in the Years of the Civil War and Foreign Intervention, 1918–1920] (Petrozavodsk: Karel.knizhnoe izd-vo, 1964), 537. The decree came into effect after its official publication on 8 June 1920, which became the "foundation date" of Soviet Karelia in official historical narratives.

49. For the "eastern Karelian question" on the agenda of the League of Nations, see *League of Nations Official Journal* 3, 2 (1922): 103–05, 107–08; 165–70.

50. Alexander Etkind, *Internal Colonization: Russia's Imperial Experience* (Cambridge, UK: Polity, 2011).

51. Alexander Etkind, Dirk Uffelman, and Ilya Kukulin, eds., *Tam, vnutri. Praktiki vnutrennei kolonizatsii v kulturnoi istorii Rossii* [There, Inside. Practices of Internal Colonization in Cultural History of Russia] (Moscow: NLO, 2012).

52. Sakari Heikkinen and Tapani Mauranen, "Nauchnaia deiatelnost Edvarda Gyllinga [Edvard Gylling's Scholarly Career]," *Skandinavskii Sobrnik. Vyp. XXXI* [Scandinavian Collection. Vol. 31] (Tallinn: Eesti Raamat, 1988), 129–33.

53. Mikko Uola, "Edvard Gylling," in *Sto zamechatelnykh finnov* [One Hundred Prominent Finns], ed. Timo Vihavainen (Helsinki: SKS, 2004), 172.

54. Pekka Kauppala, "Formirovaniie i rastsvet avtonomnoi Sovetskoi Karelii, 1918–1929: Zabytyi uspekh rannesovetskoi natsionalnoi politiki [Formation and Heyday of Autonomous Soviet Karelia, 1918–1929: A Forgotten Success of Early Soviet Nationalities Politics]," *Ab Imperio* 2 (2002): 314.

55. John H. Hodgson, *Edvard Gylling ja Otto W. Kuusinen asiakirjojen valossa 1918–1920* [Edvard Gylling and Otto W. Kuusinen in the Light of Documents 1918–1920] (Helsinki: Tammi, 1974), 89–109.

56. A letter from Edvard Gylling to Yrjö Sirola, in *Vsekarelskii s'iezd predstavitelei trudiashchikhsia karel, 11–19 fevralia 1921 g. Protokoly* [All-Karelian Congress of Representatives of Working Karelians, 11–19 February 1921. Records of Proceedings] (Petrozavodsk: Kareliia, 1990), 257–58. Here and hereafter translations from Russian and Finnish are by Alexey Golubev.

57. For more details, see Kangaspuro, *Neuvosto-Karjalan taistelu itsehallinnosta,* esp. 43–46, 87–131.

58. During the imperial period, Russian revolutionaries cooperated with Finnish nationalists to confront the tsarist government. See William R. Copeland, *The Uneasy Alliance: Collaboration between the Finnish Opposition and the Russian Underground, 1899–1904* (Helsinki: Suomalainen tiedeakatemia, 1973); and Osmo Jussila, *Nationalismi ja vallankumous venäläis-suomalaisissa suhteissa 1899–1914* [Nationalism and Revolution in the Russian-Finnish Relations, 1899–1914] (Helsinki: SHS, 1979). This cooperation included intellectual interaction that could have made Bolshevik leaders more likely to think of Karelia in terms of a separate territorial entity.

59. National Archive of Republic of Karelia (NARK), f. P-3, op. 5, d. 276,1. 22.

60. Calculations based on *Perepis naseleniia AKSSR. 1933 g. Vyp. III* [1933 Census of the Population of Karelia. Issue 3] (Petrozavodsk: Soiuzorguchiot, 1935), 16–17.

61. Calculations based on *Vsesoiuznaia perepis naseleniia. 1926, T. 1* [All-Soviet Census of 1926. Vol. 1] (Moscow: Statizdat TsSU SSSR, 1928), 178–81.

62. Takala, *Finny v Karelii,* 28.

CHAPTER 2. TWO PERSPECTIVES ON SOVIET IMMIGRATION POLICY: MOSCOW AND PETROZAVODSK

1. Roger P. Bartlett, *Human Capital: The Settlement of Foreigners in Russia, 1762–1804* (Cambridge, UK: Cambridge University Press, 1979).

2. Since Finland was a Grand Duchy of the Russian Empire, de jure in a union with Russia proper under the House of Romanovs, but not a part of it, immigration from Finland to Russian provinces was regulated by the same laws applicable to foreign nationals.

3. Galina Tarle, *Druzia strany sovetov: Uchastiie zarubezhnykh trudiashchikhsia v vosstanovlenii narodnogo khoziaistva SSSR v 1920–1925 gg.* [Friends of the Land of the Soviets: Foreign Workers' Contribution to Soviet Economic Recovery during 1920–1925] (Moscow: Nauka, 1966), 32–50. See also Annemarie H. Sammartino, *The Impossible Border: Germany and the East, 1914–1922* (Ithaca: Cornell University Press, 2010), 71–72.

4. *Dekrety Sovetskoi vlasti* [Decrees of the Soviet Power], vol. 1 (Moscow: Gospolitizdat, 1976), 298–99, 340–43.

5. Galina Tarle, "Rossiiskiie dokumenty o pravilakh v'ezda i vyezda za granitsu v 20-kh godakh XX v. (Analiz istochnokov) [Russian Documents on the Regulations of Crossing the Soviet Border in the 1920s (Analysis of Sources)]," in *Rossiia i problemy evropeiskoi istorii: srednevekovie, novoie, i noveisheie vremia* [Russia and the Issues of European History: Middle Ages, Modern, and Contemporary Time], ed. S. O. Schmidt et al. (Rostov: Rostovskii kreml, 2003), 128.

6. Ibid., 131; Tarle, *Druzia strany sovetov,* 152–54.

7. Yuri Felshtinsky, "The Legal Foundations of the Immigration and Emigration Policy of the USSR, 1917–1927," *Soviet Studies* 34, 3 (1982): 331. The author of this article was, unfortunately, completely unaware of a large body of scholarship on Western immigration to Soviet Russia and the early Soviet Union, such as works by Galina Tarle and Valerii Shishkin.

8. Quoted in Valerii Shishkin, *V. I. Lenin i vneshneekonomicheskaia politika Sovetskogo gosudarstva (1917–1923 gg.)* [V. I. Lenin and Foreign Economic Policy of the Soviet State (1917–1923)] (Leningrad: Nauka, 1977), 37.

9. Tarle, *Druzia strany sovetov,* 39.

10. Ibid., 56–70, 133; immigration figures on 66; Vadim Kukushkin, *From Peasants to Labourers:*

Ukrainian and Belarusan Immigration from the Russian Empire to Canada (Montreal: McGill-Queen's University Press, 2007), 184–87.

11. Ivan Gladkov, ed., *Sovetskoie narodnoie khoziaistvo v 1921–1925 gg.* [Soviet Economy in 1921–1925] (Moscow: Izd-vo AN SSSR, 1960), 531.

12. Moshe Lewin, *Russian Peasants and Soviet Power: A Study of Collectivization* (New York: W. W. Norton, 1975), 29.

13. See a detailed account of an immigration movement of German workers called Ansiedlung Ost and its failed attempt to establish an industrial colony in Kolomna in the chapter "Socialist Pioneers on the Soviet Frontier: Ansiedlung Ost," in Sammartino, *The Impossible Border,* 71–95. For an account of other German grassroots resettlement movements, see Julia Mahnke, *Auswanderungsvereine mit Ziel Ukraine und Sowjet-Rußland in der Weimarer Republik* [Emigration Organizations Aimed at Ukraine and Soviet Russia in Weimar Germany] (Munich: Mitteilungen des Osteuropa-Institutes, 1997).

14. Tarle, *Druzia strany sovetov,* 128–29.

15. *Sobraniie uzakonenii i rasporiazhenii rabochego i krestianskogo pravitelstva. 1917–1938* [The Collection of Laws and Decrees Issued by the Workers' and Peasants' Government] (further abbreviated as SU RSFSR), 1922, article 440.

16. Joseph P. Morray, *Project Kuzbas: American Workers in Siberia (1921–1926)* (New York: International Publishers, 1983); Liudmila Galkina, "Sozdaniie i deiatelnost avtonomnoi kolonii inostrannykh rabochikh i spetsialistov v Kuzbasse, 1921–1926 [Establishment and Operations of an Autonomous Colony of Immigrant Workers and Specialists in Kuzbass, 1921–1926]" (Candidate of Sciences diss. in Russian history, Kemerovo State University, 1997).

17. Tarle, *Druzia strany sovetov,* 209–11, 218.

18. Nikolai Shmelev and Vladimir Popov, *The Turning Point: Revitalizing the Soviet Economy* (New York: I. B.Tauris, 1990), 11–12.

19. Mikko Ylikangas, "The Sower Commune: An American-Finnish Agricultural Utopia in the Soviet Union," *Journal of Finnish Studies: A Special Double Issue, Victims and Survivors of Karelia* 15, 1–2 (2011): 51–84, esp. 51–60.

20. SU RSFSR, 1923, articles 128, 525.

21. Ibid., 1924, article 383; 1925, articles 119, 134, 152, 171; *Sobraniie zakonov i rasporiazhenii rabochе-krestianskogo pravitelstva SSSR. 1924–1937* [The Collection of Laws and Decrees of Workers' and Peasants' Government of the USSR] (further abbreviated as SZ SSSR), 1925, article 303.

22. SU RSFSR, 1926, article 458; 1927, article 130; SZ SSSR, 1927, article 95.

23. *KPSS v rezoliutsiiakh i resheniiakh s'iezdov, konferentsii, i plenumov TsK* [The CPSU in Resolutions and Decrees of Congresses, Conferences, and Plenums], vol. 2 (Moscow: Gospolitizdat, 1953), 589.

24. Zhuravliov, *Malenkiie liudi,* 27.

25. Sergey Zhuravliov and Viktoriia Tiazhiolnikova, "Inostrannaia koloniia v Sovetskoi Rossii v 1920–1930-e gody (Postanovka problemy i metody issledovaniia) [A Foreign Colony in Soviet Russia during the 1920s and 1930s (The Problem and Methods of Research)]," *Otechestvennaia istoriia* 1 (1994): 181.

26. Aleksandr Ioffe, "Deiatelnost zarubezhnykh obshchestv druzhby s Sovetskim Soiuzom [Activities of Foreign USSR Friendship Societies]," *Voprosy istorii* 3 (1966): 28; Zhuravliov, *Malenkiie liudi,* 29.

27. Koronen, *Finskiie internatsionalisty,* 130.

28. NARK, f. R-550, op. 1, d. 3/37,1. 219; col. R-115, op. 1, d. 7/70,1. 5; col. R-682, op. 1, d. 1/10,1. 5–6.

29. For English-language accounts and histories of the Civil War in Karelia, see Charles Maynard, *The Murmansk Venture* (London: Hodder and Stoughton, 1928); Nick Baron, *The King of Karelia: Col P.J. Woods and the British Intervention in North Russia 1918–1919. A History and Memoir* (London: Francis Boutle Publishers, 2007); and Alistair S. Wright, "The Establishment of Bolshevik Power on the Russian Periphery: Soviet Karelia, 1918–1919" (PhD thesis, University of Glasgow, 2012).

30. NARK, f. P-3, op. 1, d. 80,1. 79.

31. On Edvard Gylling's economic management of Soviet Karelia, see Pekka Kauppala, "Sowjet-Karelien, 1917–1941: Leistung und Schicksal eines sozialistischen Regionalexperiments [Soviet Karelia, 1917–1941: The Success and Fate of a Socialist Regional Experiment]" (PhD thesis, Albert Ludwigs University of Freiburg, 1992), especially the chapter "Der Mann an der Spitze der KTK: Edvard Gylling [The Man at the Summit of the Karelian Labor Commune: Edvard Gylling]," 50–65; Kauppala, "Formirovaniie i rastsvet"; and Nick Baron, *Soviet Karelia: Politics, Planning, and Terror in Stalin's Russia, 1920–1939* (London: Routledge, 2007), 20–23, 52–74.

32. *Krasnaia Kareliia: Sbornik materialov ofitsialnogo kharaktera* [Red Karelia: A Collection of Official Materials] (Petrozavodsk: Narkomiust AKSSR, 1925), 27–29, 45–46; Kauppala, "Sowjet-Karelien 1917–1941," 99. This privilege, though on a very restricted scale, was breaking the Soviet state monopoly in foreign trade and was discontinued in the mid-1920s.

33. Kauppala, "Formirovaniie i rastsvet," 329.

34. Iefim Gardin, *Sovetskaia Kareliia v gody vosstanovitelnogo perioda (1921–1925)* [Soviet Karelia in the Years of Reconstruction Period (1921–1925)] (Petrozavodsk: Gosizdat KFSSR, 1955), 48.

35. Kauppala, "Formirovaniie i rastsvet," 327–29.

36. Edvard Gylling, "Geroicheskoie desiatiletiie [Heroic Decade]," *Karelo-Murmanskii krai* 7–8 (1930): 4. The report, obviously, did not take into account inflation, for Soviet economic statistics had no official method for its calculation.

37. Edvard Gylling, "Biudzhetnyie prava Karelii [Budget Privileges of Karelia]," *Ekonomika i statistika Karelii* 7–8 (1926): 10.

38. NARK, f. P-3, op. 2, d. 393,1. 2.

39. NARK, f. P-3, op. 2, d. 158,1. 1.

40. Edvard Gylling, "Biudzhetnyie prava Karelii" [Budget Privileges of Karelia], *Ekonomika i statistika Karelii* 1–3 (1925): 1.

41. Sari Autio, *Suunnitelmatalous Neuvosto-Karjalassa, 1928–1941* [Planned Economy of Soviet Karelia, 1928–1941] (Helsinki: SKS, 2002), 318–19.

42. NARK, f. P-3, op. 2, d. 393,1. 9.

43. In January 1926, during a closed meeting of the Karelian *obkom* of VKP(b), Chairman Johan Järvisalo said that "we should nowhere mention about that, especially in questions regarding our economic development, as it will play in favor of [bourgeoisie], particularly in Finland." See Alexey Levkoev, "'Pravilnaia politika': Krestiianskii fon politiki finliandkogo kommunisticheskogo rukovodstva Sovetskoi Kareliii v 1920-e gg. ["The Right Policy": A Peasant Background in the Politics of the Finnish Communist Leadership of Soviet Karelia in the 1920s]," in *Natsionalnaia gosudarstvennost finno-ugorskikh narodov severo-zapadnoi Rossii (1917–1940)* [National statehood of Finno-Ugric peoples of Northwest Russia (1917–1940)], ed. A. A. Popov (Syktyvkar: KomiNTs RAN, 1996), 26.

44. Baron, *Soviet Karelia,* 63–74.

45. Nikolai Korablev et al., eds., *Istoriia Karelii s drevneishikh vremen do nashikh dnei* [History of Karelia from Ancient Times to Our Days] (Petrozavodsk: Periodika, 2001), 468.

46. Aleksandra Afanasieva, "Pervaia sredi ravnykh [The First among Equals]," *Leninskaia pravda,* 10 January 1990.

47. Ibid.

48. Alexey Golubev, "Printsipy upravleniia ekonomikoi v ekonomicheskom soznanii rukovodstva Karelii v gody NEPa (1921–1929 gg.) [Principles of Economic Management in Economic Thinking of the Leadership of Karelia during the NEP (1921–1929)]," in *Regionalizatsiia i globalizatsiia: Obshchestvennye protsessy v Rossii i na Evropeiskom Severe v XX–XXI vekakh* [Regionalization and Globalization: Social Processes in Russia and the Russian European North during the Twentieth and Twenty-First Centuries], ed. Sergey Shubin (Arkhangelsk: Pomor State University Press, 2007), 59–90.

49. Autio, *Suunnitelmatalous Neuvosto-Karjalassa,* 318.

50. Baron, *Soviet Karelia,* 151–52.

51. Markku Kangaspuro, "Finskaia epokha sovetskoi Karelii [The Finnish Era of Soviet Karelia]," in *V semie edinoi: Natsionalnaia politika partii bolshevikov i eio osushchestvleniie na Severo-Zapade Rossii v 1920–1950-e gody* [One United Family: The Nationalities Policy of CPSU from the 1920s to the 1950s and Its Implementation in Northwestern Russia], ed. Irina Takala and Timo Vihavainen (Petrozavodsk: Petrozavodsk State University Press, 1998), 129.

52. *Sbornik vazhneishikh postanovlenii za 1929–ianvar 1931 gg. po Karelskoi ASSR* [A Collection of the Most Important Decrees from 1929 to January 1931 in the Karelian ASSR] (Petrozavodsk: Narkomiust AKSSR, 1931), 55.

53. Calculations based on *Statisticheskii ezhegodnik Karelii 1922* [Statistical Yearbook of Karelia 1922], vol. 2, part 1 (Petrozavodsk: Statupravlenie AKSSR, 1923), 12–13.

54. Another ethnic group close in language and traditional cultural practices to Finns and Karelians and regarded as part of the Finno-Ugric group of peoples.

55. Calculations based on *Vsesoiuznaia perepis naseleniia 1926,* 114–15.

56. Irina Pokrovskaia, *Naseleniie Karelii* [Population of Karelia] (Petrozavodsk: Karelia, 1978), 47–48.

57. In 1929, for example, the number of workers recruited to Soviet Karelia from other Russian regions for winter timber harvesting operations amounted to 60,000 (NARK, f. R-690, op. 1, d. 17/187,1. 1).

58. NARK, f. R-690, op. 1, d. 15/163,1. 46–47.

59. Ibid.

60. NARK, f. R-690, op. 1, d. 17/181,1. 14–15, 17–18.

61. NARK, f. R-690, op. 1, d. 17/187,1. 5.

62. Ibid,1. 11.

63. Ibid,1. 15.

64. Throughout the history of North American immigration to Soviet Karelia, Soviet authorities at all levels often confused the terms "Canadian" and "American," using the latter as a synonym for "North American" (as in this quotation) and the former to refer to immigrants from both Canada and the United States.

65. NARK, f. R-690, op. 1, d. 17/187,1. 5.

66. Ibid,1. 23–24.

67. Ibid.

68. See articles in the newspapers *Krasnaia Karelia* (e.g., 24 September 1930) and *Punainen Karjala* (e.g., 30 September and 19 November 1930). At least two books were published: N. Bekrenev,

Kanadskiie lesoruby v Karelii [Canadian Lumberjacks in Karelia] (Petrozavodsk: Kirja, 1932); and V. Tonkell, *Kanadskiie lesoruby v Sovetskoi Karelii* [Canadian Lumberjacks in Soviet Karelia] (Moscow: Goslestekhizdat, 1934).

69. See, for example, NARK, f. R-690, op. 1, d. 20/222,1. 32–33; file 20/230,1. 9–10; col P-3, op. 5, d. 276,1. 24.

70. NARK, f. P-3, op. 6, d. 12774,1. 47–79.

71. Väino Järvi, "Kuulumisia Kanadan suomalaisten metsätyöarttelilta Matroosasta [News from the Finnish Canadian Logging Team in Matrosy]," *Punainen Karjala,* 7 January 1931.

72. NARK, f. R-690, op. 1, d. 15/163,1. 43.

73. SNK is an abbreviation for Sovet Narodnykh Komissarov, or Council of People's Commissars, the official title of governments (both federal and regional) in the USSR.

74. NARK, f. R-690, op. 1, d. 15/163,1. 45.

75. Sergei Kirov (1886–1934), a prominent Bolshevik leader, headed the Leningrad *obkom* of the VKP(b) at that time.

76. NARK, f. R-690, op. 1, d. 20/222,1. 32. The letter without Gylling's marginal notes was published in: *Rabochii klass Karelii v period postroeniia sotsializma v SSSR. 1926–1941,* ed. G. I. Mezentsev (Petrozavodsk: Karelia, 1984), 7–8. Vyacheslav Molotov (1890–1986), a prominent Bolshevik leader, was chairman of the Soviet government at that time.

77. NARK, f. R-690, op. 1, d. 19/213,1. 2.

78. NARK, f. P-3, op. 2, d. 790,1. 1–2.

CHAPTER 3. TO KARELIA!

1. Kostiainen, *The Forging of Finnish-American Communism,* 126.

2. For more details, see Andriainen, "Dvizheniie proletarskoi solidarnosti," 184–86; and Kostiainen, *The Forging of Finnish-American Communism,* 160–88.

3. NARK, f. P-3, op. 5, d. 276,1. 26, 28.

4. NARK, f. P-3, op. 6, d. 10792,1. 2–3.

5. Peter Kivisto, "The Decline of the Finnish American Left, 1925–1945," *International Migration Review* 17, 1 (1983): 68–74.

6. NARK, f. P-3, op. 5, d. 276,1. 27.

7. Kivisto, "The Decline of the Finnish American Left," 73. Soviet sources, not surprisingly, accused Halonen of "opposition" and "subversive" activities against the American labor movement. NARK, f. P-3, op. 5, d. 276,1. 27.

8. Alexis Pogorelskin, "Communism and the Co-ops: Recruiting and Financing the Finnish-American Migration to Karelia," *Journal of Finnish Studies* 8, 1 (2004): 28–47; NARK, f. P-3, op. 6, d. 10792,1. 6–7.

9. NARK, f. P-3, op. 5, d. 276,1. 60, 64, 68–69; NARK, f. R-685, op. 1, d. 4/40,1. 195.

10. Evgeny Efremkin, "'Karelian Project' or 'Karelian Fever'? Orders from Above, Reaction from Below: Conflicting Interests in Kremlin, Karelia, and Canada," in *North American Finns,* ed. Solomeshch and Takala, 66.

11. NARK, f. R-685, op. 1, d. 7/67,1. 14.

12. NARK, f. R-690, op. 1, d. 19/213,1. 62, 81.

13. NARK, f. R-690, op. 1, d. 23/262,1. 120.

14. NARK, f. P-3, op. 5, d. 276,1. 60, 69–70.

15. NARK, f. P-3, op. 5, d. 276,1. 51–52, 60, 69, 72.

16. Ibid.,1. 62, 72.

17. Ibid.,1. 51, 53, 62, 70, 72–73.

18. Ibid.,1. 72.

19. Ibid.,1. 63.

20. Elena Osokina, *Za fasadom "stalinskogo izobiliia": Raspredeleniie i rynok v snabzhenii naseleniia v gody industrializatsii. 1927–1941* [Behind the Facade of "Stalinist's Abundance": Distribution and the Market during the Industrialization] (Moscow: ROSSPEN, 1998), 161, 164.

21. "Kapitalovlozheniia po mestnomu budzhetu [Capital Investments in the Republican Budget]," in *Avtonomnaia Karelskaia Sovetskaia Sotsialisticheskaia Respublika. Spravochnik. 1923–1933* [Autonomous Karelian Soviet Socialist Republic. Reference Book. 1923–1933] (Petrozavodsk: Izd-vo SNK AKSSR, 1933), 80.

22. Christer Boucht, *Onnea etsimässä,* 60; NARK, f. R-690, op. 1, d. 22/254,1. 59.

23. NARK, f. P-3, op. 5, d. 276,1. 71.

24. NARK, f. R-685, op. 2, d. 205,1. 21.

25. NARK, f. P-3, op. 5, d. 276,1. 20, 81.

26. Kero, *Neuvosto-Karjalaa rakentamassa,* 83; Sakari Sariola, *Amerikan kultaan: Amerikansuomalaisten siirtolaisten sosiaalihistoria* [To American Gold: A Social History of Finnish American Immigrants] (Helsinki: Kustannusosakeyhtiö, 1982); Varpu Lindström, "'Heaven or Hell on Earth?' Soviet Karelia's Propaganda War of 1934–1935 in the Finnish Canadian Press," in *North American Finns,* ed. Solomeshch and Takala, 83–104; Efremkin, "Karelian Project."

27. Pekka Nevalainen, *Punaisen myrskyn suomalaiset: Suomalaisten paot ja paluumuutot idästä 1917–1939* [Finns of the Red Storm: Finns' Escapes to and Return from the East, 1917–1939] (Helsinki: SKS, 2004).

28. Sevander, *Red Exodus;* Sevander, *Skitaltsy.*

29. Alexis Pogorelskin, "Why Karelian Fever?," *Siirtolaisuus/Migration* 1 (2000): 25–26; Alexis Pogorelskin, "New Perspectives on Karelian Fever: The Recruitment of North American Finns to Karelia in the Early 1930s," *Journal of Finnish Studies* 1, 3 (1997): 165–78.

30. Peter Kivisto and Mika Roinila, "Reaction to Departure: The Finnish American Community Responds to 'Karelian Fever,'" in *North American Finns,* ed. Solomeshch and Takala, 17–38.

31. Esko Tommola, *Uuden maanrakentajat* [Builders of the New World] (Helsinki: Otava, 1989); Sariola, *Amerikan kultaan;* Pogorelskin, "Why Karelian Fever?"

32. Richard Hudelson and Mayme Sevander, "Relapse of Karelian Fever," *Siirtolaisuus/Migration* 2 (2000): 31–35.

33. Pogorelskin, "New Perspectives"; Kangaspuro, *Neuvosto-Karjalan taistelu itsehallinnosta.*

34. Sariola, *Amerikan kultaan;* Hannu Rautkallio, *Suuri viha: Stalinin suomalaiset uhrit 1930-luvulla* [Big Anger: Stalin's Finnish Victims of the 1930s] (Porvoo: WSOY, 1995).

35. Tuomi, "The Karelian Fever"; Kero, "Emigration of Finns."

36. NARK, f. R-690, op. 1, d. 19/213,1. 5–6.

37. Jacob M. Budish and Samuel Saul Shipman, *Soviet Foreign Trade: Menace or Promise* (New York: H. Liveright, 1931); *Embargo on Soviet Products,* Hearing in the US Congress, 19–21 February 1931, http://hdl.handle.net/2027/mdp.39015055421732.

38. *Krasnaia Karelia* 34 (1931): 3; *Krasnaia Karelia* 41 (1931): 3; *Krasnaia Karelia* 44 (1931): 2.

39. V. Suomela, *Kuusi kuukautta Karjalassa: Mitä siirtolainen näki ja koki Neuvosto-Karjalassa* [Six

Months in Karelia: What an Immigrant Saw and Experienced in Soviet Karelia] (Sudbury: Vapaa Sana Press, 1939).

40. Lindström, "Heaven or Hell on Earth?"

41. Samira Saramo, "Piecing Together Immigrant Lives: An Analysis of Personal Letters Written by North American Finns in Soviet Karelia," in *North American Finns,* ed. Solomeshch and Takala, 170–89.

42. See, e.g., V. Nurminen, "Na lyzhnoi fabrike [At the Ski Factory]," in *Na fronte mirnogo truda: Vospominaniia uchastnikov sotsialisticheskogo stroitelstva v Karelii, 1920–1940* [On the Frontline of Peaceful Labor: Memoirs of Participants of Socialist Building of Karelia, 1920–1940] (Petrozavodsk: Karelia, 1976), 43–46; H. Sundfors, "Na tselluloznom zavode [At the Pulp Factory]," in ibid., 22–25; and E. Tuomi, "Pamiatnik Iliichu [A Monument to Lenin]," in ibid., 49–52.

43. Sevander, *They Took My Father;* Sevander, *Red Exodus;* Sevander, *Of Soviet Bondage.* In this book, we refer to the posthumous Russian-language translation of her fourth book (Sevander, *Skitaltsy*), originally published in Finnish.

44. Apart from Hokkanen's memoir, they include Tuomi, "The Karelian Fever"; Boucht, *Onnea etsimässä;* Boucht, *Karjala kutsuu;* and Hokkanen and Hokkanen, *A Finnish-American Couple.*

45. Kaija Matinheikki-Kokko and Pirkko Pitkänen, "Immigrant Policies and the Education of Immigrants in Finland," in *Education and Immigration: Settlement Policies and Current Challenges,* ed. Gajendra K.Verma and Devorah Kalekin-Fishman (London: Routledge, 2002), 49.

46. See, e.g., Kalle Ranta, *Arpi korvassa ja sydämessä* [A Scar on an Ear and Heart] (Helsinki: WSOY, 2000); and Helena Miettinen and Kyllikki Joganson, *Petettyjen toiveiden maa* [The Land of Betrayed Hopes] (Saarijärvi: Gummerus kirjapaino OY, 2001). Some former immigrants, who had Canadian or American citizenship before their immigration to Soviet Karelia, returned to North America, and at least one of them published an English-language account of these events; see Komulainen, *A Grave in Karelia.*

47. Hokkanen and Hokkanen, *A Finnish-American Couple.*

48. Maria Koponen, "Zhenshchiny na lesozagotovkakh [Women in Forest Harvesting]," in *Na fronte mirnogo truda,* 80–84.

49. Olga-Maria Koponen, *Tavallisen ihmisen tarina* [A Story of an Ordinary Person] (Vaasa: Ykkös-Offset OY, 2002).

50. Ranta, *Arpi korvassa,* 42.

51. Tuomi, "The Karelian Fever," 63.

52. Quoted in Kero, *Suuren Länteen,* 278.

53. Ibid., 36.

54. Ranta, *Arpi korvassa,* 41, 36.

55. *Krasnaia Karelia,* 28 March 1932.

56. Takala, *Finny v Karelii,* 38.

57. Efremkin, "Karelian Project," 67.

58. Interview with Toini Pränny, Petrozavodsk, May 2003, in the archive of the Department of History of Northern Europe, Petrozavodsk State University.

59. Tommola, *Uuden maanrakentajat,* 267.

60. Interview with Kaarlo Ranta, Matrosy, June 2003, in the archive of the Department of History of Northern Europe, Petrozavodsk State University.

61. Nevalainen, *Punaisen myrskyn suomalaiset,* 277.

62. Ritva-Liisa Hovi, "Amerikansuomalaisten maanviljelyskommuuni Etelä-Venäjällä [Finnish American Agricultural Commune in South Russia]," *Turun Historiallinen Arkisto* 25 (1971): 283.

63. Interview with Kaarlo Ranta, Matrosy, June 2003, in the archive of the Department of History of Northern Europe, Petrozavodsk State University.

64. Boucht, *Onnea etsimässä,* 41.

65. Kero, *Suuren Länteen,* 272.

66. Interview with Dagne Salo, in *Ustnaia istoriia,* ed. Golubev and Takala, 55–56.

67. Teuvo Peltoniemi, *Kohti parempaa maailmaa* [Toward a Better World] (Helsinki: Otava, 1985), 106.

68. Anita Middleton, "Karelian Fever: Interviews with Survivors," *Journal of Finnish Studies* 1, 3 (1997): 179.

69. A Finnish name for Russian Karelia; see Chapter 1 for a more detailed discussion of the geographic context of Finnish immigration.

70. Boucht, *Onnea etsimässä,* 41.

71. Ranta, *Arpi korvassa,* 36; Pogorelskin, "Why Karelian Fever?," 25.

72. Boucht, *Onnea etsimässä,* 60.

73. Interview with Kaarlo Ranta, Matrosy, June 2003, in the archive of the Department of History of Northern Europe, Petrozavodsk State University.

74. Interview with Robert Manner, in *Ustnaia istoriia,* ed. Golubev and Takala, 137.

75. Interview with Gunnar Ingström, Chalna, June 2003, in the archive of the Department of History of Northern Europe, Petrozavodsk State University.

76. Interview with Yrjö Myllyharju, Petrozavodsk, May 2002, in the archive of the Department of History of Northern Europe, Petrozavodsk State University.

77. Early American researchers suggested 2,000, Elis Sulkanen, *Amerikan suomalaisen työväenliikkeen historia* [The History of the Finnish American Labor Movement] (Fitchburg, MA: Amerikan Suomalainen Kansanvallan Liitto, 1951), 278; from 5,000 to 7,000, Armas K. E. Holmio, *Michiganin Suomalaisten historia* [History of Finns in Michigan] Hancock, MI: Michigan Suomalaisten Historia-Seura, 1967), 411; and even 12,000 North American Finns, William Lahtinen, *50 vuoden varrelta* [During Fifty Years] (Superior, WI: American Finnish Publishers; Työmies Society, 1953), 172, emigrated to the Soviet Union. A researcher of Canadian Finnish history, Yrjö Raivio, estimated the number at 6,000 to 8,000 people; see Yrjö Raivio, *Kanadan Suomalaisten historia* [History of Finns in Canada] (Copper Cliff, ON: Canadan Suomalainen Historiaseura, 1975), 487. A Soviet work published in 1970 claimed that the number of North American immigrants was as high as 15,000; see V. F. Pimenov and R. F. Taroieva, "Etnicheskiie protsessy v Sovetskoi Karelii [Ethnic Processes in Soviet Karelia]," *50 let Sovetskoi Karelii* [Fifty Years of Soviet Karelia] (Petrozavodsk: Karelia, 1970), 226. This number corresponds more to immigration plans of the Karelian government than to their actual fulfillment. Sergey Zhuravliov's mention of "several tens of thousands of Karelians and Finns" who moved to Soviet Karelia from Canada and the United States is obviously inflated and refers, more likely, to the total number of immigrants in Soviet Karelia, including those from Finland and Sweden; see Zhuravliov, *Malenkiie liudi,* 26. In works published in the 1990s and 2000s, most authors tend to use the number suggested by Kero (5,000 to 6,000 people), *Neuvosto-Karjalaa rakentamassa,* 58, or by Takala (6,000 to 6,500 people), "Finskoie naseleniie Sovetskoi Karelii," 171.

78. Takala was the first to do so during the early 1990s. See Irina Takala, "Sudby finnov v Karelii [Fates of Finns in Karelia]," in *Voprosy istorii Evropeiskogo Severa* [Questions of History of the European North], ed. Mikhail Shumilov (Petrozavodsk: Petrozavodsk State University Press, 1991), 92–103; and Takala, "Finskoie naseleniie Sovetskoi Karelii," 150–75.

79. The database was created as part of the project Missing in Karelia (see the Preface) on the basis of

over 300 sources from the National Archive of the Republic of Karelia. The data were translated into English and are available at the website of the project, http://missinginkarelia.org.

80. We regularly encountered the names of Finnish immigrants from North America in official Soviet documents or memoirs who somehow eluded all official lists of immigrants and thus did not find their way into our database. The most probable reason is that many immigrants returned to North America or moved from Soviet Karelia to other Soviet regions in the weeks after their arrival, before they were registered and counted by the Karelian authorities.

81. Perepis naseleniia AKSSR 1933 g.

82. NARK, f. P-3, op. 6, d. 12774,1. 1–79. Collection (f.) P-3 stores documents of the Karelian *obkom* (regional committee) of the VKP(b) and KPSS, and inventory (op.) 6 of this collection contains personal files.

83. Sevander, *Skitaltsy,* 47–48.

84. NARK, f. 695, op. 1, d. 29/324,1. 2–4.

85. Aleksandr Fuks, "Na beregu ochen russkoi reki," *Karelskaia guberniia* 5 (2005): 14.

86. Perepis naseleniia AKSSR 1933 g., 16–19.

87. NARK, f. R-685, op. 2, d. 263,1. 113.

88. NARK, f. R-685, op. 2, d. 69,1. 84–85.

89. NARK, f. R-685, op. 1, d. 14/160,1. 21.

90. Calculated on the basis of NARK, f. R-685, op. 1, d. 6,1. 40–41.

91. NARK, f. R-690, op. 1, d. 19/220,1. 6.

92. Calculated on the basis of NARK, f. R-685, op. 2, d. 246,1. 1–7; NARK, f. R-685, op. 2, d. 254,1. 22–26.

93. NARK, f. P-3, op. 5, d. 276,1. 73.

94. NARK, f. R-690, op. 1, d. 22/254,1. 59.

95. The list is available online at http://www.levonius.com/Laiho_List/Laiho_List.htm.

96. Kero, *Suureen Länteen,* 131.

97. Ibid., 103, 105–06.

98. NARK, f. P-3, op. 2, d. 790,1. 6.

99. NARK, f. P-3, op. 2, file 790,1. 6.

100. NARK, f. P-3, op. 3, d. 75,1. 35; NARK, f. P-3, op. 2, d. 790,1. 66.

101. NARK, f. P-3, op. 5, file 276,1. 73.

102. Calculated on the basis of NARK, f. P-3, op. 5, file 277,1. 86–133.

103. See Takala, "Finskoie naseleniie Sovetskoi Karelii," 171; and Takala, *Finny v Karelii,* 28.

CHAPTER 4. THE FAILURE OF THE IMMIGRATION PROGRAM

1. During the Second World War, the Swedish American Line leased *MS Gripsholm* to the US Department of State, which employed it for the repatriation of American and Canadian prisoners-of-war, exchanged for German and Japanese ones.

2. NARK, f. R-685, op. 2, d. 64, 69, 246, 300.

3. NARK, f. R-690, op. 1, d. 19/213,1. 67. We do not know the exact fares that the Karelian Technical Aid Committee and the Swedish American Line agreed upon, but in 1931 the officially advertised minimum price on the route from New York to Gothenburg aboard *SS Kungsholm* was $165. See *Steamboat Bill* 45 (1988): 7.

4. NARK, f. R-690, op. 1, d. 19/213,1. 60, 68, 97; NARK, f. R-685, op. 2, d. 69,1. 26.

5. NARK, f. R-685, op. 2, d. 99,1. 26.

6. Interview with Kerttu Niemi, Petrozavodsk, October 2002, in the archive of the Department of History of Northern Europe, Petrozavodsk State University.

7. Interview with Toini Pränny, Petrozavodsk, May 2003, in the archive of the Department of History of Northern Europe, Petrozavodsk State University.

8. Interview with Kaarlo Ranta, Matrosy, June 2003, in the archive of the Department of History of Northern Europe, Petrozavodsk State University.

9. Mayme Sevander, "Severoamerikanskiie finny v Karelii [North American Finns in Karelia]," in *Kraeved: Sbornik statei* [Local History: A Collection of Articles], ed. Alevtina Rogozhina (Petrozavodsk: Verso, 2007), 141.

10. Insnab was a Soviet state organization responsible for the provision of foreign specialists and workers employed in Soviet industry with food and commodities.

11. Interview with Kaarlo Ranta, Matrosy, June 2003, in the archive of the Department of History of Northern Europe, Petrozavodsk State University.

12. NARK, f. R-690, op. 1, d. 19/213,1. 33–35, 37, 44–48.

13. The memoir of Anita Luoma, in *Ustnaia istoriia,* ed. Golubev and Takala, 146.

14. NARK, f. R-685, op. 1, d. 124,1. 32.

15. NARK, f. R-685, op. 2, d. 19/252,1. 136.

16. NARK, f. R-685, op. 1, d. 121,1. 4.

17. NARK, f. R-690, op. 1, d. 6/27,1. 18.

18. NARK, f. R-685, op. 1, d. 3,1. 71–73.

19. NARK, f. R-690, op. 1, d. 23/262,1. 6, 54.

20. NARK, f. R-685, op. 2, d. 64,1. 97.

21. NARK, f. P-3, op. 2, d. 595,1. 18–19.

22. NARK, f. R-685, op. 2, d. 64,1. 97.

23. Leningrad military district.

24. NARK, f. P-3, op. 2, d. 708,1. 1–3.

25. NARK, f. R-690, op. 1, d. 19/213,1. 19–20.

26. NARK, f. P-3, op. 2, d. 790,1. 1–2.

27. The National Archive of the Republic of Karelia has two copies of this memorandum, identical in contents but different in dates and addressees. The one of 19 May was addressed to the Central Committee of VKP(b) (NARK, f. P-3, op. 2, d. 790,1. 1–4), while the one of 20 May was addressed personally to Stalin (NARK, f. P-3, op. 5, d. 276,1. 19–23).

28. NARK, f. R-690, op. 1, d. 19/213,1. 21.

29. Ibid.,1. 8–9.

30. Finnish name of Petrozavodsk.

31. Private letter of Edvard Mason dated to 18 March 1932. NARK, f. R-685, op. 2, d. 99,1. 95.

32. NARK, f. P-3, op. 2, d. 790,1. 108.

33. NARK, f. R-685, op. 1, d. 9/97,1. 74–75, 77.

34. NARK, f. R-690, op. 1, d. 230,1. 11–13.

35. Boucht, *Onnea etsimässä,* 73.

36. Ibid., 66.

37. Aleskander Pashkov and Svetlana Filimonchik, *Petrozavodsk* (Sankt-Peterburg: Zvezda Peterburga, 2001), 87.

38. NARK, f. R-690, op. 1, d. 154,1. 63–64.

39. NARK, col. P-3, op. 2, d. 790,1. 23.

40. NARK, f. R-690, op. 6, d. 4/12,1. 218–20.

41. NARK, f. 3, op. 2, d. 790,1. 5–11, 53–64, 86–87.

42. NARK, f. R-690, op. 1, d. 22/254,1. 53.

43. Ibid.,1. 57.

44. NARK, f. 3, op. 3, d. 256,1. 29.

45. NARK, f. 3, op. 2, d. 790,1. 86.

46. NARK, f. 3, op. 3, d. 256,1. 115.

47. Ibid.

48. Interview with Yrjö Mykkänen, in *Ustnaia istoriia,* ed. Golubev and Takala, 107; Sevander, *Skitaltsy,* 69. The last of these houses was demolished in the early 2000s.

49. Sevander, *Skitaltsy,* 69.

50. Interview with Roy Niskanen, in *Ustnaia istoriia v Karelii. Vyp. 4. Kareliia i Belarus: Povsednevnaia zhizn i kulturnyie praktiki naseleniia v 1930–1950-e gg.* [Oral History in Karelia. Issue 4. Karelia and Belarus: Everyday Life and Cultural Practices in the 1930s to 1950s], ed. Alexey Golubev et al. (Petrozavodsk: Petrozavodsk State University Press, 2008), 339.

51. Interview with Paavo Alatalo, in *Ustnaia istoriia,* ed. Golubev and Takala, 87.

52. A thin soup or gruel.

53. A species of freshwater fish widespread in Northern Europe.

54. NARK, f. P-3, op. 3, d. 41,1. 43.

55. NARK, f. P-3, op. 2, d. 790,1. 23.

56. NARK, f. R-685, op. 1, d. 3/26,1. 114.

57. NARK, f. R-685, op. 2, d. 116/217,1. 115.

58. NARK, f. P-3, op. 2, d. 790,1. 9.

59. NARK, f. R-1230, op. 7, d. 6,1. 103.

60. NARK, col. P-3, op. 2, d. 790,1. 5–10.

61. Middleton, "Karelian Fever," 17.

62. Interview with Elsa Balandis, Petrozavodsk, 2007.

63. NARK, f. 3, op. 2, d. 790,1. 9.

64. See the latest scholarly account of Soviet attempts to publicize the Soviet project abroad: Michael David-Fox, *Showcasing the Great Experiment: Cultural Diplomacy and Western Visitors to the Soviet Union 1921–41* (Oxford: Oxford University Press, 2011).

65. For a more detailed account of the Soviet rationing system of the 1930s, see Osokina, *Za fasadom "stalinskogo izobiliia."*

66. NARK, f. 1230, op. 6, d. 10,1. 61.

67. NARK, f. 3, op. 3, d. 41,1. 1–3.

68. NARK, f. R-690, op. 1, d. 22/254,1. 53.

69. Such large stocks were necessary because during spring months much of northern Karelia, including Ukhta, had no transportation connection with the rest of Soviet Karelia.

70. NARK, f. R-690, op. 1, d. 22/254,1. 54–55.

71. NARK, f. R-690, op. 1, d. 23/262,1. 12.

72. See NARK, f. R-690, op. 1, d. 23/262,1. 12–13, 16, 18, 22, 25.

73. NARK, f. P-3, op. 5, d. 276,1. 62.

74. Auvo Kostiainen, "Neuvosto-Karjala ja 'Kaukaisen idän aromailta'—Suomalaiskirjeitä Venäjältä ja Neuvostoliitosta [Soviet Karelia and 'From the Steppes of a Faraway East'—Finnish Letters from Russia and the Soviet Union]," in *Maitten ja merten takaa: Vuosisata suomalaisia siirtolaiskirjeitä*

[From Across the Lands and Seas: A Century of Finnish Immigrant Letters], ed. Eero Kuparinen (Turku: Turun Historiallinen Yhdistys, 1986), 250.

75. Ibid., 242.
76. NARK, f. P-3, op. 2, d. 790,1. 7.
77. Kostiainen, "Neuvosto-Karjala ja 'Kaukaisen idän aromailta,'" 239.
78. NARK, f. R-690, op. 1, d. 230,1. 10.
79. NARK, f. R-685, op. 2, d. 90,1. 16.
80. NARK, f. R-690, op. 1, d. 19/213,1. 111–12.
81. NARK, f. P-3, op. 2, d. 790,1. 57. Such situations caused by ineffective planning and sprawling bureaucratic apparatus happened all over the Soviet Union. See, for example, a description of similar negligence of expensive equipment in Magnitogorsk in Kotkin, *Magnetic Mountain,* 60–61.
82. NARK, f. P-3, op. 2, d. 790,1. 7.
83. NARK, f. P-3, op. 3, d. 359,1. 8.
84. Ibid.
85. Ibid.,1. 12.
86. NARK, f. P-3, op. 2, d. 790,1. 59–60.
87. Golubev et al., eds., *Ustnaia istoriia,* 337.
88. Miettinen and Joganson, *Petettyjen toiveiden maa,* 20.
89. Kostiainen, "Neuvosto-Karjala ja 'Kaukaisen idän aromailta,'" 252.
90. Middleton, "Karelian Fever," 14.

CHAPTER 5. AMERICAN AND CANADIAN IMMIGRANTS IN THE SOVIET ECONOMY

1. A. M. Markevich, "Otraslevyie narkomaty i glavki v sisteme upravleniia sovetskoi ekonomikoi v 1930e gg. [Industry Commissariats and Central Offices of Industrial Management in the System of Soviet Economic Management in the 1930s]," in *Ekonomicheskaia istroiia: Ezhegodnik. 2004* [Economic History: A Yearbook. 2004], ed. L. I. Borodkin (Moscow: ROSSPEN, 2004), 118–40.
2. I. V. Stalin, *Sochineniia* [Works], vol. 12 (Moscow: Politizdat, 1949), 270.
3. I. V. Stalin, *Sochineniia* [Works], vol. 13 (Moscow: Politizdat, 1951), 177.
4. See R. W. Davis, *The Industrialisation of Soviet Russia 4: Crisis and Progress in the Soviet Economy, 1931–1933* (London: Macmillan, 1996), 18–24, 104–08, 142–301, 362–79, 466–72.
5. Yuri Kilin, *Kareliia v politike sovetskogo gosudarstva 1920–1941* [Karelia in Politics of the Soviet State] (Petrozavodsk: Petrozavodsk State University Press, 2000), 132.
6. For a detailed account of contrasting visions of the Karelian economy, see Baron, *Soviet Karelia.*
7. NARK, f. R-286, op. 1, d. 22/200,1. 12.
8. NARK, f. R-690, op. 1, d. 22/254,1. 51–52.
9. NARK, f. R-286, op. 1, d. 22/200,1. 12.
10. NARK, f. R-286, op. 7, d. 4/25,1. 12.
11. For a more detailed account, see Iosif Tonkell, *Jännesaha* [Bow Saw] (Moskova-Leningrad: Kirja, 1933), 4–7; Bekrenev, *Kanadskiie lesoruby v Karelii,* 10–12; and Kero, *Neuvosto-Karjalaa rakentamassa,* 109–15.
12. NARK, f. R-690, op. 1, d. 19/213,1. 113.
13. NARK, f. R-1632, op. 1, d. 3/39,1. 26.

14. NARK, f. R-286, op. 7, d. 23/207,1. 4.

15. Reino Kero, "The Canadian Finns in Soviet Karelia in the 1930s," in *The Finnish Diaspora I: Canada, South America, Africa, Australia, and Sweden,* ed. Michael Karni (Toronto: Multicultural History Society of Ontario, 1981), 208.

16. NARK, f. R-690, op. 1, d. 23/262,1. 25.

17. T. I. Kishchenko, "Rostki novogo na lesozagotovkakh [New Sprouts in Timber Harvesting]," in *Na fronte mirnogo truda,* 66.

18. *Traktoristin käsikirja* [A Pocket Guide of a Tractor Driver] (Petroskoi: Kirja, 1932).

19. NARK, f. R-685, op. 1, d. 1/3,1. 86.

20. NARK, f. R-286, op. 1, d. 23/208,1. 58.

21. Kishchenko, "Rostki novogo," 69.

22. NARK, f. R-690, op. 1, d. 230,1. 10; NARK, f. R-1632, op. 1, d. 3/39,1. 13; *Krasnaia Kareliia* 297 (1931).

23. *Spisok naselennykh mest Karelii. Po materialam perepisi 1933 goda* [List of Settlements of Karelia. Based on the 1933 Census] (Petrozavodsk: UNKHU AKSSR, 1935), 82.

24. P. Wissanen, "Hilli," *Karelo-Murmanskii Krai* 5–6 (1934): 53–56; Kero, *Neuvosto-Karjalaa rakentamassa,* 130–31.

25. Kishchenko, "Rostki novogo," 66–68; Autio, *Suunnitelmatalous Neuvosto-Karjalassa,* 252.

26. NARK, f. R-690, op. 3, d. 62/509,1. 67.

27. See *Krasnaia Karelia* 291 (1931), *Krasnaia Karelia* 8 and 178 (1932), *Karelo-Murmanskii Krai* 1–2 (1932): 45–48; *Punainen Karjala* 24.8 and 28.11 (1930); *Punainen Karjala* 23.7 and 14.8 (1931); *Punainen Karjala* 5.8 and 26.8 (1935); and *Punainen Karjala* 15.11 (1936).

28. Bekrenev, *Kanadskiie lesoruby;* Artturi Salo, *Amerikkalaiset metsätyömetoodit ja työvälineet* [American Forest Work Methods and Work Tools] (Petroskoi: Kirja, 1934).

29. Iosif Tonkell, *Brigady i iacheiki na lesozagotovkakh v Karelii* [Brigades and Teams in Timber Harvesting in Karelia] (Petrozavodsk: Kirja, 1932); Tonkell, *Jännesaha;* Iosif Tonkell, *Miten puutavaran kuljetusta parannetaan* [How to Improve Timber Transportation] (Moskova-Leningrad: Kirja, 1933); Tonkell, *Kanadskiie lesoruby.*

30. Iosif Tonkell, "Opyt kanadskikh lesorubov v osnuvu ratsionalizatsii lesozagotovok vtoroi piatiletki [Experience of Canadian Lumberjack as a Foundation of Rational Timber Harvesting in the Second Five-Year Plan]," *Sovetskaia Karelia* 3–4 (1932): 88.

31. See, for example, Kotkin's account, *Magnetic Mountain,* 40–71, of the administration and management of construction works in Magnitogorsk, the largest single industrial project in the Soviet Union of the early 1930s. See also Lev Trotsky, "Novyi zigzag i novyie opasnosti [A New Zigzag and New Dangers]," *Biulleten oppozitsii (bolshevikov-lenintsev)* [Bulletin of the Opposition (Bolshevik-Leninists)], 23 (1931), http://web.mit.edu/fjk/www/FI/BO/BO-23.shtml.

32. Pokrovskaia, *Naseleniie Karelii,* 74–75, 77.

33. Calculated from the database of the project Missing in Karelia (see above).

34. *Krasnaia Karelia* 11 (1932): 2.

35. NARK, f. R-685, op. 1, d. 3,1. 138; NARK, f. R-690, op. 1, d. 19/213,1. 111–17; NARK, f. R-690, op. 1, d. 23/262,1. 12.

36. The first Soviet plan for nation-wide electrification developed in 1920–21 as part of early Bolshevik visions of radical transformations of Soviet economy and society.

37. S. Grigoriev, "Na zare industrializatsii [At the Dawn of Industrialization]," in *Na fronte mirnogo truda,* 16–17; I. Iegorov, "Pervaia kondopozhskaia bumaga [First Paper from Kondopoga]," in ibid., 20–22; H. Sundfors, "Na tselliuloznom zavode [At the Pulp Plant]," in ibid., 22–25;

Svetlana Filimonchik, "Vklad Kondopogi v industrialnoie razvitiie Karelii [Contribution of Kondopoga in Industrial Development of Karelia]," in *Kondopozhskii krai v istorii Karelii i Rossii* [Kondopoga Region in the History of Karelia and Russia], ed. A. M. Pashkov (Petrozavodsk, Kondopoga: Issledovatelskii tsentr Russkii Sever, 2000), 201–07.

38. Irina Takala, "Finny v Kondopoge [Finns in Kondopoga]," in *Kondopozhskii krai,* ed. Pashkov, 211–12.

39. Ibid., 213.

40. *Krasnaia Karelia* 15.08 (1930).

41. NARK, f. R-690, op. 1, d. 22/254,1. 52.

42. *Krasnaia Karelia* 267 (1931).

43. Irina Takala, "Delo Gyllinga-Rovio [The Case of Gylling-Rovio]," in *Ikh nazyvali kr: Repressii v Karelii 20–30-kh gg.* [They Were Called C(ounter)-R(evolutionaries): Repressions in Karelia in the 1920s and 1930s], ed. Aleksei Tsygankov (Petrozavodsk: Karelia, 1992), 69.

44. Nurminen, "Na lyzhnoi fabrike," 44.

45. NARK, f. P-89, op. 1, d. 21,1. 1.

46. I. Tuomainen, "Tri goda zhizni i raboty lyzhnoi fabriki [Three Years of Life and Work in the Ski Factory]," *Sovetskaia Karelia* 9–10 (1934): 76.

47. According to the database of the project Missing in Karelia, in January 1935 137 North American Finns were employed in the ski factory: sixty-four American and seventy-three Canadian immigrants.

48. Tuomainen, "Tri goda zhizni i raboty," 75.

49. Ibid., 74–75; *Budzhet Karelskoi ASSR na 1934 g.* [Budget of the Karelian ASSR in 1934] (Petrozavodsk: NKF AKSSR, 1934), 18.

50. K. Julen, "O stroitelstve pervogo vodoprovoda v Petrozavodske [About the Building of the First Water Supply System in Petrozavodsk]," in *Na fronte mirnogo truda,* 52–53; Sevander, *Skitaltsy,* 84.

51. Julen, "O stroitelstve pervogo vodoprovoda," 54–55.

52. Calculated from the database of the project Missing in Karelia.

53. NARK, f. R-973, op. 1, d. 1/4,1. 89–93; NARK, f. R-690, op. 1, d. 254,1. 51.

54. NARK, f. R-46, op. 1, d. 2,1. 80–82.

55. Lev Trotsky, "Uspekhi sotsializma i opasnosti avantiurizma [Socialist Successes and Dangers of Adventurism]," *Biulleten oppozitsii (bolshevikov-lenintsev)* 17–18 (1930): 2, http://web.mit.edu/fjk/www/FI/BO/BO-17.shtml.

56. I. V. Stalin, *Sochineniia* [Works], vol. 14 (Moscow: Pisatel, 1997), 61.

57. Stakhanovites were particularly effective workers who were a showcase of the Soviet economy; the name comes from Alexey Stakhanov, a miner from Donbass who in August 1935 produced 14.5 production quotas.

58. Stalin, *Sochineniia,* vol. 14, 85. See the scholarly analysis of materialist and consumerist implications in Soviet social policy of the 1930s in Kotkin, *Magnetic Mountain,* 123–29, 177–79; and Fitzpatrick, *Everyday Stalinism,* 89–109.

59. Nurminen, "Na lyzhnoi fabrike," 45.

60. Ibid.

61. A song of American immigrants, author(s) unknown (Sevander, *Skitaltsy,* 67). Translated from the Russian by Alexey Golubev (the original text was Finnish, but it is not preserved). The Russian text follows:

ВЗЯЛИСЬ ЗА ДЕЛО, ВЗМЕТНУЛСЯ ТОПОР

- ТРЕСКА ТАКОГО ЛЕС НЕ ЗНАЛ ДО СИХ ПОР.

ИЗ ШАХТ И ИЗ КУЗНИЦ НАПЕРЕБОЙ

НАКОВАЛЬНИ И МОЛОТА ДОНОСИТСЯ СПОР.

СТАЛЬ КЛОКОЧЕТ В ПЛАВИЛЬНОЙ ПЕЧИ,

РАБОЧАЯ РЕСПУБЛИКА РАСПРАВЛЯЕТ ПЛЕЧИ!

МНОГО ПРЕГРАД НЕИЗВЕСТНЫХ

ПУТЬ СЕЙ ТЕРНИСТЫЙ ТАИТ — ЧТО Ж!

ЛЮД ТРУДОВОЙ ИХ ВСЕ ПОБЕДИТ!

ДЕНЬ ТОТ НАСТАНЕТ! РАБОЧИЙ НАРОД

СЧАСТЬЕ СВОИМИ РУКАМИ СКУЁТ!

62. A. Farutin, "Petrozavodsk znamenit! [Petrozavodsk Is Famous!]," *Nezavisimaia gazeta,* 14 November 2000.
63. Eino Tuomi, "Pamiatnik Iliichu [Monument to Lenin]," in *Na fronte mirnogo truda,* 49–52.
64. Sevander, *Skitaltsy,* 86–87.
65. A. Iegorov, "Petrozavodskii Iliich: 75 let s nepokrytoi golovoi [Lenin of Petrozavodsk: 75 Years without a Cap]," State Television and Radio Company of Karelia, http://petrozavodsk.rfn.ru/region/rnews.html?id=3488&rid=465&iid=2140.
66. For a scholarly account of early Soviet communes, see Dominique Durand, *Kommunizm svoimi rukami: Obraz agrarnykh kommun v Sovetskoi Rossii 1920-kh godov* [Self-Made Communism: The Image of Agricultural Communes in Soviet Russia of the 1920s] (St. Petersburg: European University at SPb Press, 2010). For communal apartments, see Ilya Utekhin, *Ocherki kommunalnogo byta* [Essays on Everyday Life in Communal Apartments] (Moscow: OGI, 2001).
67. *S Leninym v serdtse: Sb. dokumentov i materialov* [With Lenin in Heart: A Collection of Documents and Materials] (Kemerovo: Kemerovskoie kn. izd-vo, 1976), 40.
68. Ibid., 57.
69. The name Seattle resembled the Russian word *seiatel,* or "sower," a very relevant word for an agricultural commune, so it became the name of the commune in Russian. The Finnish name, Kylväjä, was a translation of the Russian name.
70. V. I. Mashezerskii et al., eds., *Ocherki istorii Karelii* [Short History of Karelia], vol. 2 (Petrozavodsk: Karel.kn.izd-vo, 1964), 209.
71. *Statisticheskii obzor. 1923–1924. Ch. 1* [Statistical Review. 1923–1924. Part 1] (Petrozavodsk: Statupravlenie AKSSR, 1925), 10; *Karelskaia ASSR za 50 let* [Fifty Years of the Karelian ASSR] (Petrozavodsk: Karelia, 1967), 63. In comparison, a dairy cow typically now produces up to 10,000 liters a year.
72. Olga Nikitina, *Kollektivizatsiia i raskulachivaniie v Karelii* [Collectivization and Dekulakization in Karelia] (Petrozavodsk: KNTs RAN, 1997), 20–21.
73. Ibid., 21.
74. "Piat let kommuny 'Säde' [Five Years of the Commune Säde]," *Krasnaia Karelia* 9 (1932): 2; I. A. Petrov, *Kommuna "Säde"* [Commune Säde] (Petrozavodsk, 1930), 6–8; V. Zlobina and L. Siikanen, "Kommunary [Communards]," in *Na fronte mirnogo truda,* 153–54.
75. Vieno Zlobina, "Kak pogasili luch [How the Ray Was Switched Off]," *Sever* 7 (1990): 159.
76. Petrov, *Kommuna "Säde,"* 10–11; Zlobina, "Kak pogasili luch," 158.
77. *Punainen Karjala,* 25 May 1933.
78. Zlobina and Siikanen, "Kommunary," 155.
79. NARK, f. R-695, op. 1, d. 29/324,l. 2–4.
80. Zlobina, "Kak pogasili luch," 159.
81. Zlobina and Siikanen, "Kommunary," 156; Zlobina, "Kak pogasili luch," 159.

82. NARK, f. R-695, op. 1, d. 29/324,1. 3.

83. See, for example, Lauri Luoto, *Lakeuksien Aunus* [Plains of Olonets] (Petroskoi: Kirja, 1933).

84. Zlobina, "Kak pogasili luch," 159.

85. NARK, f. P-207, op. 1, d. 10,1. 96.

86. Zlobina and Siikanen, "Kommunary," 157; Zlobina, "Kak pogasili luch," 160.

87. Nikitina, *Kollektivizatsiia i raskulachivaniie,* 117.

88. NARK, f. P-3, op. 2, d. 483,1. 75; NARK, f. R-690, op. 3, d. 33/252a,1. 4–7; N. A. Ivnitskii and V. G. Makurov, eds., *Iz istorii raskulachivaniia v Karelii. 1930–1931. Documenty i materialy* [From the History of Dekulakization in Karelia. 1930–1931. Documents and Materials] (Petrozavodsk: Karelia, 1991), 14–15.

89. V. A. Pashlakov, "Lesosovkhoz 'Internatsional' [Forest *Sovkhoz* 'International']," *Karelo-Murmanskii krai* 7–8 (1932): 29.

90. *Spisok naselennykh mest,* 48.

91. Pashlakov, "Lesosovkhoz 'Internatsional,'" 30.

92. NARK, f. P-3, op. 2, d. 790,1. 41.

93. NARK, f. P-33, op. 1, d. 37a and 37b.

94. *Spisok naselennykh mest,* 48.

95. Ibid., 62.

96. NARK, f. P-3, op. 2, d. 748,1. 57.

97. Kero, *Neuvosto-Karjalaa rakentamassa,* 147.

98. NARK, f. P-3, op. 2, d. 748,1. 54–55.

99. NARK, f. R-690, op. 1, d. 22/254,1. 52.

100. NARK, f. P-3, op. 2, d. 748,1. 55–56.

101. Reino Kero, "The Tragedy of Joonas Harju of Hiilisuo Commune," *Finnish Americana* 5 (1982): 10.

102. *Punainen Karjala,* 26 August 1933, 23 November 1933.

103. *Punainen Karjala,* 21 March 1934.

CHAPTER 6. NORTH AMERICAN FINNS IN SOVIET CULTURE

1. Building a new proletarian culture was a recurrent theme in Lenin's writing and public speeches. See a compilation of his texts of Soviet cultural politics in V. I. Lenin, *On Culture and Cultural Revolution* (Moscow: Progress Publishers, 1966); see also program works by Anatoly Lunacharsky, the commissar of enlightenment between 1917 and 1929: A. V. Lunacharsky, *Teatr i revoliutsiia* [Theater and the Revolution] (Moscow: Gos. izd-vo, 1924); and A. V. Lunacharsky, *Desiatiletiie revoliutsii i kultura* [The Tenth Anniversary of the Revolution and Culture] (Moscow-Leningrad: Gos. izd-vo, 1927).

2. Gayatri Chakravorty Spivak, "Can the Subaltern Speak?," in *Marxism and the Interpretation of Culture,* ed. Cary Nelson and Lawrence Grossberg (Urbana: University of Illinois Press, 1988), 271–313.

3. Kotkin, *Magnetic Mountain,* esp. 198–237; Evgeny Dobrenko, *The Making of the State Reader: Social and Aesthetic Contexts of the Reception of Soviet Literature* (Stanford: Stanford University Press, 1997); Evgeny Dobrenko, *The Making of the State Writer: Social and Aesthetic Origins of Soviet Literary Culture* (Stanford: Stanford University Press, 2000); Irina Sandomirskaia, *Kniga o*

rodine: Opyt analiza diskursivnykh praktik [The Book about the Motherland: An Experience of Analysis of Discursive Practices] (Wien: Wiener Slawistischer Almanach, 2001); Mark Steinberg, *Proletarian Imagination: Self, Modernity, and the Sacred in Russia, 1910–1925* (Ithaca: Cornell University Press, 2002); Igal Halfin, *Terror in My Soul: Communist Autobiographies on Trial* (Cambridge, MA: Harvard University Press, 2003); Jochen Hellbeck, *Revolution on My Mind: Writing a Diary under Stalin* (Cambridge, MA: Harvard University Press, 2006); Beth Holmgren, ed., *The Russian Memoir: History and Literature,* Studies in Russian, Literature and Theory (Evanston: Northwestern University Press, 2003); Igal Halfin, *Stalinist Confessions: Messianism and Terror at the Leningrad Communist University* (Pittsburgh: University of Pittsburgh Press, 2009); Ilya Kalinin, "Ugnetionnyie dolzhny govorit' (massovyi prizyv v literaturu i formirovaniie sovetskogo subiekta, 1920-e—nachalo 1930-kh godov) [The Subaltern Must Speak (A Call for Masses to Start Writing and the Making of the Soviet Subject, 1920s to early 1930s)]," in *Tam, vnutri: Praktiki vnutrennei kolonizatsii,* ed. Etkind, Uffelman, and Kukulin, 587–664.

4. I. V. Stalin, "O politicheskikh zadachakh universiteta narodov Vostoka [On the Political Objectives of the University of Oriental Peoples]," in *Sochineniia* [Works], vol. 7, by I. V. Stalin (Moscow: Gospolitizdat, 1947), 133–52, quotation on 138.

5. See, for example, Lenore A. Grenoble, *Language Policy in the Soviet Union* (Dordrecht: Kluwer Academic Publishers, 2003), 120.

6. An incredibly large body of literature is devoted to the Soviet language and nationalities policy. Our perspective is based on the following works: Walker Connor, *The National Question in Marxist-Leninist Theory and Strategy* (Princeton: Princeton University Press, 1984); Gerhard Simon, *Nationalism and Policy towards the Nationalities in the Soviet Union* (Boulder, CO: Westview Press, 1991); Yuri Slezkine, *Arctic Mirrors: Russia and the Small Peoples of the North* (Ithaca: Cornell University Press, 1994); Terry Martin, *The Affirmative Action Empire: Nations and Nationalism in the Soviet Union, 1923–1939* (Ithaca: Cornell University Press, 2001); Ronald Grigor Suny and Terry Martin, eds., *A State of Nations: Empire and Nation-Making in the Age of Lenin and Stalin* (Oxford: Oxford University Press, 2001); Francine Hirsch, *Empire of Nations: Ethnographic Knowledge and the Making of the Soviet Union* (Ithaca: Cornell University Press, 2005). For a regional perspective on the language and nationalities policy of the VKP(b)/KPSS in northwest Russia (including Soviet Karelia), see Takala and Vihavainen, eds., *V semie edinoi.*

7. E. I. Klementiev, "Iazykovaia situatsiia v Karelii: Sostoianiie, tendentsii razvitiia [Language Situation in Karelia: Current State and Tendencies of Development]," in *Karely. Finny. Problemy etnicheskoi istorii,* 113. Cf. A. I. Afanasiieva, "Sozdaniie Sovetskoi natsionalnoi avtonomii i nekotoryie voprosy iazykovogo stroitelstva [The Establishment of a Soviet National Autonomy and Some Questions of Language Construction]," in *Voprosy istorii Evropeiskogo severa: Istoriia Velikogo Oktiabria na severo-zapade Rossii* [Questions of History of European North: History of the Great October in Northwest Russia], ed. M. I. Shumilov (Petrozavodsk: Petrozavodsk State University Press, 1987), 51.

8. Esa Anttikoski, "Strategii karelskogo iazykovogo planirovaniia v 1920-e i 1930-e gody [Strategies of Language Planning for Karelia during the 1920s and 1930s]," in *V semie edinoi,* ed. Takala and Vihavainen, 208.

9. The text of the decree was published in A. I. Afanasiieva and V. I. Mashezerskii, eds., *Karelia v period vosstanovleniia narodnogo khoziaistva, 1921–1925* [Karelia during the Period of Economic Restoration, 1921–1925] (Petrozavodsk: Karelia, 1979), 59–61.

10. See a detailed discussion of political and cultural implications behind the concept Karelian-Finnish

language in Esa Anttikoski, *Neuvostoliiton kielipolitiikkaa: Karjalan kirjakielen suunnittelu 1930-luvulla* [The Soviet Language Policy: The Planning of the Karelian Literary Language in the 1930s] (Licentiate diss., University of Joensuu, 1998), 63–91.

11. *Vsekarelskii s'iezd predstavitelei trudiashchikhsia karel,* 223–27.

12. NARK, f. P-682, op. 1, d. 1/5,1. 97.

13. L. I. Vavulinskaia, ed., *Sovety Karelii, 1917–1992: Dokumenty i materialy* [Soviets of Karelia, 1917–1992: Documents and Materials] (Petrozavodsk: Karelia, 1993), 111–12.

14. Santeri Nurteva, "Problema karelskogo iazyka v natsionalnoi politike AKSSR [The Problem of the Karelian Language in the Nationalities Policy of Soviet Karelia]," *Karelo-Murmanskii krai* 3 (1927): 4.

15. I. V. Stalin, *Sochineniia* [Works], vol. 5 (Moscow: Politizdat, 1947), 240–41.

16. See more details in Simon, *Nationalism and Policy towards the Nationalities,* 20–70.

17. Calculated on the basis of *Ezhegodnik 1929 goda. Vypusk IV* [Yearbook for 1929. Issue 4] (Petrozavodsk: Statupravleniie AKSSR, 1931), 40–41.

18. A. I. Afanasieva, ed., *Kulturnoie stroitelstvo v Sovetskoi Karelii, 1926–1941* [Cultural Building in Soviet Karelia, 1926–1941] (Petrozavodsk: Karelia, 1986). A. I. Afanasieva, *Kulturnyie preobrazovaniia v Sovetskoi Karelii, 1928–1940* [Cultural Transformations in Soviet Karelia, 1928–1940] (Petrozavodsk: Karelia, 1989), 86.

19. A. A. Levkoev, *Natsionalno-iazykovaia politika finskogo rukovodstva Sovetskoi Karelii (1920–1935)* [The Nationalities and Language Policy of Finnish Leadership of Soviet Karelia (1920–1935)], preprint of a paper (Petrozavodsk: Karelsk. nauch. tsentr RAN, 1992), 12–14.

20. Ibid.

21. *Materialy i postanovlenia IV ob'iedinennogo plenuma Karelskogo oblastnogo komiteta i oblastnoi kontrolnoi komissii VKP(b), 10–13 avgusta 1929 g.* [Materials and Resolutions of the Fourth United Plenum of the Karelian Regional Committee and Regional Controlling Commission of the VKP(b), 10–13 August 1929] (Petrozavodsk: Izd-vo Karel. obl. kontr. kom., 1929), 26–28.

22. Tver Karelians are an ethnic subgroup of Karelians who live in a number of settlements in Tver, Leningrad, and Moscow regions of Russia. Large-scale resettlement of ethnic Karelians to these areas took place in the seventeenth century after the 1617 Treaty of Stolbova, when Russia ceded to Sweden vast territories to the east and north of the Baltic Sea, where Karelians were a predominant population.

23. Nikolai Marr was notorious for his so-called Japhetic theory, which claimed a universal explanation for the origins of all human languages; in the late 1920s, he introduced elements of Marxism into his theory, arguing, among other things, that languages are part of the social superstructure. His teaching became the dominant linguistic theory in the Soviet Union between 1930 and the 1950s, and opponents of Marrist theories became, on a number of occasions, subjects of repression. See Michael G. Smith, *Language and Power in the Creation of the USSR, 1917–1953* (Berlin: Walter de Gruyter, 1998), 81–102.

24. D. V. Bubrikh, *Kakoi iazyk—tverskim karelam* [What Language for Tver Karelians?] (Leningrad: LOIKFUN, 1931); D. V. Bubrikh, *Karely i karelskii iazyk* [Karelians and the Karelian Language] (Moscow: Mosoblispolkom, 1932).

25. NARK, f. P-3, op. 2, d. 560,1. 83–107.

26. Afanasieva, *Kulturnyie preobrazovaniia v Sovetskoi Karelii,* 48; *Punainen Karjala,* 7 December 1931.

27. *Vestnik TsIK AKSSR* 3 (1932): 10–11.

28. A. I. Afanasieva, "Narodnoie obrazovaniie v Sovetskoi Karelii v 1920–1930-e gody [Public

Education in Soviet Karelia in the 1920s and 1930s]," in *Natsionalnaia gosudarstvennost finno-ugorskikh narodov severo-zapadnoi Rossii (1917–1940)* [Nationhood of Finno-Ugric Peoples of Northwest Russia (1917–1940)], ed. A. A. Popov (Syktyvkar: Komi nauch. tsentr UrO RAN, 1996), 59.

29. Afanasieva, *Kulturnyie preobrazovaniia v Sovetskoi Karelii,* 47.
30. Kauppala, "Formirovaniie i rastsvet," 330.
31. Afanasieva, *Kulturnyie preobrazovaniia v Sovetskoi Karelii,* 92.
32. For a detailed account of education policy in Soviet Karelia, see Afanasieva, *Kulturnoie stroitelstvo v Sovetskoi Karelii*; Afanasieva, *Kulturnyie preobrazovaniia v Sovetskoi Karelii.*
33. Afanasieva, *Kulturnyie preobrazovaniia v Sovetskoi Karelii,* 25.
34. On the biography of Eero Haapalainen, see Irina Takala, "Eero Haapalainen—revolutsioner, zhurnalist, uchionyi [Eero Haapalainen as a Revolutionary, a Journalist, and a Scholar]," in *Politicheskaia istoriia i istoriografiia: Ot antichnosti do sovremennosti. Vyp. 2* [Political History and Historiography: From Antiquity to the Modern Age. Vol. 2], ed. G. S. Samokhina (Petrozavodsk: Petrozavodsk State University Press, 1996), 187–93. On Viktor Salo's linguistic research, see Anttikoski, *Neuvostoliiton kielipolitiikkaa,* 67–81.
35. Anttikoski, *Neuvostoliiton kielipolitiikkaa,* 70; Marja Jänis and Tamara Starshova, "Cultural and Political Contexts of Translating into Finnish in Soviet/Russian Karelia," in *Domestication and Foreignization in Translation Studies,* ed. Hannu Kemppanen, Marja Jänis, and Alexandra Belikova (Berlin: Frank and Timme, 2012), 189–209, esp. 195–97.
36. This perspective became a subject of research in a recently defended dissertation: Leonid Tereshchenkov, "Izucheniie revoliutsii 1917 goda i grazhdanskoi voiny v Karelo-Murmanskom regione v sisteme istoriko-partiinykh uchrezhdenii 1920–1930-kh godov [Studies of the Revolution of 1917 and of the Civil War in the Karelian-Murmansk Region in the System of Institutions Specializing in the History of the Communist Party]" (Candidate of Sciences diss., Petrozavodsk State University, 2010).
37. Calculated on the basis of *Statisticheskii ezhegodnik Karelii 1922* [Statistical Yearbook of Karelia, 1922], vol. 2, part 1 (Petrozavodsk: Izd-vo Statupravleniia AKSSR, 1923), 14–15.
38. Calculated on the basis of *Perepis naseleniia AKSSR 1933 g. Vypusk I* [The 1933 Census of the Population of AKSSR. Issue 1] (Petrozavodsk: Soiuzorguchiot, 1934), 18, 40–41.
39. Martin, *The Affirmative Action Empire,* 15.
40. Börje Vähämäki, "Memoir Accounts of Finnish North Americans in Soviet Karelia in the 1930s," in *North American Finns in Soviet Karelia,* ed. Solomeshch and Takala, 154–56.
41. NARK, f. P-3, op. 3, d. 210,1. 4–6. See also Pauli Kruhse and Antero Uitto, *Suomen rajan takana 1918–1944: Suomenkielisen neuvostokirjallisuuden historia ja bibliografia* [Behind the Finnish Border: History and Bibliography of the Soviet Finnish-Language Literature] (Jyväskylä: BTJ, 2008).
42. Afanasieva, *Kulturnyie preobrazovaniia v Sovetskoi Karelii,* 137; E. L. Alto, *Sovetskiie finnoiazychnyie zhurnaly, 1920–1980* [Soviet Finnish-Language Magazines, 1920–1980] (Petrozavodsk: Karelia, 1989), 16–19; Urho Ruhanen, *V vikhriakh veka: Vospominaniia i ocherki* [In Storms of the Century: A Memoir and Essays] (Petrozavodsk: Karelia, 1991).
43. Afanasieva, *Kulturnyie preobrazovaniia v Sovetskoi Karelii,* 167.
44. Ylikangas, *Rivit suoriksi,* 152–53; membership list of the Karelian Association of Proletarian Writers in NARK, f. P-3, op. 2, d. 811,1. 38–39.
45. Dobrenko, *The Making of the State Writer,* 243–94. The quotation is taken from the title of Chapter 5.

46. Santeri Mäkelä, *Elämää ikuisessa yössä* [Life in Eternal Darkness] (Ironwood: Otto Massisen kustannusliike, 1911).

47. Elena Soini, "Poeziia-utopiia finskoi immigratsii v Rossii, 1920–1930-e gody [Utopian Poetry of the Finnish Immigration in Russia, 1920s–1930s]," in *Finskii faktor v istorii i kulture Karelii XX veka* [Finnish Factor in the History and Culture of Karelia during the Twentieth Century], ed. Olga Iliukha (Petrozavodsk: KarNTs RAN, 2009), 212; this song was recorded in 1995, more than ninety years after it was written, in a documentary filmed by the Finnish Folk Music Institute: *Mestarilaulaja Erkki Rankaviita—"Laulu valittee mun"* (Kansanmusiikki-instituutti, 1995).

48. Tauno Saarela, ed., *Talonpoikainen sosialisti—Santeri Mäkelä poliittisena toimijana ja kirjailijana* [A Peasant Socialist—Santeri Mäkelä as a Politician and a Writer] (Helsinki: Työväen historian ja perinteen tutkimuksen seura, 1997), 32–35.

49. See a bibliography of Lauri Luoto's works in N. A. Prushinskaia and E. I. Takala, *Natsionalnyie pisateli Karelii: Finskaia emigratsiia i politicheskiie repressii 1930-kh godov: Bibliograficheskii ukazatel* [National Writers of Karelia: Finnish Immigration and Political Repression of the 1930s: A Bibliographic Reference Book] (Petrozavodsk: National Library of Karelia, 2005), 52–53.

50. Lauri Luoto, *Pakolaisena* [A Refugee] (Superior, WI: Amerikan suom. sosialist. kust.-liikkeiden kust., 1925); Lauri Luoto, *Valkoisen leijonan metsästäjät* [Hunters for a White Lion] (Superior, WI: Amerikan suom. sosialist. kust.-liikkeiden kust., 1926); Lauri Luoto, *Kamaran sankarit* [Heroes of the Earth] (Superior, WI: Amerikan suom. sosialist. kust.-liikkeiden kust., 1927); Lauri Luoto, *Ikuiset uhritulet* [Eternal Flame for Victims] (Superior, WI: Amerikan suom. sosialist. kust.-liikkeiden kust., 1929).

51. Evgeny Dobrenko, *Political Economy of Socialist Realism* (New Haven: Yale University Press, 2007), 189.

52. "Luoto, Lauri," in *Literaturnaia entsiklopediia. T. 6* [Literary Encyclopedia. Vol. 6] (Moscow: Izd-vo Kommunisticheskoi akademii, 1932), 637.

53. Lauri Luoto, *Jäämeri ärjyy* [The Artic Ocean Roars] (Leningrad: Kirja, 1933); Lauri Luoto, *Lakeuksien Aunus* [In the Olonets plains] (Petroskoi: Kirja, 1933).

54. See a full bibliography of Salli Lund's works in *Natsionalnyie pisateli Karelii,* ed. Prushinskaia and Takala, 50–51.

55. Mikael Rutanen, *Unohdettujen maailmasta: Kuvaus metsätyöläisten elämästä* [From the World of the Forgotten: Pictures from the Life of Forest Workers] (Superior, WI: Amerikan suom. sosialist. kust.-liikkeiden kust., 1929); Mikael Rutanen, *Taistelun säveliä: Lausuttavia runoja* [Melodies of the Battle: Runes which Should Be Uttered] (Superior, WI: Työmies Society, 1930); Mikael Rutanen, *Joukkovoima: Työttömyysaiheinen työväen romaani* [Group Strength: A Novel about Unemployment of Workers] (Worcesterm, MA: Amerikan suom. sos. kustannusliikkeiden liitto, 1931).

56. Soini, "Poeziia-utopiia finskoi immigratsii," 219.

57. Mikael Rutanen, *Työn laulu: Runoja* [A Song of Labor: Poems] (Leningrad: Kirja, 1933).

58. Auvo Kostiainen, "Matti Kurikka," in *100 zamechatelnykh finnov* [100 Prominent Finns], ed. Timo Vihavainen (Helsinki: SKS, 2004), 299–303; Kelvin Wilson, *Practical Dreamers: Communitarianism and Co-Operatives on Malcolm Island* (Victoria: British Columbia Institute for Co-Operative Studies, 2005).

59. Ruhanen, *V vikhriakh veka,* 233–36.

60. Eemeli Parras, *Pohjalta* [From the Bottom] (Fitchburg, MA: Raivaajan kirjapaino, 1910).

61. Eemeli Parras, *Villit vuoret: Nelinäytöksinen näytelmä* [Wild Mountains: A Play in Four Acts] (Hancock, MI: Työmies, 1911).

62. Eemeli Parras, *Lämmintä verta ja kylmää hikeä* [Hot Blood and Cold Sweat] (Hancock, MI: Työmies, 1914).

63. Eemeli Parras, *Valtamerien kahtapuolta: Jutelmia ja kertomuksia* [On Both Sides of the Ocean: Essays and Stories] (Petroskoi: Kirja, 1937).

64. Dobrenko, *Political Economy of Socialist Realism,* xii.

65. Eemeli Parras, *Jymyvaaralaiset* [The People of Jymyvaara] (Petroskoi: Kirja, 1933).

66. Eemeli Parras, *Jymyvaaralaiset* (Superior, WI: Työmies Society Print, 1933).

67. Armas Mashin, "Po obe storony okeana [On Both Sides of the Ocean]," *Kurier Karelii,* 19 February 2009.

68. Only one already published excerpt of the novel has come down to us: Eemeli Parras, "Maura: Katkelma samannimisest romaanista [Maura: An Excerpt from a Novel of the Same Name]," *Rintama* 7 (1937): 3–9. Its Russian translation was published simultaneously in *Karelia: Literaturno-khudozhestvennyi almanakh. Kn. 3* [Karelia: A Literary and Artistic Almanac. No. 3] (Petrozavodsk: Kargosizdat, 1937), 11–23.

69. Sakarias Kankaanpää, *Voittamattomat* [The Unbeatable] (Petroskoi: Kirja, 1934).

70. Emil Rautiainen, *Neuvostomaata rakentamassa* [Building the Soviet Land] (Petroskoi: Kirja, 1933); Emil Rautiainen, *Nuorta verta* [Young Blood] (Leningrad: Kirja, 1933); Emil Rautiainen, *Mereltä leipää hakemassa: Kertomuksia mailta ja meriltä* [Looking for Bread Overseas: Stories about Lands and Seas] (Petroskoi: Kirja, 1934).

71. See a full bibliography of Salli Lund's works in *Natsionalnyie pisateli Karelii,* ed. Prushinskaia and Takala, 47–49.

72. See a full bibliography of Ilmari Saarinen's works in ibid., 75–76.

73. "Levänen-Sandelin, V. A.," in *Pisateli Karelii: Bibliograficheskii slovar* [Writers of Karelia: A Bibliographic Glossary], ed. Y. I. Diuzhev (Petrozavodsk: Ostrova, 2006), 183–84.

74. Boris Groys, "A Style and a Half: Socialist Realism between Modernism and Postmodernism," in *Socialist Realism without Shores,* ed. Thomas Lahusen and Evgeny Dobrenko (Durham, NC: Duke University Press, 1997), 76–90, esp. 79.

75. The kantele was a traditional music instrument in both Finland and Karelia that in the nineteenth century became a Finnish national symbol.

76. Ylikangas, *Rivit suoriksi!,* 153–63.

77. Jalmari Virtanen, "Stalin," in *Rodina: Stikhi i perevody leningradskikh poetov* [Fatherland: Poems and Translations of Leningrad Poets] (Moscow-Leningrad: Sovetskii pisatel, 1937), 29; *Karelia: Literaturno-khudozhestvennyi almanakh Soiuza sovetskikh pisatelei Karelii. Vyp. 1* [Karelia: A Literary and Artistic Almanac of the Soviet Writers' Union of Karelia. Issue 1] (Petrozavodsk: Kirja, 1937), 17–32.

78. Ruhanen, *V vikhriakh veka,* 208–09. Jalmari Virtanen was arrested in February 1938 and died in one of the gulag camps in April 1939.

79. Vavulinskaia, *Sovety Karelii,* 200–01.

80. Mashezerskii et al., *Ocherki istorii Karelii,* 251.

81. Lynn Mally, *Revolutionary Acts: Amateur Theater and the Soviet State, 1917–1938* (Ithaca: Cornell University Press, 2000), 1–46; Anne Gorsuch, *Youth in Revolutionary Russia: Enthusiasts, Bohemians, Delinquents* (Bloomington: Indiana University Press, 2000), 41–79.

82. Sevander, *They Took My Father,* 24–25.

83. NARK, f. P-3, op. 6, d. 7821–22; NARK, f. R-2872; Ragnar Nyström, *Johdatus näyttämö taiteeseen* [Introduction to the Performing Arts] (Petroskoi: Kirja, 1929); P. Nikitin, "Stanovleniie teatra: K 90-letiiu so dnia rozhdeniia Ragnara Nyströma [The Making of the Theater: To the 90-Year Anniversary of Ragnar Nyström]," *Sever* 9 (1988): 100–06.

84. Yu G. Kon and N. Yu Kon, *Professionalnaia musyka Karelii: Ocherki* [Professional Music of Karelia: Essays] (Petrozavodsk: Karelia, 1995), 139.

85. Frank J. Miller, *Folklore for Stalin: Russian Folklore and Pseudofolklore of the Stalin Era* (Armonk, NY: M. E. Sharpe, 1990). For a perspective on Soviet Karelia, see Pekka Suutari, "Representation of Locality in Karelian Folk Music Activities from Composers to Singing Women: What Was Represented When Karelian Folk Music Was Performed?," in *Karelia Written and Sung: Representations of Locality in Soviet and Russian Contexts,* ed. Pekka Suutari and Yury Shikalov (Helsinki: Aleksanteri Series at Kikimora Publications, 2010), 209–28.

86. Roland Barthes, "Myth Today," in *Mythologies,* by Roland Barthes (London: Vintage, 1993), 93–149.

87. NARK, f. R-3579, op. 1, d. 1/1,1. 1–6; M. Gavrilov, *"Kantele"—gosudarstvennyi ansambl pesni i tantsa Karelskoi ASSR* ["Kantele" as the State Singing and Dancing Ensemble of the Karelian ASSR] (Petrozavodsk: Gosizdat KASSR, 1959); "Rozhdeniie Kantele: 1930-e gody [The Birth of Kantele: 1930s]," in *Kantele: Okna v istoriiu* [Kantele: Windows to History], http://history.kantele.ru/razdel1.html.

88. For Kalle Rautio, see NARK, f. P-3, op. 6, d. 9122; and A. Timonen and G. Lapchinskii, *Kompozitor K. E. Rautio* [The Composer K. E. Rautio] (Petrozavodsk: Karel.kn.izd-vo, 1964). Many American and Canadian musicians of the symphonic orchestra are mentioned in Sevander, *Skitaltsy,* 109–12. See also Pekka Suutari, "Going beyond the Border: National Cultural Policy and the Development of Musical Life in Soviet Karelia, 1920–1940," in *Soviet Music and Society under Lenin and Stalin: The Baton and Sickle,* ed. Neil Edmunds (London: Routledge, 2004), 163–80, esp. 169–70.

89. Suutari, "Going beyond the Border," 171–72; interview with Robert Manner, in *Ustnaia istoriia,* ed. Golubev and Takala, 136–43. See also the documentary *Life Saver (Hengenpelastaja),* dir. Jouko Aaltonen (Studio Illume, 2005).

90. On the making of the new Soviet body as a Stalinist political and sociocultural project, see Pat Simpson, "Parading Myths: Imaging New Soviet Woman on Fizkulturnik's Day, July 1944," *Russian Review* 63, 2 (2004): 187–211.

91. "Fizkulturu—v massy! [Physical Culture—for Masses!]," *Krasnaia Karelia* 223 (27 September 1934): 4.

92. Kotkin, *Magnetic Mountain,* 360.

93. Tim Tzouliadis, *The Forsaken: An American Tragedy in Stalin's Russia* (London: Penguin Press, 2008), 19–20.

94. Sevander, *Skitaltsy,* 116–19.

95. Tzouliadis, *The Forsaken,* 20.

96. Ibid., 20–21.

97. *Krasnaia Karelia* 201 (1 September 1934); Tzouliadis, *The Forsaken,* 15–16.

98. Lahti-Argutina, *Olimme joukko vieras vaan,* 311. Tzouliadis indicated the name of the Karelian captain as Albert Lonn (his source was the *Moscow News*); in Lahti-Argutina's *Olimme joukko vieras vaan,* which attempted to list all Finnish victims of Stalin's regime, his name is indicated as Albert Long. Lahti-Argutina's sources were NKVD files, so her variant seems more reliable.

99. Zhuravliov, *Malenkiie liudi,* 273.

100. David-Fox, *Showcasing the Great Experiment,* 285–311.

CHAPTER 7. CHALLENGES OF CROSS-CULTURAL COMMUNICATION

1. M. V. Leskinen, "Obraz finna v rossiiskikh populiarnykh etnograficheskikh ocherkakh poslednei treti XIX v. [Image of the Finn in Russian Popular Ethnographic Writing of the Last Third of the Nineteenth Century]," in *Mnogolikaia Finlandiia: Obraz Finlandii i finnov v Rossii* [Multi-Faced Finland: The Image of Finland and the Finns in Russia], ed. O. Tsamutali, P. Iliukha, and G. M. Kovalenko (Veliky Novgorod: Yaroslav Mudryi Novgorod State University Press, 2004), 154–91.

2. Ilja Solomeshch, "Rajamaa, etuvartio, käytävä, portti—eli missä kasvaa ruoččiheinä? [A Borderland, an Outpost, a Corridor, Gates—or Where Does the Swedish Grass Grow?]," in *Ajan valtimolla—mukana muutoksia: Professori Tapio Hämysen 60-vuotisjuhlakirja* [On the Pulse of Time—with Changes: A Jubilee Book to the 60th Anniversary of Professor Tapio Hämynen], ed. Marko Junkkarinen et al. (Saarijarvi: Itä-Suomen yliopisto, 2011), 133–34.

3. Irina Takala, "Repola 1922–1939 [Reboly during 1922–1939]," in *Aunuksen Repola* [Olonets Reboly], ed. Heikki Tarma (Jyväskylä: Repola-seura, 2001), 229–32.

4. See the Karelian newspapers *Izvestiia Olonetskogo Gubernskogo Soveta,* 12 May 1918, 24 November 1918; *Olonetskaia Kommuna,* 24 June 1919; and *Karelskaia Kommuna,* 6 February 1922.

5. *Olonetskaia Kommuna,* 30 April 1919, 2 May 1919, 27 June 1920; *Karelskaia Kommuna,* 29 November 1921.

6. *Krasnaia Karelia,* 21 February 1928, 2 April 1930, 18 June 1930, 20 June 1930, 21 June 1930, 10 July 1930, 2 October 1930, 3 October 1930, 8 October 1930.

7. *Krasnaia Karelia,* 30 March 1932.

8. *Krasnaia Karelia,* 28 January 1933, 23 February 1934, 29 December 1935, 29 July 1936, 27 October 1936, 9 February 1937.

9. At the height of final battles of the Russian Civil War in Soviet Karelia in early 1922, over 11,000 Karelians fled to Finland. According to information of the Karelian GPU, by August 1922 Finland had already provided refuge to 12,000 to 13,000 Karelians (NARK, f. P-3, op. 1, d. 80,1. 79). After the amnesty of 1923, the majority of them returned to Soviet Karelia. An English-language account of these events can be found in Stacy Churchill, "The East Karelian Autonomy Question in Finnish-Soviet Relations, 1917–1922" (PhD diss., University of London, 1967), published in Finnish as *Itä-Karjalan kohtalo.*

10. *Karelskaia Kommuna,* 10 January 1922; NARK, f. P-3, op. 1, d. 72,1. 60.

11. The purchase of provisions for border areas of Soviet Karelia was done in Finland until the mid-1930s because, without reliable communications, it was the only way to organize the regular supply of food to these remote territories. According to decrees of the Soviet government, provisions and certain merchandise were imported duty free. *Sobraniie zakonov i rasporiazhenii raboche-krestianskogo pravitelstva SSSR. 1924–1937* [The Collection of Laws and Decrees of Workers' and Peasants' Government of the USSR] (SZ SSSR), 1924, no. 14, article 145; SZ SSSR, 1925, no. 66, article 494.

12. A. D. Chernev et al., eds., *"Sovershenno sekretno": Lubianka— Stalinu o polozhenii v strane. T. 6* ["Top Secret": Lubianka to Stalin on the State of the Nation. Vol. 6] (Moscow: Institut rossiiskoi istorii RAN, 2002), 279.

13. NARK, f. R-689, op. 1, d. 5/52,1. 78.

14. NARK, f. R-689, op. 1, d. 8/81,1. 11; d. 15/145,1. 87, 91–82; f. P-3, op. 2, d. 365,1. 16, 62.

15. NARK, f. P-12, op. 1, d. 365,1. 65; f. R-689, op. 1, d. 8/81,1. 26, 68.

16. NARK, f. P-3, op. 2, d. 365,1. 390b.

17. Chernev et al., *"Sovershenno sekretno,"* 279.

18. NARK, f. P-3, op. 2, d. 117,1. 67.

19. NARK, f. P-3, op. 2, d. 454,1. 28–51; f. 1230, op. 8, d. 19,1. 208–12.
20. *Krasnaia Karelia* 41, 123, 291 (1931); 8, 54, 73 (1932).
21. See, for example, Ranta, *Arpi korvassa ja sydämessä*, 41–45.
22. NARK, f. R-685, op. 1, d. 2/16,1. 3.
23. Ranta, *Arpi korvassa ja sydämessä*, 36.
24. Kaarlo R.Tuomi and Sakari Määttänen, *Isänmaattoman tarina: Amerikansuomalaisen vakoojan muistelmat* [The Story of a Man without a Country: The Memoirs of a Finnish American Spy] (Porvoo: Söderström, 1984), 43.
25. On Insnab, see Chapter 4.
26. Interview with E. Rautio, 25 May 2002, in the archive of the Department of History of Northern Europe, Petrozavodsk State University.
27. NARK, f. P-3, op. 2, d. 790,1. 15; f. P-1230, op. 2, d. 9,1. 31; op. 7, d. 6,1. 123.
28. NARK, f. R-685, op. 1, d. 13/150,1. 73.
29. NARK, f. R-690, op. 1, d. 22/254,1. 10.
30. NARK, f. P-1230, op. 6, d. 10,1. 32; op. 2, d. 9,1. 35.
31. This was typical for all immigrant workers employed in the USSR. See Zhuravliov, *Malenkiie liudi,* 228–41.
32. NARK, f. P-3, op. 2, d. 790,1. 10.
33. NARK, f. R-685, op. 2, d. 12/147,1. 25.
34. *Krasnaia Karelia,* 17 September 1932.
35. *Krasnaia Karelia,* 27 August 1932.
36. See, for example, Komulainen, *A Grave in Karelia,* 24, 64.
37. NARK, f. P-1230, op. 6, d. 10,1. 22.
38. NARK, f. P-1230, op. 7, d. 6,1. 76.
39. NARK, f. P-1230, op. 6, d. 20,1. 11.
40. Saramo, "Piecing Together Immigrant Lives," 175–76.
41. Interview with Elsa Balandis, 11 April 2007, in the archive of the Department of History of Northern Europe, Petrozavodsk State University.
42. Interview with E. P. Lemetti, 28 February 2002, in the archive of the Department of History of Northern Europe, Petrozavodsk State University.
43. Ibid.
44. NARK, f. P-3, op. 2, d. 790,1. 20.
45. Zhuravliov, *Malenkiie liudi,* 149–51.
46. NARK, f. P-3, op. 2, d. 790,1. 14; NARK, f. P-1230, op. 7, d. 6,1. 86.
47. NARK, f. P-6153, op. 2, d. 1049,1. 1.
48. Sevander, *They Took My Father,* 49.
49. NARK, f. P-6153, op. 3, d. 253,1. 113.
50. NARK, f. P-3, op. 2, d. 790,1. 15; f. P-1230, op. 2, d. 9,1. 31; op. 6, d. 6,1. 123.
51. Kostiainen, *The Forging of Finnish-American Communism.*
52. NARK, f. P-3, op. 2, d. 178,1. 51; op. 2, d. 225,1. 130; f. P-16, op. 1, d. 904,1. 1.
53. Reino Kero, "The Role of Finnish Settlers from North America in the Nationality Question in Soviet Karelia in the 1930s," *Scandinavian Journal of History* 6, 1–4 (1981): 229–41; Kero, *Neuvosto-Karjalaa rakentamassa,* 53–60.
54. Pogorelskin, "Why Karelian Fever?," 25.
55. NARK, f. P-1230, op. 6, d. 10,1. 61; f. R-1532, op. 2, d. 331,1. 25; *Krasnaia Karelia,* 31 May

1931; interview with Toini Pränny, Petrozavodsk, May 2003, in the archive of the Department of History of Northern Europe, Petrozavodsk State University.

56. NARK, f. R-685, op. 2, d. 252,1. 41–42; f. P-6153, op. 2, d. 1049,1. 17.

57. Komulainen, *A Grave in Karelia,* 106.

58. Ibid., 107.

59. Interview with Yrjö Mykkänen, in *Ustnaia istoriia,* ed. Golubev and Takala, 109; interview with Robert Manner, in *Ustnaia istoriia,* ed. Golubev and Takala, 140.

60. Saramo, "Piecing Together Immigrant Lives," 178.

61. Interview with Paavo Alatalo, in *Ustnaia istoriia,* ed. Golubev and Takala, 69; interview with Yrjö Mykkänen, in *Ustnaia istoriia,* ed. Golubev and Takala, 80; Saramo, "Piecing Together Immigrant Lives," 177–81.

62. Interview with Dagny Salo, in *Ustnaia istoriia,* ed. Golubev and Takala, 64–65.

63. Interview with Toini Pränny, April 2002, in the archive of the Department of History of Northern Europe, Petrozavodsk State University.

64. See, for example, Miettinen and Joganson, *Petettyjen toiveiden maa,* 31; and interview with Toini Pränny, April 2002, in the archive of the Department of History of Northern Europe, Petrozavodsk State University.

65. Interview with Kerttu Niemi, 24 April 2002, in the archive of the Department of History of Northern Europe, Petrozavodsk State University.

66. Interview with Kaarlo Ranta, June 2003, in the archive of the Department of History of Northern Europe, Petrozavodsk State University.

CHAPTER 8. AMERICAN AND CANADIAN FINNS IN THE GREAT TERROR

1. Irina Takala, "Kansallisuusoperaatiot Karjalassa [National Operations in Karelia]," in *Yhtä suurta perhettä: Bolshevikkien kansallisuuspolitiikka Luoteis-Venäjällä 1920–1950-luvuilla* [One United Family: The Nationalities Policy of CPSU from the 1920s to the 1950s and Its Implementation in North-Western Russia], ed. Timo Vihavainen and Irina Takala (Helsinki: Kikimora Publications, 2000), 181.

2. Felix Chuev, *Sto sorok besed s Molotovym: Iz dnevnika F. Chueva* [One Hundred and Forty Talks to Molotov: From F. Chuev's Diary] (Moscow: Terra, 1991), 390.

3. Takala, *Finny v Karelii,* 123.

4. Nikolai Bugai, *The Deportation of Peoples in the Soviet Union* (New York: Nova Science Publishers, 1996), 27.

5. The policy of *korenizatsiia* in Karelia is discussed in detail in the chapter 6 of this volume.

6. See, for example, Yuri Slezkine, "The USSR as a Communal Apartment, or How a Socialist State Promoted Ethnic Particularism," *Slavic Review* 53, 2 (1994): 414–52.

7. *KPSS v rezoliutsiiakh i resheniiakh s'iezdov, konferentsii, i plenumov TsK* [KPSS in Resolutions and Decisions of the Congresses, Conferences, and Plenums of the Central Committee] (Moscow: Gospolitizdat, 1953), 564–65.

8. Oleg Khlevniuk, *1937: Protivostoianiie* [1937: Confrontation] (Moscow: Znanie, 1991), 8.

9. "O tak nazyvaemom 'natsional-uklonizme' [On the So-Called 'National Deviationism']," *Izvestiia TsK KPSS* 9 (1990): 76–84.

10. Russian "ИЗЪЯТИЕ РАЗНОГО РОДА КОНТРРЕВОЛЮЦИОННЫХ ЭЛЕМЕНТОВ," a typical phrase from documents of the 1930s that meant arrests, detentions, and deportations.

11. Matti Lackman, " Etsivä keskuspoliisi 1919–1937 [A Search for Reasonable Policy 1919–1937]," in *Turvallisuuspoliisi 75 vuotta, 1919–1994* [75 Years of Security Policy, 1919–1994], ed. Matti Simola and Jukka Salovaara (helsinki: Sisäasiainministeriö, Poliisiosasto, 1994), 11–100. The activities of the Finnish intelligence in Soviet Karelia were especially intense in the 1920s. At the turn of the 1930s, Soviet-Finnish border security was greatly improved and became nearly impenetrable. Since then, border contacts between Finnish and Karelian populations stopped being an important socioeconomic factor in border communities, though "the Finnish threat" remained an important discursive construct used by Soviet counterintelligence. See Sergey Verigin and Einar Laidinen, "Finskii shpionazh i politicheskiie repressii na severo-zapade Rossii v 1920–1930-e gg. [Finnish Espionage and Political Repression in Northwest Russia in the 1920s and 1930s]," in *Politicheskii sysk v Rossii: Istoriia i sovremennost* [Political Investigation in Russia: History and the Present Day], ed. Vladlen Izmozhnik (St. Petersburg: Izd-vo SPbUEF, 1997), 208–09.

12. See, for example, weekly reports of the GPU for 1924 in NARK, f. 689, op. 1, d. 4/41.

13. Weekly reports of the GPU for the period 9.10.24–25.08.25, NARK, f. 689, op. 1, d. 8/81,1. 178–79.

14. NARK, f. 689, op. 1, d. 8/81,1. 28–29, 178–79; f. P-16, op. 1, d. 904, 978, 980. We should also mention that the Finnish intelligence, which between 1923 and 1938 was headed by Esko Riekki, was equally attentive to its former compatriots. See, for example, Kansallisarkisto (Finnish National Archives), EK-Valpo 1. 22, 27–30; UMA, 34, 100: 89.

15. NARK, f. 689, op. 1, d. 8/81,1. 11; d. 15/145,1. 87.

16. See more details in Irina Takala, "Finnish Immigrants in the Soviet Karelia in 1920s and 1930s: A Study of Ethnic Identities," in *Challenges of Globalisation and Regionalisation. Proceedings I from the Conference Regional Northern Identity: From Past to Future at Petrozavodsk State University, Petrozavodsk 2006* (Luleå: Luleå University of Technology, 2007), 57–69.

17. Archive of the Office of the Federal Security Service (FSB) in the Republic of Karelia (hereafter Archive of the UFSB RK), d. P-18456, vol. 17,1. 166–67.

18. Ibid.

19. For this operation, Ivan Zaporozhets was decorated with the Order of the Red Banner upon the recommendation of the Karelian government. NARK, f. P-3, op. 3, d. 10,1. 84.

20. Archive of the UFSB RK, d. P-18456, vol. 17,1. 162–64.

21. Quoted in Ivan Chukhin, *Karelia-37: Ideologiia i praktika terrora* [Karelia-37: Ideology and Practice of Terror] (Petrozavodsk: Petrozavodsk State University Press, 1999), 24.

22. Archive of the UFSB RK, d. P-18456, vol. 17,1. 162.

23. Archive of the UFSB RK, f. KRO, d. 177, vol. 1,1. 331–33.

24. See more details in Takala, *Finny v Karelii*, 78–81; Oksana Repukhova, "Delo o kontrrevoliutsionnom zagovore v Karelii v 1932–1933 gg. ('Zagovor finskogo genshtaba') [Case of a Counterrevolutionary Conspiracy in Karelia in 1932–1933 ('Conspiracy of the Finnish General Staff')]," in *Korni travy: Sbornik statei molodykh uchenykh* [The Grass Roots: Collection of Articles of Young Scholars], ed. L. S. Yeremina and Y. B. Zhemkova (Moscow: Memorial, 1996), 35–44.

25. Repukhova, "Delo o kontrrevoliutsionnom zagovore," 43.

26. NARK, f. P-3, op. 3, d. 1,1. 3–4.

27. Ibid., d. 5,1.113–14.

28. Ye. A. Zaitsev, ed., *Sbornik zakonodatelnykh i normativnykh aktov o repressiiakh i reabilitatsii zhertv*

politich eskikh repressii [A Collection of Legislative and Regulatory Acts on Repression and Rehabilitation of Victims of the Political Repression] (Moscow: Respublika, 1993), 110–11.

29. See more details in Oleg Khlevniuk, *1937-i. Stalin, NKVD i sovetskoie obshchestvo* [1937. Stalin,
the NKVD, and Soviet Society] (Moscow: Respublika, 1992); and Oleg Khlevniuk, *Politburo.
Mekhanismy politicheskoi vlasti v 30e gody* [Politburo. Mechanisms of Political Power in the 1930s]
(Moscow: ROSSPEN, 1996).

30. The phrase that Soviet security organs were four years late "in the work of investigation of
the Trotskyite-Zinovievite bloc" was first used in the telegram that Stalin sent from Sochi on
25 September 1936 to the Politburo demanding that Genrikh Yagoda be replaced by Nikolai
Ezhov as commissar of internal affairs. See *Izvestiia TsK KPSS* 9 (1989): 39. Several months later
it was repeated in a resolution of the notorious February–March 1937 Plenum of the Central
Committee of the vKP(b). See *Izvestiia TsK KPSS* 3 (1989): 138.

31. Takala, "Delo Gyllinga-Rovio," 42–43.

32. NARK, f. P-3, op. 5, d. 276,1. 106–28.

33. NARK, f. P-3, op. 3, d. 314,1. 2–24.

34. NARK, f. P-3, op. 65, d. 6,1. 3–7, 11. A fifty-kilometer-wide security zone along the Finnish
border in Soviet Karelia was established by a decree of the SNK of the USSR on 19 March 1935
and by Order No. 105 of the NKVD on 4 May 1935.

35. Instead of destroyed and depopulated *kolkhozes* in the border security zone, so-called Red Army
kolkhozes were established. Their labor force was made up of Red Army soldiers who were demobilized during 1934 and 1935. NARK, f. P-3, op. 65, d. 6,1. 12–21.

36. NARK, f. P-3, op. 65, d. 6,1. 10.

37. Calculated on the basis of *Karelskaia organizatsiia KPSS v tsifrakh. 1921–1984* [Karelian Organization of the CPSU in Figures, 1921–1984] (Petrozavodsk: Karelia, 1985), 72.

38. *Krasnaia Karelia,* 14 January 1935.

39. NARK, f. P-3, op. 3, d. 252,1. 39.

40. NARK, f. P-8, op. 11, d. 663,1. 161.

41. N. S. Lebedeva, K. Rentola, and T. Saarela, eds., *Komintern i Finlandia. 1919–1943: Dokumenty*
[Comintern and Finland. 1919–1943: Documents] (Moscow: Nauka, 2003), 189–95, 197–208.

42. NARK, f. P-8, op. 11, d. 663,1. 161.

43. Ibid.

44. See NARK, f. P-3, op. 6, d. 1678.

45. NARK, f. P-3, op. 3, d. 315,1. 2, 4, 8, 17–18, 23; f. P-25, op. 1, d. 177,1. 1–27, 38–59, 63–81,
91–94, 114–24; f. P-8, op. 11, d. 663,1. 163, 171.

46. NARK, f. P-8, op. 11, d. 663,1. 163–66, 170–71.

47. NARK, f. P-3, op. 3, d. 315,1. 2–17, 25–29. For a more detailed account, see Irina Takala,
"Suomen kommunistinen puolue ja Karjala 1930-luvulla [Finnish Communist Party and Karelia
during the 1930s]," *Carelia* 9 (1994): 136–47.

48. Venla Sainio, "Manner, Kullervo," in *Suomen Kansallisbiografia,* osa 6 [Finnish National Biographies 6] (Helsinki: Suomalaisen Kirjallisuuden Seura, 2005), 489–92.

49. Takala, "Suomen kommunistinen puolue," 146.

50. See *Krasnaia Karelia,* issues for 3–10 October 1935.

51. NARK, f. P-3, op. 3, d. 299,1. 41–42.

52. NARK, f. P-3, op. 3, d. 255,1. 77.

53. Joni Krekola, *Stalinismin lyhyt kurssi* [A Short Course on Stalinism] (Helsinki: SKS, 2006),
105–10.

54. NARK, f. P-3, op. 3, d. 255,1. 132–39.

55. *Krasnaia Karelia,* 10 November 1935.

56. See Takala, "Delo Gyllinga-Rovio," 44–46; and Takala, *Finny v Karelii,* 88–89, 106.

57. Calculated on the basis of NARK, f. P-3, op. 3, d. 333,1. 6–65, 78–102.

58. Kansallisarkisto (Finnish National Archives, Helsinki), EK-Valpo 1. 27–28, 78, 93; Ulkoasiain-ministerön arkisto (Archive of the Foreign Ministry, Helsinki), 11G, 22K, 100: 89.

59. NARK, f. P-3, op. 3, d. 315,1. 31.

60. Takala, "Delo Gyllinga-Rovio," 50–51.

61. NARK, f. P-3, op. 4, d. 59,1. 33.

62. *Krasnaia Karelia,* 6 October 1935.

63. NARK, f. P-3, op. 6, d. 11076,1. 1–5.

64. Archive of the UFSB RK, collection of criminal cases (*fond ugolovnykh del*), no. P-1903, P-3164, P-9404.

65. NARK, f. P-207, op. 1, d. 10,1. 96.

66. NARK, f. P-3, op. 3, d. 315,1. 10–14; op. 50, d. 21,1. 12–15. This version was also mentioned by Kalle Siikanen's wife, Lempi Pitkälahti (Siikanen), in an interview in 1943 by Pentti Renvall, a representative of the Finnish military authorities in the occupied territories of Soviet Karelia. See Kansallisarkisto (Finnish National Archives, Helsinki), Pentti Renvallin arkisto, Itä-Karjala-aineisto, kotelo 160.

67. NARK, f. P-25, op. 1, d. 177,1. 25.

68. Here and hereafter, unless indicated otherwise, statistical data and information on individual fates of Finnish immigrants who were repressed during 1937 and 1938 are based on Eila Lahti-Argutina, *Olimme joukko vieras vaan.*

69. Propaganda or agitation that included calls for overthrowing, undermining, or weakening Soviet power or for implementing counterrevolutionary crimes; production, distribution, or storage of counterrevolutionary literature (1927 Criminal Code of the RSFSR).

70. NARK, f. R-698, op. 5, d. 65/616a,1. 9.

71. Ibid.; NARK, f. P-1230, op. 9, d. 40,1. 2.

72. These events, described as the "Doomsday of Hiilisuo," were also mentioned in the following books: Artturi Leinonen, *Punaisen aallon ajelemana: Yrjö Kultajärven seikkailut 1917–1937* [Riding a Red Wave: Adventures of Yrjö Kultajärvi 1917–1937] (Porvoo: Söderström, 1963), 183–90; and Sevander, *Skitaltsy,* 82.

73. NARK, f. P-1230, op. 9, d. 40,1. 1; f. R-698, op. 5, d. 65/616a,1. 8–30.

74. NARK, f. P-93, op. 1, d. 1,1. 40–42.

75. NARK, f. P-93, op. 2, d. 2,1. 70.

76. NARK, f. P-93, op. 2, d. 2,1. 59, 74.

77. Reino Kero, "The Tragedy of Joonas Harju of Hiilisuo Commune," *Finnish Americana* 5 (1982): 8–11. See also note 114.

78. NARK, f. P-3, op. 4, d. 59,1. 33–34; d. 57,1. 75–78, 85.

79. NARK, f. P-3, op. 4, d. 57,1. 78.

80. Rehabilitation of victims of the repressions of the 1930s to early 1950s, without written requests or complaints from victims or their relatives, began in the Soviet Union in the late 1980s, but it applied only to those convicted by extrajudicial bodies (the decree of the Presidium of the Supreme Council of the USSR of 16 January 1989). In 1991, the law "on rehabilitation of victims of political repressions" (No. 1761–1 of 18 October 1991) was passed in Russia. It

significantly expanded the number of people subject to rehabilitation, including, in particular, all those convicted under so-called counterrevolutionary articles.

81. Takala, "Delo Gyllinga-Rovio," 44–46.
82. Sevander, *They Took My Father,* 60.
83. NARK, f. P-3, op. 6, d. 10792,1. 3.
84. NARK, f. P-3, op. 5, d. 277,1. 1–8.
85. NARK, f. P-3, op. 5, d. 276,1. 60–63.
86. NARK, f. P-3, op. 5, d. 276,1. 77.
87. NARK, f. P-3, op. 3, d. 255,1. 71, 119–20.
88. NARK, f. P-3, op. 4, d. 57,1. 9.
89. Ibid.
90. "Rasstrel po raznoriadke, ili kak eto delali bolsheviki [Shot According to Orders, or How Bolsheviks Did It]," *Trud,* 4 June 1992.
91. Zaitsev, ed., *Sbornik zakonodatelnykh i normativnykh aktov,* 86–93.
92. Ivan Chukhin, "Osobaia papka: Sanktsii na pogrom [A Special File: Sanctions for a Pogrom]," *Severnyi Kurier,* 10 June 1993.
93. During the autumn and winter of 1937, a number of directives were issued that regulated repressive policies against other ethnic groups, such as Memorandum No. 49990 of the NKVD of the USSR on "the operation of repression among Latvians" (30 November 1937).
94. NARK, f. P-3, op. 4, d. 265,1. 38–43; d. 266,1. 57–62.
95. NARK, f. P-3, op. 4, d. 266,1. 1–2.
96. For more details, see Takala, "Delo Gyllinga-Rovio."
97. Archive of the UFSB RK, p/f. KRO, op. 1, p. 42,1. 95–101.
98. Archive of the UFSB RK, f. KRO, d. 168,1. 1–23 (calculations).
99. NARK, f. P-3, op. 4, d. 232,1. 23–30.
100. Takala, *Finny v Karelii,* 114.
101. Archive of the UFSB RK, f. KRO, d. 168,1. 1–23 (calculations),1. 37–42.
102. According to the 1933 census, Poles, Germans, Latvians, and Estonians in Soviet Karelia constituted about 0.2 percent each of its population (656, 623, 684, and 621 people respectively). *Perepis naseleniia AKSSR 1933 g. Vypusk I* [The 1933 Census of the Population of AKSSR. Issue 1] (Petrozavodsk: Soiuzorguchiot, 1934), xiii.
103. Archive of the UFSB RK, FSDP, p/f. KRO, op. 1, p. 42,1. 63.
104. Ivan Chukhin, "Zhestokaia statistika repressii [Cruel Statistics of the Repression]," *Severnyi kurier,* 15 January 1997.
105. Takala, *Finny v Karelii,* 116; see also Appendix 2, Table 2.
106. Archive of the UFSB RK, FSDP, p/f. Sekretariat, op. 1, p. 82,1. 52.
107. N. Gevorkian, "Vstrechnyie plany po unichtozheniiu sobstvennogo naroda [Counterplans for the Elimination of One's Own People]," *Moskovskiie novosti,* 21 June 1992.
108. Archive of the UFSB RK, f. KRO, d. 168,1. 24–31; f. SDP, p/f. KRO, op. 1, p. 52,1. 59.
109. Archive of the UFSB RK, f. SDP, p/f. KRO, op. 1, p. 53,1. 2, 10–13, 19, 73–82.
110. Chukhin, *Karelia-37,* 105–06; NARK, f. P-3, op. 6, d. 10285, 10783, 10784.
111. NARK, f. P-3, op. 6, d. 6856.
112. Archive of the UFSB RK, f. SDP, p/f. KRO, op. 1, p. 53,1. 12–14.
113. Ibid.,1. 15.
114. It is possible that the "accused Harju" mentioned in passing in this note is the aforementioned

Joonas Harju. Unfortunately, this is the only documentary evidence that can shed light on the fate of the "president of Hiilisuo."

115. That is, to condemn to death.

116. Archive of the UFSB RK, f. SDP, p/f. KRO, op. 1, p. 53,1. 26–34.

117. The phrase from a phone conversation between the head of the Third Department of the Upravleniie Gosudarstvennoi Bezopasnosti (UGB) (Directorate of State Security) of the NKVD of Soviet Karelia, Lieutenant Antonov, and the deputy head of Kalevala district office of the NKVD, Sergeant Martynov: Archive of the UFSB RK, f. SDP, p/f KRO, op. 1, p. 52,1. 81–82.

118. Archive of the UFSB RK, f. SDP, p/f. KRO, op. 1, p. 52,1. 70, 90, 162, 164, 286, 287.

119. Takala, *Finny v Karelii*, 137–38 (Appendix 2, Table 3).

120. Ibid., 119.

121. Archive of the UFSB RK, f. SDP, p/f. KRO, op. 1, p. 52,1. 209.

122. NARK, f. P-3, op. 6, d. 12774.

123. For example, the deputy head of the Kalevala district office of the NKVD, Sergeant Martynov, who had complained not long before of an "absence of material," on 2 April wrote to the head of the Third Department of the Karelian NKVD, Antonov, that, "due to a limited period before the end of [the] investigative period, we ask to sanction arrests telegraphically, so that we would be able to process cases before 15 April." Archive of the UFSB RK, f. SDP, p/f. KRO, op. 1, p. 52,1. 263.

124. Ibid.,1. 135.

125. Archive of the UFSB RK, f. SDP, p/f. KRO, op. 1, p. 54,1. 12–13.

126. Takala, *Finny v Karelii*, 138–40 (Appendix 2, Table 4).

127. Archive of the UFSB RK, FDSP, p/f. Sekretariat, op. 1, p. 82,1. 17.

128. Takala, *Finny v Karelii*, 138–40 (Appendix 2, Table 4).

129. During one of these days, more than twenty Finnish workers of the Petrozavodsk ski factory were arrested. A number of memoirs recall it as a "bloody day of the ski factory." See the memoir of Ernest Tuulensuu in Kero, *Neuvosto-Karjalaa rakentamassa*, 190; and Hokkanen and Hokkanen, *Karelia*, 92–93.

130. Archive of the UFSB RK, FDSP, p/f. Sekretariat, op. 1, p. 82,1. 1–3.

131. Ibid.,1. 20.

132. NARK, f. P-35, op. 1, d. 493,1. 108.

133. Ivan Chukhin, "Taina odnoi 'operatsii' [A Secret of One 'Operation']," *Petrozavodsk*, 7 April 1995, 12.

134. Archive of the UFSB RK, FDSP, p/f. Sekretariat, op. 1, p. 82,1. 81–82.

135. See Takala, *Finny v Karelii*, 143 (Appendix 2, Table 7).

136. See ibid., 141 (Appendix 2, Table 5).

137. Here and hereafter, we analyze data compiled in a register of Finnish victims of the Great Terror published by Lahti-Argutina, *Olimme joukko vieras vaan*.

138. Ibid., 84.

139. NARK, f. R-685, op. 2, d. 69,1. 85.

140. Takala, *Finny v Karelii*, 156–58.

141. Sevander, *Skitaltsy*, 111–12.

142. NARK, f. P-3, op. 65, d. 24,1. 6.

143. Sevander, *Skitaltsy*, 131.

144. Ibid., 133.

145. Attempted crime, preparation for a crime, travel abroad without permission from due authorities (1926 Criminal Code of the RSFSR).

146. Yu. A. Dmitriev, ed., *Pominalnyie spiski Karelii, 1937–1938: Unichtozhennaia Karelia. Ch. II. Bolshoi Terror* [Commemoration Lists of Karelia, 1937–1938: Exterminated Karelia. Part II. Great Terror] (Petrozavodsk: Pravitelstvo Respubliki Karelia, 2002), 314; Lahti-Argutina, *Olimme joukko vieras vaan,* 472.
147. A private letter of Vadim Likhachev to Irina Takala, 28 December 2009.
148. NARK, f. P-3, op. 6, d. 10791,1. 11.
149. Russian State Archive of Sociopolitical History (hereafter RGASPI), f. 495, op. 16, d. 73,1. 17.
150. RGASPI, f. 495, op. 16, dd. 64, 73.
151. RGASPI, f. 495, op. 16, d. 73,1. 16.
152. RGASPI, f. 495, op. 16, d. 64,1. 63–64.
153. NARK, f. P-3, op.5, d. 276, 277.
154. In the original document prepared by the Karelian NKVD, these 3,580 people naturalized in the USSR included not only immigrants from the United States and Canada but also those from Finland. NARK, f. P-3, op. 5, d. 276,1. 47.
155. The circular "on foreigners" was issued by the NKVD on 22 August 1937 and demanded from local authorities that residence permits to foreign nationals no longer be extended and that they be issued exit visas and expelled.
156. NARK, f. P-3, op. 5, d. 276,1. 3–18.
157. This memorandum, unfortunately, has not been preserved in the archive.
158. NARK, f. P-3, op. 5, d. 276,1. 1–2.
159. RGASPI, f. 495, op. 16, d. 64,1. 65.

CHAPTER 9. WARTIME AND AFTER

1. Archival documents of the latter half of the 1930s, as well as memoirs of and interviews with North American immigrants, give evidence of sympathy for persecuted Finns among the local population during and after the Great Terror. See Miettinen and Joganson, *Petettyjen toiveiden maa,* 31; and interview with Toini Pränny, April 2002, in the archive of the Department of History of Northern Europe, Petrozavodsk State University.
2. The Soviet position in diplomatic maneuvers preceding the outbreak of the Second World War is one of the most disputed topics in contemporary historical scholarship. On negotiations among Great Britain, France, and the USSR during the 1930s, see, for example, Jonathan Haslam, *The Soviet Union and the Struggle for Collective Security in Europe, 1933–39* (London: Macmillan, 1984). The question of Soviet-German negotiations and the Molotov-Ribbentrop Pact are addressed in all major research works on the Second World War.
3. Vladimir Nevezhin, *"Esli zavtra v pokhod . . .": Podgotovka k voine i ideologicheskaia propaganda v 30-kh—40-kh godakh* ["If We Set Out Tomorrow . . .": Preparation for War and Ideological Propaganda in the 1930s and 1940s] (Moscow: Iauza, Eksmo, 2007), 182–215.
4. Osmo Jussila, *Terijoen hallitus 1939–40* [Terijoki Government, 1939–1940] (Helsinki: WSOY, 1985); Timo Vihavainen, *Stalin i finny* [Stalin and Finns] (St. Petersburg: Zhurnal Neva, 2000), 122–38.
5. See more details in Antti Laine, "Karelo-Finskaia Sovetskaia Sotsialisticheskaia Respublika i finny [Karelian-Finnish Soviet Socialist Republic and Finns]," in *V semie edinoi,* ed. Takala and Vihavainen, 223–50; Sergey Verigin, *Kareliia v gody voiennykh ispytanii: Politicheskoiie i*

sotsialno-ekonomicheskoie polozheniie Sovetskoi Karelii v period Vtoroi mirovoi voiny 1939–1945 gg. [Karelia in the Years of War Trials: Political and Socioeconomic Situation of Soviet Karelia during the Second World War, 1939–1945] (Petrozavodsk: Petrozavodsk State University Press, 2009), 44–147.

6. Sevander, *Skitaltsy,* 165. On the question of losses in the Finnish People's Army, see also Irina Takala, "Kysymys Suomen kansanarmeijasta [A Question of the Finnish People's Army]," in *Talvisota, Venäjä ja Suomi* [Winter War, Russia and Finland], ed. Timo Vihavainen (Helsinki: SHS, 1991), 292.

7. Data of the 1939 census of the Soviet Union, http://demoscope.ru/weekly/ssp/rus_nac_39.php.

8. Laine, "Karelo-Finskaia Sovetskaia Sotsialisticheskaia Respublika," 223–50.

9. On Soviet attempts to construct literary Karelian language, see Paul Austin, "*Soviet Karelian: The Language that Failed,*" *Slavic Review* 51, 1 (1992): 16–35; Anttikoski, "Strategii karelskogo iazykovogo planirovaniia," 207–22; and Esa Anttikoski, "'Iazykovoie stroitelstvo' na severo-zapade Rossii (20-e—40-e gody) ['Language Building' in Northwestern Russia (1920s–1940s)]," *Studia Slavica Finlandensia* 17 (2000): 116–27.

10. Gennadii Kupriianov, *Otchetnyi doklad Karelskogo obkoma VKP(b) na I siezde KP(b) Karelo-Finnskoi SSR* [Summary Report of the Karelian *Obkom* of the VKP(b) at the First Congress of the Communist Party of the Karelian-Finnish SSR] (Petrozavodsk: Gosizdat K-FSSR, 1940), 97–100, 105–06.

11. Nikolai Bugai, "Sever v politike pereseleniia narodov [North in the Policy of Deportation of Peoples]," *Sever* 4 (1994): 96.

12. Pavel Polian, *Ne po svoei vole . . . Istoriia i geografiia prinuditelnykh migratsii v SSSR* [Against One's Will . . . History and Geography of Forcible Deportations in the USSR] (Moscow: OGI-Memorial, 2001), 104–14; Irina Mukhina, *The Germans of the Soviet Union* (London: Routledge, 2007), 47.

13. Polian, *Ne po svoei vole,* 114–15.

14. A. A. German, "Sovetskiie nemtsy v lageriakh NKVD v gody Veliskoi Otechestvennoi voiny: Vklad v pobedy [Soviet Germans in NKVD Camps during the Great Patriotic War: Contribution to Victory]," in *Voenno-istoricheskiie issledovaniia v Povolzhie: Sb. nauch. trud. Vyp. 7* [Military Historical Research in the Volga Region: Collection of Articles, Issue 7], ed. A. A. German (Saratov: Nauchnaia kniga, 2006), 289.

15. V. N. Zemskov, *Spetsposelentsy v SSSR, 1930–1960* [Forcibly Resettled in the USSR] (Moscow: Nauka, 2005), 95.

16. Sevander, *Skitaltsy,* 270; Paavo Alatalo, "Sylvin ja Paavon tarina," unpublished memoir, archive of the Department of History of Northern Europe, Petrozavodsk State University, 34.

17. Interview with Yrjö Mykkänen, in *Ustnaia istoriia,* ed. Golubev and Takala, 94–97; Sevander, *Skitaltsy,* 173.

18. Aate Pitkänen's story was narrated in the documentary directed by Kelly Saxberg, *Letters from Karelia* (National Film Board of Canada, 2004).

19. Aate Pitkänen to his parents, 10–12 June 1942, in the private archive of Jukka Lehesvirta. Reproduced with permission.

20. Interview with Paavo Alatalo, Petrozavodsk, 17 October 2006, record lost because of a technical failure, a summary published in *Ustnaia istoriia,* ed. Golubev and Takala, 75–77.

21. Sevander, *Skitaltsy,* 175.

22. Sevander, "Severoamerikanskiie finny v Karelii [North American Finns in Karelia]," in *Uusi Kotimaa—Novaia Rodina,* http://www.uusikotimaa.org/0/029.htm.

23. Interview with Yrjö Mykkänen, in *Ustnaia istoriia*, ed. Golubev and Takala, 96–97.

24. Sevander, "Severoamerikanskiie finny v Karelii."

25. Interview with Yrjö Mykkänen, in *Ustnaia istoriia*, ed. Golubev and Takala, 99–101.

26. Auvo Kostiainen, *Santeri Nuorteva. Kansainvälinen suomalainen* [Santeri Nuorteva. An International Finn] (Helsinki: SKS, 1983); Einar Laidinen, "Khronika presledovaniia (sudba semii A. F. Nuorteva) [A Chronicle of Persecution (Fate of the Family of A. F. Nuorteva)]," *Uchenyie zapiski Petrozavodskogo gosudarstvennogo universiteta. Obshchestvennyie i gumanitarnyie nauki* [Academic Journal of Petrozavodsk State University, Social Sciences and Humanities] 8 (2009): 24–30.

27. Nikolai Bugai, "Deportatsiia narodov [Deportation of Peoples]," in *Voina i obshchestvo, 1941–1945. V 2 kn.: Kn. 2* [War and Society, 1941–1945. In Two Volumes: Vol. 2], ed. G. N. Sevostianov (Moscow: Nauka, 2004), 313.

28. Verigin, *Kareliia v gody voiennykh ispytanii,* 280.

29. Original document in GRASPI, f. 644, op. 1, d. 64,1. 24; quoted in Nikolai Bugai, *"Mobilizovat' nemtsev v rabochiie kolonny . . . I. Stalin": Sb. dokumentov (1940-e gody)* ["To Mobilize Germans in Labor Columns . . . I. Stalin": A Collection of Documents (1940s)] (Moscow: Gotika, 1998), 44–45.

30. Bugai, "Deportatsiia narodov," 313.

31. Interview with Veikko Lekander, in *Ustnaia istoriia*, ed. Golubev and Takala, 122–23.

32. Interview with Roy Niskanen, in *Ustnaia istoriia*, ed. Golubev et al., 348–51.

33. Lahti-Argutina, *Olimme joukko vieras vaan,* 593–612.

34. Among victims of the Great Terror, second- and third-generation American and Canadian Finns constituted 23 percent (94 of 416 people) and 5 percent (17 of 323 people) respectively. If these proportions are applied to the number of American- and Canadian-born victims in Chelyabinsk (thirty-five and eight), the figure comes to approximately 300. Of course, statistical correlations can be very misleading when such low numbers are analyzed; hence, we suggest, hypothetically, dividing this figure by three to get a probable number of people who died in the Chelyabinsk labor army. If the probable number of American and Canadian victims was 100, and the total death rate in labor armies was about 20 percent, then the total number of North American prisoners in the Chelyabinsk labor camp could have been about 500. Finally, as mentioned above, it was not the only, even though the largest, of NKVD labor armies.

35. Conditions of life and work in labor armies are represented in the documentary *Life Saver* (*Hengenpelastaja*), directed by Jouko Aaltonen, studio Illume, Finland, 2005, which narrates life stories of four Finnish American musicians who, during the war, were interned in the Chelyabinsk labor camp.

36. Interview with Paavo Alatalo, in *Ustnaia istoriia*, ed. Golubev and Takala, 76, 78–79.

37. Korablev et al., *Istoriia Karelii s drevneishikh vremen,* 686.

38. Pokrovskaia, *Naseleniie Karelii,* 153.

39. Archive of UFSB of RK, f. FSDP, p. KRO, op. 1, por. 126,1. 256–57.

40. Archive of UFSB of RK, f. FSDP, p. KRO, op. 1, por. 141,1. 15–17. For a somewhat strange reason, this report of the Karelian MGB (Ministry for State Security) provides statistics only for 1,752 people, most likely only for those born outside the Soviet Union or for people of working age. Among these Finns living in Soviet Karelia, according to this list, 1,138 arrived directly from Finland, 405 from the United States, 205 from Canada, and 3 from Sweden.

41. Interview with Paavo Alatalo, in *Ustnaia istoriia*, ed. Golubev and Takala, 79; interview with Veikko Lekander, in *Ustnaia istoriia*, ed. Golubev and Takala, 128.

42. This is the observation that Alexey Golubev made during his oral history interviews in 2006 and

2007. Although the representatives of the older generation, born in the 1910s or 1920s, clearly identified themselves as Finns first and Americans or Canadians second, their children and especially grandchildren considered this just as a curious fact and did not accept their identities. This difference was reflected in their values, habits, ways of realizing their identities in material culture, and so on.

43. The observations of Irina Takala made in the Finnish community of Petrozavodsk during this period.

44. Interview with Robert Manner, in *Ustnaia istoriia,* ed. Golubev and Takala, 136–43.

45. Interview with Dagny Salo, in *Ustnaia istoriia,* ed. Golubev and Takala, 8; interview with Paavo Alatalo, in *Ustnaia istoriia,* ed. Golubev and Takala, 75.

46. Interview with Veikko Lekander, in *Ustnaia istoriia,* ed. Golubev and Takala, 129.

47. Interview with Dagny Salo, in *Ustnaia istoriia,* ed. Golubev and Takala, 60. The respondent reproduced phrases of her American relatives in English, while the interview itself was conducted in Russian.

48. Sevander, *They Took My Father,* 189.

49. Unpublished interview with Tatiana Lekander by Alexey Golubev in 2006, Chalna, Karelia, in the archive of the Department of History of Northern Europe, Petrozavodsk State University.

50. Ibid.

51. Sevander, *Skitaltsy,* 103–07.

52. Interview with Robert Manner, in *Ustnaia istoriia,* ed. Golubev and Takala, 138–39.

53. "History of Kantele," in *Kantele,* http://history.kantele.ru.

54. "Imia legendarnogo direktora uvekovechat [Name of the Legendary Principle Will Be Immortalized]," *Stolitsa na Onego,* 25 August 2008, http://stolica.petrozavodsk.ru/news/111477.html.

55. "Happy Birthday to You," *Karelia,* 15 December 2005.

CONCLUSION

1. Edgar Allan Poe, *The Works of Edgar Allan Poe* (New York: Widdleton, 1871), 45.

2. Reinhart Koselleck, *Futures Past: On the Semantics of Historical Time* (New York: Columbia University Press, 2004), 75–92, 81.

Bibliography

ARCHIVES

Archive of the Finnish Foreign Ministry (Ulkoasiainministeriön arkisto)
Archive of the Office of the Federal Security Service in the Republic of Karelia (Archive of the UFSB RK)
Finnish National Archives (Kansallisarkisto)
National Archive of the Republic of Karelia (NARK)
Russian State Archive of Sociopolitical History (RGASPI)

NEWSPAPERS AND OTHER PERIODICALS

Ekonomika i statistika Karelii
Izvestiia Olonetskogo Gubernskogo Soveta
Izvestiia TsK KPSS
Karelo-Murmanskii Krai
Karelskaia guberniia
Karelskaia Kommuna
Krasnaia Karelia
Kurier Karelii
Leninskaia pravda
Moskovskiie novosti
Nezavisimaia gazeta
Olonetskaia Kommuna
Petrozavodsk
Punainen Karjala
Rintama
Severnyi Kurier
Sobraniie uzakonenii i rasporiazhenii rabochego i krestianskogo pravitelstva
Sovetskaia Karelia
Trud
Vestnik TsIK AKSSR

PUBLISHED WORKS

Afanasieva, A. I. *Kulturnyie preobrazovaniia v Sovetskoi Karelii, 1928–1940* [Cultural Transformations in Soviet Karelia, 1928–1940]. Petrozavodsk: Karelia, 1989.

———, ed. *Kulturnoie stroitelstvo v Sovetskoi Karelii, 1926–1941* [Cultural Building in Soviet Karelia, 1926–1941]. Petrozavodsk: Karelia, 1986.

———. "Narodnoie obrazovaniie v Sovetskoi Karelii v 1920–1930-e gody [Public Education in Soviet Karelia in the 1920s and 1930s]." In *Natsionalnaia gosudarstvennost finno-ugorskikh narodov severo-zapadnoi Rossii (1917–1940)* [Nationhood of Finno-Ugric Peoples of Northwest Russia (1917–1940)], edited by A. A. Popov, 55–61. Syktyvkar: Komi nauch. tsentr UrO RAN, 1996.

———. "Sozdaniie Sovetskoi natsionalnoi avtonomii i nekotoryie voprosy iazykovogo stroitelstva [The Establishment of a Soviet National Autonomy and Some Questions of Language Construction]." In *Voprosy istorii Evropeiskogo severa: Istoriia Velikogo Oktiabria na severo-zapade Rossii* [Questions of History of European North: History of the Great October in Northwest Russia], edited by M. I. Shumilov, 49–66. Petrozavodsk: Petrozavodsk State University Press, 1987.

Afanasieva, A. I., and V. I. Mashezerskii, eds. *Karelia v period vosstanovleniia narodnogo khoziaistva, 1921–1925* [Karelia during the Period of Economic Restoration, 1921–1925]. Petrozavodsk: Karelia, 1979.

Alto, E. L. *Sovetskiie finnoiazychnyie zhurnaly. 1920–1980* [Soviet Finnish-Language Magazines. 1920–1980]. Petrozavodsk: Karelia, 1989.

Anderson, Benedict. *Imagined Communities: Reflections on the Origin and Spread of Nationalism.* London: Verso, 1983.

Andriainen, Andrei. "Dvizheniie proletarskoi solidarnosti zarubezhnykh finskikh trudiashchikhsia s Sovetskoi Kareliei [Movement of Proletarian Solidarity between Finnish Workers Abroad and Soviet Karelia]." In *50 let Sovetskoi Karelii* [Fifty Years of Soviet Karelia], 180–98. Petrozavodsk: Karelia, 1969.

———. "Zamechatelnyi primer internatsionalnoi solidarnosti [A Formidable Example of International Solidarity]." In *Voprosy istorii KPSS* [Problems of History of the CPSU], 87–101. Petrozavodsk: Petrozavodsk State University Press, 1968.

Anttikoski, Esa. "'Iazykovoie stroitelstvo' na severo-zapade Rossii (20-e–40-e gody) ['Language Building' in Northwestern Russia (1920s–1940s)]." *Studia Slavica Finlandensia* 17 (2000): 116–27.

———. "Neuvostoliiton kielipolitiikkaa: Karjalan kirjakielen suunnittelu 1930-luvulla" [The Soviet Language Policy: The Planning of the Karelian Literary Language in the 1930s]. Licentiate diss., University of Joensuu, 1998.

———. "Strategii karelskogo iazykovogo planirovaniia v 1920-e i 1930-e gody [Strategies of Language Planning for Karelia during the 1920s and 1930s]." In *V semie edinoi: Natsionalnaia politika partii bolshevikov i eio osushchestvleniie na severo-zapade Rossii v 1920–1950-e gody* [One United Family: The Nationalities Policy of CPSU from the 1920s to the 1950s and Its Implementation in Northwestern Russia], edited by Irina Takala and Timo Vihavainen, 207–22. Petrozavodsk: Petrozavodsk State University Press, 1998.

Autio, Sari. *Suunnitelmatalous Neuvosto-Karjalassa 1928–1941* [Planned Economy of Soviet Karelia 1928–1941]. Helsinki: SKS, 2002.

Avtonomnaia Karelskaia Sovetskaia Sotsialisticheskaia Respublika. Spravochnik. 1923–1933 [Autonomous Karelian Soviet Socialist Republic. Reference Book. 1923–1933]. Petrozavodsk: Izd-vo SNK AKSSR, 1933.

Baines, Dudley. *Emigration from Europe, 1815–1930.* Cambridge, UK: Cambridge University Press, 1995.

Balagurov, Ya. A., and V. I. Mashezerskii, eds. *Kareliia v period grazhdanskoi voiny i inostrannoi interventsii, 1918–1920* [Karelia in the Years of the Civil War and Foreign Intervention, 1918–1920]. Petrozavodsk: Karel.knizhnoe izd-vo, 1964.

Baron, Nick. *The King of Karelia: Col. P. J. Woods and the British Intervention in North Russia 1918–1919. A History and Memoir.* London: Francis Boutle Publishers, 2007.

———. *Soviet Karelia: Politics, Planning, and Terror in Stalin's Russia, 1920–1939.* London: Routledge, 2007.

Barthes, Roland. "Myth Today." In *Mythologies,* by Roland Barthes, 109–64. New York: Noonday Press, 1991.

Bartlett, Roger P. *Human Capital: The Settlement of Foreigners in Russia, 1762–1804.* Cambridge, UK: Cambridge University Press, 1979.

Bekrenev, N. *Kanadskiie lesoruby v Karelii* [Canadian Lumberjacks in Karelia]. Petrozavodsk: Kirja, 1932.

Birin, Viktor. *Finny Olonetskoi gubernii* [Finns of the Olonets Province]. Petrozavodsk: KarNTS RAN, 1991.

Birin, Viktor, and Irina Takala. "Finny [Finns]." In *Narody Rossii. Entsiklopediia* [Peoples of Russia. An Encyclopedia], edited by Valerii Tishkov, 370–72. Moscow: Bolshaia Rossiiskaia Entsiklopediia, 1994.

Boucht, Christer. *Karjala kutsuu* [Karelia Calls]. Helsinki: Kirjayhtymä, 1988.

———. *Onnea etsimässä: Punaisesta Karjalasta Kaukoitään* [The Search for Luck: From Red Karelia to the Far East]. Helsinki: Kirjayhtymä, 1973.

Brubaker, Rogers. *Nationalism Reframed: Nationhood and the National Question in the New Europe.* Cambridge, UK: Cambridge University Press, 1996.

Bubrikh, D. V. *Kakoi iazyk—tverskim karelam* [What Language for Tver Karelians?]. Leningrad: LOI-KFUN, 1931.

———. *Karely i karelskii iazyk* [Karelians and the Karelian Language]. Moscow: Mosoblispolkom, 1932.

Budzhet Karelskoi ASSR na 1934 g. [Budget of the Karelian ASSR in 1934]. Petrozavodsk: NKF AKSSR, 1934.

Bugai, Nikolai. *The Deportation of Peoples in the Soviet Union.* New York: Nova Science Publishers, 1996.

———. "Deportatsiia narodov [Deportation of Peoples]." In *Voina i obshchestvo, 1941–1945. V 2 kn.: Kn. 2* [War and Society, 1941–1945. Vol. 2], edited by G. N. Sevostianov, 306–30. Moscow: Nauka, 2004.

———. *"Mobilizovat' nemtsev v rabochiie kolonny . . . I. Stalin": Sb. dokumentov (1940-e gody)* ["To Mobilize Germans in Labor Columns . . . I. Stalin": A Collection of Documents (1940s)]. Moscow: Gotika, 1998.

———. "Sever v politike pereseleniia narodov [North in the Policy of Deportation of Peoples]." *Sever* 4 (1994): 92–98.

Butvilo, Andrei. "Formirovaniie territorii Kareliskoi Trudovoi Kommuny kak politicheskaia problema [The Making of Territories of the Karelian Workers' Commune as a Political Problem]." *Otechestvennaia istoriia* 3 (2009): 169–76.

Chuev, Felix. *Sto sorok besed s Molotovym: Iz dnevnika F. Chueva* [One Hundred and Forty Talks to Molotov: From F. Chuev's Diary]. Moscow: Terra, 1991.

Chukhin, Ivan. *Karelia-37: Ideologiia i praktika terrora* [Karelia-37: Ideology and Practice of Terror]. Petrozavodsk: Petrozavodsk State University Press, 1999.

Churchill, Stacy. "The East Karelian Autonomy Question in Finnish-Soviet Relations, 1917–1922." PhD diss., University of London, 1967.

———. *Itä-Karjalan kohtalo 1917–1922: Itä-Karjalan itsehallintokysymys Suomen ja Neuvosto-Venäjän välisissä suhteissa 1917–1922* [The Fate of Eastern Karelia, 1917–1922: The Question of Self-Government in Eastern Karelia in the Finnish-Soviet Relations, 1917–1922]. Porvoo: WSOY, 1970.

Connor, Walker. *The National Question in Marxist-Leninist Theory and Strategy.* Princeton: Princeton University Press, 1984.

Copeland, William R. *The Uneasy Alliance: Collaboration between the Finnish Opposition and the Russian Underground, 1899–1904.* Helsinki: Suomalainen tiedeakatemia, 1973.

Danielsen, Rolf. *Norway: A History from the Vikings to Our Own Times.* Oslo: Scandinavian University Press, 1995.

David-Fox, Michael. *Showcasing the Great Experiment: Cultural Diplomacy and Western Visitors to the Soviet Union 1921–41.* Oxford: Oxford University Press, 2011.

Davis, R. W. *The Industrialisation of Soviet Russia: Crisis and Progress in the Soviet Economy, 1931–1933.* London: Macmillan, 1996.

Dekrety Sovietskoi vlasti [Decrees of the Soviet Power]. Vol. 1. Moscow: Gospolitizdat, 1976.

Diuzhev, Yu. I., ed. *Pisateli Karelii: Bibliograficheskii slovar* [Writers of Karelia: A Bibliographic Glossary]. Petrozavodsk: Ostrova, 2006.

Dmitriev, Yu. A., ed., *Pominalnyie spiski Karelii, 1937–1938: Unichtozhennaia Karelia. Ch. II. Bolshoi Terror* [Commemoration Lists of Karelia, 1937–1938: Exterminated Karelia. Part II. Great Terror]. Petrozavodsk: Pravitelstvo Respubliki Karelia, 2002.

Dobrenko, Evgeny. *The Making of the State Reader: Social and Aesthetic Contexts of the Reception of Soviet Literature.* Stanford: Stanford University Press, 1997.

———. *The Making of the State Writer: Social and Aesthetic Origins of Soviet Literary Culture.* Stanford: Stanford University Press, 2000.

———. *Political Economy of Socialist Realism.* New Haven: Yale University Press, 2007.

Durand, Dominique. *Kommunizm svoimi rukami: Obraz agrarnykh kommun v Sovetskoi Rossii 1920-kh godov* [Self-Made Communism: The Image of Agricultural Communes in Soviet Russia of the 1920s]. St. Petersburg: European University at SPb Press, 2010.

Efremkin, Evgeny. "'Karelian Project' or 'Karelian Fever'? Orders from Above, Reaction from Below: Conflicting Interests in Kremlin, Karelia, and Canada." In *North American Finns in Soviet Karelia in the 1930s,* edited by Ilya Solomeshch and Irina Takala, 55–82. Petrozavodsk: Petrozavodsk State University Press, 2008.

Engle, Elois. *Finns in North America.* Minneapolis: Lerner Publications Company, 1975.

Engman, Max. *Förvaltningen och utvandringen till Ryssland, 1809–1917* [Administration of Finland and Finnish Immigration to Russia, 1809–1917]. Helsingfors: Tryckericentralen, 1995.

———. *Petersburgska vägar* [Roads to St. Petersburg]. Esbo: Schildt, 1995.

Engman, Max, and Sune Jungar. "Pereselencheskoiie dvizheniie iz Finlandii v Rossiiu v 1809–1917 gg. [Resettlement Movement from Finland to Russia in 1809–1917]." In *Materialy VI Sovetsko-finliandskogo simposiuma istorikov: Rossiia i Finliandiia 1700–1917* [Materials of the Sixth Soviet-Finnish Symposium of Historians: Russia and Finland in 1700–1917], edited by I. S. Kukushkin and I. P. Shaskolskii, 115–38. Leningrad: Nauka, 1980.

Etkind, Alexander. *Internal Colonization: Russia's Imperial Experience.* Cambridge, UK: Polity, 2011.

Etkind, Alexander, Dirk Uffelman, and Ilya Kukulin, eds. *Tam, vnutri: Praktiki vnutrennei kolonizatsii v kulturnoi istorii Rossii* [There, Inside: Practices of Internal Colonization in Cultural History of Russia]. Moscow: NLO, 2012.

Ezhegodnik 1929 goda. Vypusk IV [Yearbook for 1929. Issue 4]. Petrozavodsk: Statupravleniie AKSSR, 1931.

Felshtinsky, Yuri. "The Legal Foundations of the Immigration and Emigration Policy of the USSR, 1917–1927." *Soviet Studies* 34, 3 (1982): 327–48.

Filimonchik, Svetlana. "Vklad Kondopogi v industrialnoie razvitiie Karelii [Contribution of Kondopoga in Industrial Development of Karelia]." In *Kondopozhskii krai v istorii Karelii i Rossii* [Kondopoga Region in the History of Karelia and Russia], edited by A. M. Pashkov, 201–07. Petrozavodsk, Kondopoga: Issledovatelskii tsentr Russkii Sever, 2000.

Fitzpatrick, Sheila. *Everyday Stalinism: Ordinary Life in Extraordinary Times: Soviet Russia in the 1930s.* New York: Oxford University Press, 1999.

———, ed. *Stalinism: New Directions.* New York: Routledge, 2000.

Galkina, Liudmila. "Sozdaniie i deiatelnost avtonomnoi kolonii inostrannykh rabochikh i spetsialistov v Kuzbasse, 1921–1926 [Establishment and Operations of an Autonomous Colony of Immigrant Workers and Specialists in Kuzbass, 1921–1926]." Candidate of Sciences diss., Kemerovo State University, 1997.

Gardin, Iefim. *Sovetskaia Kareliia v gody vosstanovitelnogo perioda (1921–1925)* [Soviet Karelia in the Years of Reconstruction Period (1921–1925)]. Petrozavodsk: Gosizdat KFSSR, 1955.

Gavrilov, M. *"Kantele"—gosudarstvennyi ansambl pesni i tantsa Karelskoi ASSR* ["Kantele" as the State Singing and Dancing Ensemble of the Karelian ASSR]. Petrozavodsk: Gosizdat KASSR, 1959.

Gelb, Michael. "'Karelian Fever': The Finnish Immigrant Community during Stalin's Purges." *Europe-Asia Studies* 45, 6 (1993): 1091–1116.

German, A. A. "Sovetskiie nemtsy v lageriakh NKVD v gody Veliskoi Otechestvennoi voiny: Vklad v pobedy [Soviet Germans in NKVD Camps during the Great Patriotic War: Contribution to Victory]." In *Voenno-istoricheskiie issledovaniia v Povolzhie: Sb. nauch. trud. Vyp. 7* [Military Historical Research in the Volga Region: Collection of Articles. Issue 7], edited by A. A. German, 278–300. Saratov: Nauchnaia kniga, 2006.

Gladkov, Ivan, ed. *Sovetskoie narodnoie khoziaistvo v 1921–1925 gg.* [Soviet Economy in 1921–1925]. Moscow: Izd-vo AN SSSR, 1960.

Golubev, Alexey. "Printsipy upravleniia ekonomikoi v ekonomicheskom soznanii rukovodstva Karelii v gody NEPa (1921–1929 gg.) [Principles of Economic Management in Economic Thinking of the Leadership of Karelia during the NEP (1921–1929)]." In *Regionalizatsiia i globalizatsiia: Obshestvennye protsessy v Rossii i na Evropeiskom Severe v XX-XXI vekakh* [Regionalization and Globalization: Social Processes in Russia and the Russian European North during the Twentieth and Twenty-First Centuries], edited by Sergey Shubin, 59–90. Arkhangelsk: Pomor State University Press, 2007.

Golubev, Alexey, and Irina Takala, eds. *Ustnaia istoriia v Karelii: Sbornik nauchnykh statei i istochnikov. Vypusk 2. Severoamerikanskiie finny v Sovetskoi Karelii 1930-kh gg.* [Oral History in Karelia: A Collection of Articles and Sources. Issue 2. North American Finns in Soviet Karelia in the 1930s]. Petrozavodsk: Petrozavodsk State University Press, 2007.

Golubev, Alexey, et al., eds. *Ustnaia istoriia v Karelii. Vyp. 4. Kareliia i Belarus: Povsednevnaia zhizn i kulturnyie praktiki naseleniia v 1930—1950-e gg.* [Oral History in Karelia. Issue 4. Karelia and Belarus: Everyday Life and Cultural Practices in the 1930s to 1950s]. Petrozavodsk: Petrozavodsk State University Press, 2008.

Gorsuch, Anne. *Youth in Revolutionary Russia: Enthusiasts, Bohemians, Delinquents.* Bloomington: Indiana University Press, 2000.

Grenoble, Lenore A. *Language Policy in the Soviet Union.* Dordrecht: Kluwer Academic Publishers, 2003.

Groys, Boris. "A Style and a Half: Socialist Realism between Modernism and Postmodernism." In *Socialist Realism without Shores,* edited by Thomas Lahusen and Evgeny Dobrenko, 76–90. Durham: Duke University Press, 1997.

Halfin, Igal. *Stalinist Confessions: Messianism and Terror at the Leningrad Communist University.* Pittsburgh: University of Pittsburgh Press, 2009.

———. *Terror in My Soul: Communist Autobiographies on Trial.* Cambridge, MA: Harvard University Press, 2003.

Harpelle, Ronald, Varpu Lindström, and Alexis Pogorelskin, eds. *Karelian Exodus: Finnish Communities in North America and Soviet Karelia during the Depression Era.* Beaverton, ON: Aspasia Books, 2004.

Heikkinen, Sakari, and Tapani Mauranen. "Nauchnaia deiatelnost Edvarda Gyllinga [Edvard Gylling's Scholarly Career]." In *Skandinavskii sbornik. Vyp. XXXI* [Scandinavian Collection. Vol. 31], 127–37. Tallinn: Eesti Raamat, 1988.

Hellbeck, Jochen. *Revolution on My Mind: Writing a Diary under Stalin.* Cambridge, MA: Harvard University Press, 2006.

Hirsch, Francine. *Empire of Nations: Ethnographic Knowledge and the Making of the Soviet Union.* Ithaca: Cornell University Press, 2005.

Hobsbawm, Eric. *Nations and Nationalism since 1780: Programme, Myth, Reality.* Cambridge, UK: Cambridge University Press, 1990.

Hodgson, John H. *Edvard Gylling ja Otto W. Kuusinen asiakirjojen valossa 1918–1920* [Edvard Gylling and Otto W. Kuusinen in the Light of Documents]. Helsinki: Tammi, 1974.

Hoglund, Arthur W. "Finnish Immigrant Letter Writers: Reporting from the US to Finland, 1870s to World War I." In *Finnish Diaspora II: United States,* edited by Michael G. Karni, 13–31. Toronto: Multicultural History Society of Ontario, 1981.

———. *Finnish Immigrants in America, 1880–1920.* Madison: University of Wisconsin Press, 1960.

Hokkanen, Sylvia, and Laurence Hokkanen, with Anita Middleton. *Karelia: A Finnish-American Couple in Stalin's Russia, 1934–1941.* St. Cloud, MN: North Star Press, 1991.

Holmgren, Beth, ed. *The Russian Memoir: History and Literature.* Evanston: Northwestern University Press, 2003.

Holmio, Armas K. E. *Michiganin Suomalaisten historia* [History of Finns in Michigan]. Hancock, MI: Michigan Suomalaisten Historia-Seura, 1967.

Hovi, Ritva-Liisa. "Amerikansuomalaisten maanviljelyskommuuni Etelä-Venäjällä [Finnish-American Agricultural Commune in South Russia]." *Turun Historiallinen Arkisto* 25 (1971): 281–300.

Hudelson, Richard, and Mayme Sevander. "Relapse of Karelian Fever." *Siirtolaisuus/Migration* 2 (2000): 31–35.

Ioffe, Aleksandr. "Deiatelnost zarubezhnykh obshchestv druzhby s Sovetskim Soiuzom [Activities of Foreign USSR Friendship Societies]." *Voprosy istorii* 3 (1966): 15–30.

Iukhneva, Natalia. *Etnicheskii sostav i etnosotsialnaia struktura naseleniia Petersburga, vtoraia polovina XIX—nachalo XX v.* [Ethnic Composition and Ethnosocial Structure of the Population of St. Petersburg in the Second Half of the Nineteenth and Early Twentieth Centuries]. Leningrad: Nauka, 1984.

Ivnitskii, N. A., and V. G. Makurov, eds. *Iz istorii raskulachivaniia v Karelii. 1930–1931. Documenty i materialy* [From the History of Dekulakization in Karelia. 1930–1931. Documents and Materials]. Petrozavodsk: Karelia, 1991.

Jänis, Marja, and Tamara Starshova. "Cultural and Political Contexts of Translating into Finnish in Soviet/Russian Karelia." In *Domestication and Foreignization in Translation Studies,* edited by Hannu Kemppanen, Marja Jänis, and Alexandra Belikova, 189–209. Berlin: Frank and Timme, 2012.

Jungar, Sune. "Finlandskiie remeslenniki v Sankt-Peterburge [Finnish Artisans in St. Petersburg]." In *Remeslo i manufaktura v Rossii, Finliandii, Pribaltike* [Artisanship and Manufactory in Russia, Finland, and Baltic States], edited by N. Ye. Nosov, 90–99. Leningrad: Nauka, 1975.

———. *Från Åbo till Ryssland: En studie i urban befolkningsrörlighet 1850–1890* [From Åbo to Russia: A Study of Urban Population Mobility]. Åbo: Åbo Akademi, 1974.

Juntunen, Alpo. *Suomalaista kulttuuria Nevan rannoilla: Piirteitä Pietarin suomalaisen siirtokunnan kulttuurielämästä 1900-luvun alussa* [Finnish Culture on Banks of the Neva River: Features of Cultural Life of Finnish Immigrants in St. Petersburg in the Early Twentieth Century]. Turku: Turun yliopisto, 1970.

Jussila, Osmo. *Nationalismi ja vallankumous venäläis-suomalaisissa suhteissa 1899–1914* [Nationalism and Revolution in the Russian-Finnish Relations, 1899–1914]. Helsinki: SHS, 1979.

———. *Terijoen hallitus 1939–40* [Terijoki Government, 1939–1940]. Helsinki: WSOY, 1985.

Jussila, Osmo, Seppo Hentilä, and Jukka Nevakivi. *From Grand Duchy to a Modern State: A Political History of Finland since 1809.* London: C. Hurst and Company, 1999.

Kalinin, Ilya. "'Ugnetionnyie dolzhny govorit' (massovyi prizyv v literaturu i formirovaniie sovetskogo subiekta, 1920-e—nachalo 1930-kh godov ['The Subaltern Must Speak' (A Call for Masses to Start Writing and the Making of the Soviet Subject, 1920s to Early 1930s)]." In *Tam, vnutri: Praktiki vnutrennei kolonizatsii v kulturnoi istorii Rossii* [There, Inside: Practices of Internal Colonization in Cultural History of Russia], edited by Alexander Etkind, Dirk Uffelman, and Ilya Kukulin, 587–664. Moscow: NLO, 2012.

Kangaspuro, Markku. "Finskaia epokha sovetskoi Karelii [The Finnish Era of Soviet Karelia]." In *V semie edinoi: Natsionalnaia politika partii bolshevikov i eio osushchestvleniie na severo-zapade Rossii v 1920–1950-e gody* [One United Family: The Nationalities Policy of CPSU from the 1920s to the 1950s and Its Implementation in Northwestern Russia], edited by Irina Takala and Timo Vihavainen, 123–60. Petrozavodsk: Petrozavodsk State University Press, 1998.

———. *Neuvosto-Karjalan taistelu itsehallinnosta* [The Struggle of Soviet Karelia for Autonomy]. Helsinki: SKS, 2000.

Kankaanpää, Sakarias. *Voittamattomat* [The Unbeatable]. Petroskoi: Kirja, 1934.

Karelia: Literaturno-khudozhestvennyi almanakh Soiuza sovetskikh pisatelei Karelii. Vyp. 1 [Karelia: A Literary and Artistic Almanac of the Soviet Writers' Union of Karelia. Issue 1]. Petrozavodsk: Kirja, 1937.

Karelskaia ASSR za 50 let [Fifty Years of the Karelian ASSR]. Petrozavodsk: Karelia, 1967.

Karelskaia organizatsiia KPSS v tsifrakh. 1921–1984 [Karelian Organization of the CPSU in Figures. 1921–1984]. Petrozavodsk: Karelia, 1985.

Kauppala, Pekka. "Formirovaniie i rastsvet avtonomnoi Sovetskoi Karelii, 1918–1929: Zabytyi uspekh rannesovetskoi natsionalnoi politiki [Formation and Heyday of Autonomous Soviet Karelia, 1918–1929: A Forgotten Success of Early Soviet Nationalities Politics]." *Ab Imperio* 2 (2002): 309–37.

———. "Sowjet-Karelien 1917–1941: Leistung und Schicksal eines sozialistischen Regionalexperiments [Soviet Karelia 1917–1941: The Success and Fate of a Socialist Regional Experiment]." PhD diss., Albert Ludwigs University of Freiburg, 1992.

Kero, Reino. "The Canadian Finns in Soviet Karelia in the 1930s." In *The Finnish Diaspora I: Canada, South America, Africa, Australia, and Sweden,* edited by Michael Karni, 203–13. Toronto: Multicultural History Society of Ontario, 1981.

————. "Emigration of Finns from North America to Soviet Karelia in the Early 1930's." In *The Finnish Experience in the Western Great Lakes Region: New Perspectives,* edited by Michael G. Karni, 212–21. Turku: Institute of Migration, 1975.

————. *Neuvosto-Karjalaa rakentamassa: Pohjois-Amerikan suomalaiset tekniikan tuojina 1930-luvun Neuvosto-Karjalassa* [Building Soviet Karelia: North American Finns as the Introducers of New Technologies in Soviet Karelia in the 1930s]. Helsinki: SHS, 1983.

————. *Suomalaisina Pohjois-Amerikassa: Siirtolaiselämää Yhdysvalloissa ja Kanadassa* [Finns in North America: Life of Immigrants in the United States and Canada]. Turku: Siirtolaisuusinstituutti, 1997.

————. *Suuren Länteen: Siirtolaisuus Suomesta Yhdysvaltoihin ja Kanadaan* [To the Great West: Immigration from Finland to the United States and Canada]. Turku: Siirtolaisuusinstituutti, 1996.

————. "The Tragedy of Joonas Harju of Hiilisuo Commune." *Finnish Americana* 5 (1982): 8–11.

Khlevniuk, Oleg. *1937: Protivostoianiie* [1937: Confrontation]. Moscow: Znanie, 1991.

————. *1937-i. Stalin, NKVD, i sovetskoie obshchestvo* [1937. Stalin, the NKVD, and Soviet Society]. Moscow: Respublika, 1992.

————. *Politburo: Mekhanismy politicheskoi vlasti v 30e gody* [Politburo: Mechanisms of Political Power in the 1930s]. Moscow: ROSSPEN, 1996.

Kilin, Yuri. *Kareliia v politike sovetskogo gosudarstva 1920–1941* [Karelia in Politics of the Soviet State]. Petrozavodsk: Petrozavodsk State University Press, 2000.

Kirkinen, Heikki, Pekka Nevalainen, and Hannes Sihvo. *Karjalan kansan historia* [History of the Karelian People]. Porvoo: WSOY, 1994.

Kivisto, Peter. "The Decline of the Finnish American Left, 1925–1945." *International Migration Review* 17, 1 (1983): 68–74.

————. *Immigrant Socialists in the United States: The Case of Finns and the Left.* Rutherford, NJ: Fairleigh Dickinson University Press, 1984.

Kivisto, Peter, and Mika Roinila. "Reaction to Departure: The Finnish American Community Responds to 'Karelian Fever.'" In *North American Finns in Soviet Karelia in the 1930s,* edited by Ilya Solomeshch and Irina Takala, 17–38. Petrozavodsk: Petrozavodsk State University Press, 2008.

Klementiev, E. I. "Iazykovaia situatsiia v Karelii: Sostoianiie, tendentsii razvitiia [Language Situation in Karelia: Current State and Tendencies of Development]." In *Karely. Finny. Problemy etnicheskoi istorii* [Karelians. Finns. Problems of Ethnic History], 112–24. Moscow: Russian Academy of Sciences, 1992.

Komulainen, Ernesti. *A Grave in Karelia.* New York: Braun Brumfield, 1995.

Kon, Yu. G., and N. Yu. Grodnitskaia. *Professionalnaia musyka Karelii: Ocherki* [Professional Music of Karelia: Essays]. Petrozavodsk: Karelia, 1995.

Konkka, Unelma, ed. *Puteshestviia Eliasa Lönnrota: Putevyiie zametki, dnevniki, pisma 1828–1842 gg.* [Elias Lönnrot's Travels: Travel Notes, Diaries, Letters from 1828 to 1842]. Petrozavodsk: Karelia, 1985.

Koponen, Olga-Maria. *Tavallisen ihmisen tarina* [A Story of an Ordinary Person]. Vaasa: Ykkös-Offset OY, 2002.

Korablev, Nikolai, et al., eds. *Istoriia Karelii s drevneishikh vremen do nashikh dnei* [History of Karelia from Ancient Times to Our Days]. Petrozavodsk: Periodika, 2001.

Koronen, Matvei. *Finskiie internatsionalisty v borbe za vlast Sovetov* [Finnish Internationalists in the Struggle for Soviet Power]. Leningrad: Lenizdat, 1969.

Koselleck, Reinhart. "Begriffsgeschichte and Social History." In *Futures Past: On the Semantics of Historical Time,* by Reinhart Koselleck, 75–92. New York: Columbia University Press, 2004.

Kostiainen, Auvo. *The Forging of Finnish-American Communism 1917–1924: A Study in Ethnic Radicalism.* Turku: University of Turku, 1978.

———. *Loikkarit: Suuren lamakauden laiton siirtolaisuus Neuvostoliittoon* [Border Hoppers: Illegal Immigration to the Soviet Union during the Great Depression]. Helsinki: Otava, 1988.

———. "Neuvosto-Karjala ja 'Kaukaisen idän aromailta'—suomalaiskirjeitä Venäjältä ja Neuvostoliitosta [Soviet Karelia and 'From the Steppes of a Faraway East'—Finnish Letters from Russia and the Soviet Union]." In *Maitten ja merten takaa: Vuosisata suomalaisia siirtolaiskirjeitä* [From Across the Lands and Seas: A Century of Finnish Immigrant Letters], edited by Eero Kuparinen, 209–61. Turku: Turun Historiallinen Yhdistys, 1986.

———. *Santeri Nuorteva: Kansainvälinen suomalainen* [Santeri Nuorteva: An International Finn]. Helsinki: SKS, 1983.

Kotkin, Steven. *Magnetic Mountain: Stalinism as a Civilization.* Berkeley: University of California Press, 1995.

KPSS v rezoliutsiiakh i resheniiakh s'iezdov, konferentsii, i plenumov TsK. T. 2 [KPSS in Resolutions and Decisions of the Congresses, Conferences, and Plenums of the Central Committee. Vol. 2.]. Moscow: Gospolitizdat, 1953.

Krasnaia Kareliia: Sbornik materialov ofitsialnogo kharaktera [Red Karelia: A Collection of Official Materials]. Petrozavodsk: Narkomiust AKSSR, 1925.

Krekola, Joni. *Stalinismin lyhyt kurssi* [A Short Course on Stalinism]. Helsinki: SKS, 2006.

Kruhse, Pauli, and Antero Uitto. *Suomen rajan takana 1918–1944: Suomenkielisen neuvostokirjallisuuden historia ja bibliografia* [Behind the Finnish Border: History and Bibliography of the Soviet Finnish-Language Literature]. Jyväskylä: BTJ, 2008.

Kukushkin, Vadim. *From Peasants to Labourers: Ukrainian and Belarusan Immigration from the Russian Empire to Canada.* Montreal: McGill-Queen's University Press, 2007.

Kupriianov, Gennadii. *Otchetnyi doklad Karelskogo obkoma VKP(b) na I siezde KP(b) Karelo-Finnskoi SSR* [Summary Report of the Karelian *Obkom* of the VKP(b) at the First Congress of the Communist Party of the Karelian-Finnish SSR]. Petrozavodsk: Gosizdat K-FSSR, 1940.

Lackman, Matti. "Etsivä keskuspoliisi 1919–1937 [A Search for Reasonable Policy 1919–1937]." In *Turvallisuuspoliisi 75 vuotta, 1919–1994* [75 Years of Security Policy, 1919–1994], edited by Matti Simola and Jukka Salovaara, 11–100. helsinki: Sisäasiainministeriö, Poliisiosasto, 1994.

Lahti-Argutina, Eila. *Olimme joukko vieras vaan: Venäjänsuomalaiset vainonuhrit Neuvostoliitossa 1930-luvun alusta 1950-luvun alkuun* [We Were Just a Group of Visitors: Russian Finnish Victims of Soviet Repression from the 1930s to the Early 1950s]. Turku: Siirtolaisuusinstituutti, 2001.

Lahtinen, William. *50 vuoden varrelta* [During Fifty Years]. Superior, WI: American Finnish Publishers; Työmies Society, 1953.

Laidinen, Einar. "Khronika presledovaniia (sudba semii A. F. Nuorteva) [A Chronicle of Persecution (Fate of the Family of A. F. Nuorteva)]." *Uchenyie zapiski Petrozavodskogo gosudarstvennogo universiteta. Obshchestvennyie i gumanitarnyie nauki* 8 (2009): 24–30.

Laine, Antti. "Karelo-Finskaia Sovetskaia Sotsialisticheskaia Respublika i finny [Karelian-Finnish Soviet Socialist Republic and Finns]." In *V semie edinoi: Natsionalnaia politika partii bolshevikov i eio osushchestvleniie na severo-zapade Rossii v 1920–1950-e gody* [One United Family: The Nationalities Policy of CPSU from the 1920s to the 1950s and Its Implementation in Northwestern Russia], edited by Irina Takala and Timo Vihavainen, 223–50. Petrozavodsk: Petrozavodsk State University Press, 1998.

Laine, Antti, and Mikko Ylikangas, eds. *Rise and Fall of Soviet Karelia: People and Power.* Helsinki: Kikimora Publications, 2002.

Lavrushina, Natalia. "Iz istorii poiavleniia severoamerikanskikh finnov v Karelii v nachale 1930-kh godov [From the History of Immigration of North American Finns to Karelia in the Early 1930s]." In *Karely. Finny. Problemy etnicheskoi istorii* [Karelians. Finns. Problems of Ethnic History], 176–89. Moscow: Russian Academy of Sciences, 1992.

Lebedeva, N. S., K. Rentola, and T. Saarela, eds. *Komintern i Finlandia 1919–1943: Dokumenty* [Comintern and Finland 1919–1943: Documents]. Moscow: Nauka, 2003.

Leinonen, Artturi. *Punaisen aallon ajelemana: Yrjö Kultajärven seikkailut 1917–1937* [Riding a Red Wave: Adventures of Yrjö Kultajärvi 1917–1937]. Porvoo: Söderström, 1963.

Lenin, V. I. *On Culture and Cultural Revolution.* Moscow: Progress Publishers, 1966.

Leskinen, M. V. "Obraz finna v rossiiskikh populiarnykh etnograficheskikh ocherkakh poslednei treti XIX v. [Image of the Finn in Russian Popular Ethnographic Writing of the Last Third of the Nineteenth Century]." In *Mnogolikaia Finlandiia: Obraz Finlandii i finnov v Rossii* [Multi-Faced Finland: The Image of Finland and the Finns in Russia], edited by A. N. Tsamutali, O. P. Iliukha, and G. M. Kovalenko, 154–91. Veliky Novgorod: Yaroslav Mudryi Novgorod State University Press, 2004.

Levkoev, A. A. *Natsionalno-iazykovaia politika finskogo rukovodstva Sovetskoi Karelii (1920–1935)* [The Nationalities and Language Policy of Finnish Leadership of Soviet Karelia (1920–1935)]. Preprint of a paper. Petrozavodsk: Karelsk. nauch. tsentr RAN, 1992.

———. "'Pravilnaia politika.' Krestiianskii fon politiki finliandkogo kommunisticheskogo rukovodstva Sovetskoi Karelii v 1920-e gg. ['The Right Policy.' A Peasant Background in the Politics of the Finnish Communist Leadership of Soviet Karelia in the 1920s]." In *Natsionalnaia gosudarstvennost finno-ugorskikh narodov severo-zapadnoi Rossii (1917–1940)* [National statehood of Finno-Ugric peoples of Northwest Russia (1917–1940)], edited by A. A. Popov, 23–28. Syktyvkar: KomiNTs RAN, 1996.

Lewin, Moshe. *The Making of the Soviet System: Essays in the Social History of Interwar Russia.* New York: Pantheon, 1985.

———. *Russian Peasants and Soviet Power: A Study of Collectivization.* New York: W.W. Norton, 1975.

Liedes, Liisa A., and Uuno Vesanen. *Suomalainen helluntaiherätys Pohjois-Amerikassa* [The Awakening of the Pentecostal Movement in North America]. Vancouver: Mission Press Society, 1994.

"Liitteenä V. Keynään laatima ja sovittama kansallisuuskartta Itä-Karjalasta ja Kuollan Niemimaasta [Attached Ethnic Map of Eastern Karelia and Kola Peninsula, Prepared and Arranged by V. Keynäs]." In *Karjalan oikeus* [The Right to Karelia], appendix (*liitenä*). Helsinki: Otava, 1921.

Lindquist, Herman. *A History of Sweden: From Ice Age to Our Age.* Stockholm: Norstedts, 2006.

Lindström, Varpu. "The Finnish Canadian Communities during the Decade of Depression." In *Karelian Exodus: Finnish Communities in North America and Soviet Karelia during the Depression Era,* edited by Ronald Harpelle, Varpu Lindström, and Alexis E. Pogorelskin, 15–27. Beaverton, ON: Aspasia Books, 2004.

———. "'Heaven or Hell on Earth?' Soviet Karelia's Propaganda War of 1934–1935 in the Finnish Canadian Press." In *North American Finns in Soviet Karelia in the 1930s,* edited by Ilya Solomeshch and Irina Takala, 83–104. Petrozavodsk: Petrozavodsk State University Press, 2008.

Lindström, Varpu, and Börje Vähämäki. "Ethnicity Twice Removed: North American Finns in Soviet Karelia." *Finnish Americana* 9 (1992): 14–20.

Lunacharsky, A. V. *Desiatiletiie revoliutsii i kultura* [The Tenth Anniversary of the Revolution and Culture]. Moscow-Leningrad: Gos. izd-vo, 1927.

———. *Teatr i revoliutsiia* [Theater and the Revolution]. Moscow: Gos. izd-vo, 1924.

Luoto, Lauri. *Ikuiset uhritulet* [Eternal Flame for Victims]. Superior, WI: Amerikan suom. sosialist. kust.-liikkeiden kust., 1929.

———. *Jäämeri ärjyy* [The Artic Ocean Roars]. Leningrad: Kirja, 1933.

———. *Kamaran sankarit* [Heroes of the Earth]. Superior, WI: Amerikan suom. sosialist. kust.-liikkeiden kust., 1927.

———. *Lakeuksien Aunus* [Plains of Olonets]. Petroskoi: Kirja, 1933.

———. *Pakolaisena* [A Refugee]. Superior, WI: Amerikan suom. sosialist. kust.-liikkeiden kust., 1925.

———. *Valkoisen leijonan metsästäjät* [Hunters for a White Lion]. Superior, WI: Amerikan suom. sosialist. kust.-liikkeiden kust., 1926.

Mahnke, Julia. *Auswanderungsvereine mit Ziel Ukraine und Sowjet-Rußland in der Weimarer Republik* [Emigration Organizations Aimed at Ukraine and Soviet Russia in Weimar Germany]. München: Mitteilungen des Osteuropa-Institutes, 1997.

Mäkelä, Santeri. *Elämää ikuisessa yössä* [Life in Eternal Darkness]. Ironwood, MI: Otto Massisen kustannusliike, 1911.

Mally, Lynn. *Revolutionary Acts: Amateur Theater and the Soviet State, 1917–1938.* Ithaca: Cornell University Press, 2000.

Markevich, A. M. "Otraslevyie narkomaty i glavki v sisteme upravleniia sovetskoi ekonomikoi v 1930e gg. [Industry Commissariats and Central Offices of Industrial Management in the System of Soviet Economic Management in the 1930s]." In *Ekonomicheskaia istroiia: Ezhegodnik 2004* [Economic History: A Yearbook 2004], edited by L. I. Borodkin, 118–40. Moscow: ROSSPEN, 2004.

Martin, Terry. *The Affirmative Action Empire: Nations and Nationalism in the Soviet Union, 1923–1939.* Ithaca: Cornell University Press, 2001.

Mashezerskii, V. I., et al., eds. *Ocherki istorii Karelii* [Short History of Karelia]. Vol. 2. Petrozavodsk: Karel.kn.izd-vo, 1964.

Materialy i postanovlenia IV ob'iedinennogo plenuma Karelskogo oblastnogo komiteta i oblastnoi kontrolnoi komissii VKP(b), 10–13 avgusta 1929 g. [Materials and Resolutions of the Fourth United Plenum of the Karelian Regional Committee and Regional Controlling Commission of the VKP(b), 10–13 August 1929]. Petrozavodsk: Izd-vo Karel. obl. kontr. kom., 1929.

Matinheikki-Kokko, Kaija, and Pirkko Pitkänen. "Immigrant Policies and the Education of Immigrants in Finland." In *Education and Immigration: Settlement Policies and Current Challenges,* edited by Gajendra K. Verma and Devorah Kalekin-Fishman, 48–73. London: Routledge, 2002.

Maynard, Charles. *The Murmansk Venture.* London: Hodder and Stoughton, 1928.

Meinander, Henrik. *Istoriia Finlandii* [History of Finland]. Moscow: Ves' Mir, 2008.

Mezentsev, G. I., ed. *Rabochii klass Karelii v period postroeniia sotsializma v SSSR. 1926–1941.* Petrozavodsk: Karelia, 1984.

Middleton, Anita. "Karelian Fever: Interviews with Survivors." In *Melting into Great Waters: Papers from Finnforum V,* edited by Varpu Lindström, Oiva Saarinen, and Börje Vähämäki. Special issue of *Journal of Finnish Studies* 1, 3 (1997): 179–82.

Miettinen, Helena, and Kyllikki Joganson. *Petettyjen toiveiden maa* [The Land of Betrayed Hopes]. Saarijärvi: Gummerus kirjapaino OY, 2001.

Miller, Frank J. *Folklore for Stalin: Russian Folklore and Pseudofolklore of the Stalin Era.* Armonk, NY: M.E. Sharpe, 1990.

Morray, Joseph P. *Project Kuzbas: American Workers in Siberia (1921–1926).* New York: International Publishers, 1983.

Mukhina, Irina. *The Germans of the Soviet Union.* London: Routledge, 2007.

Na fronte mirnogo truda: Vospominaniia uchastnikov sotsialisticheskogo stroitelstva v Karelii, 1920–1940

[On the Frontline of Peaceful Labor: Memoirs of Participants of Socialist Building of Karelia, 1920–1940]. Petrozavodsk: Karelia, 1976.

Nevalainen, Pekka. *Punaisen myrskyn suomalaiset: Suomalaisten paot ja paluumuutot idästä 1917–1939* [Finns of the Red Storm: Finns' Escapes to and Return from the East 1917–1939]. Helsinki: SKS, 2004.

Nevezhin, Vladimir. *"Esli zavtra v pokhod . . .": Podgotovka k voine i ideologicheskaia propaganda v 30-kh—40-kh godakh* ["If We Set Out Tomorrow . . .": Preparation for War and Ideological Propaganda in the 1930s and 1940s]. Moscow: Iauza, Eksmo, 2007.

Niinistö, Jussi. *Heimosotien historia 1918–1922* [The History of Kindred Wars 1918–1922]. Helsinki: SKS, 2005.

Nikitin, P. "Stanovleniie teatra: K 90-letiiu so dnia rozhdeniia Ragnara Nyströma [The Making of the Theater: To the 90-Year Anniversary of Ragnar Nyström]." *Sever* 9 (1988): 100–06.

Nikitina, Olga. *Kollektivizatsiia i raskulachivaniie v Karelii* [Collectivization and Dekulakization in Karelia]. Petrozavodsk: KNTs RAN, 1997.

Nironen, Jarmo. *Suomalainen Pietari* [Finnish St. Petersburg]. Vantaa: Novomedia, 1999.

Nyström, Ragnar. *Johdatus näyttämö taiteeseen* [Introduction to the Performing Arts]. Petroskoi: Kirja, 1929.

"O tak nazyvaemom 'natsional-uklonizme' [On the So-Called 'National Deviationism']." *Izvestiia TsK KPSS* 9 (1990): 76–84.

Ollila, Douglas J. "From Socialism to Industrial Unionism (IWW): Social Factors in the Emergence of Left-Labor Radicalism among Finnish Workers on the Mesabe, 1911–19." In *The Finnish Experience in the Western Great Lakes Region: New Perspectives,* edited by Michael G. Karni, 156–71. Turku: Institute of Migration, 1975.

Osokina, Elena. *Za fasadom "stalinskogo izobiliia": Raspredeleniie i rynok v snabzhenii naseleniia v gody industrializatsii, 1927–1941* [Behind the Facade of "Stalinist's Abundance": Distribution and the Market during the Industrialization, 1927–1941]. Moscow: ROSSPEN, 1998.

Parras, Eemeli. *Jymyvaaralaiset* [The People of Jymyvaara]. Petroskoi: Kirja; Superior, WI: Työmies Society Print, 1933.

———. *Lämmintä verta ja kylmää hikeä* [Hot Blood and Cold Sweat]. Hancock, MI: Työmies, 1914.

———. *Pohjalta* [From the Bottom]. Fitchburg, MA: Raivaajan kirjapaino, 1910.

———. *Valtamerien kahtapuolta: Jutelmia ja kertomuksia* [On Both Sides of the Ocean: Essays and Stories]. Petroskoi: Kirja, 1937.

———. *Villit vuoret: Nelinäytöksinen näytelmä* [Wild Mountains: A Play in Four Acts]. Hancock, MI: Työmies, 1911.

Pashkov, Aleskander, and Svetlana Filimonchik. *Petrozavodsk.* Sankt-Peterburg: Zvezda Peterburga, 2001.

Peltoniemi, Teuvo. *Kohti parempaa maailmaa* [Toward a Better World]. Helsinki: Otava, 1985.

Perepis naseleniia AKSSR. 1933 g. Vyp. III [1933 Census of the Population of Karelia. Issue 3]. Petrozavodsk: Soiuzorguchiot, 1935.

Pervaia Vseobshchaia perepis naseleniia Rossiiskoi imperii. 1897 g. T. I. Arkhangelskaia guberniia. [First General Census of the Population of the Russian Empire. Vol. 1. Arkhangelsk Province]. Moscow: Tsentralnyi statisticheskii komitet MVD, 1899.

Petrov, I. A. *Kommuna "Säde"* [Commune Säde]. Petrozavodsk, 1930.

Pimenov, V. F., and R. F. Taroieva. "Etnicheskiie protsessy v Sovetskoi Karelii [Ethnic Processes in Soviet Karelia]." In *50 let Sovetskoi Karelii* [Fifty Years of Soviet Karelia], 214–47. Petrozavodsk: Karelia, 1970.

Pogorelskin, Alexis. "Communism and the Co-ops: Recruiting and Financing the Finnish-American Migration to Karelia." *Journal of Finnish Studies* 8, 1 (2004): 28–47.

———. "New Perspectives on Karelian Fever: The Recruitment of North American Finns to Karelia in the Early 1930s." *Journal of Finnish Studies* 1, 3 (1997): 165–78.

———. "Why Karelian Fever?" *Siirtolaisuus/Migration* 1 (2000): 25–26.

Pokrovskaia, Irina. *Naseleniie Karelii* [Population of Karelia]. Petrozavodsk: Karelia, 1978.

Polian, Pavel. *Ne po svoei vole . . . Istoriia i geografiia prinuditelnykh migratsii v SSSR* [Against One's Will . . . History and Geography of Forcible Deportations in the USSR]. Moscow: OGI-Memorial, 2001.

Prushinskaia, N. A., and E. I. Takala. *Natsionalnyie pisateli Karelii: Finskaia emigratsiia i politicheskiie repressii 1930-kh godov: Bibliografīcheskii ukazatel* [National Writers of Karelia: Finnish Immigration and Political Repression of the 1930s: A Bibliographic Reference Book]. Petrozavodsk: National Library of Karelia, 2005.

Raivio, Yrjö. *Kanadan Suomalaisten historia* [History of Finns in Canada]. Copper Cliff, ON: Canadan Suomalainen Historiaseura, 1975.

Ranta, Kalle. *Arpi korvassa ja sydämessä* [A Scar in the Ear and Heart]. Helsinki: WSOY, 2000.

Rasila, Viljo. *Istoriia Finlandii* [History of Finland]. Petrozavodsk: Petrozavodsk State University Press, 2006.

Rautiainen, Emil. *Mereltä leipää hakemassa: Kertomuksia mailta ja meriltä* [Looking for Bread Overseas: Stories about Lands and Seas]. Petroskoi: Kirja, 1934.

———. *Neuvostomaata rakentamassa* [Building the Soviet Land]. Petroskoi: Kirja, 1933.

———. *Nuorta verta* [Young Blood]. Leningrad: Kirja, 1933.

Rautkallio, Hannu. *Suuri viha: Stalinin suomalaiset uhrit 1930-luvulla* [Big Anger: Stalin's Finnish Victims of the 1930s]. Porvoo: WSOY, 1995.

Repukhova, Oksana. "Delo o kontrrevoliutsionnom zagovore v Karelii v 1932–1933 gg. ('Zagovor finskogo genshtaba') [Case of a Counterrevolutionary Conspiracy in Karelia in 1932–1933 ('Conspiracy of the Finnish General Staff')]." In *Korni travy: Sbornik statei molodykh uchenykh* [The Grass Roots: Collection of Articles of Young Scholars], edited by L. S. Yeremina and Ye. B. Zhemkova, 35–44. Moscow: Memorial, 1996.

Ruhanen, Urho. *V vikhriakh veka: Vospominaniia i ocherki* [In Storms of the Century: A Memoir and Essays]. Petrozavodsk: Karelia, 1991.

Runeberg, Johan Ludvig. *The Tales of Ensign Stål*. Princeton: Princeton University Press; New York: American Scandinavian Foundation, 1938.

Rutanen, Mikael. *Joukkovoima: Työttömyysaiheinen työväen romaani* [Group Strength: A Novel about Unemployment of Workers]. Worcester: Amerikan suom. sos. kustannusliikkeiden liitto, 1931.

———. *Taistelun säveliä: Lausuttavia runoja* [Melodies of the Battle: Runes that Should Be Uttered]. Superior, WI: Työmies Society, 1930.

———. *Työn laulu: Runoja* [A Song of Labor: Poems]. Leningrad: Kirja, 1933.

———. *Unohdettujen maailmasta: Kuvaus metsätyöläisten elämästä* [From the World of the Forgotten: Pictures from the Life of Forest Workers]. Superior, WI: Amerikan suom. sosialist. kust.-liikkeiden kust, 1929.

S Leninym v serdtse: Sb. dokumentov i materialov [With Lenin in Heart: A Collection of Documents and Materials]. Kemerovo: Kemerovskoie kn. izd-vo, 1976.

Saarela, Tauno. *Suomalaisten kommunismin synty 1918–1923* [Birth of Finnish Communism 1918–1923]. Tampere: KSL, 1996.

Saarinen, Oiva W. *Between a Rock and a Hard Place: A Historical Geography of the Finns in the Sudbury Area.* Waterloo: Wilfrid Laurier University Press, 1999.

Sainio, Venla. "Manner, Kullervo." *Suomen Kansallisbiografia* 6 [Finnish National Biographies 6], 489–92. Helsinki: Suomalaisen Kirjallisuuden Seura, 2005.

Salo, Artturi. *Amerikkalaiset metsätyömetoodit ja työvälineet* [American Forest Work Methods and Work Tools]. Petroskoi: Kirja, 1934.

Sammartino, Annemarie H. *The Impossible Border: Germany and the East, 1914–1922.* Ithaca: Cornell University Press, 2010.

Sandomirskaia, Irina. *Kniga o rodine: Opyt analiza diskursivnykh praktik* [The Book about the Motherland: An Experience of Analysis of Discursive Practices]. Wien: Wiener Slawistischer Almanach, 2001.

Saramo, Samira. "Piecing Together Immigrant Lives: An Analysis of Personal Letters Written by North American Finns in Soviet Karelia." In *North American Finns in Soviet Karelia in the 1930s,* edited by Ilya Solomeshch and Irina Takala, 170–89. Petrozavodsk: Petrozavodsk State University Press, 2008.

Sariola, Sakari. *Amerikan kultaan: Amerikansuomalaisten siirtolaisten sosiaalihistoria* [To American Gold: A Social History of Finnish American Immigrants]. Helsinki: Kustannusosakeyhtiö, 1982.

Sbornik vazhneishikh postanovlenii za 1929—ianvar 1931 gg. po Karelskoi ASSR [A Collection of Most Important Decrees from 1929 to January 1931 in the Karelian ASSR]. Petrozavodsk: Narkomiust AKSSR, 1931.

Sevander, Mayme. *Of Soviet Bondage.* Duluth: OSCAT, 1996.

———. *Red Exodus: Finnish-American Emigration to Russia.* Duluth: OSCAT, 1993.

———. "Severoamerikanskiie finny v Karelii [North American Finns in Karelia]." In *Kraeved: Sbornik Statei* [Local History: A Collection of Articles], edited by Alevtina Rogozhina, 132–42. Petrozavodsk: Verso, 2007.

———. *Skitaltsy: O sudbakh amerikanskikh finnov v Karelii* [Wanderers: Fates of American Finns in Karelia]. Petrozavodsk: Petrozavodsk State University Press, 2006.

———. *They Took My Father: A Story of Idealism and Betrayal.* Duluth: Pfeiffer-Hamilton, 1991; reprinted, Minneapolis: University of Minnesota Press, 2004.

Sevostianov, G. N., et al., eds. *"Sovershenno sekretno": Lubianka—Stalinu o polozhenii v strane. T. 6* ["Top Secret": Lubianka to Stalin on the Situation in the USSR. Vol. 6]. Moscow: IRI RAN, 2002.

Shishkin, Valerii. *V. I. Lenin i vneshneekonomicheskaia politika Sovetskogo gosudarstva (1917–1923 gg.)* [V. I. Lenin and Foreign Economic Policy of the Soviet State (1917–1923)]. Leningrad: Nauka, 1977.

Shmelev, Nikolai, and Vladimir Popov. *The Turning Point: Revitalizing the Soviet Economy.* New York: I.B. Tauris, 1990.

Sihvo, Hannes. *Karjalan kuva: Karelianismin taustaa ja vaiheita autonomian aikana* [The Picture of Karelia: The Background and Stages of Karelianism during the Autonomous Time]. Helsinki: SKS, 1973.

Simon, Gerhard. *Nationalism and Policy towards the Nationalities in the Soviet Union.* Boulder, CO: Westview Press, 1991.

Simpson, Pat. "Parading Myths: Imaging New Soviet Woman on Fizkulturnik's Day, July 1944." *Russian Review* 63, 2 (2004): 187–211.

Slezkine, Yuri. *Arctic Mirrors: Russia and the Small Peoples of the North.* Ithaca: Cornell University Press, 1994.

———. "The USSR as a Communal Apartment, or How a Socialist State Promoted Ethnic Particularism." *Slavic Review* 53, 2 (1994): 414–52.

Smith, Jeremy. *The Bolsheviks and the National Question, 1917–1923*. London: Macmillan, 1999.

Smith, Michael G. *Language and Power in the Creation of the USSR, 1917–1953*. Berlin: Walter de Gruyter, 1998.

Soini, Elena. "Poeziia-utopiia finskoi immigratsii v Rossii, 1920–1930-e gody [Utopian Poetry of the Finnish Immigration in Russia, 1920s–1930s]." In *Finskii faktor v istorii i kulture Karelii XX veka* [Finnish Factor in the History and Culture of Karelia during the Twentieth Century], edited by Olga Iliukha, 208–31. Petrozavodsk: KarNTs RAN, 2009.

Solomeshch, Ilja. "Rajamaa, etuvartio, käytävä, portti—eli missä kasvaa ruoččiheinä? [A Borderland, an Outpost, a Corridor, Gates—or Where Does the Swedish Grass Grow?]." In *Ajan valtimolla— mukana muutoksia: Professori Tapio Hämysen 60-vuotisjuhlakirja* [On the Pulse of Time—with Changes: A Jubilee Book to the 60th Anniversary of Professor Tapio Hämynen], edited by Marko Junkkarinen et al., 127–34. Saarijärvi: Itä-Suomen yliopisto, 2011.

Solomeshch, Ilya, and Irina Takala, eds. *North American Finns in Soviet Karelia in the 1930s*. Petrozavodsk: Petrozavodsk State University Press, 2008.

Spisok naselennykh mest Karelii. Po materialam perepisi 1933 goda [List of Settlements of Karelia. Based on the 1933 Census]. Petrozavodsk: UNKHU AKSSR, 1935.

Spivak, Gayatri Chakravorty. "Can the Subaltern Speak?" In *Marxism and the Interpretation of Culture*, edited by Cary Nelson and Lawrence Grossberg, 271–313. Urbana: University of Illinois Press, 1988.

Stalin, I. V. *Sochineniia* [Works]. Vol. 5. Moscow: Politizdat, 1947.

———. *Sochineniia*. Vol. 7. Moscow: Gospolitizdat, 1947.

———. *Sochineniia*. Vol. 12. Moscow: Politizdat, 1949.

———. *Sochineniia*. Vol. 13. Moscow: Politizdat, 1951.

———. *Sochineniia*. Vol. 14. Moscow: Pisatel, 1997.

Statisticheskii ezhegodnik Karelii 1922 [Statistical Yearbook of Karelia 1922]. Petrozavodsk: Statupravlenie AKSSR, 1923.

Statisticheskii obzor. 1923–1924. Ch. 1. [Statistical Review. 1923–1924. Part 1] Petrozavodsk: Statupravlenie AKSSR, 1925.

Steinberg, Mark. *Proletarian Imagination: Self, Modernity, and the Sacred in Russia, 1910–1925*. Ithaca: Cornell University Press, 2002.

Sulkanen, Elis. *Amerikan suomalaisen työväenliikkeen historia* [The History of the Finnish American Labor Movement]. Fitchburg, MA: Amerikan Suomalainen. Kansanvallan Liitto, 1951.

Suny, Ronald Grigor, and Terry Martin, eds. *A State of Nations: Empire and Nation-Making in the Age of Lenin and Stalin*. Oxford: Oxford University Press, 2001.

Suomela, V. *Kuusi kuukautta Karjalassa: Mitä siirtolainen näki ja koki Neuvosto-Karjalassa* [Six Months in Karelia: What an Immigrant Saw and Experienced in Soviet Karelia]. Sudbury: Vapaa Sana Press, 1939.

Suutari, Pekka. "Going beyond the Border: National Cultural Policy and the Development of Musical Life in Soviet Karelia, 1920–1940." In *Soviet Music and Society under Lenin and Stalin: The Baton and Sickle*, edited by Neil Edmunds, 163–80. London: Routledge, 2004.

———. "Representation of Locality in Karelian Folk Music Activities from Composers to Singing Women: What Was Represented When Karelian Folk Music Was Performed?" In *Karelia Written and Sung: Representations of Locality in Soviet and Russian Contexts*, edited by Pekka Suutari and Yury Shikalov, 209–28. Helsinki: Aleksanteri Series at Kikimora Publications, 2010.

Takala, Irina. "Delo Gyllinga-Rovio [The Case of Gylling-Rovio]." In *Ikh nazyvali KR: Repressii v Karelii 20–30-kh gg.* [They Were Called Counterrevolutionaries: Repressions in Karelia in the 1920s and 1930s], edited by Anatoly Tsygankov, 34–73. Petrozavodsk: Karelia, 1992.

————. "Eero Haapalainen—revolutsioner, zhurnalist, uchionyi [Eero Haapalainen as a Revolutionary, a Journalist, and a Scholar]." In *Politicheskaia istoriia i istoriografiia: Ot antichnosti do sovremennosti. Vyp. 2* [Political History and Historiography: From Antiquity to the Modern Age. Vol. 2], edited by G. S. Samokhina, 187–93. Petrozavodsk: Petrozavodsk State University Press, 1996.

————. "Eldoradoa etsimässä: Tarina ennen sotia Neuvosto-Karjalaan valtavesien takaa saapuneista amerikansuomalaista [The Search for El Dorado: A Story of American Finnish Immigrants to Soviet Karelia in the Interwar Period]." *Carelia* 3 (1993): 4–25.

————. *Finny v Karelii i Rossii: Istoriia vozniknoveniia i gibeli diaspory* [Finns in Karelia: The History of Birth and Death of the Diaspora]. St. Petersburg: Izdatelstvo Zhurnal Neva, 2002.

————. "Finskiie pereselentsy v Karelii i na Kolskom poluostrove [Finnish Settlers in Karelia and in the Kola Peninsula]." In *Pribaltiisko-finskiie narody Rossii* [Baltic and Finnic Peoples of Russia], edited by Evgenii Klementiev and Natalia Shlygina, 522–32. Moscow: Nauka, 2003.

————. "Finskoie naseleniie Sovetskoi Karelii v 1930-e gg. [Finnish Population of Soviet Karelia in the 1930s]." In *Karely. Finny. Problemy etnicheskoi istorii* [Karelians. Finns. Problems of Ethnic History], 150–75. Moscow: Russian Academy of Sciences, 1992.

————. "Kansallisuusoperaatiot Karjalassa [National Operations in Karelia]." In *Yhtä suurta perhettä: Bolshevikkien kansallisuuspolitiikka Luoteis-Venäjällä 1920–1950-luvuilla* [One United Family: The Nationalities Policy of CPSU from the 1920s to the 1950s and Its Implementation in Northwestern Russia], edited by Irina Takala and Timo Vihavainen, 161–206. Helsinki: Kikimora Publications, 2000.

————. "Kysymys Suomen kansanarmeijasta [A Question of the Finnish People's Army]." In *Talvisota, Venäjä ja Suomi* [Winter War, Russia and Finland], edited by Timo Vihavainen, 287–94. Helsinki: SHS, 1991.

————. "Loikkareiden kohtalo Neuvosto-Karjalassa asiakirjojen kuvaamana [The Fate of Border Hoppers in Soviet Karelia as Described in Archival Documents]." In *Kahden Karjalan välillä: Kahden Riikin riitamaalla* [Between Two Karelias: On the Land Disputed by Two Powers], edited by Tapio Hämynen, 173–80. Joensuu: Joensuun yliopisto, 1994.

————. "Repola 1922–1939 [Reboly during 1922–1939]." In *Aunuksen Repola* [Olonets Reboly], edited by Heikki Tarma, 229–32. Jyväskylä: Repola-seura, 2001.

————. "Sudby finnov v Karelii [Fates of Finns in Karelia]." In *Voprosy istorii Evropeiskogo Severa* [Questions of History of the European North], edited by Mikhail Shumilov, 92–103. Petrozavodsk: Petrozavodsk State University Press, 1991.

————. "Suomen kommunistinen puolue ja Karjala 1930-luvulla [Finnish Communist Party and Karelia during the 1930s]." *Carelia* 9 (1994): 136–47.

Takala, Irina, and Timo Vihavainen, eds. *V semie edinoi: Natsionalnaia politika partii bolshevikov i eio osushchestvleniie na severo-zapade Rossii v 1920–1950-e gody* [One United Family: The Nationalities Policy of CPSU from the 1920s to the 1950s and Its Implementation in Northwestern Russia]. Petrozavodsk: Petrozavodsk State University Press, 1998.

Tarle, Galina. *Druzia strany sovetov: Uchastiie zarubezhnykh trudiashchikhsia v vosstanovlenii narodnogo khoziaistva SSSR v 1920–1925 gg.* [Friends of the Land of the Soviets: Foreign Workers' Contribution to Soviet Economic Recovery during 1920–1925]. Moscow: Nauka, 1966.

————. "Rossiiskiie dokumenty o pravilakh v'ezda i vyezda za granitsu v 20-kh godakh XX v. (Analiz istochnokov) [Russian Documents on the Regulations of Crossing the Soviet Border in the 1920s (Analysis of Sources)]." In *Rossiia i problemy evropeiskoi istorii: Srednevekovie, novoie, i noveisheie vremia* [Russia and the Issues of European History: Middle Ages, Modern, and Contemporary Time], edited by S. O. Schmidt et al., 119–42. Rostov: Rostovskii kreml, 2003.

Tereshchenkov, Leonid. "Izucheniie revoliutsii 1917 goda i grazhdanskoi voiny v Karelo-Murmanskom regione v sisteme istoriko-partiinykh uchrezhdenii 1920–1930-kh godov [Studies of the Revolution of 1917 and of the Civil War in the Karelian-Murmansk Region in the System of Institutions Specializing in the History of the Communist Party]." Candidate of Sciences diss., Petrozavodsk State University, 2010.

Tommola, Esko. *Uuden maanrakentajat* [Builders of the New World]. Helsinki: Otava, 1989.

Tonkell, Iosif. *Brigady i iacheiki na lesozagotovkakh v Karelii* [Brigades and Teams in Timber Harvesting in Karelia]. Petrozavodsk: Kirja, 1932.

———. *Jännesaha* [Bow Saw]. Moskova-Leningrad: Kirja, 1933.

———. *Kanadskiie lesoruby v Sovetskoi Karelii* [Canadian Lumberjacks in Soviet Karelia]. Moscow: Goslestekhizdat, 1934.

———. *Miten puutavaran kuljetusta parannetaan* [How to Improve Timber Transportation]. Moskova-Leningrad: Kirja, 1933.

Traktoristin käsikirja [A Pocket Guide of a Tractor Driver]. Petroskoi: Kirja, 1932.

Trotsky, Leon. "Novyi zigzag i novyie opasnosti [A New Zigzag and New Dangers]." *Biulleten oppozitsii (bolshevikov-lenintsev)* 23 (August 1931), http://web.mit.edu/fjk/www/FI/BO/BO-23.shtml.

———. "Uspekhi sotsializma i opasnosti avantiurizma [Socialist Successes and Dangers of Adventurism]." *Biulleten oppozitsii (bolshevikov-lenintsev)* 17–18 (November–December 1930), http://web.mit.edu/fjk/www/FI/BO/BO-17.shtml.

Tuomi, Kaarlo. "The Karelian Fever of the Early 1930s: A Personal Memoir." *Finnish Americana* 3 (1980): 61–75.

Tzouliadis, Tim. *The Forsaken: An American Tragedy in Stalin's Russia.* London: Penguin Press, 2008.

Uola, Mikko. "Edvard Gylling." In *Sto zamechatelnykh finnov* [One Hundred Prominent Finns], edited by Timo Vihavainen, 172–75. Helsinki: SKS, 2004.

Utekhin, Ilya. *Ocherki kommunalnogo byta* [Essays on Everyday Life in Communal Apartments]. Moscow: OGI, 2001.

Vähämäki, Börje. "Memoir Accounts of Finnish North Americans in Soviet Karelia in the 1930s." In *North American Finns in Soviet Karelia in the 1930s,* edited by Ilya Solomeshch and Irina Takala, 152–69. Petrozavodsk: Petrozavodsk State University Press, 2008.

Vavulinskaia, L. I., ed. *Sovety Karelii 1917–1992: Dokumenty i materialy* [Soviets of Karelia 1917–1992: Documents and Materials]. Petrozavodsk: Karelia, 1993.

Verigin, Sergey. *Kareliia v gody voiennykh ispytanii: Politicheskoiie i sotsialno-ekonomicheskoie polozheniie Sovetskoi Karelii v period Vtoroi mirovoi voiny 1939–1945 gg.* [Karelia in the Years of War Trials: Political and Socioeconomic Situation of Soviet Karelia during the Second World War, 1939–1945]. Petrozavodsk: Petrozavodsk State University Press, 2009.

Verigin, Sergey, and Einar Laidinen. "Finskii shpionazh i politicheskiie repressii na severo-zapade Rossii v 1920–1930-e gg. [Finnish Espionage and Political Repression in Northwest Russia in the 1920s and 1930s]." In *Politicheskii sysk v Rossii: Istoriia i sovremennost* [Political Investigation in Russia: History and the Present Day], edited by Vladlen Izmozhnik, 198–211. St. Petersburg: Izd-vo SPbUEF, 1997.

Vihavainen, Timo. *Stalin i finny* [Stalin and Finns]. St. Petersburg: Zhurnal Neva, 2000.

———, ed. *Sto zamechatelnykh finnov* [One Hundred Prominent Finns]. Helsinki: SKS, 2004.

Vsekarelskii s'iezd predstavitelei trudiashchikhsia karel, 11–19 fevralia 1921 g. Protokoly [All-Karelian Congress of Representatives of Working Karelians, 11–19 February 1921: Records of Proceeding]. Petrozavodsk: Karelia, 1990.

Vsesoiuznaia perepis naseleniia 1926. T. 1 [All-Soviet Census of 1926. Vol. 1]. Moscow: Statizdat TsSU SSSR, 1928.

Wilson, Kelvin. *Practical Dreamers: Communitarianism and Co-Operatives on Malcolm Island.* Victoria: British Columbia Institute for Co-Operative Studies, 2005.

Wright, Alistair S. "The Establishment of Bolshevik Power on the Russian Periphery: Soviet Karelia, 1918–1919." PhD diss.,, University of Glasgow, 2012.

Ylikangas, Mikko. *Rivit suoriksi! Kaunokirjallisuuden poliittinen valvonta Neuvosto-Karjalassa 1917–1940* [Straighten Your Ranks! Political Control over Literary Writing in Soviet Karelia during 1917–1940]. Helsinki: Kikimora Publications, 2004.

————. "The Sower Commune: An American-Finnish Agricultural Utopia in the Soviet Union." *Journal of Finnish Studies: A Special Double Issue, Victims and Survivors of Karelia* 15, 1–2 (2011): 51–84.

Zaitsev, Ye. A., ed. *Sbornik zakonodatelnykh i normativnykh aktov o repressiiakh i reabilitatsii zhertv politicheskikh repressii* [A Collection of Legislative and Regulatory Acts on Repression and Rehabilitation of Victims of the Political Repression]. Moscow: Respublika, 1993.

Zemskov, V. N. *Spetsposelentsy v SSSR, 1930–1960* [Forcibly Resettled in the USSR]. Moscow: Nauka, 2005.

Zetterberg, Seppo, ed. *Suomen historian pikkujättiläinen* [A Small Giant of the Finnish History]. Helsinki: WSOY, 2003.

Zherbin, A. S., ed. *Karely Karelskoi ASSR* [Karelians of the Karelian ASSR]. Petrozavodsk: Kareliia, 1983.

Zhuravliov, Sergei. *Malenkiie liudi i bolshaia istoriia: Inostrantsy moskovskogo Elektrozavoda v sovetskom obshchestve 1920-kh—1930-kh gg.* [Little People and Big History: Foreigners from Moscow's Elektrozavod in the Soviet Society of the 1920s and 1930s]. Moscow: ROSSPEN, 2000.

Zhuravliov, Sergey, and Viktoriia Tiazhiolnikova. "Inostrannaia koloniia v Sovetskoi Rossii v 1920–1930-e gody (Postanovka problemy i metody issledovaniia) [A Foreign Colony in Soviet Russia during the 1920s and 1930s (The Problem and Methods of Research)]." *Otechestvennaia istoriia* 1 (1994): 179–89.

Zlobina, Vieno. "Kak pogasili luch [How the Ray Was Switched Off]." *Sever* 7 (1990): 157–60.

Index

Ahokas, Eelis, 130–31
Alatalo, Paavo, 161, 191, 205, 212–14
All-Karelian Congresses of Soviets, 91
anti-immigrant sentiment, 110–17
Antonen, Eero, 75
Arkhangelsk province, 5–7, 9, 12, 73, 91, 141, 178
Aronen, Kalle, 29, 31, 132–33, 152–53

Balandis, Elsa, 62, 104, 116, 191
Balitskii, Vsevolod, 55
Barents Sea, 7
Belomorsk, 160–61
border and borderlands (between Russia and Finland), xii, 6, 8, 9, 12–20, 23, 54–56, 83, 91–92, 96, 110–12, 114, 121–24, 126–27, 133, 135–37, 140–42, 150, 157–59
Boucht, Christer, 58
Bubrikh, Dmitry, 93–94
Buck, Tim, 151
Bukharin, Nikolai, 20
Bushuev, Pavel, 129
Buy (town), 8

Central Executive Committee: of Soviet Karelia, 91, 162; of the USSR, 94
Chalna, 167, 169
Chelyabinsk, 163, 213
Chicago, Illinois, 46, 104
Chicherin, Georgy, 12
Chudov, Mikhail, 127, 129, 130
civil war in Karelia, 8, 10, 18–19, 83, 111–12
Cleveland, Ohio, 46, 150
Cobalt, Ontario, 42, 83
Comintern, xi, 27–28, 33, 127–30, 151, 153, 154, 158
Communist Party of Canada, 23, 29, 151–54
Communist Party USA, 27–29; 41, 100
Communist Party USSR, 8, 17, 28, 55, 63, 69, 94, 98, 109, 123, 128, 139, 173; Central Committee (including Politburo), 94, 96, 122, 125, 126, 129, 134–36, 142, 153; Karelian Regional Committee (*obkom*) 12, 20, 31, 42, 44, 50, 55, 93, 102, 125–30, 133, 135–36, 151, 153, 183;

Leningrad Regional Committee (*obkom*), 20, 55, 123, 185; local cells in Karelia, 130–32; Sixteenth Congress of, 17–18, 22, 28, 69, 122; Twelfth Congress, 92
Corgan, Oscar, 29, 31, 34, 57, 132–33, 148–49
Corgan, Pavel, 168
Council of People's Commissars (government) of Soviet Karelia, 12, 18–22, 25, 29–30, 33, 54–57, 94–96, 123, 127
cultural activities, 21, 67, 80, 85, 89–107, 116, 119, 159, 165, 167–68

dancing groups, 85, 102, 103–4, 119
Detroit, Michigan, 37, 41, 46, 66, 76, 104, 107
Dimitrov, Georgi, xi, 151–52

economy of Soviet Karelia: agriculture, 19, 82–88, 131; autonomous budget, 18–21; construction industry, 75–76; First Five-Year Plan, 20–21, 61, 63, 69–71, 74, 76, 79–80; forest industry,18, 22, 70–74; infrastructure projects, 76–77; modernization plans, 18–21, 74; shortage of labor force, 8, 18, 21–22, 74, 127, 141
education in Soviet Karelia, 38, 68, 72, 90–95, 118, 127, 162, 165
Ekman, Kalle, 75
Erola, Arho, 142
Ewen, Tom, 151, 153–54
Ezhov, Nikolai, 129, 134, 136, 137, 140–42, 207

Finland: civil war, 4, 7–8, 10, 99–100, 103; Karelianism, 9–10, 13, 99; as a model for Soviet Karelia, 20; nationalism, 9–13, 91, 96, 101, 118–19; territorial claims for Karelia, 10, 12–13
Finnish Communist Party, 13, 28; Central Committee, 129–30, 133–34; support groups, 127–31
Finnish communities in North America, xi, 1–4, 99–100, 102, 116; cooperative movement, 4, 28; ethnic radicalism, 4, 27, 36, 39, 100, 118, 119; "Karelian fever," 24–25, 27, 29–33, 97; reaction to the "Karelian fever," 34–35, 151; recruitment campaign to Soviet Karelia, 18, 22–23, 25, 28, 29, 31, 33, 36–39, 46, 49, 53–58, 97, 102, 118